# BE A HOBBIT, SAVE THE EARTH

## The Guide to Sustainable Shire Living

### STEVE BIVANS

Shireness Publishing
St. Paul
2014

For more information about Be a Hobbit and other works by Steve
Bivans, subscribe to his email list at
**Subscribe to Be a Hobbit!**
**http://eepurl.com/Vghp5**
and find him online at
**www.stevebivans.com**

To my daughter, Samantha Noël, my Eówyn and my heroine, there is none braver and none more beautiful in all the histories of this Earth, or of Middle Earth.

Love, Dad

# TABLE OF CONTENTS

# ACKNOWLEDGMENTS

One thing I have learned in my 48, almost 49 years of life is that there are no planned trajectories, no itineraries that last longer than the time it takes to put down the pen. As I say in the chapter *Barbequing With Lesbians*, one cannot coerce things into being; neither can one predict where a path will lead, "Be careful stepping outside your door, Frodo" indeed. A book of this nature and size is never the product of one mind and will. In that sense I am not the author of this book; it might be more accurate to call me a *channeler*, if that didn't bring up visions of some new-agey swami with a deck of tarot cards and a crystal ball. No, I'm not claiming *divine inspiration*. What I will claim is that I have been influenced by so many people over the decades, either directly through conversation and adventures — with friends and enemies — or indirectly through the words and art of enlightened individuals I've never met in person — through books, films, television, and music. I'd love to thank them all but since I'm an older Hobbit and my memory isn't that good — plus I've already written 500 pages — I'll keep it short.

Thanks to the late Professor, J.R.R. Tolkien for revealing a world to me that pulled me out of darkness into light. To Daniel Quinn who gave me the key to the Ring so many years ago. To my friend, Michele Newton Latham who posted the "30 Questions to answer before you die" on her Facebook page last year. Little did she — or I — know the effect they would have. Thanks to Sharon Fischlowitz who reminded me of Mr. Quinn's work and set me in the right direction. Thanks to my brother, Tim Bivans, for walking through Mordor with me all those many years ago. Thanks to my mother and father who—despite years worrying that they'd failed—taught me compassion for my fellow man and to always *try* to do what is right even if I frequently failed to do it. Thanks to Heather Anne Muster, Kendra McAnally & Michael Broome for your generous support of the project. Thank you Linda & Greg Felt for all the things you have done for Patience, Duke, and I and your support for the book. It would not have happened without you. Thanks to Duke for your twelve year old perspective and for being the face of Be a Hobbit in so many Facebook posts. Thanks to my daughter, Samantha, for being an inspiration to me in so many ways I cannot enumerate. Thanks to James Coplin for being a friend through green Shire pastures and blackest Moria, and to his lovely wife, Heidi. Your home has been an oasis of South Farthing hospitality without which I'm not sure I would have survived. Thanks, also, to the Coffee Pit Writing Club: James—again, Adam Blackler and Alisha Volante for being my *Inklings*. I look forward to many more Mondays of cheap Chinese food, laughs, microwave timers, Black Jesuses, and the occasional *face slap*—y'all know what I'm talkin' about. Thanks and much love to my good friends Monk Moeschl and Kitty West—Monk for being my Bombadil and for the intense philosophical discussions throughout the years, even if I was often guilty of 'waiting to speak' instead of listening—Kitty for being Goldberry/ Galadriel/ Gamgee, for your songs, your laughter, and your positivity—the Light of Eärendil to all who know you.

Lastly and most importantly, thank you to my beautiful girlfriend, Patience, who has earned her name time and again, and has seen my darkest Dwarfy days as well as my sunniest Hobbity ones. Thank you for the moral support through this journey, as well as the long hours listening to me rant, reading draft after draft, marking out extraneous commas, cleaning up my orcish phrases, and for the insightful discussions—even if many of them came too early in the morning and before your java. Oh yeah, and thanks for the popcorn and cornbread with lots of honey butter! I love you.

# THANK YOU!

To the following Hobbits, Wizards, Dwarves, Elves, Men and Women of Middle Earth, I give my undying thanks for your support for Be a Hobbit during the Kickstarter Campaign. Without your help and support, this book would not have happened. Thank you!

## Most Generous Hobbitses!

Greg & Linda Felt
Dr. Kendra McAnally & Michael Broome
Dr. Heather Anne Muster

## Party Tree Attendees
Whitney-Lehr & Christopher Flynn
(Hurricanes Baby!)
Cameron Parkhurst & Sharon Fischlowitz

### Council of Elrond
Dr. Richard J Edgar
Brandon Foat
Kimm Mosier-Pastrana
Sam & Linda Bivans
(heretofore referred to as 'mom' and 'dad', Thanks
mom n dad! )

### Fellowship of the Ring
Timothy McLamb
Craig Johnson
James Coplin (BBQ Master)
Tim Taylor
Kristi Swanson

...it is now exactly twenty years since I began in earnest to complete the history of our renowned Hobbit-ancestors of the Third Age. I look East, West, North, South, and I do not see Sauron; but I see that Saruman has many descendants. We Hobbits have against them no magic weapons. Yet, my gentle Hobbits, I give you this toast: To the Hobbits. May they outlast the Sarumans and see spring again in the trees.

**J.R.R. Tolkien, in a speech in Rotterdam, 1958.**

# Introduction

I'm a Hobbit. Yes, I know I look like a human, except maybe in the morning when I first wake up, when I look—and probably smell—much more like an orc. I definitely grunt in the Black Speech for 30 minutes or more, until I manage to stumble to the kitchen, fry up a couple eggs, some sausage, and toast some bread, onto which I scrape plenty of butter. I've been accused, not inaccurately, of being more Dwarvish: warlike, belligerent, greedy and self-centered. I suspect that somewhere back in my lineage, one of my ancestors probably lived in a cave, ate fire-roasted shanks of pork, drank kegs of ale, which dribbled down his hairy chin while he rested his posterior on sacks of dragon-gold. Or was that me, last night?

I'm not really a dwarf, or an orc. I'm much too tall for either. At slightly over 6 feet tall, most of my friends would probably say that I look more like one of the Rohirrim: long, curly blonde hair, salt n pepper goatee, blue eyes, and an overly serious scowl. I have to admit that I would probably look more at home on the back of a horse, with spear in hand, smashing into waves of orc-flesh on the Pelennor, than tiptoeing through tulips in the Shire. In the 'real world,' I'm a teacher, trained in Viking military history. I love reading, researching, and writing about martial subjects. I've dreamt of wild adventures: riding into battle like Theoden or fighting my way out of stony rooms full of gnashing orcs in Moria, so that's certainly part of my nature. And by appearance, that's what you would think, too.

Other than my belly—evidence of very few skipped second breakfasts—and my hairy feet—which thankfully remained covered 7 to 8 months of the year—no one would ever know to look at me that I'm a Hobbit. Truth be told, however, I would rather be blowing smoke rings from my pipe, reading a dusty tome in my little home study—and occasionally tiptoeing through tulips; just don't tell any of my friends. My favorite days include activities like looking out the window at snow falling, sipping a cup of warm cocoa, or sitting in my garden, drinking a cold beer on a summer afternoon, dreaming of second breakfast, or sixth supper. In fact, one day at work not long ago, I was thinking to myself, "You know what I *really* love the most in life? Food." Yep, just food. I love the cooking of food, the eating of food, the talking about food, the thinking about food, and the dreaming about food. Food, food, food. That's what I love. Can there be anything more Hobbity than that? I reckon not.

But I'm not writing a cookbook. I might do that one day, but that's not what this book is about. This book is about how we all can learn to live more like Hobbits—simply, hospitably, bravely, with a sense of respect and awe for Nature—and, in so doing, save this Middle Earth, much as little Frodo and his companions did so very long ago.

## Why THIS book, and why NOW?

Our Middle Earth, Mother Earth, is dying. A dark power is assaulting her daily. Her species, both plant and animal, are disappearing at an alarming rate. Her great rivers, lakes and oceans are steaming with pollution. Poisonous fumes belch into her atmosphere, trapping heat upon her surface, raising the levels of her seas, disturbing her weather patterns, whipping up ever more massive storms and droughts. Hordes of orcish exploiters wielding massive chainsaws are felling her forests so quickly that they may not last another 50 years. I won't belabor the point. For most of you, you already know these things, in general, if not in exhaustive detail. I will cover it in brief detail in part one, *Mordor is at the Door*, but even there, I will only give you the briefest glimpse of the *iceberg*. There are plenty of books on *what is wrong* with the earth. Suffice it to say for now, the Shire is burning. But *why* is this happening?

Why would we, the human species, with so much professed intelligence, devour, devastate, and destroy the ecological system supporting our very existence? In this book, I assign the underlying cause of our insanity to the evil power of the One Ring. Yes, the Ring does exist, metaphorically at least. But *what* it is, and *where* it resides, is not so obvious, because it is an ancient cultural myth, long forgotten, hidden in the long, dark of our collective 'Moria'. Forgotten, but just as powerful and destructive as it ever was. And the Ring has nothing to do with religion, not directly anyway. Neither is it some kind of new age boogyman, or a gift from Marvin the Martian. The Ring is cultural, and it's entirely the product of perfectly 'normal' *homo sapiens sapiens*; to understand it is not to abandon one's religious beliefs, or beliefs in boogymen or martians—though you may abandon, hopefully, some of your key cultural preconceptions.

You may be asking, "Why do we need to know *why* we are destroying our planet? Is it really important to know the cause? Isn't it enough to know that we *are* doing it, and to just *stop?*" I suppose that the point could be made that on a personal level, knowing the underlying cause of our insanity isn't that important. We could, after all, just choose to treat the earth with respect, recycle our garbage, put up solar panels on our houses, grow our own food or buy organic and local produce, join protest rallies at city hall, at the White House or Downing Street. Certainly all those are good ideas, which I will discuss in the last part of the book. But I will argue here, that unless we really know *why* we are screwing up our precious planet, we really can't change the course of our actions in an effective way. Knowing why is a transformative experience, and at the heart of real change. We must first change our *minds*, our way of thinking. Then, and only then, we can begin to live as Hobbits should, as *stewards* of the Earth, and do as Tolkien challenged us to do, to "outlive the Sarumans and see spring again in the trees." I would add that in order to defeat the power of the Sarumans and Saurons, we must first bring Shire-ness to the Earth, by repairing our scoured Shires, our communities.

All of that brings us to the primary subject of this little book: how to '*be*' a Hobbit. In Part III, *Saving the Earth: Sustainable Shire Living*, I will attempt to do what so many modern, eco-preachy books have not: to lay out in extensive detail just *how*, and *what*, we can do, individually and collectively, to carry the One Ring to Mount Doom and toss that evil thing away, once and for all. I will also make a case for why I think it's possible for individual Hobbits, like you, and me, to *save the Earth*. It will take a massive, collective fellowship of humanity to accomplish this task. But the journey begins with the first step outside your door, as Bilbo said, "It's a dangerous business, Frodo, going out your door. You step onto the road, and if you don't keep your feet, there's no knowing where you might be swept off to."

# Why Tolkien?

This book could be written in infinitely different ways, and the ideas should be shouted from rooftops, in every language; it is essential that the message gets out, because our future depends upon it. There are numerous authors shouting similar messages to their audiences. That being said, one must choose an audience, or have none at all, so one day, while contemplating on which direction to go, I stumbled into the Hobbits.

### Applicability vs Allegory

I chose to apply Tolkien's world as a lens through which to view our own, for a couple of reasons. First, the story is applicable. Tolkien's Middle Earth was under attack by a dark, mysterious force that threatened to lay waste to all in its path. Our earth is also under attack though the *dark power* is not as obvious as it might seem. As in *The Lord of the Rings*, the solution to the problem is a simple one, if arduous, dangerous and nearly impossible. Frodo, with the help of the Fellowship, was charged with carrying the Ring to its source to let it drop into the abyss whence it came: simple, but not easy. In the real world, we are all Frodo; we must each discover the true nature of our Ring, be willing to destroy it, and come home to our Shire and clean *it* up.

The other reason I have chosen Tolkien, other than the fact that I'm an enormous fan of his books—having read most of them some 7 or 8 times through—is that I truly believe that J.R.R. would approve of my *ends*, if not entirely of my *means*. This is where I will probably lose some of the Tolkien purists. I understand your reluctance. Many fans of his books, have taken umbrage with critics, and movie directors, for polluting Tolkien's stories with insertions of allegory, cutting key chapters, or adding unnecessary characters and scenarios. Tolkien, himself was outspoken about people—especially other scholars—attempting to read 'allegory' into his books. It's not extreme to say that he detested the attempts to find hidden meaning within his works. Tolkien, while shunning *allegory*, did acknowledge that *applicability* was always a possibility when reading works of literature, "That there is no allegory does not, of course, say there is no applicability. There always is." Thanks, Professor Tolkien, for the leeway!

The reason I think the renowned professor would approve of my *ends*, is that my ends are the protection, and eventual redemption of our poisoned planet. Tolkien was, at heart, a lover of Nature. He was an outspoken defender of all things green and growing, both in his fiction and in his personal and professional life. His books exude his love of natural things: trees, forests, streams, rivers, fields, mountains, the sea, animals of all species (with the possible exception of wolves and spiders). His detest for those who would destroy in the pursuit of power is evident, as well. Describing orcs he wrote: "It is not unlikely that they invented some of the machines that have since troubled the world, especially the ingenious devices for killing large numbers of people at once, for wheels and engines and explosives always delighted them" (*The Hobbit*, 73). Much more could be said about Tolkien and his love of Nature; much of it has already been written, and a sense of it will come across as we travel along through the book.

### Plus Tolkien has already done it...

If these reasons weren't enough to convince you that I'm not profaning the good professor's life work, then I will refer you, again, to the epigraph of this book:

> I look East, West, North, South, and I do not see
> Sauron; but I see that **Saruman has many**
> **descendants**. We Hobbits have against them no magic
> weapons. Yet, my gentle Hobbits, I give you this toast:
> To the Hobbits. May they outlast the Sarumans and
> see spring again in the trees.

I love this quote. In it, the author himself applies his work to the modern world in much the same way that I propose to do it here in this book. In fact, I have adopted part of it as my life's purpose, since Tolkien himself has charged us with a mission: to see spring again in the trees. Should we not all aspire to that? I think so. I have added to his words to construct my own purpose: *To bring Shire-ness to the Earth, and spring again to the Trees.* I hope that by the end of the book, it will be part of your purpose as well.

## The Earth Depends on Tolkien's Message

The most important reason I have chosen Professor Tolkien's works for this project is that the message I hope to impart to you is, I believe, the most important one that you need to hear at this very moment in history. To reach the largest audience possible it is necessary to target the message. If I were to write this in a general way — without Tolkien's assistance that is — I might reach a very small segment of people already concerned about the environment, governmental corruption, pollution, over-population, etc., looking for new books on the subject. Thankfully, Tolkien's audience is a massive, global group of people, who should be, in my opinion, receptive to the ideas in this book. Most of us Tolkien fans already *live* in Middle Earth. In a very real sense, we view our world as an extension of Tolkien's and wish that we were in fact, there. Many of us have travelled to that distant land and have never really returned. To view our modern world through such a lens isn't a stretch, I think.

This is important, because if this message does not rapidly spread over the earth, and if it is not taken to heart and put into action, the Earth that the esteemed author loved so well, and the one that we should love at least as much as he, will not much longer sustain our existence. Middle Earth, Mother Earth, will reject us, and as a species we will perish or, at the very least, be reduced to a remnant of our current population. Even if that were to happen, and the odds are stacking against us — much as they were against Frodo and his world — 'the survivors would still need to know the information I hope to pass along here. Because if they do not it is a distinct possibility that they will only rise from the ashes to form new civilizations on the same flawed premises on which ours was conceived. How much better it would be, for us all, if we take the little Hobbits of The Shire as our models and save the Earth.

# PART I

## MORDOR IS AT THE DOOR

# I

# MORDOR IS AT THE DOOR: OUR BURNING SHIRE

"My news is evil." Then he looked about him, as if the hedges might have ears. "Nazgul," he whispered. "The Nine are abroad again. They have crossed the River secretly and are moving westward. They have taken the guise of riders in black." —*LOTR, The Council of Elrond*

We're flirtin' with disaster,
y'all know what I mean
And the way we run our lives,
it makes no sense to me
I don't know about yourself
or what you want to be, yeah
When we gamble with our time, we choose our
destiny —Molly Hatchet, *Flirtin' With Disaster*

Mordor is kicking *in* our door, is more accurate. It is no longer just *away*, a problem for some other person, living in some Third World country. The Black Riders are burning *our* Shire. I will not spend undue time attempting to convince you that our future is dark. I'm going to assume you know that the Earth is in peril or you wouldn't be reading the book. But it's important to give you a glimpse of what is going on, so that you know what we're facing, and what needs to be done, in order to clean up the Shire.

The news is certainly dire. Here are a few facts to give you some perspective. In the next two to three minutes, about the time it takes to read this page, the following things will happen:

- 30 Tons of plastic will be dumped into the Earth's oceans.

- The U.S. will dump over 1000 pounds of toxic chemical waste into their waterways.

- Somewhere, 14 people, lacking clean water, will die.

- 130 acres of tropical rainforest will be destroyed.

- 8 million dollars will be spent on militaries worldwide.

- Private interests will spend $5,500 to *influence* members of the U.S. Congress.

- 2 people, in the U.S., will die because they lack adequate health insurance.

At the beginning of Frodo's story all seems well as if the Shire had been, was, and would forever be, just the green, fertile, rolling hills all Hobbits took for granted: *their* Shire. Sure, there were rivalries, especially between Bilbo and his relations, the Sackville-Bagginses, but overall the Shire was the model of peace and contentment. Chief concerns were how the pipe weed might turn out this year, or just how big was Bilbo's eleventieth birthday celebration going to be. There was no thought of war, disease, death or darkness. These things were of much concern for the other races of Middle Earth, for whom the Hobbits gave little heed: dwarves, big folk, elves and wizards. War and violence were things that happened far, far away, or long, long ago. There was no need to fret about such things. Best to tend to the garden and get ready for afternoon tea.

Such was the situation for most of us, in the western world anyway, at least after the turbulent events of WWII. The post-war years were a boom, especially for those of us living in the fertile farmlands of the United States. There were plenty of jobs again, money rolling in, children to feed, new houses to build and pay for in the suburbs: no more nasty city living for the middle class. As time went on, things also improved for war-torn Europe. Prosperity reigned, and capitalism seemed all that it was ever promised to be for the West that is.

In Middle Earth, things were not, of course, as peaceful as Hobbits liked to think. We know that Sauron had returned, and that he had summoned his Black Riders, the cold and frightening Nazgul, nine of them, to spread their fear outward from Mordor into the rest of Middle Earth. Unaware of the danger, the Shire went on as before but the rest of the world was suffering from the ravages of the riders and the looming darkness of Mordor. As in Middle Earth, on our Earth, many places have been suffering similar crises for decades, if not centuries. They were battle fields long ago and continue to be so today. But even the modern Shire (the West) is now feeling the effects of centuries of uncontrolled greed and resource gathering. That greed has led to a plague of despair and devastation.

## The Nine: Our Modern Ringwraiths

In our world, the Black Riders symbolize what I consider the nine major dangers that face our planet. Why nine? It's a large enough number to cover at least categorically, the main problems we face. There may seem to be an infinite number of problems in the world, but they really all fall within one of these nine broad categories: Ignorance & Want, Corruption, Violence, Waning Energy, Food, Disease, Pollution, and Climate Change. We will cover each in the order of importance. In many ways these issues build, one upon another, much in the way one builds a house of cards. Yank the first card at the bottom and the entire structure will come down in a crash. I have omitted the first card in our house of cards, The One Ring, which we will discuss in Part II. Once we pull that card out—as when Sauron's Ring fell into the fires of Mt. Doom—all will come crashing down; then it's just a matter of cleaning up the debris. But let's begin our story *in* the debris itself. We'll begin our journey with one man's story in the depths of Moria and the darkness of Shelob's Lair.

# 2

# THE POWER OF 'STORY':
# A MODERN HOBBIT'S JOURNEY

"Beren now, he never thought he was going to get that Silmaril from the Iron Crown in Thangorodrim, and yet he did, and that was a worse place and a blacker danger than ours. But that's a long tale, of course, and goes on past the happiness and into grief and beyond it — and the Silmaril went on and came to Eärendil. And why, sir, I never thought of that before! We've got — you've got some of the light of it in that star-glass that the Lady gave you! Why, to think of it, we're in the same tale still! It's going on. Don't the great tales never end?"

"No, they never end as tales," said Frodo. "But the people in them come, and go when their part's ended. Our part will end later — or sooner." — *LOTR*: II, *The Stairs of Cirith Ungol*

If you should go skating
On the thin ice of modern life
Dragging behind you the silent reproach
Of a million tear-stained eyes
Don't be surprised when a crack in the ice
Appears under your feet.
You slip out of your depth and out of your mind
With your fear flowing out behind you
As you claw the thin ice. — Pink Floyd, *The Thin Ice*

A young man, 25 years old, lay on a stained futon cushion, ripped and worn on a cold linoleum kitchen floor in a roach-infested apartment. There was no bed, there was no kitchenette table with cushioned chairs on which to sit and spread butter over so much toast. There was no place to eat second breakfast, or first breakfast. The fridge hummed in the corner; it was mostly empty, maybe a few beers left, a half empty package of Winn Dixie brand bologna. A few slices of stale bread sat on the counter, in a crumpled plastic bag. There was little else of substance in the room, only the futon, dust, dirt, and cock-roaches, roaches the size of Texas, as tough as leather. Littering the floor were numerous crushed beer cans and empty bottles, a haphazard pile of pizza boxes, a bag of garbage, no garbage can, a sink full of dishes covered in mold.

The man was not unemployed; just underemployed. He had a slave-wage, burger-flipping job at a fast food chain. In the bathroom, just off the kitchen, over the shower rod, one of his two work shirts — wet from washing in the dirty sink — dripped on the floor, which had not been swept or mopped in months, if ever. The smells of urine, stale beer, and mold pervaded the place. His younger brother was asleep down the hall in the one bedroom, on the one bed. The brother *was* unemployed and had been for months.

The young man on the kitchen floor had collapsed from despair, from depression, from disillusionment, from a broken heart. The world, which he once believed to be a place of beauty and possibility had disappeared. He had lost his marriage, his self-esteem, his dreams and his hope. In his mind, there was no light there was only darkness. Darkness and the dank kitchen floor and the sweat-stained futon and the roving cock-roaches. He wept, sobbed silently, so no one would hear and think him weak. He was doubled up in a position he hadn't been in since the day before he was born. Tears no longer came, just gut-wrenching sobs that left an ache.

Through the sobs, he could hear strains of Pink Floyd, "Is there anybody out there..." echoing down the hall from the front room, also covered in beer cans, bottles and tops, pizza boxes, and cigarette butts. The light fixture on the ceiling was full of beer bottle caps and pull tabs, tossed there in a mindless game. There were so many that they prevented most of the light from escaping, even when the light was on. But it was off, like the lights of the man's future. He was utterly alone and in the dark. His essence was fading away, like some Gollum in the deep, dark places of the World. The man could have been any one of a billion souls on this Earth, but he wasn't. The man was me.

## The Black Magic of Storytelling

In many ways the story of this book is the story of my own life, as it relates to J.R.R. Tolkien's great story. But we are *all* story tellers, even if we don't realize it. Each of us has a story to tell, and we in fact *do* tell it all the time, usually to ourselves, internally, in our heads. And for most of us it is a very, very dark story indeed, full of negativity that we repeat over and over *ad nauseum*, until we believe it and manifest our own negative reality. If we think negatively, we will have negative lives. Trust me on this one, I *know*. But the converse is also true: we can *rewrite* our stories, and make them positive! Most of the negative stuff in our stories is *dragon-shit* anyway.

Throughout the book, I will share some of my story with you, in the hopes that it will help you to think about the one you carry around in your own skull, and to begin to pull it apart, and examine it more critically. We'll also discover, in Part II, that our civilization has a *collective* story, and it is exceedingly dark and negative, though there are glimmers of hope in the darkness. In Part III, we'll look at how we can rewrite our stories, both personal and collective.

## My Personal Mordor

Much as Frodo and Bilbo's stories, my story has a beginning: a happy childhood and peace at home, not unlike the Hobbits in their idyllic Shire. Then, in the middle, like the fateful night when Gandalf tossed the Ring into Frodo's fireplace—sweeping him off on his dark adventure—the fabric of my life came apart in a flash: crisis, disillusionment, despair, and struggle. And the end? Well, I'm not dead yet, so the end is still in question, or at least the *means* to the end is. But the end for our purposes is the very words you're reading right now: this book. The story of how *Be a Hobbit* came to be written is very much my story, and it probably began the day I was born, though I'll try not to bore you with pages of my childhood, tip-toeing in the tulips of my metaphorical Shire. Don't worry, I won't depress you with every detail of my life; this isn't my autobiography but I will share a few of my experiences when they serve as an example.

## The Beginning

Like the Hobbits in The Shire, I had a happy childhood, a Shire-like childhood, if you will. My mom and dad, who were model parents — however you want to measure that — were Salvation Army officers, which means preachers, or ministers. Contrary to what many think, the Salvation Army is not just a social, charitable organization that rings bells at Christmas. They do that, of course, and I did it many, many times in my youth and early adulthood, but it is at heart a church. So my brothers and I grew up in an atmosphere of religion and charity work. We rebelled against both at times, as children and teenagers do. I tell people all the time that there are two kinds of preacher's kids: ones that become preachers themselves, and my kind. At one point in my life, early adulthood, I rejected almost everything my parents had ever taught me.

My rejection of religion, and many of society's conventions, came as the result of books that challenged much that I thought I knew about the world. Unfortunately for my parents, I was born with a questioning mind. I tell people all the time that there's nothing more dangerous on Earth than a good question. Once a question lodges itself in the brain, there's really no getting it out until you find a suitable answer for it. And very strong questions require very strong answers, backed up with stronger evidence.

I won't go too much into *why* I rejected my upbringing, but a process that began with reading and questioning was then reinforced by the struggles of being a young father in my early tweens (twenties), money (the lack thereof), and divorce. I chose to drown most of that pain and stress in copious amounts of alcohol, which of course did nothing to solve the problems. What I did manage to do during that period, however, was to read insatiably. I read a butt-load of Stephen King's books, *The Stand*, being my favorite. I was in a very nihilistic mindset at the time, and King's vision of a post-apocalyptic world, nearly devoid of people was attractive to me.

In my mind at the time, the problem with the world was that it was filled with too many stupid and ignorant people and if they all disappeared one day it would be fine with me. I was in a very negative mental state, and the more I read, the darker the World appeared to me. I read everything I could get my hands on, especially non-fiction; history, religion, philosophy, new-*agey*, old *agey*, you name it, I read it. What I really wanted to know was, "If Christianity isn't the answer, if there is no God, then why are we here?" This led to an endless stream of further questions, but at the heart of all of them was "What possible *purpose* does our seemingly ruined species serve on this rock in space?" So I read. And read. While I am neither a card-carrying atheist, nor a preacher, religion is important to my story and the story of how this book came to be. My rejection of any and all belief was part of my spiral downward much as Frodo was dragged down by the power of the Ring. I was carrying my own Ring at the time: a ring of despair, fear, ignorance, want, and rage, which pulled me ever downward.

**A Light in Dark Places**

I was drowning in negative emotions, groping through a metaphorical dark tunnel in the side of a mountain, trying to get through to the other side—which in my twisted mind was probably just as bad or worse than the tunnel itself. As far as I was concerned the other side was just more darkness. I didn't know it then, but I was Frodo, lost in Cirith Ungol headed for certain death in the webs of Shelob's Lair. I could not see a path through my negativity, it enveloped me like the darkness that surrounded Frodo. In a very real sense, I had been spun into a spider's web, awaiting the hunger of the beast of my own making.

Then one day, someone suggested a book that I had heard of before. Everyone had heard of it, I suppose. I'm not sure who it was that turned me on to *The Hobbit* first, possibly it was my brother, Tim, who was living with me at the time in that roach-infested apartment in New Bern, NC. I don't remember, which is strange, because normally my mind is a steel trap, but I reckon drinking a minimum of twelve Olympia beers per day, and God only knows how much liquor on the weekends, might just blur the memory a bit. I wouldn't recommend it as a cure for depression. But I survived. Because like Frodo, a faithful companion came to rescue me with the Light of Eärendil, Tolkien's wonderful books, and I could see again. Yes, I was still in a tunnel but I was not alone. I had a Samwise and I had hope, if only the smallest glimmer.

So I picked up *The Hobbit*. And I began to read. I was swept off to a green, green Shire in a far, far land, and my soul has never returned. I suppose it never will. Yes, my soul at the time wandered more in the smoking wastelands of Mordor or the Dead Marshes than Hobbiton, but wandering in Middle Earth, was superior to my own world in every way.

After ripping through *The Hobbit*, I read *The Lord of the Rings*, and the darkness of that story enveloped me in a way that is impossible to explain. I was *THERE*, in a very real sense. The fear was palpable in the presence of the black-cloaked Ringwraiths, and I could taste the sulfurous fumes of Mt. Doom. I could smell the sweat of horses and hot leather and hear the clash of battle as I rode with the Rohan on the fields of the Pelennor. I bled and died with the sun-king, Theoden. I rose again with Eowyn's defiance of the Witch King. I soared with the Eagles as they swept the broken and bloody body of Frodo and his companion Samwise the Brave from the smoking crags of the fiery mountain. There has never been such a story, and I don't think there ever shall be again.

## Our Earth is Broken: Heroes Needed

The game designer, Jane McGonigal, who'll we'll discuss in more detail later, argues that the real world is broken. It doesn't work the way it should; real life is mundane, stressful as hell, and not all that exciting. It's the routine that stresses us out. Life has no *meaning*, no *purpose*. We get up, we go to work, we eat, we sleep, and we repeat. Where is the adventure? And that's why so many of us are drawn to games, especially video and computer games. In the game world we can escape our mundane existence and become heroes. We can save the Earth every day! But in the real world? There're just traffic jams and bills to pay. No heroes to be seen. McGonigal suggests that we should make the real world, reality, more like a game. I agree, with an addendum. What makes games great, any game, is the story. Real life should be more like a game with an epic, heroic storyline, you know, something like Hobbits saving the Earth!

What I'm proposing is that those of us who love Tolkien's stories, write ourselves *into the his story*, become *part of the story*, or better yet, make *his* story part of *our* individual and collective story We should view *our story* through the lens of Tolkien's. In this way, we can transform ourselves from Modern *Humans*, to Modern *Hobbits*, thereby saving ourselves *and* the Earth.

It's not an exaggeration to say that Tolkien saved my life with his books. At the time I was so low and angry and defiant that without such a story I might never have aspired to be anything but a belligerent, destructive, orc of a man, or at best, a really pissed off dwarf. It took me ten years or more to work my way out of Mordor, but I did and that was the result of my encounter with a some Hobbits, some wizards, some Elves and ole Tom Bombadil, but you're gonna have to wait for that part of the story. During my dark period, my Mordor, I began to see that our world was very much like the burning scoured Shire that Frodo and his companions found when they returned from saving Middle Earth from the clutches of Sauron. What they found, much like my life in my tweens (twenties), was that their homeland had been ravaged by the greed and vindictiveness of Saruman, who had brought his own industrial version of Mordor to the once green fields of the Shire. So that is where we shall begin, at the end if you will, in the burning, crumbling ruins of our civilization, with the evil work of the Nine Black Riders. That journey begins at the foot of the Two Towers of Barad Dur and Orthanc, for they are both problem and cause, root and branch of all that is dark in this world: Ignorance, and

Want. Warning, it is a very dark story, but don't despair; we have the light of the Elves with us. We will come through the tunnel, destroy that Ring, clean up our Shire, and return the spring to the Trees.

# 3

# THE TWO TOWERS: SEEDS OF THE GARDEN OF MORDOR

Frodo and Sam gazed out in mingled loathing and wonder on this hateful land. Between them and the smoking mountain, and about it north and south, all seemed ruinous and dead, a desert burned and choked. They wondered how the Lord of the realm maintained and fed his slaves and his armies. Yet armies he had. —*LOTR: 'The Land of Shadow'*

"Oh, Man! Look here. Look, look, down here!" exclaimed the Ghost.

They were a boy and girl. Yellow, meagre, ragged, scowling, wolfish; but prostrate, too, in their humility. Where graceful youth should have filled their features out, and touched them with its freshest tints, a stale and shriveled hand, like that of age, had pinched, and twisted them, and pulled them into shreds. Where angels might have sat enthroned, devils lurked, and glared out menacing. No change, no degradation, no perversion of humanity, in any grade, through all the mysteries of wonderful creation, has monsters half so horrible and dread.

"Spirit! are they yours?" Scrooge could say no more.

"They are Man's," said the Spirit, looking down upon them. "And they cling to me, appealing from their fathers. This boy is *Ignorance*. This girl is **Want**. Beware them both, and all of their degree, but most of all beware this boy, for on his brow *I see that written which is Doom*, unless the writing be erased. Deny it!" cried the Spirit, stretching out its hand towards the city. "Slander those who tell it ye! Admit it for your factious purposes, and make it worse! And bide the end!"

"Have they no refuge or resource?" cried Scrooge.

"Are there no prisons?" said the Spirit, turning on him for the last time with his own words. "Are there no workhouses?" The bell struck twelve. —Charles Dickens, *A Christmas Carol*

The captain of the Nazgûl, the chief of the Nine Black Riders of Mordor, was the Witch King of Angmar, an ancient and evil lord who ruled the northern lands of Middle Earth. He was originally a Númenorean, who in the Second Age, left the island kingdom of Númenor, and came to Middle Earth to serve as a servant to Sauron, and as such, he and his followers and kinsmen were forever known as the Black Númenoreans. He was personally responsible for the downfall of the northern kingdom of Arnor, and the demise of Aragorn's inheritance as King of Arnor. He symbolizes for us Fear & Ignorance, Greed & Want: the roots of the other Nine Black Riders of our World. He was a sorcerer of great power, impervious to wounds sustained from mortal men. It is significant, for our comparison that he was eventually brought to ruin by a woman and a tiny Hobbit, not by the great and powerful.

# Ignorance and Fear: the Roots of Barad Dur

True education is a kind of never ending story — a matter of continual beginnings, of habitual fresh starts, of persistent newness. —J.R.R. Tolkien

We are all born ignorant, but one must work hard to remain stupid. —Benjamin Franklin

Timendi causa est nescire (Ignorance is the cause of fear). —Seneca, *Natural Questions*

There's probably no deeper root cause of the suffering on Earth than Ignorance. As the Ghost of Christmas Present warned Scrooge, "most of all beware this boy [ignorance], for on his brow I see that written which is Doom, unless the writing be erased. Deny it!" Can you deny it? I don't think so. If you do then you are practicing the most insidious kind of ignorance, the willful kind, the kind where one knows of the truth, the facts, and chooses to ignore them or to disbelieve them. There are really three kinds of ignorance: simple, enlightened or *higher*, and willful. Only two of them are particularly dangerous: simple and Willful Ignorance. The other, *higher*, we'll return to much later. Simple ignorance just means that someone is unaware of the facts or truth or some particular knowledge. Everyone is guilty of this one. It's not possible to know everything or be aware of everything. As long as we are aware of our simple ignorance we can be open to learning new things. Ignorance—no matter how often it serves as a substitute—isn't the same thing as stupidity. The former has to do with *what* one knows; the latter, stupidity, refers to one's *ability* to know: their level of intelligence. Intelligence and knowledge are not synonymous either. In fact, the most insidious kind of Willful Ignorance is that practiced by highly intelligent people.

To be intelligent and somewhat knowledgable, and then to ignore evidence, is practicing Willful Ignorance. I do it. You do it. Everyone does it. But we shouldn't, and we should stop, because it fuels many—if not all—of the ills on the planet. We shall see, in Part II, that it is also the root of the One Ring. Ignorance also leads to fear which is one of the most destructive things on Earth. So anything we can do to combat Willful Ignorance will in turn remove Fear which can only be a positive thing. Ignorance and Fear lead people to retreat into their own *fortresses*, to build Barad Durs in their own minds, if you like. These fortresses are constructed on our own misconceptions about *how the world works*, and *why other people do what they do*. We *think* we know the answers to those questions, but usually, we're completely ignorant to their true motivations. We have constructed myths to explain why the World is so messed up and why other people think *wrongly*, but they are just myths.

We are being willfully ignorant of their perspective. We rarely take time to walk in their shoes, to see things through their eyes.

Objectivity is not an easy thing to come by. It's very hard to view the world from another's perspective. We aren't them. We can never *really* see the World from a perspective different than our own. This idea reminds me of an interview I once saw with George Harrison, the guitar player for the Beatles. The interviewer was trying to grasp George's perspective on the crazed mania that the group experienced in the early days of the band. He asked George, "So, what was it like to be a Beatle?" George, in his typical, Zen-master wisdom, answered with a question, "What was it like to *not* be one?" Precisely! What indeed? We can never really know what it's like to be someone else. But that doesn't mean we shouldn't try.

While we can't experience life through any perspective than our own, we can empathize with other people. We can use our imaginations to compare their experiences and stories to our own, or to people close to us. Most of us—even if it has never happened to us—can empathize with another human being who's lost a loved one. Most of us, once we get to adulthood, have dealt with loss in some way or another. And the idea of loss is key to understanding others because it's something that everyone, everywhere has to face. It is common not only to humans but to all living things, though other living things may experience it much differently.

Much of our Fear, is based in the fear of loss. We fear losing our own lives. We fear death for our family and friends. We fear the loss of our means of survival. In the Western World that's tied up in the way we make money to support ourselves and families. In many parts of the World, it's more basic: food and water. We fear violence, oppression. We fear *others*. Our fear of other human beings is very much rooted in Ignorance. We don't understand them. There are many reasons for this ignorance. They have a different religion, are of a different race, have strange customs, eat strange food. So we fear them. It seems—if we are to believe our news sources—and we shouldn't—that we should fear everyone, even our own family members. But this fear has run out of control. It is rampant, and we need to get control of it. Fear is an insidious, nasty thing and it's killing the

Earth and us. In the words of President Franklin Delano Roosevelt, "We have nothing to fear, but fear itself." In Part II, we'll come back to Fear, and look at why it's so pervasive in the human species, and how that led to the creation of the One Ring.

### Chicken or the Egg: What Came First? Ignorance or Fear?

So Ignorance is the root of Fear. But what is the root of Willful Ignorance? If we can get at that, then we can unravel much of the World's problems, and our own. It is the job of every Hobbit, every human, to do just that. If you accomplish nothing else in your life, if you manage to eliminate Willful Ignorance, in all its manifestations, you will have lived a successful life. It is no easy task.

Let's tackle our premise first. *Is* Ignorance the root of Fear? Or is it the other way around? Are we talking about chickens and eggs? Possibly. Here's my two cents, and I'm quite certain it's not the first or last word on the subject. I think that the root of Willful Ignorance, is Fear. We'll return to that in a minute. But the root of Fear, is Simple Ignorance, at least I think that our original Fear is rooted in simply not understanding the World around us: not knowing. It might be easier to grasp it if we look at a hypothetical scenario.

Let's say we are humans living at the dawn of time, at the beginning of the species. We have just migrated to a new area to follow animal migration patterns or because of climate changes. So we move into this new area where there are strange plants and strange animals maybe even other humans or relatives of humans, living there already. We know nothing about them. We are simply ignorant of our new surroundings. This engenders a certain amount of trepidation, of Fear. Really, I don't even think we have to go back that far, other than to realize that the roots of this kind of fear go that far back. We've all experienced such fear in our own lives. We have to start a new job or go to a new school or move to a new city, or state, or country. We don't know anyone. Will they like us? What kind of food do they have there? Will my new boss be a jerk? These are all fears based on ignorance: Simple Ignorance. Usually, we find out that our new boss is okay, the food in the new country is pretty good and that there are friendly kids in our new school—but not always. Sometimes that Fear lingers, or is reenforced by negative experiences.

Such Fear, once it works its way into our minds, can lead to Willfull Ignorance especially if it runs contrary to our preconceived notions and belief systems. But Simple Ignorance isn't the only root of Fear. Fear is also born out of what we *do know*. I have a fear of snakes. Some snakes can and will kill you. Lightning can kill you. Some people have a fear of crossing the street; traffic can definitely kill you. Death by traffic, death by lightning, and death by snake are *real things*, not unknown to humans. So some fear is based upon what we know, not ignorance. But those very real fears become Willfull Ignorance when we disregard the evidence that suggests that most of us will not die from snake bites or lightning strikes and refuse to cross that street or walk in the woods. Buttloads of us will die from traffic related accidents, however, because we disregard the evidence that proves that wearing a seat belt or looking both ways before crossing the street is a good idea. Simple Ignorance and real knowledge can lead to Fear. Fear of the unknown or an overinflated fear of what we *do* know can, and often does lead to Willfull Ignorance which manifests itself in a number of ways.

## The Black Gates of Belief

The most prevalent manifestation of Willful Ignorance seems to be when facts run up against an entrenched belief system. We're all guilty of this one. I'm going to go out on a limb and say *all*, because I'm fairly certain of it. We all have a perspective on the World, how it works and why it works that way. Even if we *admit* to a lack of knowledge, we usually *act* as if we *do* know. Religious dogma is the most common example of this kind of Willful Ignorance. If our religious beliefs contradict what we hear we usually reject the new information out of hand. It's either relegated to *just wrong, conspiratorial, misinformed,* or my favorite, *spawn of Satan*. Religion is fine. Faith in a higher power is okay, too, as long as it is a force for good. If it resists change for resistance sake, if it is based on Willful Ignorance of the facts, or of logic, then it is useless and should be abandoned in favor of a religion, or version of the same religion that *is* a force for good and based on logical principles. If a sentient Creator made us, *he, she, it* gave us minds to use. Let's use them. But to do that effectively, we have to open them up. A closed mind — a willfully ignorant mind — is just protein rotting in a box of bone.

### Fear of Error: I Can't Possibly Be *Wrong*!

Once we are certain of our beliefs we hold onto them for dear life. They become not just *beliefs* but an integral part of *who we are*. We internalize what we believe. Our identity is bound up in our beliefs about the World how it works, and why it is that way in much the same way that Sauron's essence and power was bound up in the One Ring. To admit that a long held perspective was wrong is a very, very difficult thing to do. When our beliefs run into contradictory logic or facts a sort of *cognitive dissonance* sets in; things don't add up. Fear and Willful Ignorance are the result. It's painful. There's a feeling of loss, of grief even, to let go of it. "I can't possibly be wrong!" we tell ourselves. "I know I'm right!" This fear of losing our identity is an integral part of Willful Ignorance. Once an idea lodges itself in the mind it *becomes* a part of *who we are*, and to shed that is to cut off a part of ourselves, like slicing off our own finger to get rid of the Ring. But neither Sauron nor Frodo lost the Ring to conscious choice. It was cut *from* them; both losing a finger in the process. It is nearly impossible for someone else to do that for *us*. The facts can be presented to us but it is up to us whether we choose to set aside our core beliefs and open our minds to new ones. To do that we have to overcome the fear of being alone.

### Conformity: But My Friends Say Different

> "But all my friends are doing it!"
> "If your friends told you to jump off a bridge,
> would you do it?" — Traditional Mom-ism

The worst evidence I ever attempted to use in an argument with my mother was to suggest that, "all my friends are doing it." Nope. Not gonna work. That went nowhere, and it went there fast. But most of us don't stop using it as an excuse for doing, thinking, and continuing to believe erroneous things — to be

Willfully Ignorant in other words—long into our adulthood. This is based solidly in Fear, the fear of being alone, of going our own direction, of going against the grain, being the Lone Wolf. Most people are simply *not* Lone Wolves. I'm not, though I will disagree with friends. But most disagreements between friends tend to end the friendship, and send us off looking for new friends who think more akin to us. It's difficult to maintain a friendship if you have differences of belief on core ideals. So we tend to flock together with people of like mind, and that is another thing that reinforces our belief systems and our Willfull Ignorance. It's crucial to the work of saving the Earth that we Hobbits learn to disagree and continue to be friends, neighbors, and allies. This takes patience, understanding, compassion: things that seem to be in short supply these days.

## Overload: I Don't Have Time to Learn That

No one has any time anymore. We're all so busy it seems. The pace of life has accelerated to such a degree that we're all running around like the proverbial chicken with no head. "Have to get the kids to soccer, and dance, and football, and their 18th Century, Impressionist Art Class! No time for dinner! I'll text ya later! totes luv!" At the same time, we're bombarded with butt-tons of information, all streamed at us at light speed on our computers, televisions, cell phones, and pads. It's enough to give us all migraines. We're overloaded and overwhelmed. We simply don't have *time* to learn anything new, especially negative stuff like *what's wrong with the world*. "The world's messed up, got it, move on." And even if we had time to read about it, what would we read? There's so much conflicting information to sift through it's hard to tell the truth from the lies, from just the ignorant, or stupid. So to simplify it all, we get our news and information in digested form from television, and from the internet. Some people still read newspapers but fewer and fewer do. And their reliability is in serious question, too. The problem with getting news from the old sources is that they have been tainted by corporate ownership, Greed, in other words. They only show us the news they want us to see and with the spin they want to put on it. There's less and less *real* news on the major networks and news outlets. They've been overrun by pundits who spout out propaganda from one perspective or another. As a result, we *think* we know what's going on, when we really don't. But most of us don't have time in a day to critically sift through all the news that's out there, so our misconceptions continue.

## Misunderstanding: I *Know* What You Believe, and It's Wrong

Another key way that Willful Ignorance shows its ugly head is in our certainty that we know what the other person, side, or camp believes and that what they believe is simply *wrong*. We hear what we expect to hear from our opponents in an argument. How many times have you gotten into an argument, either in person or on Facebook, when you didn't really read what the other person said before you already had a rebuttal in mind? Be truthful now. I've done it so many times that I'd like to flog myself. I argued, in one of my blog articles, that we should have some kind of app connected to electrodes that are in turn attached to our genitals so that when we reach to respond to some idiot's post on Facebook, it sends a mild, yet painful charge to our nether regions. I'm not completely certain that it wouldn't be a good idea. Better yet, probably, would be our own restraint when entering into a discussion of a sensitive topic, especially politics.

The problem isn't the discussion of politics but the fact that instead of actually *listening* to what the other person has to say we're trying to figure out how to interject what *we have to say*, before they've even said it. That's because we think we already know what they're going to say or what they *mean*. Doing this is a projection of your *own* Willful Ignorance into the discussion where you will probably point out your *opponents* Ignorance. It's the pot calling the kettle black. I've seen almost *no* discussion where this isn't happening on both sides. This happens because we disregard the other persons perspective; we are ignorant of their experiences. We devalue theirs and over-value our own. It is important to remind ourselves, constantly, that people hold opposing viewpoints for a variety of reasons not all of them invalid, or ignorant, or stupid.

For example, racism, an insidious problem in the World, isn't *all* based on ignorance, be it willful or simple. It's based on many things including inherited belief systems. But too often it is reinforced by negative, personal experiences in interactions with the other race. This goes both ways, by the way. Racism isn't *just* white against those of color. It's also those of color against whites, and color on color. I've seen it manifest itself in all kinds of ways. But the point is that not all negative attitudes about the other race are based on misconceptions; they can be based on real experience. However, those experiences are often generally applied to *every one* of that particular race. The specific incident or experience becomes a stereotype. Instead of, "That African-American/Caucasian/Hispanic man mugged me!" it becomes "All African-American/Caucasian/Hispanic men are muggers!" Of course my example is a stereotype of sorts as well. Things never happen so simply. Most people who are truly racist were raised to be that way by their parents. This was reinforced by the language of their peers and the other people of the community. Then all negative interactions with the other race lent credence for what one already *knew to be true.*

When addressing a false belief system like racism we tend to discount everything the other person is saying because their viewpoint is simply *wrong.* I'm not going to argue here, or ever, that racism *isn't'wrong.* It is. But that doesn't get us very far if we want to find a solution to it. Yes, it's wrong. Great. Now what do we do? What we do is find out *why* the other person thinks the way they think. At the same time, we have to realize that *right,* or *truth* isn't always on one side or the other. If the other side didn't have real experiences to draw upon, their belief system would soon collapse in upon itself. It could not be maintained. Often members of both sides perpetuate the stereotypes which further fuels the beliefs on either side. For example, skin-head racists waving Nazi flags perpetuates the idea that whites are racist. Obviously they don't represent *all* whites but they come to symbolize a mentality. This is further reinforced by actions of authority figures, like the police in Fergusson, Missouri and other places where non-whites, especially those who *dress the wrong way,* are targeted for harassment. Sometimes this escalates into real violence as in the case in Fergusson. There are also, of course, numerous examples of violence perpetrated by people of color which fuels the distrust and reinforces racist sentiment among those who already held racist belief systems, giving them a platform and something to point to to make their case.

I'm not going to attempt to solve racism here. I'll talk a bit more about it in Part III when we get to the solutions to these problems—and there *are* solutions to racism, just as there are to all the other problems presented in this boo— and to those that I've overlooked or neglected to mention. But in order to solve them we first must be able to look within ourselves and make some very hard decisions about what we *really know* about our supposed enemies and opponents. Do we really know what they're thinking? Have we tried to understand their perspective? to put ourselves in their shoes? Or have we lost all ability to empathize with those unlike us. Are they really unlike us?

### Lack of Empathy or Compassion: Survival of the Fittest! So sayeth Darwin!

As I said above, it's impossible to truly see the World though another person's perspective. At best, we can empathize with them or if we've experienced a similar trauma or pain, sympathize with them. Much of the time it seems that humanity as a whole has lost the ability to do that. I could launch into one of those *old guy* speeches here, about how it was so awesome in the olden days, but I'm pretty sure that's not true, so I won't. I think people have always had a hard time feeling empathy and compassion for others. Maybe our modern, electronic world is syphoning off even more of our compassion. Technology does seem to disconnect us more than connect. Where it should expedite the ability to connect with each other, it seems instead to allow us to do the opposite—*disconnect* at lightning speed.

The lack of compassion and empathy is itself rooted in Fear and Ignorance. The fear comes from a vague belief that other people are out to take what we have, whether that be our hard-earned cash, our reputation, our security or simply our time. The ignorance can be Simple Ignorance—we fear what and who we don't know—or it can be Willful: "I don't *want* to know" or think I *already* know what they think or want. This lack of compassion has reared its ugly head many times but is no more prevalent than our collective tendency to blame the poor for being poor. "They're poor/homeless/jobless because they want to be, or because they're not ambitious enough, or they didn't take advantage of free education, *ad nauseum.*" There's a certain Social Darwinian logic implied, if not explicit, in such an argument. It seems to argue that if one is poor, one deserves to be so, because they are unfit to be successful. They are poor because they aren't the *fittest; ergo,* if they're going to die, "they'd better do it, and decrease the surplus population." Thank you, Charles Dickens.

How does such a callous mentality develop? It behooves us to discover the answer. Without the answer we'll never be able to counter callous mentalities like racism, bigotry, and religious prejudice. In Scrooge's case, his callousness was developed over a lifetime of experience tainted with a drive for *gain,* Greed. Such Greed leads to the other spectre under the robe of the Spirit of Christmas Present: Want.

# Want and Greed: Orthanc and the Destabilizing Force of Unchecked Capitalism

"Desire is the root of all suffering." —The Buddha

What good is it for a man to gain the whole world, yet forfeit his soul? —Jesus, *The Bible, Gospel of Mark* 8:36

And as for he who is stingy and holds back.
And denies goodness.
We will make the difficult path for him.
And his wealth will not avail him when he demises.
—The Koran, 92:9-11

He that hasteth to be rich hath an evil eye, and considereth not that poverty shall come upon him. — *The Bible, Proverbs* 28:22

"There is a sufficiency in the world for man's need but ·not for man's greed." —Mahatma Gandhi

"He who is not contented with what he has, would not be contented with what he would like to have." — Socrates

"There is no crime more onerous than greed,
No misfortune more devastating than avarice.
And no calamity that brings with it more grief than
insatiability." — *The Tao De Jing*, Chapter 46

"Don't get me wrong
Try getting me right
Your face is OK
But your purse is too tight
I'm looking for pound notes, loose change, bad checks,
anything
Gimme some money, gimme some money." —Spinal
Tap, *Gimme Some Money*

## In the Kitchens of Isengard

"Hold it steady now!" I said to my partner, Deshaun, on the
other side of the mop well.

"There are no f'n handles on this thing man!" Deshaun
replied.

"I know, so pay attention!"

It was 1990, in New Bern, N.C. Both of us were standing on
a slick, greasy tile floor, in the mop well, in the back of the only
Burger King in town. It was late night, probably about 10
o'clock or so, closing time. We had been charged with cleaning
the fryers that night, a crappy job, handling 360 degree
vegetable oil. In order to clean the fryers, and dispose of it after
it had already been filtered and reused a couple of times, you
had to roll the filter vat back to the rear of the store, and dump it
into a round, steel pot—basically a big-assed stock pot, so you
could carry that out to the big, plastic barrels outside and dump
it again so that some company could come pick it up and do
with it whatever it was they did. I didn't know, and quite
frankly, didn't care at the time. I was getting paid minimum
wage to stick frozen patties of 'beef' into the back of a broiler
machine all day long, pick them up on the other end with tongs,
put them between two buns—which also went through the
machine—and then into a steamer table, where they sat,
supposedly for no more than ten minutes—actually much
longer—before someone ordered a Whopper with cheese, and

then I, or some other wage-slave would pick it out of the steam table, put it on some plastic-coated *wax* paper, assemble it, nuke it for about 5 seconds, and then toss it up into the rack for the slave up front to serve it up to some sap who had just wasted his money on overly-processed food, to wash down with some sugary drink.

So, Deshaun and I were standing in the mop room, and I was standing in the mop well, you know, the section of floor recessed about 4 inches to catch mop water when you pour out the big mop bucket. In the middle of the well was a drain, for the aforementioned water. Pouring hot grease into a round pot would be difficult enough, if you had a funnel, and if the vat you were pouring from had a spout or something. But it didn't. In fact, the filter vat, itself stainless steel, was a rectangular box, on small casters—so you could roll it to the back. It had once been fitted out with handles on either side so that the employee lucky enough to be assigned the job could pick it up without burning himself to hell. I'll repeat, it *once* had handles. It no longer did. So what my compatriot and I were actually faced with was a disaster waiting to happen, compounded by the fact that neither of us had ever been assigned to this task before, so there was going to be a very steep learning curve, or I should say, *deep* learning curve, as it turned out.

Instead of handles, we both had kitchen towels in our hands, to keep from burning the skin off our fingers and palms when we picked up the vat. So I turned to Deshaun and said, "Ok, on 3, pick it up with me and let's do this slow and carefully."

"Ok man."

"One, two, three. Umphh." It was heavy, probably about 5 gallons of grease, so at least 40 pounds. We slowly began to tip the front over the big stock pot in the well. The hot grease edged its way to the rim, and slowly began to pour over the top. That's when things picked up quickly, and I mean very quickly. Because grease doesn't pour well from a rectangular receptacle into a round one: square peg, round hole. But more importantly than the geometry of the situation was the nature of liquid and pouring. If you don't pour fast enough initially, it will just run down the front, and onto the floor, table or counter, or...the hands holding the receptacle, which is what happened in our case: my right hand. When 360 degree grease hits your hand, something uncontrollable occurs: you drop whatever is in said hand. In my case, that meant the vat of grease. I let it go, and true to Newton's Law, it went down, went down hard, emptying its contents into the mop well, filling it up to about a 2 inch depth in about 1 second of time. This was the same mop well I was standing in. I might have been spared a great deal of pain by my shoes.

But I was not. My *shoes* were nearly unrecognizable as such. Thanks to the generosity of my employer, I hadn't purchased new shoes in a couple of years, and since I didn't have a car, most days I walked the 3 miles to work and back, 6 days a week. That puts a great deal of wear and tear on a pair of Walmart special tennis shoes, so that by the time my shoes met the boiling grease, on that night in 1990, there were essentially no soles on the bottoms, and holes on the top too. When I say no soles, I actually mean it. The front end of the soles were completely worn away from walking. So when that grease filled the well, it filled my shoes, from the bottom up.

Needless to say, I came out of the grease, like, well, greased lightning. Howling for Deshaun to turn on the water hose! I'm pretty sure he had never seen a white boy move so fast in his life. I was out of the well, and my *shoes* in about 2 seconds and standing in the hallway outside the mop room over a floor drain, yelling, "Damn it man, give me the f'n hose!"

Well, I hosed my smoking feet off, which were already blistering, and then went back to work, despite the manager telling me that I could go home. I needed the extra minutes on the paycheck to survive, especially since the next day I couldn't get the same *shoes* on my feet to walk the 3 miles back to work. I was there the second day though. Missing work meant missing dinner. I was eventually fired from that stellar job because, hungry one day, I snuck a couple of chicken tenders to the back of the store and ate them, and was caught by the manager, who promptly fired me.

I only tell this story here to illustrate what so many people go through every day, in the U.S., and other places in the world, just to scrape a meager paycheck and keep the wolves at bay. Meanwhile, the owner of the store lived in the posh section of town, drove a Cadillac, and only dropped into the store to 'fix' the broken ice machine that he had purchased used years before to save a few dollars. And to give us advice on how to make french fries properly as if he had ever actually made any in the real world. Then he would leave us in the rundown kitchen with the broken ice machine, faulty ventilation system, and unsafe fryer grease vat. He made millions over the years; I made minimum wage, walked the soles out of my shoes, and waded in boiling fryer grease. So do many other workers, still. And since I was one of them I can tell you that they aren't all lazy, uneducated, unambitious bums.

## Beware of *Want*: Wealth Inequality and Saruman's Greed

> "Man," said the Ghost, "if man you be in heart, not adamant, forbear that wicked cant until you have discovered *What the surplus is*, and *Where it is*. Will you decide what men shall live, what men shall die? It may be, that in the sight of Heaven, you are more worthless and less fit to live than millions like this poor man's child. Oh God! to hear the *Insect on the leaf pronouncing on the too much life among his hungry brothers in the dust!*" (italics/bold-mine) — Charles Dickens, *A Christmas Carol*

"The poor are just lazy." I hear this sentiment all the time. Sometimes it's verbalized exactly that way, sometimes just implied, but it's rampant. And I've been guilty of thinking it for a very long time, until recently. It has been—if I had to be honest and admit it—my underlying assumption about wealth distribution in America since I was a child. Unfortunately, I'm not the only person with this assumption.

When I peruse Facebook, I run into it daily. Some friend of mine, or friend of a friend, spouting off a retort, usually in rebuttal to some 'liberal' meme—pointing to the imbalance of wealth in this country—with the underlying message—if not explicitly so—that the poor in this country are just plain lazy and scamming the welfare system. Where does this mentality come from? I don't know where most people obtained theirs, but recently I was able to dig deep enough to find the source of my own affliction. It was Christmas, 1976. As I mentioned in the introduction, my parents are retired Salvation Army Officers. They worked tirelessly at that calling for over 40 years.

One December, probably about 1976 or so—I would have been about 10 years old—I was helping my parents set up the annual Toy Store. The Salvation Army does this every year. A sizable portion of the Christmas Kettle fund goes toward providing toys for underprivileged kids. The rest of the fund is allocated towards other social work throughout the year: food, clothing, shelter, utilities, etc., for those in need. My brother, Dave, and I were helping my mom and dad organize the Toy Store and to distribute toys to the parents that came to pick up toys for their kids. Back then, some of those toys were used, or what we might call 'recycled' toys. It was our job to sort through these—pausing ever so often to inspect (play with) the occasional G.I. Joe with the KungFu Grip, or X-wing Fighter, and to divide them by appropriate age and gender. We then put them into bags for the pickup day.

When the day of the Toy Store came, we helped to hand out the bags to the parents and, sometimes, carry them out to their car. And this is when the seed of welfare scam and lazy poor people was planted in my young mind, where it grew into a Mirkwood Forest of myth. There were two ladies, who had come together—a younger African American lady, and an older one, maybe her mother, I don't know—who came in to pick up bags for 3 or 4 kids, presumably the younger lady's children. There was nothing remarkable about the two women. I remember nothing about how they were dressed or what they looked like—it was a long time ago. But when they were finished choosing bags of toys my mom asked me if I would help carry them out to their car. I did, and that's when it happened.

When I got out to the parking lot beside the building, the older lady opened up the trunk of a more-or-less, brand new, shiny, maroon Cadillac into which I put the toys. I was stunned, shocked, amazed and at once disillusioned. In one instant, all my assumptions about poor people were seismically altered. I was 10 remember. In my young mind, poor people didn't drive Cadillacs; rich people did. My family didn't have a Cadillac, that's for sure. Here was someone picking up free toys for their children and driving off with them in the trunk of their rich person's car. For the majority of the rest of my life—until very recently, actually—my view of the poor in this country, and indeed every country, was that they were one of, or a combination of, four things: lazy, disabled, uneducated—because they were lazy—or scamming the system. There's only one problem with that assumption; it's all but completely false.

## What's the Truth? Where are the real welfare scams?

Yes, there are a few poor people scamming government systems and the systems set up by non-profits like the Salvation Army. It's true. Given the chance, some people scam systems. But the poor aren't the ones really scamming it; the richest 1% of the country are. Every year, the top 'earners' in this country hoard more wealth to themselves, while the rest of us are left with the crumbs of the pie. That used to be mainly a problem for those so-called lazy poor people, but not anymore. Now the middle class are inexorably slipping into the ranks of the poor who were never lazy to begin with.

## How can this be?

Because the wealth created in this country is trickling: not down—as most conservatives think—but UP. Nearly 50% of Americans are now considered lower income, while the elite at the top, the 1%, have seen increases in income grossly out of touch with the snail-paced increase in average wages. That's not just wages for the so-called, 'unwashed masses' at the bottom, but wages for educated, skilled workers as well. The average 1 percenter makes about 400 times what the average *working* American makes. Let me repeat that—400 TIMES! About 400 people in the U.S. hold wealth equal to the amount held buy the lowest half of U.S. citizens, or about 180 Million people. Six heirs of the Walmart fortune hold as much wealth as the bottom 42 percent of the U.S. population.There is no other country on Earth with that kind of wealth disparity: not one.

Worldwide the disparity is even worse. The richest 85 people on Earth, hold more wealth than the bottom 50%! That's 85 people compared to 3.5 BILLION! So, about 1 percent of 1 percent of the population of the United States holds enough wealth to obliterate poverty in the country, and 85 people on Earth could eliminate it for the entire planet.

## Why don't they end poverty?

That's a very good question. They would argue and do argue, much as Mitt Romney did during his disastrous and shameful campaign for president in 2012, that the lower half of the population is simply lazy and/or unambitious, and therefore inferior to the other 50%, or more accurately, inferior to the 1%. But I think we have addressed that falsity. How then can this inequality be justified? It cannot by any argument based at all on logic. Those at the top simply do not work that hard if they work at all, and many do not. Most of them produce nothing, unless you count the rhetoric about how they are necessary to provide jobs for those of us at the bottom. What jobs? Are they referring to the minimum-wage, poverty-slave-wage-jobs *created* by companies like Walmart? Most of Walmart's employees are part-timers, so the company can avoid paying for benefits. These workers are a small part of a larger problem in America and elsewhere; they are *underemployed*. Many of them are on public welfare assistance because if they weren't their families would starve. In some cases, they are starving anyway because the food they can afford is basically junk. So instead of requiring Walmart and every other employer in the U.S. to pay livable wages to their employees, the taxpayers — and by taxpayers, I mean the middle class or what's left of it, because the ultra rich don't pay their share of taxes — have to supplement the wages that employers won't pay their workers just so they won't starve to death. It's a ridiculous situation.

If all that wealth were actually recirculated — either by creating millions of new jobs rebuilding our crumbling infrastructure at a livable wage, or by at least *spending* it — then the elite could at least make the argument sound more plausible, but that's simply not the case. This is the so-called 'trickle down' theory. I confess that I used to believe in the so-called 'Trickle Down' theory, but I've seen very little evidence of trickling. If anything, the wealth, in defiance of Newtonian physics, is trickling up, if indeed 'trickle' is the right word to describe it. I suspect that it's more akin to the flow over the great Niagara Falls or the Falls of Rauros pouring into the pockets of those at the top. But they aren't creating new jobs and the top 1% simply don't spend 400 times as much as everyone else. They don't eat 400 times as much food, or drive 400 cars, or have 400 times as many pairs of shoes—well not most of them anyway. Mostly they just hoard that wealth in offshore accounts so they don't have to pay taxes on it. Occasionally they invest it, or *speculate* on markets, like they did with real estate market creating a massive *bubble* like the one that burst in 2007. It's going to happen again because they're *at it again* thanks to the bailouts that we gave the banks. Not one banker has even been charged with a crime for that collapse. Instead, they all got bonuses while millions of hardworking, middle class Americans joined the hardworking poor, and slipped into homelessness or at the very least, lost what wealth they once had.

When the corporations—owned, operated and invested in by the 1%—feel that American taxes are too onerous—even though they are historically low, these same corporations purchase companies in other countries so they can pick up stakes and move out to avoid paying their fair share while they continue to sell their products in the U.S.! The process, called a corporate *inversion* has become increasingly popular in recent days. The most recent being Walgreen's Pharmacies who planned in 2014 to purchase a company in Switzerland and move out while leaving their retail stores in America in full operation. Thankfully, public outcry via social media was so loud that they backed out of the idea and fired the man who came up with it, as if it were solelly his fault. The damage to their reputation might be impossible to repair though. Time will tell.

And those two ladies with the Cadillac back in 1976? My dad attempted to explain it to me that day—though it didn't sink in until recently. Perhaps, he told me, the older one was giving a ride to the younger one as a charitable act. They may not have even been related. Who knows. I just assumed that the older one was the mother. Assumptions are the most dangerous things we can have because more often than not they're baseless. Whether the older lady was or was not the mother, or whether the younger lady was or was not scamming the system, it's not the poor we should blame. Those at the top who are hoarding wealth while expecting the rest of us to support the employees that they refuse to pay a livable wage, are the lazy-assed scammers.

**Couldn't we just tax the rich more?**

This sounds like an easy enough and simple solution. The problem is that when the liberals in the country push for taxes on the wealthiest, it never really happens. What happens instead — thanks to the lobbyists in Washington, paid for by the top 1% — is that taxes increase for those in the middle of the economic ladder, and so instead of the middle class businessman siding with the rest of the population against the top 1%, they tend to side with those at the top who make ridiculous arguments about how taxes will harm their business. Taxes on middle class businesses do hurt the economy, and quickly. Middle class businesses simply don't run on a large profit margin contrary to what a lot of us might think. For instance, the owner of a McDonald's franchise might consider herself lucky to walk away with 10% of his gross sales at the end of the year. While this is nothing to sneeze at, the overhead of running the place means that if she pays too much for wages she will not make a profit at all and her restaurant will have to close. This is why most franchise owners are so against a raise in the minimum wage in the U.S. And this is the argument they and other small business owners use to justify paying their workers poverty wages.

What is the solution then? Where is all that money going? Why can't they afford to pay their workers a livable wage? Quite simply, it is because the corporations are raking in record profits every year, to pay fat dividends to their stockholders. To maximize their profits and dividends they take fees from the franchise owners, though that is not where most of the profit originates, not these days. Back in the early days of franchises, the 50s and 60s, even up into the 80s, corporations like

McDonalds and others took a small percentage of the gross sales of each franchise, usually only about 1%. That doesn't sound like a lot, but when you add that up over 1000s of restaurants it's a lot of dragon gold.

But in the 80s things started to change. Corporate headquarters of all the big franchises discovered that they could maximize their profits if they centralized control over the supply to each franchise. Before this time, a local franchise like a Kentucky Fried Chicken, for example, would buy its chicken and other produce from local suppliers in the community. Most of the other supplies — plates, cups, napkins, etc. — were purchased from corporate headquarters. But in the 80s, when big corporations like Pepsi Co. and others began to scoop up smaller corporations like KFC and Taco Bell they began to require that the franchisees purchase ALL of their supply from central headquarters, including the meat and produce. The effect of this was to shift money that once recirculated into the local economies of each individual town and city into the pockets of the corporate shareholders, via central headquarters, where they also shaved their share off the top. So the vast majority of the money that we spend in franchises is usurped by the *mother ship* so to speak; it does not buy yachts for the local owner. That's not to say that some of them don't make a good profit, but they work pretty hard to get it, unlike the shareholders who do little to nothing to produce that wealth.

Meanwhile, the person cooking your burger or breading your chicken in a hot, greasy kitchen, emptying vats of boiling hot grease, mopping up floors can't even afford to eat in the restaurant where he or she works because they aren't paid enough to even pay their bills. As I mentioned in my story earlier, I was fired from that Burger King for eating a chicken tender without paying for it. Now, to be fair, I didn't pay for it, and the rules certainly stated that termination was the immediate punishment for said infraction. But quite frankly, I was hungry. Now, I wasn't going to starve to death if I didn't eat that fried piece of 'chicken', or whatever it actually was. No, I would have survived to sweat another day in my polyester uniform and my 'air-conditioned' shoes. The point I'm making is that this is a common rule in many franchise restaurants.

Employees have to pay for their food, most of the time, full price. No free meals, just 8 plus hours of sweat for minimum wage.

Many of them—who work at more than one job, because the owner can't afford to pay for their health benefits if he hires them full-time—have to sign up for welfare and food stamps in order to feed their families. So, instead of the corporation taking care of their employees, i.e., paying them a living wage, we have to support their employees via tax dollars. So who is really getting the welfare? I would argue that it is the shareholders of the corporations. We are supporting their employees because they refuse to do so. So when the wealthy complain about people scamming the welfare system, we should all take a moment to think, and then say, "Uh, yeah. You are!" Sure, there a few poor people out there scamming welfare. I've seen it myself, but the real scam comes from those with plenty who essentially steal their profits from the sweat of their poor employees and then expect those of us in the middle class to pay the difference between their employees' paltry wages and what it actually takes to survive. Here are some figures on wages in comparison with corporate taxes, provided by Gar Alperovitz, from his book, *What Then Must We Do?: Straight Talk about the Next American Revolution*:

> ...for almost 40 years, there has been only a minuscule, token change in weekly earnings for most Americans—approximately one-tenth of 1 percent per year for roughly 80 percent of all wage and salary workers. Private production and nonsupervisory workers made an average of $18.74 per hour in 1973 (in 2011 dollars); by 2011—thirty-eight years later—this had edged up only to $19.47. Corporate taxes have steadily declined: from 32.1 percent of federal revenues in 1952 to 15.5 percent of such revenues in 1972 to 10.2 percent in 2000 to 7.9 percent in 2011. Corporate taxes as a share of GDP declined from a modest 6.1 percent in 1952 to 2.1 percent in 2000 to a mere 1.2 percent in 2011."

Wealth inequality has risen steadily in the 20th Century. According to the Worldwatch Institute—an organization of academics who keep track of issues for the planet—"the richest 10 percent of people have, on average, nine times the income of the poorest 10 percent."

## Debt: Saruman's Shell Game

One of the things driving this inequality is the increase in debt that most of us are under. Debt is actually a tool to increase wealth for those who already have it, at the expense of those who do not. While there is not time or space here to go into the history of debt and money—I would suggest reading David Graeber's book, *The History of Debt: the First 5000 Years*, if you're interested in a fascinating examination of wealth—it is important to know how it works in today's market. Banks are, by law, supposed to keep a percentage of all their deposits in reserve. That was traditionally at least 10%, but these days that is not always the case. The rest of the money they can lend out as loans to people, businesses, or foreign governments. But that's not the trick to making money. The trick—and you won't believe this when I tell you—is that they then take the debt that is owed to them, and deposit *it* into another bank, who can then turn around and lend out *that* debt, after reserving a percentage, as another loan! Let me try to simplify this. It's a real shell game, so pay close attention. Only a wizard like Saruman or Sauron could pull this off, but here it is again, in slow motion. 1. You put money into savings. 2. The bank loans out most of that money to someone else. 3. They deposit that person's debt in another bank. Not money, mind you, but debt, as if it were money they already had. 4. The second bank then lends out most of that *money/debt* to someone else. 5. The second bank then can take that debt and deposit it in another bank, who treats this debt as actual money. 6. The process keeps going, forever, *ad infinitum*.

Now, if you go through that process slowly you will notice that at a minimum, banks essentially create money out of debt, each and every time they go through this process and they do it every day, everywhere. Not only do *people* put money into banks—who play the shell game with it—but *governments* loan or credit money to the banks to do the same thing.

> For example, if a government credits $1 million to a bank and the fractional reserve requirement is 10 percent, banks can create $9 million in new money, for a total money supply of $10 million. In this way, most money is today created as interest-bearing debt . Total debt in the United States— adding together consumers, businesses, and the government— is about $50 trillion. This is the source of the national money supply. —Worldwatch Institute, *State of the World 2013: Is Sustainability Still Possible?*

The money that banks lend out doesn't actually exist! They are lending out debt, and turning it into money! We are all in the wrong business! This is truly a shell game people.

What this means is that it is not the U.S. Government that prints money. Banks *print* it every time they make a new loan. This of course drives up the price inflation of products which we have to pay every time we go to the grocery store or the gas pump. The inflation creates more profits for big businesses and for the banks. It's a win/win situation for those at the top, while the rest of us pay the price. If all this seems too incredible to be true, I hope you will check up on it for yourself. There is plenty of information online about it. The banks are *banking* on the unfortunate fact that most of us don't have time to pay attention to what they're doing. Make the time. It is a matter of life and death and I'm not exaggerating on that. And don't for a second believe that the government is in control of all this.

## Taking the 'Fed' Out of Federal

The Federal Reserve is supposed to regulate this, but just what is the Federal Reserve? Entire books have been written on it. While the name suggests that it is a government bank, it is not. Yes, the head of the reserve is appointed by the President, but the institution is actually run by the big private banks in the country. Yes, I said that correctly. Private banks make all the decisions about debt, money, interests rates, and inflation. These private banks control nearly all the wealth in the country. According to Worldwatch, "In 1994, the five largest U.S. banks held 12 percent of total U.S. deposits. By 2009 they held nearly 40 percent. The country's 20 largest banks control almost 60 percent of bank assets." And for those of you not living in

America, fear not, this is a global reality. Even if the regulations on banks are different in other countries, they can create money in American banks and American banks lend their money to businesses and countries around the world, each time creating more money. So much of the so-called *money* sitting in a bank in Switzerland, is actually debt, owed by someone in Iowa, or California, or North Carolina, or 47 other states.

## Myth of the 'Free' Market: Saruman's Welfare Check

The top *earners* in the country use as their mantra the idea of the *Free Market*, as if it were some religious concept to which we should all bow down. They argue that a free market will automatically even out and keep check on greed and abuses by big business through what Adam Smith coined as the *Invisible Hand*. Smith, an 18th Century economist, and the equivalent to economics that Darwin is to evolutionary science, argued that if allowed to work freely, the economy would self regulate. Well, that's what most modern big businessmen *think* Smith said, but what they leave out is that Smith also argued that government intervention was necessary to moderate the tendency of greed and profit to drive industry to do horrible things to its workers.

What's interesting is that most *free*-marketers don't seem to want a free market at all, but a *status quo* market. The market in the United States is anything but free. If it were, big business would have to survive without corporate welfare to the tune of about $1 trillion (that's trillion) in government subsidies, the majority of which, about $650 billion, go to the fossil fuel industry! They are living off of the public dole on subsidies totaling billions of dollar—that we hand out either directly, or through tax breaks for their big corporations—with the false assumption that they are *creating jobs*. They are not. They are creating yachts, Leer Jets, and McMansions with swimming pools. So the uber-rich in the U.S. aren't *earning* their profits; those were given to them, by us. Hobbits need to stand up and demand that pay back the welfare they've been squandering for decades, start creating livable wage jobs, or we will dissolve them!

Saruman has bewitched us and our lands are overrun with Ringwraiths in the form of big bankers who tell us that if we will just borrow their gold they will look out for us. They take our wealth, shuffle it around in a real-life shell game which we never win, while they create more and more debt which creates more and more money for them. And then, with our money in their pockets — the fictional money they created out of thin air — they can turn it to *good* use dominating the very entity that might be able to keep them in check: the governments of the world.

# 4

# WORMTONGUE & THEODEN: THE CORPORATE CORRUPTION OF POLITICS

"There are pockets of wealth in this country. Mostly those pockets are in the politicians' pants."
Jarod Kintz, *How to construct a coffin with six karate chops*

"It could probably be shown by facts and figures that there is no distinctly native American criminal class except Congress." Mark Twain

"We have the best congress money can buy." Mark Twain

From Isengard, Saruman sent his 'lobbyist', Wormtongue, to poison the ear of King Theoden of Rohan, whom he bewitched with lies and promises of friendship until the old king withered and rotted on his throne. Years of foul council from Saruman via Wormtongue effectively ground royal decisions to a halt. Theoden could no longer tell friend from foe as we discover when Gandalf returns with Aragorn, Legolas, and Gimli to meet with the king. Instead of talking directly to the king Gandalf finds himself speaking through the twisted mouth of Wormtongue:

> The wise speak only of what they know, Gríma son of
> Gálmód. A witless worm have you become. Therefore
> be silent, and keep your forked tongue behind your
> teeth. I have not passed through fire and death to
> bandy crooked words with a serving-man till the
> lightning falls. — *LOTR*: II, *The King of the Golden Hall*

Luckily for Middle Earth, and the kingdom of Rohan the wizard was able to break the spell on the old king, and bring him back to his true nature.

In a similar way, the Sarumans of our world are rapidly taking control of access to government. The most damaging aspect of wealth inequality is the extent to which the wealth flowing upward to the 1% at the top has overtaken and corrupted our political system. In an ideal political system the people have a voice in government, a voice with weight. The American form of republican democracy is in theory designed to do just that. In reality, however, the system is ruled by big money originating from several sources but ultimately, from big business. There are many interest groups lobbying the representatives in Washington, but the loudest voice comes from multibillion dollar corporations who can afford to spend millions, even billions, to influence policy makers to vote for laws that protect and extend their interests and profits.

Most of us are aware of this ugly truth, but sometimes it's easy to forget that the root of the political problems aren't Democrats or Republicans—however much we may argue and disagree on that point—but the *money* that inevitably ends up in the pockets of Democrat and Republican *politicians*. I have stated many times, usually in some drawn-out, politicized, Facebook rant that while there are Democrat and Republican *people*, there are very few Democrat or Republican *politicians*. They are nearly all *corporate* politicians. I know that's a gross oversimplification and generalization but the essence of the statement is true however many exceptions to the rule one might find to contradict it. The number of freethinking, idealistic politicians in our nation's capitol can probably be counted on two hands, and I'm probably being generous. The point is, the system is corrupt—which we can all probably agree on—and it's corrupted by a massive river of money flowing through the halls of congress and the White House, though the situation isn't restricted to the U.S., of course.

It might be helpful to think about the situation in a hypothetical way. Imagine for a moment, that you are one of the 1%. You own stock in myriad companies, maybe you're even a CEO of one. You've never really worked a day of hard labor in your life—unless you count staring at the stock ticker on your computer screen and doing lunch with your peers as *work*—and all those millions, nay billions, are yours to roll around in. Imagine that there are two political rivals, one Republican, one Democrat, running for a U.S. Senate seat that traditionally controls a committee overlooking the doings of your favorite industry. You have a couple of choices if you want to influence the outcome of the election. You can pour a great deal of money into one campaign or the other, hoping that your choice wins, which would be quite the gamble, because what if he/she doesn't win? Or, you could *donate* a more modest sum to both candidates, attend several dinners in their honor, shake their hands, have cocktails together, you get the picture. Then you could sit back and relax. In the end it matters not which one wins. You will still have the ability to pick up the phone, or have one of your minions do it, call the illustrious senator and request he or she vote in your favor. This is the ancient art of hedging your bets. Amateur gamblers bet on one horse to win. Smart businessmen aren't really gamblers; they bet on several to win, place or show. In the end, if you play the game this way, you can't lose. While the people at the bottom—many of whom don't even know their playing a game—will always leave the track with empty pockets.

Yeah, I know, call me a cynic. But this is exactly how the system works! The politicians know it, the corporations know it, and the media knows it. For some reason, though, the average voter is slow to figure this out. It's not the voters fault. The two parties know exactly how to whip up the dander of their members against the other party. That's not to say there is no difference at all between the parties. As I said above, most voters *do* fall into one of the party platforms, and can be quite passionate about it, as is evident to anyone who's spent an hour reading their friends' social media posts. I'm sure you've seen, as I have, old friends of many years slinging mud and insults at each other over political issues. Many a friendship has ended as a result. I've been guilty of such arguments too, most of us probably have.

Saruman managed to introduce discord into the kingdom of Rohan, too. Thanks to his lies there was strife between Theoden and his nephew, Eomer. It's unfortunate that we argue with each other over politics because the solution to the world's problems is unlikely to come from our political systems, at least not as those systems are currently functioning, if *functioning* is even remotely the right word to use—I suspect that it would be more accurate to say **dys-**functioning.

### Super Pacs: Wargs in the Village!

When Bilbo escaped Gollum and the orcs in the Misty Mountains—sans a few buttons—he found his companions not far away and all was well. But as Gandalf warned them, the orcs would come looking for them when the sun retired, so they better move along. By nightfall, they found themselves scrambling up tree tops to avoid a ravenous pack of wargs who had surrounded them on all sides! As Gandalf was able to discern from their growling speech they had been organized to come together under the instruction of the Great Goblin to raid human settlements along the river. Now one warg is bad enough, but when they come in packs they're hard to beat. Luckily for Bilbo and his friends, they had Gandalf and the great Eagles to help them out of this sticky wicket!

One of the most insidious institutions to arise in American politics in the last decade or so is the spectre of the Super Pac, a largely anonymous group of individuals—usually millionaires, or billionaires—ravenous wargs who pool their money to run their own political ads supporting one candidate or political agenda while demonizing and attacking the opposition. This has been upheld and reenforced as *constitutional* by the Citizens United decision of the Supreme Court, who seem to be completely undermined as an institution themselves.

## Saruman's Court: Wargs United and Corporate *People*

In early 2010, the Supreme Court of the United States, in a disastrous decision known now by the name of the group that brought it to court, *Citizens United*, essentially declared that corporations had the same rights as individuals when it came to contributing money to political campaigns. In other words, corporations *are people*. Thanks to this decision, big business has managed to complete their domination of much of the political arena, spending billions to attack opponents while supporting their own candidates. If that decision wasn't damaging enough, the Supreme Court backed it up again in early 2014 with a ruling that essentially removed any limits on what corporation-people could spend on campaigns. There can be no democracy or a republic under such a system. As the old saying goes, money talks, and in this case the rest of us walk.

In short, the Supreme Court has decreed that the United States is now, officially, an **oligarchy**. A study carried out by Princeton and Northwestern Universities, agrees:

> The central point that emerges from our research is that economic elites and organized groups representing business interests have substantial independent impacts on U.S. government policy, while mass-based interest groups and average citizens have little or no independent influence. Our results provide substantial support for theories of **Economic Elite Domination** and for theories of Biased Pluralism, but not for theories of Majoritarian Electoral Democracy or Majoritarian Pluralism.

Thanks to Citizens United, these Super Pacs have completed the corruption of American politics, a process that began a very long time ago. And the corruption of corporate money isn't restricted to politics. In order to keep the lid on their shady dealings, they also use it to control the very source of information that might shed light on their doings: the media.

## Mass Media: the Corporate Wormtongues

All this big money has corrupted more than just our political systems. In order to keep all this money-shuffling out of sight and mind, some of it must be employed to control the dissemination of news. Thanks to the internet, this has become, for the most part, an impossible task. Most of the media in the U.S. is controlled by about 6 corporations. The corporate sector has spent hundreds of millions of dollars on political campaigns since the 1990s, while laws restricting consolidation of media outlets have steadily weakened, allowing more and more consolidation. In their 2013 rankings, Reporters Without Borders ranked the U.S. at #32 worldwide in their Press Freedom Index. The descendants of Benjamin Franklin didn't even make it into the top 30! Franklin and Jefferson surely must be tossing in their graves! How did a country based on such lofty ideals allow its *free* press to be dominated by so few? A free press, free from central control, is an essential part of a democratic system. How else can the people be informed enough to vote on important issues? If it were not for the internet, our modern 'voice of Gandalf,' if you will, many major news stories would go unnoticed.

If you think I'm exaggerating, I offer this case in point. In 2009, during the global financial crisis, the people of Iceland peacefully ousted their government, arrested their president, closed the private banking industry, sent them packing, and in a referendum voted to default on all debts owed to foreign banks. U.S. media was strangely silent. Most Americans learned of this story via the internet, and largely through social media like Facebook and Twitter. There are numerous other examples, but if the media cannot be trusted to cover the peaceful revolution of a normally stable country like Iceland, what can they be trusted to cover? What possible reasons could they have for not covering such a story? The only answer that seems to make sense is that the Saruman CEOs and stockholders of U.S. media outlets—who are also CEOs and stockholders of many other large corporations—were afraid, as they should have been, that the American people might do the same thing in the U.S.!

All this corruption leaves the American people, and people of other countries around the world in similar situations, feeling helpless, depressed, despondent, angry, frustrated and in many cases, apathetic. Gar Alperovitz, in his book *What Then Must We Do?: Straight Talk about the Next American Revolution*, points out that around 80% of Americans do not believe their representatives have their best interests at heart, and are instead more concerned about the special interests groups who wine and dine them—translate, *"bribe them."* The same percentage of Americans, 4 out of 5, believe that the wealthiest people and corporations have entirely too much power.

This is not a pretty picture for *democracy* in America. We will leave the topic of corruption for now by pointing out, as Mr. Alperovitz has, that in order to find political solutions to some of the world's biggest problems we need systemic changes to our corrupt political system. We will come back to this topic in part three of the book where I will suggest what I believe to be the best solution to the juggernaut of corporate influence. And guess what, it has to do with money.

All this corruption leads to self-serving decisions by corporate-owned representatives in governments around the world. This leads to illogical, wasteful, destructive, and deadly consequences. The rest of Part One will focus on those consequences starting with the most prominent, violence and the destruction of our sense of community.

# 5

# LOSS OF SHIRE-NESS: VIOLENCE AND THE DISINTEGRATION OF COMMUNITY

"We have become Middle Men, of the Twilight, but with memory of other things…we now love war and valour as things good in themselves, both a sport and an end; and though we still hold that a warrior should have more skills and knowledge than only the craft of weapons and slaying, we esteem a warrior, nonetheless, above men of other crafts." — *LOTR*, *'The Window on the West'*

Mother, mother
There's too many of you crying
Brother, brother, brother
There's far too many of you dying
You know we've got to find a way
To bring some lovin' here today —Marvin Gaye, *What's Goin' On*

I got God on my side
And I'm just trying to survive
What if what you do to survive
Kills the things you love

Fear's a powerful thing, baby
It can turn your heart black you can trust
It'll take your God filled soul
And fill it with devils and dust. — Bruce Springsteen,
*Devils and Dust*

# War

The most fearful of the Black Riders in our world would seem to be the spectre of violence on all levels, from domestic abuse to war between nations. It is the most sensational of our world problems, certainly, and draws the most attention. Fear of it spreads like a disease through our societies. It leads us to seek protection and security, to plead for government intervention in the creation of new institutions and drives us into even more wars. But violence isn't a cause; it is a symptom of an errant mentality. It can be eliminated, or at the very least, we can eliminate much of the roots of that evil tree. No, all violence will not disappear. People, and nations will always argue, and sometimes come to blows. But it should be an aberration, not the norm. As we'll see much later, it is *not* a fundamental aspect of humanity.

On the larger scale, wars seemed to have subsided in the world, at least from the Western point of view, after WWII. This did not last long. As 1950s turned into the 1960s, cracks in the defenses appeared, even in the western world. New wars, Korea and Vietnam, led many people, especially the youth of the world, to question whether violence and war was the answer to the new threat of communism. At the same time, minorities around the world and in particular in the U.S. rose up to demand a fairer share of society's pie and a voice on the issues impacting them. Violence erupted in many places, even in the 'peaceful' heartland of the United States. Massive, deadly riots broke out in many major cities, like Detroit in the summer of 1968, after the assassination of Martin Luther King Jr, and on college campuses, like that of Kent State in Ohio. Oppressed nations around the world rose up in rebellion against totalitarian regimes. While deaths from war have dropped in the 21st Century, war and violence continues in places like Afghanistan, Iraq, Syria, the Ukraine and in the streets of cities like Ferguson, Missouri. There are reasons to question the statistics. Keeping accurate records of deaths from violence has always been difficult to do. We can be sure that many deaths from war, and other violence, go unrecorded.

At the beginning of Tolkien's stories, Hobbits in The Shire seem to have lived without the threat of violence for a very long time. There were certainly disputes, the Sackville-Bagginses had their issues with Bilbo and Frodo, and weren't afraid to vocalize them. These never led to violence, however. The only battle recorded in Shire memory was the Battle of Greenfields when the goblins came out of the North, long, long ago, and Old 'Bullroarer' Took smashed off the skull of Golfimbul the goblin king which rolled into a rabbit hole, ending the battle and inventing the game of golf in one stroke: the first *hole in one*, in recorded history. But that was almost 300 years in the distant past and a story to tell little Hobbits.

War didn't appear again in the Shire until the evil CEO, Saruman, or 'Sharky' as he was called by his orcish followers, arrived to set up his corporate headquarters and open up factories belching smoke into the air. Thanks to his greed and avarice, he pitted Hobbits against Hobbits, men versus men, and men versus Hobbits. It was not until the four Hobbit heroes returned to their ravaged homeland that things were put to right—but not without further violence. Frodo, who had lost the taste for violence—if he ever had obtained it—refused to actively participate in the fighting. Merry and Pippen were more pragmatic, taking charge of the uprising to boot ole Saruman out on his ass. War, at that point had become inevitable due to Saruman's greed and obstinance. War is what he got, if a couple of days of violence count as a war, which I suppose by Hobbit standards it would.

In our modern world, Saruman has "many descendants," as Tolkien pointed out in his speech in 1958, and they have long been in control of our modern Shire. Corporate greed has led to a gulf of separation between those who hold the wealth and those who do not. On the international level, war is the result when one side is pushed to a point where personal safety is over-ridden by Fear for the immediate and future safety and necessities of the community, much as it was for the Hobbits in the Shire. Violence in all its forms, contrary to popular belief, is rarely motivated by differences in religion or ethnicity though it can be manipulated that way, with Fear. Driving that fear are economic inequalities and political disenfranchisement, or the perception that one has been disenfranchised. Never for a moment forget that perception is as good as reality.

An idea need not be true, only perceived to be true, to be powerful. In a culture of Fear people look at those who are different as *other*, a threat to their very existence or the continued existence of their own way of life, their culture, their religion, their safety, and their freedom. Fear is almost always driven by a lack of understanding. And the fear runs on both sides, many times multiplying with each new action till it tips over into violence. Violence then reinforces Fear, creating a super-storm which leads to war, eventually exhausting the energies of one or both sides till an equilibrium is reached, or both sides are so depleted it becomes impossible to prosecute the war and the war ends, leaving destruction in its wake, like a Class 5 tornado ripping through a midwestern town.

I hesitate to even bring up the word Terrorism because it is such a loaded term these days but even terrorism is an extension of this same scenario. The only thing that might distinguish this form of violence from war proper would be the intentional targeting of non-combatants: women, children and the elderly, but even that definition falls apart when you look at modern, *proper* wars, where so-called civilized countries, like Britain and the United States have indiscriminately bombed entire cities knowing well that they were full of non-combatants. This is not in anyway to excuse or condone the use of indiscriminate violence and war against the innocent but an attempt to understand the underlying causes that drives it. One need not agree with the methods of one's enemy, i.e., Al Qaeda, to examine the reasons such violence is employed. It pays to know what drives it so that, theoretically at least, we can find ways to remove the underlying causes.

The root of most *proper* war, i.e., wars carried out by sovereign nations, is usually greed, or revenge. Regardless of the excuses given, when it comes down to it, most modern wars—and many if not all ancient ones—were really disputes over resources. Would the United States have intervened in Iraq in 1991, or 2004 if Iraq lacked resources that the U.S. needed—vast oil reserves—and if the U.S. had not recently suffered from a terrorist attack? Would Alexander the Great have invaded the Persian Empire if they were not the repository of tons of gold, and the traditional enemy of all Greek speaking peoples? Probably not.

## Microcosms of War: Violence in the Home

Suicides are rampant. In 2010, the Center for Disease Control reported over 38,000 suicides in the United States, which made it the 10th leading cause of death. Suicide can be a symptom of many things of course, but poverty, abuse, a sense of hopelessness, and lack of support from family, friends, or community, are common contributors. People who feel disconnected from society, for whatever reason, are more susceptible to taking their own life. Abuse of family members, spouses, children, significant others, is a widespread tragedy. Most of us, maybe all of us, know people who have suffered from abuse, if we haven't suffered it personally. I had a wonderful childhood, with loving, supportive parents, but many of my friends had a very different experience.

Domestic violence seems to be on the rise, though there are problems with measuring such an insidious and secret practice. The evidence, in broken marriages, battered spouses and children must lead us to the conclusion that the violence is rampant in many homes around the world. Some of this may be the tendency of our major news outlets to push sensational stories of violence upon us in the belief that bad news is what *sells*. Again, poverty and despair are contributors to this unfortunate, and horrible issue, though abuse and violence certainly occurs daily in wealthy homes as well; the rich are not immune from those mental diseases. Despair and depression are contributors no matter what the economic situation may be. A contagion of aberration is also at work with abuse. Abused often grow up to become abusers themselves. Violence begets violence.

## Crime and Punishment and the New Slavery

Crime is often fueled by inequalities of wealth between the privileged elite and those on the bottom of the wage scale. As job prospects fall and the wealth is siphoned to the top, the poor scramble to find ways to survive; many times this means resorting to illegal means: drug trafficking, prostitution, burglary, and theft. Crime rates are on the rise again, thanks in large part to the economic collapse in 2007-8. This increase in crime, mostly non-violent, has led to the largest per capita prison population in the United States: over 700 people for every 100,000! The only other country that comes close to this is Russia, with just over 600. The prison population has exploded from about 300,000 in the 1970s to over 2,000,000 today. About 25% of all prisoners, worldwide, are in the U.S.: a country with only 5% of the world's population. Can it continue to call itself the 'land of the free'? Or should it more accurately be renamed, the land of the incarcerated?

One wonders if this push is due in large part to the privatization of U.S. prisons. Starting in the mid 1980s, private investors began pushing for the privatization of prisons in the U.S. Currently, they house about 10% of all prisoners, and are pushing for more. Privatization is not limited to prisons, as we'll see later on. If corporations run the prison system, and then lobby the state and federal governments for more laws, are they not creating more customers? Every law made creates another criminal, or thousands, or millions. There are enough laws on the books already. That is one of the problems. The more laws written the more convoluted the situation becomes.

It has long been the case that even highly educated people are ignorant of the vast majority of laws, even those pertaining to their individual situations. There are simply too many laws. This is even true for the legal profession! There are no lawyers who keep up with all the laws. Law, as a profession has long been specialized to the point of absurdity. Each section of the law has been divided multiple times so that to practice law means to practice a very small segment of it, dealing with increasingly specialized topics. If the lawyers can't keep up with the law, who can? Certainly the average citizen struggling to pay bills can't be expected to do it. Laws should not be that complicated, or numerous. Without systemic change the proliferation of laws will remain the norm. Laws need not be so numerous, or complicated. They exist, or they're supposed to exist, to protect one person from the greed and violence of another. Many laws these days seem to exist to perpetuate both greed and violence by protecting not the victims but the perpetrators. Such laws need to be repealed.

Other crimes, violent ones, are also exacerbated if not created by the despair that has set in thanks to increasing pressures of economics in the 20th and 21st Centuries. While most of us tend to think of slavery as something that died in 1865, it is alive and well in the 21st Century. Human trafficking, as it's called now, is on the rise around the world, and not just in Third World countries. According to a report by the International Labor Organization, through the auspices of the United Nations, there are about 20.9 million people worldwide who are essentially, if not actually, slaves. The most alarming statistic in the report estimated that in 2010, about 27% were children, many of them pressed into illegal prostitution. While violence, on a small scale, is probably part of human nature, what is driving all this institutionalized violence?

## Loss of Shire-ness

Crime and violence can be fueled by many things: racism, hatred, religious beliefs, revenge, ignorance, and want. But what it always signals is a breakdown in community. This is more evident on the micro scale, in neighborhoods, for example, than it is on the international level, but it is essentially the same thing. Much of the time it is fueled by economics. Small crime is committed in most cases by those at the bottom of the economic scale, who are simply attempting to survive, by any means at hand or lashing out at perceived enemies—those with more resources. When people lose hope, when they can no longer feed their families or themselves they become desperate and will do whatever it takes to survive, whether that be stealing or selling drugs.

Poverty itself is a form of violence. It is not a natural state of human affairs, regardless of what some might argue. Not all people on earth have 'poor' living among them. Most of the populations that you and I see on a daily basis do, but all those populations are part of the same dominant culture, something we'll discuss more in section two of the book. Poverty can be eliminated. If enough people on earth agreed to focus on the problem, and took the necessary steps, it would disappear in short order. Until this issue is addressed we will continue to have a break down of community. Community can be rebuilt, however, and communities, or Shires, can take on big issues like poverty, and moderate its effects if not eliminate it altogether. It is our job to look out for each other, not necessarily because we love each other, or that it's the right thing to do—although we should, and it is—but because if we do not, violence and crime will ensue.

**Let Hatred Go**

It's time to step back and reexamine our hatred and let wrath subside. Are we striking out against the real problems: ignorance, fear, want, greed, and political disenfranchisement or just trying to find the most immediate scapegoat on which to lay the blame? Are we so busy blaming our fellow Hobbits that we've forgotten who is really behind the fouling of our Shire? Are we personally guilty of greed? Most of us are, to an extent. We need to reexamine our own desires, and make sure they are really *needs* instead of just *wants*. Poverty could be wiped out world wide, if enough modern Hobbits just said, "No! We will not stand for it anymore," or if those at the top of the economic ladder really wanted to do so. I would suggest that they really do not, no matter how much a few of them might talk about finding solutions. "Put your money where your mouth is," as they say. But it is uncontrolled Greed, and a desire to rule that drives many of those at the top, and as long as that is the case, violence and crime will follow as sure as night follows day. Just as Tolkien's Saruman lusted for power, so do modern Sarumans. They realized long ago that the key to *power* is *energy*. Thanks to them, and to our own addiction to it, we are destroying our planet, and ourselves.

# 6

# ORTHANC-OIL INCORPORATED: OUR WANING ENERGY RESOURCES

> Coal, oil and gas are called fossil fuels, because they are mostly made of the fossil remains of beings from long ago. The chemical energy within them is a kind of stored sunlight originally accumulated by ancient plants. Our civilization runs by burning the remains of humble creatures who inhabited the Earth hundreds of millions of years before the first humans came on the scene. Like some ghastly cannibal cult, we subsist on the dead bodies of our ancestors and distant relatives. —Carl Sagan, *Billions & Billions: Thoughts on Life and Death at the Brink of the Millennium*

One of the most insidious industries on the planet is the fossil fuel industry. Since the early 20th century, the world has seen a growing dependence on coal and oil to fuel our ever expanding populations. Not only are these sources of energy used for lighting our homes and running our vehicles, but also to pump billions of tons of plastics into the world, and to make dangerous, destructive petrochemicals, for every purpose you can imagine, including to spray on our food supply—with the pretense of *protecting* it, and increasing yield in order to eradicate hunger on the planet. Yet every year, the world produces more and more food – mostly poisoned via those same petrochemicals: pesticides, herbicides and fertilizers – and still large sections of the word's population are starving.

We consume these fuels as if they will last forever while ignoring the effects on the environment or our own health. But these sources of energy will not last forever, even if we could afford to keep polluting the environment to do it. They are running out – especially oil. The best way to illustrate this is to look at the energy *return* – the amount of oil extracted – compared to energy spent – of oil burned in order to extract new oil. In the 1930s, the industry could extract 100 barrels of oil, while only burning 1 in the process, a ratio of 100:1. By the 1960s that ratio had dropped to about 50:1. Today it is down to around 11:1. So we are burning one barrel of oil for every 11 we bring to the surface. Estimates by economists and the industry itself say that when that ratio drops to below about 8:1 the industry will probably walk away from oil *production*. However, the consumer may walk away from it long before then. As costs of extraction go up so do prices paid at the pump when you fill up your gas tank as well as the price of electricity fueled by oil. Oil will simply become too expensive to burn, even if the industry can squeeze the last drops from the earth which is precisely what they are trying to do with the process called *fracking*.

Fracking, or *hydraulic fracturing* is a process in which high pressure liquids are pumped deep into the Earth to create fractures in rock formations to release trapped natural gas and oil that would otherwise be impossible to reach with traditional drilling methods. The liquids used are water, mixed with sand and other chemicals. There are so many things wrong about this process that whole books have been written on it. We'll return to the topic in a later chapter, where we'll discuss the environmental issues in more depth, but for the purpose of this chapter the main problem with fracking is that we need to be looking for alternative sources of energy not drilling for more oil. But oil is not the only fossil fuel we depend on; there is also coal.

The coal industry, long a blight on the environment, continues to rape the earth in the pursuit of more profit, while leveling mountains in places like West Virginia and poisoning the air and water. There does seem to be more coal left to mine if we can stomach the process of bringing it up from the Earth. More on that later. According to government figures, the supply in the United States should last another 190 years or more, but I'm not sure I trust government estimates considering how well they do with other simple math problems. Even if we *can* mine it, we probably *shouldn't*. When oil runs out, not too far down the road, the price of coal is likely to skyrocket. For now, in America at least, oil and coal are the *cheapest* source of energy but that's a deceptive reality.

The reason coal and oil are cheaper is due to two factors. One, the industries are subsidized by the government with tax dollars extracted from the American people. The oil industry, at least, has fought back against this idea of subsidies, pointing out that they aren't really subsidies but tax breaks/incentives to offset the costs of doing business, etc. While some of this may be technically true, it's really just a smoke screen to say, "Hey y'all, we're really not any different, than say, Walmart, or McDonald's, or your mom's bakery. We're just taking advantage of the same tax write-offs that everyone else gets." This is the tone of the fossil fuel industry's argument. Of course, they use much slicker verbiage, but the message is the same. This might be an effective argument, if it were not for the fact that Walmart's and McDonald's business practices are also questionable, especially when it comes to paying their employees, as mentioned earlier. The comparison to our mother's bakery is absurd, of course. I made that one up.

If not for these subsidies/tax breaks, the oil industry might close up shop sooner, which would be good for alternative sources of energy, like solar and wind, which have not received the same balance of incentives/subsidies. These breaks give fossil fuels an unfair advantage over cleaner alternatives struggling to break the stranglehold that oil and coal have on the market. Essentially, the industry is receiving *welfare* — much as other huge corporations — while at the same time recording record profits. It's wrong, no matter how you look at it. In 2008, during the world-wide, economic collapse, ExxonMobil recorded profits of $11.68 billion in the second quarter alone! Ironically, companies like ExxonMobil, Walmart, and McDonalds, and their uber-rich stockholders consistently lobby and argue against other forms of welfare for those who are at the bottom of the economic scale, many who are the working underemployed, some of whom work for the fossil fuel industry itself and certainly work for companies like Walmart and McDonald's.

The second reason that coal and oil are cheaper than other energy sources is the simple fact that these industries, much the same as most corporations, don't actually calculate *ALL* the costs of doing business. They *export* many of their costs or refuse to acknowledge them as costs at all. For instance, the cost of air and water pollution, as well as the health risks involved in the extraction and consumption of their products. While the fossil fuel industry rakes in record profits their products and the extraction processes are creating massive pollution worldwide. None of this gets recorded in their Excel Spreadsheets! WE pay the costs in ruined landscapes, poisoned water, air, and increased health costs. We'll get into this more in a later chapter, when we see the effects of all this burning. It's not a pretty picture. The lust for power between the Two Towers of Isengard and Barad-dur is driving the destruction of Middle Earth and its primary target isn't the environment, but our food supply.

## Oil Shortage and Food

Did you know that about 60-70% of the world's food supply is dependent on fossil fuels? No? Me either until recently. The subject is not well known to the public, but without oil and gasoline farmers in the United States — the biggest agricultural producer — will not be able to sustain their production levels. It takes 10 calories of fossil fuel energy to produce, transport and store 1 calorie of food in the United States. This includes the fuel for vehicles to plow, harvest, store, and transport the produce and meat to market, as well as all of the petro-chemicals employed to fertilize and protect them from insects and weeds.

Without fossil fuels, most of that 70% will no longer be grown. What will the world look like without it? Quite frankly, it will collapse into anarchy. This might sound like an intro to a section about how we should increase fossil fuel extraction, not decrease it, but I will never argue that, due to the issues already raised in this chapter. Fossil fuels should go the way of the dinosaur; which is kind of ironic, since — as Carl Sagan pointed out above— they once *were* dinosaurs. They served their purpose, for good or ill. While they may be important to the over-production of food it's time to find alternatives to these methods of agriculture before we run out of fossil fuels, and before we poison everything on the planet. In the next chapter, we'll examine this axis of evil, the alliance of fossil fuels, chemical companies and the food we eat. Sauron is planting some nasty stuff these days and if we Hobbits don't put a stop to it, he will soon overrun Middle Earth with poisonous food if he doesn't succeed in poisoning all of the air and water first.

# 7

# ORC-ADE & SAURON'S SLOP: GMOS, CHEMICALS AND THE POISONING OF OUR FOOD SUPPLY

Several orcs laughed. Uglúk thrust a flask between his teeth and poured some burning liquid down his throat: he felt a hot fierce glow flow through him. The pain in his legs and ankles vanished. He could stand…

His head swam, but from the heat in his body he guessed that he had been given another draught. An Orc stooped over him, and flung him some bread and a strip of raw dried flesh. He ate the stale grey bread hungrily, but not the meat. he was famished but not yet so famished as to eat flesh flung to him by an Orc, the flesh of he dared not guess what creature. — *LOTR*: II, *The Uruk Hai*

Rain on the scarecrow Blood on the plow
This land fed a nation This land made me proud
And Son I'm just sorry there's no legacy for you now
Rain on the scarecrow Blood on the plow
Rain on the scarecrow Blood on the plow —John Mellencamp, *Rain on the Scarecrow*

While it's hard to choose a winner when it comes to the most destructive aspects of fossil fuels—air pollution, water pollution, corruption of our governments—it just might be what it's done to our food supply. Companies like Monsanto and others introduced the use of petrochemicals into modern agriculture following the Second World War with the idea that they could increase farmers' yields and supposedly end world hunger. I'm not sure that their motivations were so pure. They developed new chemical fertilizers, herbicides like RoundUp, and pesticides like the infamous DDT, to assist in this goal. DDT was so destructive to the ecosystem, that Rachel Carson, in her 1962 book, *Silent Spring* argued that if we didn't stop using this evil chemical, pretty soon there would be no birds left and this would have catastrophic ramifications to our entire system. Luckily, enough people in America heeded her warnings to accomplish the banning of DDT. Unfortunately, there are still many other nasty chemicals being introduced into the food supply and the environment that have not been banned or even really tested. Proponents of this new method of agriculture argue that these chemicals are *needed* to combat pesky weeds and insects that have become resistant to a new breed of crops, GMOs, as they're known, which were engineered themselves to resist weeds, pests and disease.

In order to increase crop yield, in the 1970s seed companies like Monsanto began to use the new discoveries of biological science to genetically modify the structure of our food supply. The first products came to the market in the 90s. The experiments worked, of course, and food supply rocketed along with the human population, driving the need for more food. The new technology of genetic engineering created prettier, tougher, more disease resistant and pest resistant crops. They also were able to resist the chemicals, like Roundup, that were being sprayed on them to keep down weeds. The term for these new super crops has become GMO, or genetically modified organisms.

This is a bit misleading though, as most crops that existed before these new ones were also modified genetically through ancient means of cross pollination, cross breeding, etc. The old way is much slower, as it only modifies one crop or animal at a time, in a small area, and therefore takes longer to achieve the aims. Changes were introduced much slower, and over time, essentially mimicking the process of natural evolution. The new GMOs however, are not just 'modified', they are 'engineered' artificially in a lab by removing and changing the actual genetic structure at a molecular level to instantly create a new strain of a particular organism, be it vegetable, fruit or animal. This new gene structure then runs rampant within the population forever changing the original species and its basic properties. The argument put forth by the industry is that GMOs are a good thing because they allow farmers to produce more food in less time and in less space, therefore feeding more people. Meanwhile, these new crops infect non-GMO crops grown nearby by farmers who are trying to grow traditional, and many times, organic crops.

Monsanto has even tried to sue these farmers for stealing their technology, and in some cases, has won. Pushing back against this are some farmers that have tried to sue Monsanto for poisoning non-GMO crops. They have had little to no success because Monsanto and their rivals exert massive influence in the halls of government and the court systems at the highest levels. The Deputy Director of Food Safety, Michael R. Taylor, is a former Vice President for Public Policy for, none other, than Monsanto Corporation. Supreme Court Justice, Clarence Thomas also used to work for Monsanto in the 1970s. Yes, that's a long time ago but I have friends from the 70s, and they still have influence over me and they don't have billions of dollars to spend to do it—though it would be nice if they did. So just how is the FDA going to impartially test GMO crops when the guy in charge of the testing is a former vice president for the very company who makes the majority of genetically modified seeds? Answer: There *is* no way. And if a lawsuit makes its way to the Supreme Court, which it has, are we to believe that Judge Thomas's former connection to the defendants has no influence on his decision?

If a head honcho at the FDA and a Supreme Court Justice weren't enough, the probable candidate for President of the United States in 2016, Hillary Clinton, has recently come out in defense of GMOs. This is particularly frightening, because if she runs she is certainly the one to beat for that office. Her support for GMOs shouldn't be surprising, since her former law firm,

Rose Law Firm, was a representative for Monsanto. These situations are the very reason that government jobs used to be ruled by conflict of interest policies, and still should be.

Of course, if their political connections fail to get them what they want, Monsanto, and the other chemical/seed companies have their own Ring-wraithish armies of high-priced lawyers to defend their insidious practices. More successful than the farmers who have tried to sue Monsanto directly have been the few farmers that have decided instead to sue their GMO-planting neighbors. Since they seemed unable to beat the industry's lawyers in court, they decided to take on the GMO growers themselves. There is a war going on in the U.S. over the protection of our food supply. Currently one could say that Mordor and Isengard are winning, but Hobbits are fighting back in growing numbers. This must continue. It wouldn't hurt to have a few Boromirs and Aragorns, not to mention a few sweaty Gimlis, join the fight, too!

## Safe or Not?

Monsanto's wraith-lawyers argue that there is little evidence their crops aren't safe. This is simply untrue. There is a growing body of evidence from unbiased laboratories around the world — labs not under the GMO thumb — pointing to a myriad of issues with GMOs. Even if these new crops and animals *were safe*, we would not know. The government tests are invalidated due to conflicts of interest, as mentioned. Their claim is a smoke screen, anyway. The burden of proof has always been on the manufacturer to demonstrate the safety of their products, not on the government or other private interests to prove the opposite. There has simply not been enough independent, unbiased study to prove that they are safe, and that is enough to call for a ban on them, worldwide. In fact, many countries, especially in Europe, have already banned Monsanto's GMO seeds and their chemical products, and more join the list every year.

Besides the effect of GMO foods on our health and the future of non-GMO species, there is the poisoning of the GMO crops themselves, and the water used to irrigate them, through the use of pesticides and herbicides that are liberally sprayed over them. A recent study revealed that Monsanto's RoundUp—a chemical linked to a laundry list of physical maladies and cancers—is in the blood stream of pretty much every person on Earth! It is one of the most dangerous of chemicals, and most popular. I'll admit, I've used it many times in my own yard on pesky weeds. It definitely kills them, but who knows what damage I've done to my own health, not to mention the health of my family, and the wildlife around me. If there is ONE THING, in this entire book that I hope you take away and incorporate into your life, it's the rejection of RoundUp. Just don't use it, please. If you have any left in your garage, take it to the local hazardous waste disposal center and get rid of it. Do not just pour it out, or put it in the regular garbage!

## Old Man Willow and Mirkwood Spiders: Super Weeds and Monster Pests

Roundup is sprayed in large quantities on GMO produce, where it enters our food supply, regardless how much we try to wash it off down the sink. It cannot be washed off; it is in the cells of the plant. It is not safe, no matter how much Monsanto wants to argue that it is. And they are developing new poisons, because the insects and weeds are evolving to resist Roundup and the new genetically modified foods, also largely designed in the forges of Mordor, i.e., Monsanto's laboratories.

To combat these new super pests and super weeds, Dow Chemical has developed a new strain of GMO soybeans and corn, under the brand Enlist, to withstand a stronger herbicide, 2, 4-D, an ingredient for an orcish chemical they developed during the Vietnam War to defoliate the jungles of Southeast Asia, so that the U.S. Army could see the Vietcong and North Vietnamese Army moving around on the jungle floor. Known by its popular name, Agent Orange, for its color, the army sprayed it liberally on the virgin jungles to amazing and orcish effect. It certainly worked to open up the jungle, but it has also been directly linked to numerous cancers and other maladies suffered not only by the Vietnamese, whom the U.S. dumped it on, but also by the foreign troops, the U.S., British, and

Australian troops that came into contact with the chemical. It is one of the nastiest chemicals ever developed. Dow's new 'Enlist' GMO crops, they argue, are a *final solution* to the new super weeds, created by the RoundUp-ready crops developed by their competitors at Monsanto. The USDA has already approved them for use, against a ground-swell of public opinion. Our government simply isn't listening to us.

During a Facebook discussion awhile back, I posted something to the effect that we didn't need GMOs and that no one did. While this was a generalization, I refused to retract it when a friend of a friend argued that I shouldn't speak for everyone, and that we shouldn't, "throw out the baby with the bathwater." I would argue that the last thing we need on this planet, is a lot of two-headed babies. Toss the water, and whatever's in it. GMOs simply *have not*, and I would argue further, probably *never will be* demonstrated to be safe, and we do not need them. They are in fact a large part of the world's problems, by fueling overpopulation and centralizing food control in the hands of a few corporations: corporations responsible for poisoning not only our bodies, but our minds through advertising, our communities by encouraging isolation, our governments through bribery, and the very resources upon which our existence depends with invasive plant species, chemical pesticides, herbicides, and fertilizers.

If you have to wear a hazmat suit to raise crops, why would you ever eat them? If you're afraid of getting that crap on your skin, how much more insane would it be to put it in your mouth! Seriously? I often wonder, and I wish someone would research it if they haven't already, whether the CEOs of Monsanto, Dupont, etc., eat GMO products and feed them to their families, or if they send out their 'personal shoppers' to the local farmer's market to bring home fresh, organic produce every week? I suspect the latter. I'm quite sure they all have reverse osmosis water systems in their mansions. Let me put it bluntly, if I haven't been clear so far. The day the CEO of Monsanto guzzles a gallon of Roundup, is the day I'll consider buying their products, maybe.

If for no other reason than to bring down Monsanto, and Dow, and a handful of other monolithic corporations, boycotting their products would be a noble thing to do. But the best reason to boycott them, is because they are unhealthy. I will suggest to you that it is quite possible that many of our modern health problems stem from what we eat. Remember the old saying, "You are what you eat." Merry and Pippin were forced to drink Sauron's Orc-Ade, which did keep them *alive* for awhile, but it was Treebeard's healing Entwash that helped to bring them back to full health. There is nothing more important than our health. This is something you hear people say all the time, but it seems we forget it every time we go grocery shopping, or pull into a drive-thru at a fast food, or what I like to call, orc-food restaurant.

Stop to think, fellow Hobbits, about what you're putting into your mouth and calling *food*. Is it really? Or is it some dreadful concoction from the sulfur laden labs of Mordor or Isengard? Even close proximity to the agents of Mordor could lead to horrible sickness, and possibly death, if not treated quickly, as Merry, Eowyn and Farmamir, and Frodo all experienced. Luckily for our heroes, there were healers of great power to nurse them back to health. Where shall we turn for healing? Will we have Aragorns to save us? Or has the ancient art of healing been lost?

# 8

# HOUSES OF HEALING: DISEASE, ALLERGIES, AND THE FORGOTTEN KINGSFOIL

So at last Faramir and Eówyn and Meriadoc were laid in beds in the Houses of Healing; and there they were tended well. For though all lore was in these latter days fallen from its fullness of old, the leechcraft of Gondor was still wise, and skilled in the healing of wound and hurt, and all such sickness as east of the Seas mortal men were subject to. Save old age only. For that they had found no cure; and indeed the span of their lives had now waned to little more than that of other men...But now their art and knowledge were baffled; for there were many sick of a malady that would not be healed; and they called it the Black Shadow, for it came from the Nazgul. And those who were stricken with it fell slowly into an ever deeper dream, and then passed to silence and deadly cold, and so died. —LOTR: III, *The Houses of Healing*

Well the doctor comes 'round here with his face all bright
And he says "in a little while you'll be alright"
All he gives is a humbug pill, a dose of dope and a great big bill

Tell me how can a poor man stand such times and
live. —Bruce Springsteen, *How Can a Poor Man Stand
Such Times and Live*

# Where's the Damned Kingsfoil Already?

I hate going to the doctor. I know that's a typical male response.
Why? Because I know before I get there, a couple of things. One,
it's going to cost me more than I want to pay. Two, I'm going to
have to wait to be seen, and I hate waiting for anything. I tell
people all the time that, "Patience, is my girlfriend, not one of
my virtues." I also know, or assume—usually correctly—that
my doctor is going to try to push some drug on me and I'm
probably going to tell her, "Hell no!" That's usually the end of
the conversation, more or less.

When I first came to grad school at the University of
Minnesota, I was a 20 year victim of a disease suffered by the
majority of people on Earth: lack of health insurance. I was 41
years old, over-weight, out of shape, and exhausted. I had
known for some time that I was also suffering from sleep
apnea—a common affliction these days. Basically, you are
unable to sleep, because your windpipe shuts off when you drift
off to the *land of La*, so your brain keeps waking you up to
breathe. Apparently one needs oxygen to sleep, who knew. You
don't usually know this process is happening; gradually you
just start to suffer from the lack of real sleep. By the time I got to
Minnesota, I was almost suicidal. All I wanted to do—my first
month of graduate school when there's simply no time for it
anyway—was to sleep. But it was the one thing that was a
complete waste of time. Luckily for me, the graduate program at
the University of Minnesota has excellent health insurance, or it
did when I was teaching and studying there. So after a few
weeks of scheduling, tests, etc., I finally managed to get a CPAP
machine (constant positive air pressure) that kept my windpipe
open and allowed me to sleep. The transformation was
astounding. Sleep was awesome! Who knew? But that wasn't
my only problem.

## It's a S.A.D., Sad World

I also went to see a doctor because I had diagnosed myself with Seasonal Affective Disorder, or SAD, for short. This was due in large part to the complete lack of sunlight in Yankeeland during the 8 months of winter. Ok, it's not quite 8 months, maybe 7. It was February, the first brutal winter up here, when I was sitting at a local diner for breakfast one morning a couple days before my birthday—when one *should* be happy—that I told some one, "I f'n hate February!" So I went back to my doctor and I told her that I thought I was suffering from SAD, so she posed some questions to me, like "Do you cry like a girl more than twice a week?" Sorry that was a low shot, and probably a bit sexist, but that's what it felt like, and the way I experienced the question. I was like, "No, but I'm pretty pissed off all the time and I f'n HATE February, and where the hell is the sun!?"

So she agreed that I did indeed have SAD and promptly tried to prescribe anti-depressants for me. I shot back, like a Chinese, ping pong champion, "I will blow my brains out, before I ever take one of those damned things." She was a bit taken aback, as you can imagine, and asked why? I told her that a few years before I had watched helplessly as one of my good friends and neighbors gasped his last breath after swallowing every pill in his house the night before—unbeknownst to the entire family—days after his doctor had upped his dosage of antidepressants. My friend was dead, basically because his doctor had no clue what was causing a series of seizures that he had been suffering from. He was depressed about his mental state, and the anti-depressants probably pushed him over the edge. So, no, I would not be taking anti-depressants, thank you very much. I then asked her about *happy lights,* or full spectrum light therapy, something I had heard about from colleagues in my department at the university, and had researched myself, online. She then, reluctantly—after I suggested it—said that some people had found those useful, but she didn't know much about them. I thanked her for her *assistance,* with just a bit of sarcasm in my voice, then went home, ordered a happy light which arrived a couple days later. It works like a charm. And the side effects? Well, it doesn't make me want to kill myself. I love my happy light. I still hate going to the doctor, and the dentist, but that's a story for another day.

What my story illustrates, I think, is an experience not unlike many people have when they visit their doctors. My doctor had not even considered alternatives for my treatment. It was just, "Ok, you're sick. Here's a pill." Fortunately for me I knew better, and I'm kind of a pain in the ass — thanks to my mother (you should see *her* when *she* goes to the doctor) — so I went home and ordered my own happy light, and ignored my doctor's sales pitch for drugs. Unfortunately, many people, especially in the U.S. have been duped by the drug companies, the ad agencies, and their doctors into believing that modern science can solve all medical problems with a little pill. Guess what? It can't.

## Un-natural Long Life: the Magic of the Ring

> I am old, Gandalf. I don't look it, but I am beginning to feel it in my heart of hearts. *Well-preserved* indeed!" he snorted. "Why, I feel all thin, sort of *stretched*, if you know what I mean: like butter that has been scraped over too much bread. That can't be right. — *LOTR*: I, *A Long Expected Party*

Everyone is aware of the proliferation of diseases these days, from heart disease, to cancer, to mental disease. It's the hottest topic in the U.S. with the new Affordable Health Care Act on everyone's mind. I'm not here to argue for or against it. The idea of health insurance for everyone — especially in a country with supposedly so much wealth — makes sense. The best way to achieve it is the question. The one thing that has not been addressed by the ACHA is the rising costs of health care in the U.S. Health care is simply too expensive for the average person. Even if you can get an appointment with one, most of us cannot afford to visit a doctor on a regular basis to help prevent the onset of disease or other health issues. And when issues arise, we can't afford to pay the hospital bills that are the result of a lack of preventative medicine. It's a Catch 22 situation. Meanwhile, the drug companies are making record profits selling us drugs with side effects as long as our arm, while doctors struggle to pay their insurance premiums, jacked up by insurance companies — also making money hand over fist — who dictate what procedures are covered and how much the doctor can charge for them, while dropping long-time, paying customers, and refusing to pay for many procedures on the basis of *pre-existing* conditions and the like. What a mess.

We all see report after report about how people are overweight, out of shape — though, as a Hobbit I take offense to this, since *round* IS a shape — hooked on junk food, soda drinks, sugar, and coffee. The blame for all of this is being pushed onto the individual — who obviously has to shoulder some of it — while ignoring the fact that the majority of what we have to choose from food-wise or drink-wise is loaded with high fructose corn syrup — made from GMO corn laden with RoundUp — sodium, and a myriad of man-made chemicals and preservatives, all to enhance color, keep it from rotting on the shelf, and to inject some flavor into a *food* that has had the life processed out of it to the point that its nutrition level is essentially negative. Meanwhile, those who are theoretically trained to stem this tide of disease, doctors — many of which got into medicine for good reasons — are leaving in droves because of the work-hours, pay, insurance costs, and a system essentially run by drug and insurance companies and an ever encroaching government with no real idea how to fix the problems, other than to introduce mandates about insurance.

## Poisoned Pills for Profit

The lack of insurance, while a problem, isn't the heart of the issue. The real issue is that the entire system is based on maximizing *profit*, which often leads to conflicts of interest when making decisions about a patient's health. Most of us blame our doctors for the problems. This is unfortunate, even though there are bad doctors out there; I've certainly seen some. As demonstrated in my personal story, my last doctor seemed more of a drug pusher than anything else. That's one of the big complaints most of us have these days as we realize that every time we turn around there's another ad on TV or the radio trying to push another man made drug-chemical down our throat, promising to cure everything from heart disease to hang nails. And we all wonder why our teenagers, hell, ourselves, look to drugs—both legal and illegal—for recreation and relief from stress?

We live in a drug culture! Drugs are everywhere and touted as the panacea for every ailment in our society. We have drugs for hyper children, drugs for depression—some of the most insidious drugs ever—, drugs for allergies, drugs for acne, drugs for emphysema and drugs for erectile disfunction— maybe the most useful of them all. And let's not forget the side effects of these wonder drugs! It's cliche to even talk about drug advertisements and the laundry list of side effects tacked onto the end of them, usually rattled off at warp speed by someone on loan from the local auction house. I've seen ads for acne medicines that include side effects that are potentially fatal! Seriously? "Hey! Buy our Acne-Magic Drug! You'll have crystal clear skin! In your coffin!" What the hell is wrong with us? And don't tell me that every doctor out there really knows all these possible side effects, or better yet, the reactions between one miracle drug and the next. If the late, great Robin Williams's suicide can teach us anything, it might be that drugs can kill, even those that it is meant to cure. More often than they should, they do.

Insurance companies, meanwhile, are making a killing— pun intended—off of the medical industry. Contrary to what they might say publicly about Obamacare, they are doing just fine, thanks in part to their powerful lobby in congress. Insurance companies in the United States more or less dictate what treatments, drugs, and tests that patients can receive, because they simply refuse to pay for many of them. It's not up to doctors anymore, and many of them are leaving the profession, disillusioned and depressed.

## Doctors in Distress

Most doctors, I'm sure, entered the profession for a couple of reasons. One, they truly found the work fascinating and meaningful. They dreamed of helping people and making a difference in the world, and many of them have, in both small and enormous ways. Two, there has always been the alleged lure of money, in the United States anyway. Most doctors are paid fairly well, though most of us have an overinflated idea of just how much they are compensated. If you add up the long years of schooling, the student loans, the stress of medical school, the long hours worked as an intern and then as a doctor, being on call, and the increasingly negative and mistrusting attitude of patients—like me—towards their profession, the money isn't nearly as enticing. Personally, I'm not sure why anyone would want to go through all of that for any amount of money.

And now, doctors have lost almost all control over the care they offer their patients, including what they prescribe, and the tests and treatments they can offer. Contrary to what most of us think, they also have little control over what they charge. Insurance companies and other entities routinely overcharge and double charge patients for treatments and tests. The doctor's name usually appears on the bill even if the doctor has never seen the bill, or signed off on it. To further muddy the waters, and take power away from doctors, insurance companies and drug companies have nearly obliterated the title of *doctor* all together.

I challenge you, when you're watching TV the next time and a drug ad comes up, to pay close attention to the language they use when they talk about doctors. Do they actually use the word, *doctor*, or have they substituted it for the newest, nebulous term, *provider*? The term provider has no defined meaning. It could mean a doctor, a nurse, an orderly, or maybe even the janitor? It's a watering-down of a precise term for a more general one. Doctors have medical degrees, which they spent many years and many tens of thousands, sometimes hundreds of thousands of dollars to achieve. *Provider* has no precise definition. It essentially means, 'some person, possibly in a white, or pink lab coat thingy, who might or might not poke you with needles, slip a thermometer up your ass, take your blood pressure, and ask you if you've been abused—by someone other than your provider—had sex recently, smoked tobacco, or drank too much bourbon, then overcharge you for the *pleasure* of the experience.' I should work for Webster's.

Somewhere in the history of the end of the 20th century, Saruman worked his dark magic on the medical profession in the United States, and I suspect, a great deal of other countries, though nowhere does Greed rule more than in America. It's unfortunate, that while more doctors will be needed to treat all the new patients that Obamacare and an increasing population with decreasing health will demand, those same doctors are reevaluating their decisions to practice medicine and leaving in large numbers. I suppose we'll be ok though; we still have all those *providers* to take care of us when Mother Nature finally gets tired of us crapping in her yard and decides to give us a spanking. It's time to examine the driving force behind most of the Earth's problems: our bulging human population.

# 9

# ORCSES EVERYWHERE: OVER POPULATION AND THE CONSUMPTION OF NATURE

> Within your culture as a whole, there is in fact no
> significant thrust toward global population control.
> The point to see is that there never will be such a
> thrust so long as you're enacting a story that says the
> gods made the world for man. For as long as you
> enact that story, Mother Culture will demand
> increased food production today- and promise
> population control tomorrow. —Daniel Quinn,
> *Ishmael: An Adventure of the Mind and Spirit*

Many of the issues facing the Earth today are driven by the
ever-expanding human population, which puts increasing
pressure on the resources of the planet. Currently just over 7
billion and climbing, experts predict that at the current rate of
growth—which is slowing a bit, especially in developed
countries—we will still reach 9 to 10 billion by the middle of this
century. Can our Earth sustain such a number? At our current
state of consumption of energy, water, and food, it cannot. The
average U.S. citizen consumes energy, water and other
resources at a rate 5 times more than the Earth would sustain if
everyone on the planet consumed at the same rate. The numbers

simply do not add up. Either we will find alternative ways to filter fresh water from salt water, heat, cool, and light our homes, transport ourselves and our necessities, and feed ourselves, or a massive catastrophe of untold proportions is looming in our very near future. This is not some religious, fanatical, prediction. It is based on hard science and agreed upon by the vast majority of the scientific community.

Human population has always increased, but in the last 200 years or so, since the dawn of the Industrial Revolution, we have exploded across the globe thanks in large part to our machines and the fossil fuels that run them. These fuels have enabled us to multiply our food production, transport that food, store that food, and cook that food more efficiently. As mentioned earlier in the book, new fertilizers, pesticides, and herbicides, have allowed us to ramp up food production in the 20th century to levels unheard of in human history. In the Medieval period—the period I study when I'm not writing about how to be a Hobbit—a farmer was lucky to manage a yield of 3:1, or 4:1 from his seed. Today we have increased that geometrically to over 400:1. What does this have to do with over-population?

Food equals people. People are made of food. You are what you eat. This is scientifically true not just a quaint saying to get you to eat your broccoli, though I've personally never wished to *be* broccoli. Scientists know this to be true, or at least those who are paying attention. More food equals more people. Less food would equal less people. "But people are starving!" you say. Yes, many are, but that has nothing whatsoever to do with the lack of food on Earth. There is plenty of food to feed every single person living on this planet, because if there were not, they wouldn't exist, in fact, they could NOT exist, because people are made of the very food they eat.

The problem has never been *not enough* food, but the lack of adequate distribution of food resources. More importantly, in this age of mass transportation, it is not that we can't produce enough food to feed everyone, or get it to them; it is simply that not everyone can *afford* to pay for the food produced. Monsanto, Syngenta, and the other Saurons of our Earth would have us believe that we need their GMO crops, and orcish pesticides, herbicides, and fertilizers to feed the starving billions. But every year, they produce record crop yields, record profits, and record numbers of starving people. Why is this? Simply because Sauron couldn't care less about feeding the starving billions. What they care about is *MAKING BILLIONS*, of dollars, that is.

## Where does all this food go?

The simple answer is: into landfills. Did you know that nearly 40% of the food produced in the United States alone, every year, goes into the garbage? Yes, I said 40%. Absolute fact. We waste nearly half of what we produce, yet corporate farms are still advocating for more orcish crops to feed the starving billions. Here's an idea. Why don't we stop wasting food, and actually ship it to those starving people? Or better yet, maybe we should teach those people how to raise their own food, sustainably, so they can feed themselves! Then we won't *need* Sauron's crops anymore!

All this would help to solve the problem of world hunger, but it would not solve the problems driven by over-population. Because unless we find a way to curb, slow down, and gradually reduce the human population on Earth we are still headed for disaster. Because in order to feed more and more people, we have to consume finite resources to do it. This might sound a bit counterintuitive, because the things we eat are produced over and over again: animals and plants. Yes, we *produce* new animals and plants every year, and it seems that we could theoretically keep doing that infinitely, but that is not the case. Because we live in a closed system, not an open one.

The Earth has only so much biomass. It does not continually create more. In order to feed ourselves, we must consume some of that biomass, which turns it into more humans. Humans are essentially storing biomass taken from other plants and animals. Basically, an equivalent amount of biomass is used up to create every human. In order to plant more food we have to turn land that was once supporting other life—plants and animals—into farmland, or grazing land so that we can consume those plants or animals. The more people there are, the more farm and grazing land we need, and the less trees, plants, and other wild animals can exist. We consume their natural habitat, every time we create a new farm. Eventually, we will run out of land to turn into farms, but long before that environmental disasters stemming from this ever growing expansion will either seriously curb, or eliminate our species from existence altogether. We will have essentially *eaten ourselves into extinction.*

This is not a popular subject, I know. It's a very unsettling one, because people want the problem to go away so they don't have to think about it. It seems impossible to solve. It isn't, but it seems that way. We will not attempt to solve it here. We'll come back to it in the last section of the book. There are solutions, and they are not destructive or diabolical. I promise. In the next chapter, we'll look more closely at what our expanding population is doing to our environment. And guess what? It's ain't good.

# 10

# ANDUIN WEEPS & FANGORN BURNS: THE DESTRUCTION OF MOTHER NATURE

He [Saruman] and his foul folk are making havoc now. Down on the borders they are felling trees— good trees. Some of the trees they just cut down and leave to rot—orc-mischief that; but most are hewn up and carried off to feed the fires of Orthanc. There is always a smoke rising from Isengard these days.
— *LOTR*: II, *Treebeard*

## A Great Hewing and Burning

As mentioned in an earlier chapter, one of the largest—if not *the* largest—sources of pollution comes from fossil fuels. Burning coal, oil, and natural gasses, releases carbon monoxide, a greenhouse gas, into the atmosphere. Most of us have heard a great deal about this. $CO_2$ in the atmosphere traps heat, which causes what has been coined as global warming. We will address global warming and climate change later. Fossil fuels also create a great deal of other pollution. Air quality is an obvious problem. It doesn't take a genius to figure out that breathing in CO2 and Carbon Monoxide is bad for you. In fact, if you suck in the latter for several minutes it will kill you. But this is what we are releasing into our air, every time we crank up our vehicles or the power plant cranks up its generators to light up our homes. Essentially, in a larger sense we're all sitting in our cars in a very large garage, with the door down and the engines running. Eventually, something bad is going to happen if we don't stop the engine or find something else to put in the tank.

Not only does oil poison the air but it finds it's way into our water supply as well. I could write an entire book, and books have been written, on the numerous oil spills into our rivers, lakes, and oceans over the last 100 years. Most of us can at least remember the BP spill in the Gulf of Mexico a few years ago and the debacle that clean up was, as well as the lies and coverups that BP employed to shift blame away from the dangerous and illegal shortcuts that they had been using to bring their product to the surface. All the while, small businesses trying to recover from Hurricane Katrina, including small, local fishermen, were losing their livelihoods in the name of oil profits. At the same time, millions of fish, birds, and other wildlife were dying, suffering, and washing up on oil soaked beaches. Beach communities, Shires if you will, desperately trying to draw tourists back after the destruction of Katrina, now had a new disaster to deal with: a man-made one.

If that incident was isolated, it would be one thing, but we all know it isn't. Oil is spilled on a regular basis, all around the world, even if the major news outlets *forget* or neglect to cover them. I won't go into example after example. A quick Google search, or browse of your friends' Facebook posts will probably provide you with enough to keep your head shaking for a while.

## What the 'Frack' are we Doing?!

The oil industry is so desperate to extend their profits, that in the last few years they have resorted to extreme efforts to extract the last few drops of oil from U.S. deposits using a method called fracking, which we mentioned earlier. There seems to be no limit to what the industry will do to extend their reign over the world's energy supply. Even industry experts know that this will not last indefinitely; oil is becoming more and more expensive to extract. Continuing to burn oil is simply not an option; we need to be looking for alternative sources of energy to begin with, not drilling for more oil. But the expense of extraction isn't the only, or even the main, argument against fracking.

The main problem is that the chemicals employed are highly toxic. And these chemicals seep into the water supply. Much of the water used for drinking and watering agricultural crops comes from aquifers deep in the Earth's crust. This water is slowly replaced and collected over centuries, sometimes millennia, but fracking is almost certainly poisoning some of the larger aquifers in the U.S. While the industry's scientists try to assure the public that the process if perfectly safe, there are many experts who say that this is just not so, and that there has not been sufficient testing of the new process to prove that it is not irreparably damaging our water supply. According to a 2012 article in *Scientific American*:

> ...220,000 well inspections found that structural failures inside injection wells are routine. From late 2007 to late 2010, one well integrity violation was issued for every six deep injection wells examined — more than 17,000 violations nationally. More than 7,000 wells showed signs that their walls were leaking.

Not only is fracking polluting the water but there is growing evidence that it is also upsetting geological faults deep underground causing an upswing in minor earthquakes. So the official *jury* might still be out on fracking, but quite frankly, I don't think we need a jury. The burden of proof should be on the industry to *prove* that their new process is safe. They have not and probably never will, most likely because it's *not* safe and cannot be proven to be so. But remember, oil is not the only fossil fuel we depend on; there is also coal.

# The Ashes of Mordor: Sauron Coal Incorporated

Burning coal, contrary to what the industry's *clean coal* advertising campaigns might suggest, creates many of the same air pollution issues as burning oil. It is also a major source of water pollution. Coal ash spills and leaks of the toxic chemicals used to 'clean' coal, are becoming a frequent news item. The massive chemical spill into the water supply in West Virginia is still a problem months after the event and there have been other recent incidents in North Carolina too. The incident in January of 2014, in West Virginia, where 7500 gallons of the toxic chemical, 4-methylcyclohexanemethanol—try saying that one three times backwards—was leaked into a local river, left over 300,000 local residents without clean drinking water for days. Even after the state declared the water safe to drink, many residents were complaining of the quality of the water, and are still wary.

The following month, February of 2014, in North Carolina, coal ash ponds from one of Duke Power's plants suddenly burst and flooded the Dan River with an estimated 40 tons of coal ash slurry and an undetermined volume of chemically-poisoned water, essentially choking off the river and poisoning it beyond recognition, killing fish down the entire length of the river. As of the writing of this book, a federal investigation has been launched into Duke Power's practices and possible coverups of known issues leading up to the disaster. Even the governor of N.C., Pat McCrory, and several of his cabinet—who seem to be setting new world records for ineptness, and corruption—have been drawn into the investigation. The governor was once an employee of Duke Power and there are allegations that he may have turned a blind eye to known violations by his former employer. Only time will tell whether these allegations prove to be true.

What's almost comical, if it weren't so ridiculous and criminal, is Duke Power's push to ask the citizens of the state to pay for the cleanup of their mess! This, while they have reaped record profits for years, breaking the laws, and covering up their activities. I saw a Facebook post by a friend of a friend who actually attempted to defend the company's request for public funds to clean up the mess, by arguing that it was the public's demand for cheap energy that drove Duke Power to cut corners on safety. Really? This kind of guilt shell game, where the consumer is blamed for the abuses and criminal activities of the supplier is ridiculous, and a breach of logic. If Duke Power had come to its customers and said, "Hey y'all,—they talk like that in the south y'all know—these laws are kind of expensive to follow. Let's take a vote to see if we want to follow them or not," then my social media acquaintance might have an argument. However, there was no such *vote* to break the laws and ignore safety practices. Duke Power, in the pursuit of Greed for its shareholders—some of which I'm sure aren't even citizens of the state—decided to try to skate by and ignore some of the laws and safety practices. As a result, they have nearly destroyed the ecosystem of one river in the great state of North Carolina. They should pay to clean it up.

Of course, one way or another, we will all, worldwide, pay the cost in the long run. Such destruction is nearly impossible to clean up once it is suffered. The fish will not come back to life, though hopefully the species will survive in other rivers. If only these incidents were isolated, but alas they are not. As with oil spills, coal ash is a hot topic on Google and Facebook, as well. You will find no end of articles to read if you are so inclined to research it further and are in the mood for crappy news.

## The Road Runs Ever On...and Off...

Fossil fuels find other ways to get into our water supply as well. As our cars run over the roads, they emit pollution that sticks to the road surfaces, most of which are constructed with fossil fuel ingredients. When it rains, those chemicals run off into ditches on the side of the roads. Where does that run off to? Guess where: our rivers and ultimately into our oceans. This form of pollution, I'm afraid, *is* partly the public's fault. Though we aren't given many viable alternatives of transportation, most of us do choose to drive vehicles that burn gasoline, a fossil fuel. It's also true that the oil industry continues to fight alternatives to their juggernaut on transportation, but there are ways to minimize the consumption of oil for that purpose. We'll discuss those in the last section of the book, but for now, it is important to point out that there are alternatives out there, and new, fascinating innovations are coming.

The pollution of the water supply presents many issues, of course. One is that we drink water, bathe in it, and wash our clothes and dishes in it, to name a few. We also need it to eat because plants, much like us, are mostly water, or as the crystalline inhabitants of Velara III on Star Trek once said of humans, we are "ugly bags of mostly water." I couldn't pass that one up, since Patience is a big ole Trek geek, and it's one of her favorite quotes of all time. But I digress, so yes, our plants need water, preferably water without poisons in it.

Only a very small portion of the Earth's water is drinkable, fresh water. Less than 1% of the water on Earth is non-frozen, fresh water, and about 30% of that 1% is stored in groundwater beneath our feet. That leaves us with about .7 % of the water on Earth that is easily accessible for all those things I mentioned above. And we are poisoning it? We're also poisoning the other .3%, the groundwater with the process of fracking. Mother Nature is weeping, as are her rivers. And it's not just oil, coal ash, and chemicals poisoning our waters; oil, in the form of plastic is polluting the oceans and our seafood supply.

# The Funeral of Boromir, Plastic Jugs, the Mississippi, and Oceanic Garbage Patches

> His cloven shield, his broken sword,
> they to the water brought.
> His head so proud, his face so fair,
> his limbs they laid to rest;
> And Rauros, golden Rauros-falls,
> bore him upon its breast.
> O Boromir! The Tower of Guard
> shall ever northward gaze
> To Rauros, golden Rauros-falls,
> until the end of days.
> —*LOTR*: II, *The Departure of Boromir*

The funeral of Boromir has always been one of the most beautiful parts of Tolkien's great story. It's a powerful image: the fallen warrior, in his mail, his battered weapons and broken Horn of Gondor clenched upon his chest, laid out in an elven boat, surrounded by the weapons of his foes, swept away down the great river to float past cities, farms and fields. I awoke last night—at 2:15 AM—to this image in my head, for some reason. I woke up thinking about Boromir's funeral, and then a question popped into my head. "Where does ole Boromir end up?" and "What the hell does that have to do with the book I'm trying to write?" Then it hit me. It's all about plastic! Hang with me here people; that's just how my brain works.

## A Tale of Two Rivers

Let's follow the path of two objects if you will, down two different rivers, one, Tolkien's—the Anduin, and one *real*—the Mighty Mississippi. I will try not to digress too far on whether the Anduin might be more *real*, though I could probably stretch that into a chapter all by itself. Anyway, we have two rivers. Into one we gently nudge Boromir's funeral canoe, piled high with his large corpse, his gear, the bloodied and bent weapons of his orcish victims, maybe a few orc heads, use your imagination. Off he goes, down the great river Anduin. Into the second we throw a milk jug. I know, it's not quite as poetic, but that is actually the point. Let's say I drive over to Minneapolis and chuck one of my jugs into the great American river, the river that in many ways belonged to another great writer, Mark Twain. So, now we have two objects floating along great rivers. So hitch up yer Huckleberry britches and let's float along with them.

Boromir and his funeral trophies were swept in the current towards the golden falls of Rauros, and by some miracle prone to warrior funerals, he, his canoe, and all its contents were not separated or crushed upon the rocks below, but continued in the elven boat, over the torrent and on to southern lands, his homelands of Gondor. At some point he passed through the smoking ruins of Gondor's former capitol city, Osgiliath, recently overrun by hordes of nasty orcs and trolls, where his younger brother, Faramir, half dreaming, glimpsed his shadowy bier as it slipped past in the morning mists.

At some point earlier, perhaps in a particularly jouncy rapid, the cloven remnants of his great horn, the Horn of Gondor, fell from the boat and drifted to the muddy banks of the great river, where guards of the great city discovered them, and guessed that Boromir was no more. The vessel slipped ever on and on, southward leaving the gleaming white tower of Ecthelion in the distance, where his fretting father yearned for news of his favored son. Onward Boromir's body raced, past the port city of Pelargir, the great Bay of Belfalas, and into the Western Sea.

Meanwhile, my milk jug bounces along over the not-so-impressive St. Anthony Falls, past the two towers of the University of Minnesota: the Social Science building and Heller Hall. Trust me, these are not Barad Dur and Isengard. Though to look at them, one might guess they were built by the modern Sauron, Stalin, during the cold war.

So the little jug jounces along past cliffs and parks, the great cities of St. Louis, Memphis, Vicksburg which–like Osgiliath–was once a smoking ruin itself after the Yankees left in 1865—no I'm not comparing them to orcs or trolls, ok, just a little—past the moss-covered trees, and whiskey-scented streets of New Orleans, and out into the Gulf of Mexico. There our little jug is picked up by the Loop Current, a mini gyre—a vortex current— eventually to be swept away by the Gulf Stream, around sunny Florida's oranges, north past Georgia peaches, Myrtle Beach-es, the Hatteras Lighthouse, through the Graveyard of Ships, and eventually reaching what's known as the North Atlantic Subtropical Gyre.

The NASG is a current vortex in the Atlantic Ocean. What it does, is collect an enormous amount of debris, especially plastic. How much debris? Such great volume that it is commonly referred to as the North Atlantic Garbage Patch, an area stretching from roughly the latitude of Virginia to that of Cuba! West to East, it spans most of the Atlantic from North America to the Azores. This is not the only such 'patch' on earth. There are at least 5 major ones, the largest by far, the Great Pacific Garbage Patch, is about the twice the size of Texas, and lies between California and Hawaii.

So what happens to our two cargoes over time? Well, we can safely assume that there were no plastics in Boromir's canoe, though I'm sure, given enough time, Sauron or Saruman would have developed such nasty things. Boromir's body began to decompose immediately after death, and within a few weeks at sea, what was not consumed by sharks, slowly dissolved and become part of the ocean. His clothing of natural fibers slowly rotted and joined him. His gear, especially the iron, sank to the bottom of the sea. His sword, covered in silt, probably lasted a very long time indeed, possibly centuries, but caused no real harm, and eventually, over millennia rusted and disappeared. His wooden boat sank in a storm, was crushed by the pressures of the deep and dissolved into nothingness.

On the other hand, our little jug, constructed of man-made plastic, will never truly bio-degrade. What will happen, over time, is that it's structure will break down into smaller and ever smaller particles, much of which will be consumed by unsuspecting marine life: birds, fish, plankton, turtles. Many of these poor creatures will die a nasty death. Many will not. Instead they will be eaten by a larger creature, who may in turn be gobbled by a larger one, until one day, months or years later, they end up on our plate, in a seafood restaurant, in some quaint little sea-side town like the ones I love so much back home in North Carolina. Yuck.

**The Moral of the Story is...**

Patience, when presented with my Boromir funeral/plastic jug idea was completely confused at first, befuddled to the point where we ended up arguing in the kitchen, at 5:30 AM one morning. To be fair, it was too early in the morning for such discussions, and my presentation was seriously lacking. Instead of waiting for her to wake up, drink her ritual cup of coffee, and let her **read** what I had written, I just blindsided her with it: a bolt out of the blue, "Hey! So Boromir is pushed into a river, and just like a plastic jug in the Mississippi, they end up in the ocean! Get it?"

Needless to say, she did not. She screwed up her face in a *WTF* look, while I was standing there dumbstruck, with an emphasis on the *dumb*, wondering to myself, "What the heck is wrong with her? This idea is absolute genius!?" Then, slowly, I began to realize that while the idea might be clever — probably not genius — my delivery was, well, not so clever.

Part of the problem, as she explained on the way to work later, was that she, as an English Literature type person was expecting more allegory, or some deeper meaning connecting Boromir and the plastic jug. After dropping her off at work, and on the way to mine, I gave it some more thought. After cogitatin' on it for a bit, I came to the conclusion that she was right. Here's what I came up with. While there are similarities between the two events — both are 'stuff thrown into a river that end up in the ocean — there are far more differences, and they are significant, even crucial.

The scenarios are different in two fundamental ways: intent and result. The intent motivating both acts is very different indeed. Aragorn and company were performing a funeral ritual for a fallen comrade. The act is meant to pay respect for Boromir's life, bravery, deeds and accomplishments. It is to remember him as the great defender of Gondor and its people, and honor his final stand against the forces of Saruman in a desperate, bloody defense of the two Hobbits, Merry and Pippin. The funeral of Boromir is respectful and mindful toward the sacrifice the great warrior had made, and with a realization that they are returning him to Nature, where he will eventually become *part* of Middle Earth in a very real way. The occasion is ritualized by surrounding his body with funeral trophies or *grave goods* — the weapons of the enemies — and with song.

On the other hand, throwing a plastic jug into the Mississippi, even if it accidentally drops from our trash can, lacks intent. There is no ritual, though one might argue, as Patience did with me, that taking out the garbage is a *ritual*. I completely disagreed, and I think I convinced her in the end that the word has been abused for so long that *ritual* has come to stand for *habit*, and usually not a beneficial one. They are NOT synonymous. The plastic jug reaches the river, not through ritual but by habit, the habit of tossing things that have been used only once. There is no remembrance of the jug's accomplishments, but an immediate forgetting of them. Where there should be mindfulness and respect–for Nature, if not for the jug–there is only mindlessness and disrespect: disrespect for Nature, and quite frankly, for our own future and the future of our children and grandchildren on this planet. Once our jug is tossed, it goes *away*, never to be contemplated again. It is simply waste: disregarded, discarded, and forgotten.

The problem is that there *is* no *away*. All things end up somewhere, if out of sight and mind. If they are no longer in our backyard, they are in someone's: your neighbor's down the road, in the next state, or in the middle of the ocean. They will return to us in very nasty ways, quite possibly in our fish n chips. That is, if we haven't already suffocated from lack of oxygen, or died of heat stroke thanks to the destruction of our sole oxygen supply: the trees.

# Fangorn is Burning: the Deforestation of Earth

> Many of those trees were my friends creatures I had known from nut and acorn; many had voices of their own that are lost for ever now. And there are wastes of stump and bramble where once there were singing groves. I have been idle. I have let things slip. It must stop! — *LOTR*: II, *Treebeard*

One of the most destructive and stupid things we, as a species, are doing to this planet is eradicating the forests of the world. Every year, we destroy about 18 million acres of forest worldwide, an area equal to the size of the state of West Virginia, or the country of Ireland. It is estimated that by the end of the 21st century, there will be no more rainforests. Can we afford to do this? The answer is an emphatic *no*. The human species and thousands of others will be extinct if we do not stop and do something to promote new tree growth, worldwide. There is no greater threat to our future existence than the threat to the very air we breathe. The rain-forests — indeed all forests and the trees within them — supply us with the oxygen that keeps us alive. About 20% of the World's oxygen is produced in the Amazon alone. At the same time, trees consume $CO_2$, one of the most destructive of the greenhouse gases that contribute to global warming and climate changes.

Just as men, orcs, and dwarves were slowly whittling away at the great forests of Middle Earth—Fangorn, Mirkwood, and the Old Forest—we are following suit. However, we have technologies and tools of destruction that Saruman and Sauron would kill their own mother to have, if in fact they had mothers. What will we do when all the trees are all gone? The answer: die. Why are we doing this in the first place? Answer: Cheap beef and coffee, to name the two biggest causes. We will discuss both in Part III, when we discuss food in more depth but much of the rain-forest cut down today is to make room for one or both of those crops. The beef mostly goes to U.S. fast-food restaurant suppliers. So every time you eat a McDonald's burger you're killing a tree somewhere in the world, and Treebeard weeps. Sorry for the guilt trip, but it works, so I'm punching below the belt on this issue. Anything to get the job done. Plus, it's really crappy beef. To give McDonald's some credit they have recently started to work on this issue but only time will tell whether they are truly serious about solving the problem or just paying lip service to it.

In Middle Earth, the biggest destroyer of trees, other than probably Sauron, was Saruman, who cut them down by the thousands from the edges of Fangorn to feed the fires of his forges at Isengard. It was knowledge of this treachery that drove the Ents to march to war against the wizard. But that's not all the White Wizard was up to. He was also diverting and damming up the river Isen to keep it from flooding his evil, subterranean workshops and labs where he practiced genetic engineering on orcs to create a new race: the Uruk Hai.

We are also diverting and damming up rivers, worldwide, for many reasons, but usually to produce hydro-electric power. While the reasons are understandable, the consequences are devastating for millions of people, animals, and ecosystems. Every time a dam is built, it floods the lands above the dam, lands almost always inhabited by communities of people, some who had been there for thousands of years. Some of those dams are being overwhelmed by seasonal runoff of land that will no longer absorb the rains that fall upon them. The resulting runoff swells rivers downstream, while leaving parched earth behind.

# Desolation of Smaug: the Desertification of Earth

> They knew that they were drawing near to the end of their journey, and that it might be a very horrible end. The land about them grew bleak and barren, though once...it had been green and fair. There was little grass, and before long there was neither bush nor tree, and only broken and blackened stumps to speak of ones long vanished. They were come to the Desolation of the Dragon, and they were come at the waning of the year. — *The Hobbit, On the Doorstep*

One of the major problems facing humankind, and indeed all life on the planet, is the desertification of once green and fertile land. The U.N. estimates that every year we lose about 30 million acres (12 million hectares) to encroaching desert. This is not a subject that gets much press, and as such, most people are unaware of the extent of the problem or its significance. There have always been *natural* deserts caused by geographical features and climate shifts, but desertification is a man-made process whereby areas that receive seasonal, yet adequate, annual rainfall are turning to desert due to human intervention. Like the great serpent, Smaug, we are burning and destroying the Earth.

The causes of this are controversial, though the U.N. and most of the scientific community have traditionally attributed the phenomenon to several factors: deforestation and stripped grasslands for agriculture, intensive farming practices which deplete the topsoil, and over-grazing by livestock. Scientists and government agencies around the world have been attempting to discover the causes and to find ways to thwart the ever encroaching deserts. They have, up to this point in time, failed quite miserably.

The continued desertification of the Earth has been argued, by a small group of scientists, to be a major contributor to climate change. The South African scientist, Alan Savory is one of them. He argues, logically, that plants, grasses especially, hold carbon in the soil. This is not disputed. He reasons that if we can find a way to halt and then reverse desertification that it will have a larger effect on greenhouse gasses than even the transition away from fossil fuels—which he is in favor of doing as well. This point has been argued against, but it seems mostly to be a point of degree, and not of substance. In other words, the argument is over *how much* difference it would make if we could reclaim land that has been desertified.

Deserts in places with significant rainfall also add to the problem of waning fresh water, something that is becoming a major issue on Earth, as mentioned above. Grasslands, forests, even agricultural plants if cultivated properly help to store fresh water and return it the atmosphere to fall again as rain. Trees are especially good at this but so are other plants, in particular, wild grasses. They help to slow rainwater down as it moves over the land towards creeks and rivers and absorb a great deal of it into their roots where it is used to fuel photosynthesis. These grasses then feed wild animals and grazing livestock. More on that later. Much of that stored water is then evaporated slowly into the atmosphere instead of running off into our oceans, where it mixes with salt water. Trees and plants supply about 10% of the water in our atmosphere. Private interests, Sarumans, are cutting them down faster than they can be replenished, and at the same time, laying claim to our water supplies.

## Privatization of Water

If desertification weren't bad enough to threaten our water supply, big corporations are sweeping in to claim rights to the remaining sources of fresh water on the planet. They've realized that the future of business is the control of water resources, not oil, which we've already discussed, is waning. Fresh water is a precious commodity which will only become more so as the

Earth's population increases. Leading this charge is the Nestlé Corporation, who's CEO, Peter Brabeck, recently said that access to water isn't a human right. Yes, that is the gist of his statement, but I'll let you decide for yourself:

> The one opinion, which I think is extreme, is represented by the NGOs, who bang on about declaring water a public right. **That means as a human being you should have a right to water. That's an extreme solution.**

Extreme? Yeah, I'd say it was, but it's Brabeck's statement that's extreme. To be somewhat fair, he has tried to back-pedal from that statement recently, even though he says it isn't actually back-pedeling. He tries to point to other work that he and his company have done to try to make water accessible to Third World countries, etc.

The real truth comes out when you put his company under scrutiny and see what they are actually *doing* around the world, and that is to pressure governments, local, and national to sell, give, or lease them rights to water resources, so they can corner the market on fresh water, instead of that remaining a public *right*. What it sounds like, from Brabeck's statements, is that he's an elitist Saruman who thinks he can spout a few philanthropic words here and there, as if we'll be mesmerized by his bullshit. I have news for you Mr. Brabeck; it ain't workin'! What he's actually doing is part of a larger movement by international corporations, the Sarumans of the World, to lay claim to the *Commons*, the things that were once owned, and shared by everyone, in common. Monsanto is doing a similar thing with agriculture, and the very seeds that are needed to feed us. If we don't put a stop to it soon, they will lay claim to everything we need to survive.

The grasslands, forests, rivers, and lakes are disappearing at an alarming rate. Can we survive if this continues unabated? Will there be Lake Towns in our future? Or will there only be the Desolation of the dragon in the waning of our species? Will Mother Nature suffer our destruction much longer? The evidence suggests that she is very unhappy with us. It's not nice to fool Mother Nature even if it's possible. What happens when she discovers our transgressions? At some point, in the near future we're going to finally piss off the Treebeards and the rest of the Ents on our earth, with our stupid attempts to *fix* Mother Nature. I suspect they will call an Entmoot. It's quite possible that they've already called it, since it does take a very long time for them to make a decision. When they finally come to consensus, we are all in trouble. Remember what happened to Isengard? That is the subject of the last chapter in Part I.

# 11

# MARCH OF THE ENTS: SARUMAN'S TREACHERY AND THE DANGERS OF CLIMATE CHANGE

We come, we come with roll of drum: ta-runda runda
runda rom!
We come, we come with horn and drum: ta-runa runa
runa rom!
To Isengard! Though Isengard be ringed and barred
with doors of stone;
Though Isengard be strong and hard, as cold as stone
and bare as bone,
We go, we go, we go to war, to hew the stone and
break the door;
For bole and bough are burning now, the furnace
roars - we go to war!
To land of gloom with tramp of doom, with roll of
drum, we come, we come;
To Isengard with doom we come!
With doom we come, with doom we come! —*LOTR*:
II, *Treebeard*

If it keeps on rainin', levee's goin' to break,
If it keeps on rainin', levee's goin' to break,
When The Levee Breaks I'll have no place to stay. —
Led Zeppelin, *When the Levee Breaks*

# Mother Earth is Angry

The climate of the Earth is changing, and doing so quickly. This is a controversial topic with most of the public because, quite frankly, the fossil fuel industry is paying so-called scientists to publish bogus reports to suggest that the Earth is not heating up or at least not heating up due the burning of their products. Among real scientists there is nearly unanimous consensus that both are true. Thousands of scientists are in agreement that the planet is definitely heating up and that <u>humans are the cause, or at the very least exacerbating a natural phenomenon,</u> accelerating what nature is prone to do.

"But it seems colder where I live?" I hear this all the time, especially here in Minnesota, where the last two winters have been very cold and harsh. I also read similar things on Facebook from my friends in North Carolina where they have had exceptionally cold, wet winters and summers the last couple of years. This is a conflation of two things: weather—which is localized, and climate—which is global. If you examine climate and temperature maps of the planet, the rest of the planet is recording record heat. Climate is changing and it is not cooling down, though some areas are experiencing momentary cooling. Heat has to dissipate somewhere, and it will drive temps down in some places, while it increases in general.

The damning evidence in support of warming is found in the waning of the polar ice caps, and the receding glaciers. Both poles, North and South, are quickly melting and the great glaciers, like the ones in Glacier National Park, are receding at alarming rates. There's only one thing that makes ice melt: heat. Nothing else does, unless it's lots of salt. Thousands of scientists are in agreement on the fact that the earth is heating up and that we are an important part of that process.

## The Mouths of Sauron

So who is writing all the counter arguments? There are a handful—in comparison to the thousands who are on the other side of the so-called 'argument'—who are claiming that the whole *global warming thing* is just a ploy by *green* companies to make money off of an unsuspecting public. Who are these green companies? Why is it that most of these so-called-scientists seem to be getting pay checks from fossil fuel companies? As Colonel Fletcher said in the *Outlaw Josie Wales*, "Don't piss down my back, and tell me it's rainin'." When it comes to this particular subject, the rain is indeed warm, and kind of ammonia-y smelling.

After every oil spill, coal ash spill, the fossil fuel industries try to reassure us that their products are perfectly safe, that all will be well, while the price of their product steadily climbs, and the pollution they release into nature increases every second of every day. I realize that my defense here is *ad hominem*, to a degree, but why should we believe anything the fossil fuel industry's *scientists* have to say? I would suggest that if they will lie and cover up crimes and facts when it comes to pollution in one area, that they will do so in all cases, including questions of climate change. It is really common sense to disregard their *scientists*. They are mouthpieces for propaganda from Sauron himself, like the Mouth of Sauron at the Black Gates of the Morannon; they spew lies and deception in hopes to hypnotize their listeners. Do not be drawn in by their lies. Yes, the weather where you live might be a bit cooler and wetter than usual, but there are vast areas of the planet that are heating up quickly. For instance, this winter, 2013-14, while the Central Plains and east coast of the U.S. have experienced near record cold, snow and rain the west coast is going through a major drought and near record heat. So are many places on Earth.

I challenge you, if you are in doubt about this, to do some research for yourself. The World Watch report for 2013 details the climate change phenomena, and will give you a better look at the dire situation that we are facing, as well as many ideas about how we might fight it. I will warn you ahead of time, the picture is not pretty, and the report tends to be paralyzing. You must resist this Denethorian paralysis, however. Giving up, just because the road is tough, is not an option. If Frodo and Sam gave up because the quest seemed impossible, where would Middle Earth have been? We too must not give up, no matter how difficult the task might seem. If we do, and the predictions do come true, we are looking at a world that will be very hostile to human survival. Sea levels are already rising, and will continue to do so. Most of the Earth's human populations live on or near the oceans and around rivers. An increase of around 7 degrees Fahrenheit would sink most of those areas under oceans, seas, and rivers. Look at a map of the U.S. population, and see where they live, and then compare that to predictions of sea rise in the next century. It's sobering. "If it keeps on rainin', levee's goin' to break…"

Sea rise is only one danger of climate change. One of the most devastating changes is the loss of the polar ice caps. In brief, when all that fresh water melts into the salty oceans it lowers the salt content in the great ocean currents. It is the salt that holds the sun's heat in the water and in fact, drives the entire current. With lower salt levels the currents will slow down, which will change the weather on the planet in more chaotic ways, creating massive storms like continental sized hurricanes to dissipate all the heat trapped in the oceans. Situations like this have occurred in the Earth's past, though not in the memory of modern humans. Our ancestors were here, of course, but they did not have writing technology 12,000 years ago. Essentially, if we do nothing to slow down or stop our influence on increasing temperatures we can expect to see some devastating climate events, more destructive than we have ever seen in recorded history. It's possible that these things will happen at some point in the near future anyway. If so, then we need to start preparing for a very different world.

## Higher Temps, Less Food

One area that is already being affected by rises in temperature, is our ability to grow food. This has not been a problem in the Untied States, but in many places in the world, they have seen a marked decrease in rain during the 20th and 21st centuries, to the point that they are suffering from famine. Even minor changes in temperature can be devastating to our food supply. Plants are very susceptible to minor changes in climate and crop failures are current events stories. The Black Death in the 14th century was preceded by a period of colder weather, the Little Ice Age, which had first caused massive crop failures across Europe and other areas as well. The Great Hunger, as it is now called, subjected Europeans to a scarce diet for decades leading up to the introduction of the Black Plague in the middle of the century.

The results were nothing short of Biblical. Anywhere from 30-50% of the population of Europe — not to mention other areas in the Middle East and Africa where numbers are harder to estimate — perished in horrible agony, leaving the survivors in a very different world. Most of us have either experienced or seen crop failures if not pandemic disease during our lifetime, in other places, if not where we live. It was a crop failure in Russia during the 1970s that spurred the U.S. government to encourage farmers to plow more land, even marginal lands, to increase our exports of grain with far reaching effects on our soil and the pollution of our rivers and oceans due to erosion and chemicals running off of these expanded farms. As mentioned already, the world's food supply is heavily dependent on fossil fuels. If oil becomes to expensive to burn or make chemicals with — which in my opinion would be a good thing — and at the same time, temperatures rose to the point where crops failed either due to extreme droughts — something we're already experiencing in some areas — or extreme moisture, the result could be catastrophic indeed.

## Stormcrow or Timely Advisor?

The dangers of doing nothing when it comes to climate change are far worse than accepting that the problem is real, and working to slow or reverse the damage done already. Even if the projections of doom are overstated, it is foolish to ignore thousands of scientists who tell us that we are in grave danger. That's what we pay them for! Even if the scope of the problem turns out to be less than predicted, the efforts to clean up our pollution should be considered the right thing to do anyway. Are there really any of us who would seriously argue that we are not doing grave damage to our planet through burning fossil fuels and dumping tons of plastic into the soil, not to mention our oceans?

Wouldn't it be prudent to just accept the advice of the majority of the scientific community, prepare for the worst, and hope that it does not come, than to just ignore their advice all together? If 100 well-respected firemen inspected your house and told you that it was a firetrap due to faulty wiring, would you ignore them all, if one drunken fireman with a lighter and a can of gasoline in his hands said all the others were lying and exaggerating? Would it be prudent to ignore Gandalf, Aragorn, Legolas, and Gimli if they came to your court to warn you of impending war? I think not. But this is exactly what the minority of so-called *scientists* are asking us to do while taking checks from the Sarumans running the fossil fuel industry. They are nothing more than Wormtongues spewing serpentine lies, "It will be ok, keep driving your gas powered cars however much you want! Turn on all your lights and burn as much electricity as you can! There will always be plenty! It doesn't really affect the environment. Ignore all those other scientists, those Stormcrows; we're the real scientists. We have your best interest at heart. Do you really want to live without power? What about your precious car? How will you get to work? Those other people are just alarmists. We are your real allies."

It all sounds a lot like the drivel spewing from Saruman's mouth when confronted in his tower of Isengard, by his enemies, Gandalf, Theoden, and Aragorn. But they did not fall for his lies and we shouldn't either. If the warnings turn out not to be founded, we will still have cleaned up our planet and our children's Earth will be a much better place to live in. We really need no dire predictions to consider living a greener life. Green is better than black anyway. I say this as I look out the window at the spring snowmelt in St. Paul. There are few things as ugly as black snow melting. At least it's melting. Much of that black is from the asphalt scraped from the street, made primarily of fossil fuels covered in fossil fuel residue leaked from cars who constantly spew more of it into the air. All this will melt, and run off into the rivers along with tons and tons of debris that has been trapped all winter in mounds of this snow, waiting to begin its journey to the oceans.

Is this really the world we want to leave our children? Hell, is it the world WE want to live in? Not I. It's time to stop listening to Saruman and start cleaning up his messes. It may in fact be too late to avoid a significant increase in global temperatures, as it was in fact too late to save the Shire from the ravages of Saruman! But the Hobbits did not stop at the borders, despair and turn around. No, they marched to the center of the smoking Shire, Merry blasted his horn, Hobbits rallied, and they kicked Saruman's ass out of town! Despair is for those who would be buried, and lack the courage to fight back, however little that effort might seem. All efforts are needed, from the smallest Hobbit to the largest and bravest.

So suck it up fellow Hobbits. Things are dire indeed but we must not give in to despair. There is a reason behind all the destruction we see every day and thankfully, it is not complex though its history certainly is. Whether you knew it or not, you and I, and every member of our culture are sheltering the One Ring. It's in our homes and more accurately, in our own minds. Once we dig it out of that old forgotten chest in the basement of our collective memories we can carry it to Mount Doom and toss it into the chasm whence it came. In the next section, we begin our journey to land of Mordor, where the shadows lie.

# PART II

## THE ONE RING:
## A HISTORY OF WHY THINGS ARE
## THE WAY THEY ARE

# 12

# The One Ring:
# A History of Why Things Are
# the Way They Are

Three Rings for the Elven-kings under the sky,
Seven for the Dwarf-lords in their halls of stone,
Nine for Mortal Men doomed to die,
One for the Dark Lord on his dark throne
In the Land of Mordor where the Shadows lie.
One Ring to rule them all, One Ring to find them,
One Ring to bring them all and in the darkness bind them
In the Land of Mordor where the Shadows lie
—J.R.R. Tolkien, *The Lord of the Rings*

Love is a burning thing
And it makes a fiery ring
Bound by wild desire
I fell into a ring of fire.
—Johnny Cash, *Ring of Fire*

When Tolkien's great story, *The Hobbit*, begins, Sauron's One Ring had been lost for time immemorial, forgotten by those with short memories, but not by all. In the minds of the *natives* of Middle Earth, the Elves, memory of it lingered like a dark nightmare, a thin, stretched story of a time long past. Galadriel and Elrond remembered it, all too well. Elrond had been present when it was hacked from the hand of Sauron in the great battle before the Black Gates, some 3000 years before. He was there when Isildur was unable and unwilling to return it to the fires of the mountain, choosing instead to keep it as his precious. After it was lost in the great river, Anduin, Elrond and others thought or hoped that it might never be found again, that it had been swept out to sea where it would be lost forever.

Sauron had certainly not forgotten his most precious possession, and in secret — existing for millennia as a misty spectre — he longed for its return that he might become corporal again and make his bid to conquer and rule all of Middle Earth. But for most of the races of Middle Earth such things were long lost in the mists of time. But it had not been lost forever. Silently it lay in the muck of the great river, as seasons turned to years, years to centuries and centuries to millennia. For two thousand five hundred years it slept, until a Hobbit-like creature, Deagal, scooped it from the river's bed while fishing. Unfortunately for him, he had chosen a twisted fishing-mate, his *friend*, Smeagal, who promptly strangled him in a sudden rage of desire to posses the shiny trinket of evil. The Ring, in Smeagal's hands, found it's way to an even darker hiding place where it waited in utter darkness, for another five hundred years until an unlikely Hobbit stumbled across it in the dark while on a quest for a fortune of dragon's gold. Out of the roots of the mountain the Ring emerged, into the light, and back into memory, and to its dark purpose.

Our culture also has a Ring, forged deep in the mists of time as well. So long ago, that few now know that it exists. It is not a physical ring of course. It is metaphorical. It is our central myth. Didn't think we had one? Yeah, me too. But I was wrong. Let me tell you the story of how it was revealed to me, and guess what; it was in a book. And like Bilbo's story, it all began with the lust for Fame and Fortune...

# 13

# In Search of Fame and Fortune: On the Finding of the Ring

"First I should like to know a bit more about things," said he, feeling all confused and a bit shaky inside, but so far still Tookishly determined to go on with things. "I mean about the gold and the dragon, and all that, and how it got there, and who it belongs to, and so on and further."

"Bless me!" said Thorin, "haven't you got a map? and didn't you near our song? and haven't we been talking about all this for hours?"

"All the same, I should like it all plain and clear," said he obstinately, putting on his business manner (usually reserved for people who tried to borrow money off him), and doing his best to appear wise and prudent and professional and live up to Gandalf's recommendation. "Also I should like to know about risks, out-of-pocket expenses, time required and remuneration, and so forth"—by which he meant: "What am I dong to get out of it? and am I going to come back alive?" — *The Hobbit, An Unexpected Party*

Just about a year ago
I set out on the road
Seekin' my fame and fortune

Lookin' for a pot of gold
Things got bad and things got worse
I guess you know the tune
Oh Lord, stuck in Lodi again —Creedence Clearwater
Revival, *Lodi*

We must be willing to let go of the life we planned so
as to have the life that is waiting for us.
—Joseph Campbell

# Fame and Fortune

"You guys brought in $150 at the door," Sam informed me as he counted off the bills, though my memory of that gig is pretty foggy. He continued, "Minus $50 for beer..." which instantly explained the *fogginess*.

"But, I thought beer was a buck a piece tonight?"

"Yeah, it was." Sam laughed, "But you guys pasted off a case each!" Visions of the *Blues Brothers* flashed through my brain.

"No way man! Really?"

"Yeah, really."

So I took the $100 bucks, stumbled out the door. So ended the first official gig of the Bivans Brothers, and one of the more lucrative I might add. We had just played The Metropolitan Club in New Bern, North Carolina—just picture "Rawhide" in the *Blues Brothers*, sans chicken wire, and you've pretty much got it. It was 1991, I think, and we were both highly intoxicated, Tim and I, to say the least. I'm still not sure how we both managed to drink 25 beers a piece while playing a 3 hour gig— without being hooked to an IV bag—but apparently that's what we did and we were off on our bid for fame and fortune.

**Chasing the Dream: Losing One's Feet in the Stream**

Once upon a time, I wanted to be famous. Rich and famous actually. I fancied myself a rock star. I dreamt of limos, world travels, sex, drugs, and Rock-n-Roll. I know, it wasn't an original dream, not particularly creative as dreams go but I was tired of being broke and wondering where my next meal was coming from. I was already in debt, and felt that if I didn't *score big* I would never get out of the hole. Fear drove me, the fear of falling back into despair, into the hell-hole I had recently escaped. I had escaped, narrowly, but my mind was very much still in Mordor, Moria, and Shelob's Lair. What I needed was to shoot straight to the top, then I could even the score with those whom I owed and get even with those who owed me! And, I could get off of that metaphorical futon in the kitchen floor. I say *metaphorical*. I was still sleeping on it, but had upgraded from the kitchen to the middle of the living room—not much of an improvement, but hey, you take what you can get, right? I wanted off of the *real* futon, too, but that wasn't enough; I wanted to erase it from my memory. The futon had come to symbolize my situation in life, and I was done with it.

So my brother, Tim, and I formed an acoustic duo, then eventually a band. We had been raised in a musical family. The Bivans family had been singing and playing instruments for a few generations at least, and we were no different, well, except for the rock-n-roll, drinking thing—that's pretty much frowned upon in the family. But pursuing music as a career seemed a natural choice for us. We began our *long way to the top* back in 1991 by playing that gig at The Metropolitan. We wrote our own songs and covered everything from Jimmy Buffett, to Kiss, to the theme from Scooby Doo. Were we any good? I reckon we were all right. We could clear out a redneck bar faster than anyone. More than once we began the night in some country, redneck dive, filled with farmers, bikers, painters, wife-beaters, and father-rapers. By the end of the night there would be us, our girlfriends, and usually the bartender. I guess hippie-dippie songs aren't that popular with rednecks. One night at the Backdoor Tavern, another *classy joint* in New Bern, the patrons got so bored with us that they actually put money into the juke box, WHILE WE WERE PLAYING! That was it! I looked at Tim, said, "We're f'n outta here!" So we packed up in a huff, got our money, and left. Good times man.

So I spent a few years chasing that dream, pushing it actually. It was during this period that I obtained a moniker: Genghis Khan. Tim coined it; after listening to me rant, rave, coerce and bitch about something one day, he turned to me and said, "Man, you're like Genghis Khan!" It stuck. I adopted it and mimicked my new hero. I continued to push and coerce every situation, from my personal life, to jobs, to the band, and to an organization I created out of thin air one day while delivering pizzas: The Greenville Musicians' Guild.

I won't go too much into that, other than to say that in order to promote my own band, I came up with the idea of promoting ALL the musicians in the area, which it turns out, is a pretty Hobbity thing to do though I was definitely more Dwarf than Hobbit at the time. "Smash it through," was my motto. "Make it fit! Get'er done! Get the hell outta the way, I'm comin' through!" Obstacles beware! I was a piece of work for many years. I probably still am, though a better piece and of better workmanship, I hope.

My coercive nature was in many ways my reaction to the negative, dark story of my mid-tweens. I was tired of being the victim, of being on the bottom. I was bound and determined to be on *top*, no matter the costs, to my health, to the sanity of those around me, and I damned sure didn't care about the rest of the idiots and assholes on the planet. It was a recipe for disaster, but that cake was still in the oven, and as far as I could see it wouldn't be on a plate for years; and I didn't care. My apathy for the world was running at its highest. The world was going to hell in a hand-basket, but I was out to get mine before it caught fire. And I went after it tenaciously. In the end it was my fear of losing and my drive for fame and fortune, not unlike Bilbo and his dwarves, that led me into Boli's Pizza one afternoon in early 1997.

### In the House of Tom Bombadil

Boli's Pizza — which doesn't exist anymore — was a college-town joint on 5th Street in Greenville, NC. Frequented by crazed, drunken Pirates from East Carolina University, it was a hang-out and favorite of all downtowners and students. They had live music there on the weekends; my brother and I played the joint regularly. One afternoon in early 1997, I walked into Boli's to have a few beers. The place was pretty busy, or at least the small bar area was. There was only one stool left at the bar, so I took it. I have never regretted that moment since, because I sat down next to a monk.

*The Monk,* actually. I don't know who was sitting on my right that day — I don't think I said two words to him — but the guy on my left introduced himself right off, "Hey there! Have a seat! I'm Monk," and shook my hand firmly.

"So, that's actually your *name?* Or a *nickname?*" I asked.

"That's what my friends call me," he said with a grin.

Monk was, and still is, a below average sized guy, though he's much thinner these days than ever he was back then. Thick, graying black hair, rugged, cheerful face — a happy squint to his eyes, and an authentic smile and laugh that attracted me to him immediately; you might say he was a modern Bombadil in nature, though with a touch of dwarf and not a tiny bit of Hobbit lurking in the smile. I didn't know it then, but about a year later, in a different bar — while playing NTN trivia — I discovered that he was also an enormous Tolkien fan, and had always identified with Tom Bombadil. I guess in that first meeting, some part of me sensed his inner, Old Forest spirit, because we hit it off instantly.

We talked for sometime that first day before the conversation turned to music — it always did with me back then since I was constantly pushing the band and the Guild everywhere I went. Up to that point the conversation was more about how awesome Zeppelin was, and the Beatles, etc., until I let it slip that I was in a band myself.

Monk's ears perked up, "You ever been to the Reunion?"

I said I had not, to which he replied, "I'm in charge of it this year, and we're always looking for new bands." And now MY ears were perkin' like an Elf running across the Riddermark tracking a band of orcs towards Isengard.

"Reeeally?" I said, "Well let me give you my card!"

## A Chance Meeting with Elves in the Forest

The Reunion was an annual, music, camping, party event somewhere in NC. It had its beginnings in Greenville though, back in the 70s. It was an invite only party, and it was very hard to get into. It had become legendary; most everyone in the local party scene had heard of it, but few had been. Basically, you had to know someone that knew someone, and then get lucky enough to get an invite from one of them. And here I was, sitting next to *The Man* in charge of the upcoming event! After shoving my card into his palm, I told him that the Bivans Brothers would be very interested in rocking the event! That one moment, sitting down on the only empty bar-stool in Boli's Pizza, changed everything. I had no idea at the time just *how* things would change — though in my mind I thought it might be our next big break — but it was a change nonetheless. It was *not* our big break; it was only the beginning of the change for me. And it was not fame and fortune that I found, well, not fame anyway. I did find a fortune.

What I found in that fateful choice of barstool, was a life-long friend, and a friendship beyond any price, even the price of Frodo's mithril hauberk, all the silver in Moria, or the soot-covered loot of Smaug the Magnificent in his lair under the Lonely Mountain. Thanks to Monk's generosity, and his own innate ability to read character — even character buried under mountains of Fear, Ignorance, anger, hate, and apathy — that year I experienced the Reunion for the first time, and I've never forgotten it, nor shall I. What I found there was a group of people who had a dream, a dream of a better world. Were they perfect little hippies and tree-huggers? No. But they were all seekers of something better. It was a Council of Elrond, of sorts. All free-races were welcome. Some of them were Hobbits: Bagginses, some Tooks, some Brandybucks and Gamgees. Some of them, the ones like me, with *issues*, were Ted Sandymans, Sackville-Bagginses, and Boromirs seeking a fight with the *powers that be*. Some of them were Elves, some Dwarves, and some wizards. Some of them were veterans of foreign wars, especially the dark one in the jungles of Vietnam. All of them were veterans of life: scarred and beautiful.

The only thing separating these people from the rest of us, was that they were actively seeking something better than what our society had to offer. Some of them seem to have found it, some of them not. But most of them were aspiring to something more, and that made me want to search for different answers to my questions and to push a little less, coerce a little less, hate a little less, fear a little less, and to start *caring* again. And that was a big change; it cannot be over-stated. Before sitting on that stool next to Mr. Bombadil, I lacked almost all empathy for the world, or at least I thought I did. He saw something else in there. What he saw, I think, was a soul that probably cared *too much*, and had seen some very dark days, and he identified with that having seen much himself, things much darker than I've ever seen. But he saw that my anger was a product of despair for the world, fear of failure, and my own negative story, and *THAT* could be mended with some help from his Elven and wizard friends in the woods. As we've all heard, the opposite of love is not hate, far from it; it's apathy. Thanks to that meeting, I was beginning to shed my apathy, and regain my humanity.

## Better Questions, Different Answers

Monk and I, as well as my small group of friends began to question many of our previous assumptions about how things worked, though there was still a vein of angst, anger, and fear running through our discussions. We were looking for causes. We were looking for reasons. We were looking for conspiracies. I had been chasing conspiracies around every corner for years at that point. They all seemed to merge into one big conspiracy in my mind. But eventually I discovered that there is no *one big conspiracy*, no One Ring of conspiracies. That would mean that those who are the greediest and most avaricious in our civilization are able to put aside their greed and avarice long enough to cooperate with their direct competitors. They don't work that way, not usually. It's easier to envision that all of them are working for their own self interests, that sometimes those self interests intersect, and that their interests almost frequently run contrary to the interests of the public at large.

The great thing about my group of new friends—those Elves, Dwarves, wizards, and Hobbits—was that any subject was fodder for discussion: religion, philosophy, politics, war, violence, love, money, sex, food—always food. As a result of these conversations I began to read in different directions. I found authors who weren't all negative, who had a very different perspective on the Earth, and our place in it. And then I stumbled on a book that blew the back of my skull right out, and changed the way I viewed the world forever. I had discovered a *magic ring*.

## Our One Ring: the Root of Our Story

The author of this book argued that human storytelling had originated as an extension of hunting. Success for early hunters, he contended, was dependent upon their ability to track game across varied landscapes. In order to do that they had to learn to read clues left behind, in other words, to read animal tracks and other clues in order to determine patterns of movement. But gathering clues isn't enough to track game. You then have to put those clues together to make sense of them. In other words, what do the clues and the tracks, *tell you*? And *THAT* is where storytelling begins. Piecing together clues, is storytelling, and this ability, a learned ability, was a *Eureka* moment in the development of humankind. From that moment forward, we have been telling stories, and many of them are based on Fear and faulty assumptions—much as my own story was—and that is the root of *OUR RING*, the subject of Part II. We are telling ourselves a very negative story, and it is destroying our Earth, and our civilization.

# 14

# THE HISTORY OF THE RING, THE BIRTH OF FEAR, AND THE GREAT FORGETTING

"Hold it up!" said Gandalf. "And look closely."

As Frodo did so, he now saw fine lines, finer than the finest pen strokes, running along the ring, outside and inside: lines of fire that seemed to form the letters of a flowing script. They shone piercingly bright, and yet remote, as if out of a great depth.

"I cannot read the fiery letters,' said Frodo in a quavering voice.

"No," said Gandalf, "but I can. The letters of Elvish, of an ancient mode, but the language is that of Mordor, which I will not utter here." — *LOTR*: I, *The Shadow of the Past*

The worldview we transmit to our children today is fundamentally the same as the worldview transmitted to children four hundred years ago. The differences are superficial. Instead of teaching our children that humanity began just a few thousand years ago (and didn't exist before that), we teach them that human history began just a few thousand years ago (and didn't exist before that). Instead of teaching our children that civilization is what humanity is all about, we teach them that civilization is what history is all

about. But everyone knows that it comes to the same
thing. —Daniel Quinn, *The Story of B*

The book I stumbled upon back in 1999 was Daniel Quinn's *Ishmael: an Adventure of the Mind and Spirit.* The central idea of the book was that our culture, modern civilization, was based on a flawed story, a dark mythical purpose, one that we'd forgotten we even had not unlike the One Ring in Middle Earth. According to Quinn, our culture's *central myth* has been forgotten for nearly 10,000 years. He argues that our culture, what he calls *Taker* culture, originated first in the Fertile Crescent some 10,000 years ago when humans first discovered agriculture, the period we now know as the Agricultural Revolution.

Ok, I want you do something before you read any further in this book. I seriously want you to do it so don't just cheat and keep reading. Take some time, 10 minutes, an hour, a day, whatever it takes to answer this question: What *is* the central myth of our culture? By myth, I mean the absolute central idea or *story* driving almost everything we do. Not the American story, the European story, the Asian story, but the story of all our cultures? <u>PUT DOWN THE BOOK AND THINK NOW</u>.

If you're like me, you cheated. Maybe you actually tried to think about it for a few seconds. Maybe you even got up out of your chair, got a drink, pondered the question for a few minutes, rolled it around in your brain while you relieved yourself in the bathroom, and gave up. That's okay. Sit back down and we'll get started.

If you were unable to come up with an answer to the question, it's not surprising. The clues are all around us, but we are so used to seeing them and hearing them that they've ceased to be clues anymore. Daniel Quinn points out that there is something fishy about the way we, meaning our culture, looks at history. According to Quinn we have a collective memory, or better put, amnesia—what he calls The Great Forgetting— thanks to something that happened far back during the dawn of civilization. So it's perfectly understandable if you were unable to come up with the answer. Actually, it would be surprising if you did. Quinn took many years to come up with an answer to that question.

There seems to have been a disconnect between our culture's *story* and our so-called *prehistoric* ancestors and their story. This is most evident by the simple fact that we refer to their story, i.e., what happened before the agricultural revolution as, *pre-history*. Somewhere, deep in our past we forgot how we came to be the way we are and just accepted that our way of living was the only *right* way to live.

"What way of living, you ask? People all over the world live in thousands of different ways! My culture isn't the same as people in Europe, or Asia, or Africa! That's absurd." There is indeed a great deal of absurdity going on but it's not the idea that we all have one way to live, regardless of where we live. I say all of us, but really I mean about 99.99% of the population of the earth. The overwhelming majority of the Earth's population is all part of one culture, because it is based on a central myth or *story* formed in the dawn of civilization. The myth, Quinn argues, is so engrained in our collective psyche that we do not even know it when we hear it, which we do, everyday, in hundreds of different ways. It invades every aspect of our life. It's in our entertainment, our schooling, our workplace, even our food, especially our food. It's like Sauron's One Ring sleeping on the bottom of the Anduin or trapped in the roots of the Misty Mountains in the greasy clutches of the creature Gollum. We can't see it but it's there all the same.

For the sake of time I'll do my best to summarize the key points of Quinn's books. If you are still curious, and I hope you are, read them—*Ishmael* for starters. It will probably blow the back of your head off, if what I tell you next does not. The central myth and story of our culture, worldwide, is simply that, **"The world was created for man, and man was meant to rule it."**

Examine this idea for a moment and let it sink in. Does this not explain why our culture, both west and east, does the destructive things that it does? Collectively, we live by this assumption every day. As mentioned earlier our populations increase exponentially every year. We are over-running the planet's resources, polluting it, ravaging it, consuming it. Why?

Why would any sane culture do such things to its environment? The answer is painful, I'm afraid. No sane culture **would do that,** *ergo,* our culture is insane. Most of us have heard the quote from Albert Einstein, "The definition of insanity is doing the same thing over and over and expecting different results." Unfortunately, he never actually said it, though the quote is appropriate for our context. What he did say was "The Earth is the insane asylum of the Universe," which might even be *more* accurate. Our culture lost its sanity somewhere a long time ago and forgot that it was insane, if it ever realized it to begin with. Every year, year after year, century after century, we follow the same patterns, expecting things to improve, but have they? If you think things on Earth are fantastic you're probably not reading this book to begin with. Mordor is at our door. But how did this happen? How did we lose our sanity? What did sanity even look like? By the way, the first quote probably came from the Basic Texts of Narcotics Anonymous, which is also appropriate. Our story, our culture is like a drug; we're addicted to it in every sense of the word.

Quinn contends that our myth originated sometime after the introduction of agriculture, probably around the time that the former nomadic tribes in the Fertile Crescent settled down and began to build villages, towns, and cities: the birth of Civilization. The history of cities reaches back to about 8000 B.C., but really began to spring up in earnest around 5000 B.C. around the Tigris and Euphrates rivers. A similar phenomenon happened in the other great civilization centers: China and the Indus River Valley. It is in those places, Quinn says, that at some point, the idea developed that their way of living, i.e., settled agriculture, was the only RIGHT way to live.

This could have been a result of the rise of centralized government and religious power figures: kings and priests, who needed to legitimize their right to rule. To do so, they may have invented the idea that the gods *deeded* the earth to humans to rule. It must have seemed that this was right because the more food they grew the faster their population increased which in turn gave them the power, especially military power, to expand into more territories and take land from those who were not settled: herders and hunter-gatherers. Quinn refers to this new form of agriculture as **Totalitarian Agriculture** and the culture springing from it as, *Taker* culture. At its very core is the idea that everything on the planet belongs to humans and therefore they may do with it as they will, for their own ends, regardless of the consequences to other species, both plant and animal.

But *Takers*, contrary to our cultural myth, were not the only culture on earth, nor are we still. As Quinn points out, humanity had existed in one form or another for almost three million years before the *Taker* culture arrived on the scene! Homo sapiens have been around at least 100,000 years! What were they doing all that time? If we accept our own myth, the answer would be *not very much*. Most people would say that those early humans, even those exactly like us, were just kind of waiting around to discover agriculture so they could do something useful.

But that is our cultural myth speaking to us, what Quinn calls the voice of Mother Culture, whispering in our ears "Don't pay attention to those *prehistoric, primitive* peoples. They were wasting time running around in rotted loin cloths, grubbing around in the dirt for roots, picking berries, chasing prey all day and night, nearly starving to death, a hair's breadth in front of famine, living in mud huts and filth, unhealthy and miserable. You are happy! You have everything they wished for!" This image of so-called *primitive* and prehistoric cultures is so common in our culture that most of us never stop to think how ridiculous it really is. A select group of educated people know—academically at least—that this image is inaccurate but for the most part, even *they* still believe it on some deep subconscious level.

Most of us have bought into the political philosopher, Thomas Hobbes's maxim that life in the past, especially the distant past was "nasty, brutish, and short." But this is simply not true, and anthropologists have known this for some time. Quinn points it out as well; he calls these so-called *primitive* peoples *Leaver* cultures. In contrast to our central myth, *Leavers* do not believe that the world was created exclusively for their benefit; instead, they see themselves as a part of the earth and its circle of life. If the Elton John song from *The Lion King* is playing in your head, I apologize—unless of course you loved that movie — but there's a lot of truth in the song, the movie, and the idea.

*Leavers* understand the circle of life and live by the code that you take what you need, only what you need, and leave the rest alone. That doesn't mean they never take too much. Sometimes they do. There is certainly evidence that ancient humans hunted some species to the point, and sometimes beyond the point, of extinction, especially when they moved into a new area where they had not been before. With our tool-making ability, humans have an unfair advantage over most species, and sometimes even *Leavers* take too much. But when they do, or did, they paid a price and usually learned their lessons or suffered the destruction of their way of life.

## The Great Forgetting, the Forbidden Tree of Fried Chicken, and the Slighted Vegetarian

You might be wondering why you've never heard of *Takers* and *Leavers* before. Well, for one, they are terms invented by Quinn. Another reason, is that our culture has a case of amnesia, what Quinn calls the Great Forgetting. Almost all traces of this early period, when our culture was born, has been lost in the mists of history. But there are traces of it left, and in two stories that most of us know: Adam & Eve in the Garden of Eden and the tragic tale of Cain and Abel, or as I like to refer to them, the Forbidden Tree of Fried Chicken, and the Slighted Vegetarian. Hey, it's my book, and the Tree is supposed to represent something that you want, but can't have, or shouldn't, and it's damned hard to find decent fried chicken up here in Yankeeland — and with my cholesterol I probably shouldn't eat it anyway — so I apologize if I sound irreverent. That's just the way I am.

Just to refresh your memory, in case it's been too many years since Sunday School class, I'll give you the Hobbit-Digest version. It's been awhile for me too. In the beginning, so the story goes, God created the Earth, and to *rule it* he created Adam and Eve and placed them in a paradise where they did not have to wash dishes, slave over the stove, or commute 40 miles to work every day. All their needs were supplied. There was only one rule: thou may not eat from the Fried Chicken Tree. Well, we all know that Eve loved fried chicken or at least she dreamed about it a lot, so one day this snake told her, "Come onnn girl! You can have *one pieccccce*! God'll never missss it. You sssshouldn't lissssten to him anyway. He'ssss only trying to keep you from being like him!" — because we all know that great fried chicken will bring instant enlightenment. Well, the rest is history, or myth. Thanks to her lust for fried chicken she and her husband were tossed out of the Garden, and forced to till the Earth for food the rest of their lives. All their children were also cursed to do the same.

Adam and Eve had a couple of sons, Cain and Abel. I'll keep this one short. Abel was a sheperd and Cain was a farmer. God came to the brothers and told them that he wanted a tribute from their labors. Abel killed his best lamb and offered it; Cain brought some veggies and some grain he had grown himself. God favored Abel's and shunned Cain's gift. Apparently, God is a carnivore. Who knew? Personally, I would have favored Abel's gift as well; I love meat. But I've always thought this story was odd. Why would God look down his nose at Cain's gift? I mean, he worked really hard on it I'm certain. Sure, I would rather have roasted meat too but it seems a bit harsh to turn down the gift of a hard working farmer!

I have argued, in some classes I've taught, that these two stories demonstrate a conflict that existed between hunter-gatherers and the new agriculturalists that were springing up in the Fertile Crescent in the centuries after the invention of agriculture. The problem with this explanation is that the book containing the stories, the *Old Testament*, is a book produced by a *Taker* culture: the Jews/Israelites, who certainly practiced settled agriculture, at least by the time they got around to writing these stories down. The stories clearly suggest that the God of the *Old Testament* had a low regard for agriculture. God seems to have been a supporter of nomadic, animal husbandry, the ancient way of life of many in the region before the spread of agriculture and to some extent, even today. Why would God hate agriculture? If he did, why would agriculturalists include this story in their religious texts? Quinn has a plausible explanation for the first question at least; the story isn't a *Taker* story, it's a *Leaver* story.

What the story suggests is that during the expansion period of Totalitarian Agriculture, many *Leaver* peoples were either destroyed, or absorbed into the *Taker* juggernaut. *Leavers* could not understand why anyone would settle down and commit themselves to such a laborious life trying to keep plants alive in the burning Middle Eastern heat. In order to explain why this was happening they came up with a story, a myth that these new peoples had somehow angered the gods—or their single God—and were cursed to live a painful life toiling in the dirt for food: the story of Adam and Eve cast from the Garden.

Just in case you're wondering, agriculture is the most laborious way to make a living. Ask any farmer and he or she will tell you. It takes an enormous amount of energy and time to feed a population via Totalitarian Agriculture. In contrast, most *Leaver* cultures spend only 2 to 3 hours per day gathering, growing, or hunting for food. This is a surprise to most of us who aren't anthropologists studying so-called primitive cultures. It's a truth, nevertheless. If you don't believe me check it out for yourself. There's plenty of information out there on it. So to sum it all up, the first couple in history had pissed off their god to no end and were then banished to a life of driving tractors, farm subsidies, Dust Bowls, Woodie Guthrie songs, and no fried chicken.

In contrast, *Leaver* cultures, under the constant threat of extermination have survived for 3 million years! As if to stick their finger in Hobbes's eye, they have survived despite our culture's attempts to eradicate them or absorb them and turn them into good little agriculturalists. They are a highly successful culture. If they weren't, if their lives really were "nasty, brutish, and short" they would have developed a better way of living, or willingly adopted ours. Many of them have tried agriculture and abandoned it, sometimes after several hundred years of experimenting, and determining that it just didn't work for them. Others quit after suffering massive disasters, like the introduction of European diseases that followed in the wake of the Conquistadors in the 15th century. The Spanish explorers chronicled the existence of city-sized villages of Natives, from Mexico all the way up into the American Mid-West. When later explorers returned to these areas in the 17th and 18th centuries, they could not find these settlements, only small tribal villages, practicing what modern anthropologists would call *hunter-gathering*. The myths that were passed down in these remnant tribes suggest that it was an epic sickness, a plague, that wiped out their great population.

Hobbes was writing in the middle of the 17th century, during the disastrous English Civil War, when life was indeed very hard especially for those at the bottom. But what he got wrong was the assumption that the way Europeans lived, or most of the world that he knew, was the *only* way to live, and he assumed, incorrectly, that those living a different way were even worse off, i.e., Africans, Native Americans and other indigenous tribes known to him. Contrary to our perceptions they are not living in squalor and filth. They certainly live at a different level of creature *comfort* than we are accustomed to, that's for sure, but they are usually a great deal happier than those of us in the so-called *civilized world*. Yes, most of these groups may have a life expectancy lower than the average, rich, populations of the world, but usually they are much healthier and live longer than their poor, *Taker* counterparts in much of the Third World. Our perceptions of *Leaver* peoples isn't based on fact; it's based on ignorance, and many times, Willful Ignorance. Where does this originate? Usually in Fear.

## Ignorance, Fear and Our Drive to *Tame* the Wild

When our culture, *Taker Culture*, sees empty land or forests, we see wasted land that needs to be tamed. It is *wild* and we want to tame it. Why? Because deep down we fear the wild. We fear nature. In fact, Fear, is probably part of the DNA of all humans, as is negativity in general. Why? Think about it for a moment. If you were an early human, living in a wild world, in Nature, Fear, or at least a very healthy *respect* for the dangers around you would be advantageous to your survival. Dr. Martin Seligman, in his book, *Flourish: A Visionary New Understanding of Happiness and Well-being,* argues that in early humans, the ability to visualize negative scenarios and prepare for them, allowed those people, and their DNA to survive disasters like the Ice

Age. But of course, this would also allow them to survive simple, personal dangers like being eaten alive by lions, tigers, and bears. Those who did not have a healthy fear of the wild, of Nature, were less likely to pass their DNA along to the next generation, in other words, the survival of the *fraidy cats*, if you will. So our ancestors passed down their proclivity to negative thinking, and Fear, to us.

But at a certain point fear is no longer a useful thing to have. Like I try to tell people all the time, a little fear is a good thing, but too much will kill you just as bad as none at all. If you're crossing the street a little fear might prompt you to look "left, right, then left again," as we were all taught in school and by our parents. As a result, most of us reading this book managed *not* to be flattened by a semi-truck while running to catch the Ice-cream Man. But, however, if our fear is such that we *never cross the street* we might die of loneliness, starvation, or the stress that comes from such fear, or the lack of ice cream, which would really suck. Fear of Nature can also keep you alive, as long as it reminds you to pack a coat, a flashlight, some duct tape, and a Swiss Army Knife for your hiking trip. Nature can kick your ass, sure. But too much fear leads to destruction of that which we fear, and that is not a good thing, for Nature, or for us.

**Progress and Manifest Destiny**

To our culture, wild land is exactly that, wild. When Europeans arrived in the New World, they saw a land teaming with wildlife and untamed wilderness that could be made *useful*, the basic idea of Manifest Destiny, which is only an extension of 'the world belongs to us,' which allowed European Americans to push ever further into the continent, killing, burning, and chopping everything in sight. If a competing species, say a wolf, killed one of their chickens or pigs, they did not kill the guilty wolf. Out of Fear, they hunted down ALL the wolves, almost entirely to extinction. Fear of *want* and hunger is one of the things that drove them to expand into the wild, Native American, *Leaver* lands in the Mid West, where Europeans tried to extinguish them as well sometimes with smallpox-infested blankets, and bullets. When killing the Natives directly proved difficult, *civilized* Americans attacked the Natives's food supply, namely, the great buffalo herds, hiring crack shots like Buffalo Bill to hunt them down indiscriminately until there were almost none left. This same Fear is what drove the Agricultural Revolution to begin with, we can be sure. Fear of starvation, even if they weren't experiencing it. Those early tribal leaders and kings, Saurons, were able to play upon the people's fears and to present them with an alternative: settled agriculture and cities, ideas backed up by the power that those things gave to the early *Takers*.

To the early *Taker* settlers, and really in our minds today, land that is being unused for something—agriculture, cities, homes, businesses—is basically wasted. There is no *progress*, and progress is what we want. Now, before you tree-huggers drag out your ropes to lynch me—which is kind of a funny image anyway, I mean, where would you hang me? From a tree?—I am not speaking about individuals in our culture. Some of you are well aware of what we are doing to our environment these days, if not WHY we are doing it. I'm trying to explain why. Why do we do it? Because our central myth compels us to. I'm not trying to pass blame off on *the devil* if you will, just trying to explain what drives us to be so destructive. We have an almost genetic predisposition to exploit our environment to our own uses and to ignore the consequences to other species, and the consequences to our own existence. Our myth is not, however, genetic; it is a learned story. We know this because we aren't the only culture on Earth. *Leavers* do not think this way; only *Takers* do.

Leavers look at the same *wilderness*, and see Paradise. They see food lying around waiting to be picked up when they need it. They see animals as both their family and their food. They do not declare war on species that compete with them. Yes, if they are attacked by a wolf, they will kill it, and then eat it. They kill animals, not for sport, but rather to feed themselves, and they let none of it go to waste. They do not believe in progress; it's not part of their story.

## Not Lothlórien

Before you get the idea that I'm idealizing *Leaver* culture to sound like some kind of pre-Columbian paradise—where everyone danced around naked, hugged each other and the trees, without war, violence, hatred, or jealousy—let me state that *Leavers* have some of the same problems we do. They are not perfect humans. There *are* no perfect humans. They fight, argue, and some times kill each other. Sometimes they go to war with other tribes. What they do have that we do not is a way of living that is in better balance with their environment, not at war with it. And they've been that way for a very long time indeed: for at least 100,000 years, if not millions. *Leavers* aren't saints, just sustainable. That is very good news for us. Our culture isn't the only one; it's not the only way to live and certainly not a very good one. But we can change that; it's as simple as changing our minds. **The Earth does NOT belong to us**. **We belong to the Earth**, though she is growing tired of our attitude.

## A Wake Up Call from Gandalf

The clock is ticking. It's time we start asking ourselves some very important questions, life and death questions. What will we do when we have consumed THIS planet? Will we find the energy and technology to *Star Trek* our asses into the final frontier, into space where we can colonize another unfortunate spinning rock? What then? Will we export *Taker* culture to a galaxy far, far away? Will we consume the entire universe, one star system at a time? Isn't that like taking our trash to the street and hoping that the garbage man takes it *away*? As mentioned earlier, there is no *away*. This is the only Earth we have. We must save it, or perish. We must destroy this Ring we carry, this *Taker* mentality. We must destroy it, truly destroy it, and toss it into the heat of Mount Doom. Hopefully we will not need to lose a finger to be shed of it. Frodo's task was in some ways far more difficult, physically for sure. To destroy our Ring, we must only decide that we no longer want to think in a destructive way.

"That's all peachy and creamy," you say, "But what the hell do we do once we change our minds and destroy the Ring?

What then? How do we fix the damage we have done to our Earth?" That, my fellow Hobbit, is the central question this book is designed to answer. All in good time.

## Return to the Jungle?

"Do you expect us to sell off all our possessions and move into the forest or jungle and live like nasty, brutish, savage indigenous peoples?"

Absolutely not. This is a question often posed to Daniel Quinn by his readers, who are often left with the same sense of "Ok, we know what's wrong and why, but what do we do now?" Quinn, like most gurus, Elves, or crusty old wizards, is elusive when it comes to giving direct advice. Most of the time he answers such questions with a simple, "You don't have to do anything." Or he advises us to be creative and find solutions. When asked if we should all move into the wild, he usually replies, "What wild? It doesn't exist anymore!" We can't all move off-the-grid, out into some fictional wilderness, even if we could find such a place. If we did, it would no longer be wilderness.

It's frustrating at times but I suspect that that is Quinn's goal: to frustrate us. He's very Socratic, or Gandalf-ic in that way. I know when I read his works originally, 15 years ago or so, I had the same reaction. Subsequently, I spent the next 15 years trying to ignore what was wrong with the world because I could not see any way that one person could change it. If I had had a map like Thorin's or a guide like Gandalf or brave companions like Aragorn, Boromir, Legolas, and Gimli, I might have found my way to Mt. Doom earlier and been able to clean up my part of the Shire years ago. Oh well, nothing can be done about the past; we simply must push ahead and hope that we can do what needs to be done in time. Like the advice from an ancient Chinese proverb.

When a sage was asked, "When is the best time to plant a tree?"

"Twenty years ago!"

"When is the second best time to plant a tree?"

"Today!"

## Setting Off for Mordor

Faced with the terrifying facts as they were presented at the Council of Elrond, Frodo, a tiny Hobbit from "a far green country," a creature of comfort, not a stony warrior, or great wizard of power, searched deep within himself, realized what he must do, sucked up the courage to stand and say, "I will take it, but I do not know the way." Thankfully, Frodo had friends that did know the way and so do we. In the next section, we'll take stock of our allies and our enemies. Before we can get to work cleaning up we need to understand with what, and whom we're up against and who is on *our* side. We must face our fears and mock them. Then we must form our Fellowship, for the task is far too dangerous and difficult to do alone. It would be prudent to heed the wise words of Gandalf the Grey, "It would be well to trust to their friendship than to great wisdom."

# 15

# COUNCIL OF ELROND: FELLOWSHIP AND FOES

The Company of the Ring shall be Nine; and the Nine Walkers shall be set against the Nine Riders that are evil. With you and your faithful servant, Gandalf will go; for this shall be his great task, and maybe the end of his labours. Legolas shall be for the Elves; and Gimli son of Gloin for the dwarves...For men you shall have Aragorn son of Arathorn, for the Ring of Isildur concerns him closely...Boromir will also be in the Company. He is a valiant man."

It is true that if these Hobbits understood the danger, they would not dare to go. But they would still wish to go, or wish that they dared, and be shamed and unhappy...in this matter it would be well to trust rather to their friendship than to great wisdom. Even if you chose for us an elf-lord, such as Glorfindel, he could not storm the Dark Tower, nor open the road to the Fire by the power that is in him. —*LOTR*: I, *The Council of Elrond*

I've always thought that one of the most interesting and instructive exercises is to observe the way that the various characters in Tolkien's great story react to the presence of the Ring, especially the nine members of the Fellowship. The manner in which each interacted with its power reveals much about their particular character and suggests insightful, modern parallels that might be useful in the attempt to destroy **our Ring**. In this way we can view our own world and the people around us through the lens of Middle Earth. Remember, these connections aren't necessarily ones that Tolkien would have made, or in all likelihood, approve of—though as I pointed out in the introduction, he did allude to such connections in his letters, speeches, and conversations with friends. Whether or not he would approve, let's do it anyway. I mean, at this point, we're already so far down the proverbial *rabbit hole*, or better yet, mines of Moria, there's no use turning around now. Let's do as Bilbo and Frodo might, and just keep walking. If we're lucky, we'll emerge from the mountain with a clearer understanding of just how pervasive the power of the Ring really is. And while we're at it we can begin to form our own modern Fellowship of the Ring. We'll begin with the most powerful characters, the wizards.

## Wizards, Scientists, and Philosophers

The race of wizards in *The Lord of the Rings* is a fascinating one, and one that has been written about extensively. In Tolkien's universe, the wizards, the Istari, were of the race of Maiar, ranking just under the Valar, or the gods, who all lived in Valinor, far to the West in the Western Sea. We are told by Gandalf that five wizards were sent to Middle Earth to help the other races in their struggle with Sauron. There was also a sixth wizard working in Middle Earth, but we'll get to him in a minute. This race had enhanced powers to manipulate their environment, for the purpose of good, though at least two of them chose to employ their talents otherwise.

If we look to our modern world for comparisons, I would liken the wizards to great scientists, or philosophers, who can either use their knowledge and influence for great good, or great evil. Unfortunately, much of the technological advances and philosophies that have been developed by modern wizards have been designed for more nefarious purposes, as in the case of weapons of war, or were at least utilized for nefarious ends or had unintended consequences that turned out to be more damaging than helpful, as in the case of fossil fuels and some genetic research. Even the purely scientific discoveries of Charles Darwin were twisted by Hitler who used them to argue for the existence of, and the perpetuation of what he termed, the *master race*.

Philosophers have fared little better. Karl Marx, who saw communism as the ultimate political achievement of mankind argued that the prerequisite steps—Feudalism, Merchantilism, Capitalism, and Socialism—were essential to achieve Communism, if it hoped to succeed. Whether Marx's steps and process was right or not—and he was definitely wrong about a lot of things, especially his loose interpretation of history—we will probably never know because Vladimir Lenin held other ideas. To achieve his totalitarian objectives, Lenin and his fellow Bolshevik revolutionists murdered, assassinated, and bullied their way to the top of the Russian political heap, a heap composed of the rotting corpses of Russian comrades, especially those of the Menshevik Party, and the Bourgeoise. All of this carnage was inflicted in order to skip those *necessary* steps in the process that Marx had argued for.

In *LOTR* there are only two characters that match this level of evil: Morgoth of the Valar, and his servant, Sauron, the Dark Lord of Mordor. Science and philosophy can also do great good, as we'll see, but first we'll see how it's being twisted for the purposes of Power, Greed, and Fear.

## Sauron: Dark Lord of Mordor and World's First *Taker*

At the center of Tolkien's great story is the Ring, which we have established as applicable to our culture's central story, "The world was made for man, and man is here to conquer and rule it." If we entertain the Garden of Eden myth as a record of this moment in our misty past then the serpent in Eden might be symbolized by the evil defiler of Middle Earth, the fallen Valar, Morgoth, though I think Sauron is a better fit. While Morgoth does not appear in *LOTR* his presence is felt through his servant, Sauron, his closest devotee and messenger, who fashions the Ring and fills it with his malice. We should think of Morgoth as the darkest side of mankind's nature, one that most of us would rather not think about. Morgoth is akin to the spirit that drove the Holocaust. It is Sauron, however, that acts as an ancient *Führer*, the instrument of that malicious spirit. It is Sauron after all who fashions the Ring to accomplish Morgoth's goal of covering the earth in darkness and evil.

Sauron, who escaped the disaster of Numenor's fall, set himself to work, in Gondor, sweet talking the Elves into assisting him in a new project. He was especially crafty when it came to making rings. With the help of Elven smiths, Sauron designed the Nine rings for the kings of men and Seven for the Dwarves with the intention of crafting the One Ring to rule them all. To craft the One Ring, however, he trusted no one but himself, so in secret he labored away in Oroduin, the fiery mountain of Mordor to hatch his dark plan

## The Serpent and the Tree

Sauron, who's name in Quenya—one of the Elven languages of Middle Earth—means "abhorred," might also have been derived from the Greek root, *saur*, meaning of course, serpent or lizard, i.e., *dino-SAUR*. We can then think of Sauron as the serpent of the Garden of Eden, symbolic of some long, forgotten king-philosoper-scientist who convinced the ancestors of our culture that Totalitarian Agriculture was a gift from the gods and that it would give them the knowledge of 'good and evil', or as Daniel Quinn puts it, "the knowledge of <u>who should live and who should die.</u>" Did Tolkien intend for Sauron to mirror the serpent in Genesis? Probably not, but the comparison is useful to us. This early king-philosopher-scientist whose name is lost to time, is the progenitor of our culture, *Taker* culture, and we are his offspring, the children of Totalitarian Agriculture and Totalitarian Civilization, the expansive city-building mentality that over ran ancient Mesopotamia, the Indus River Valley, ancient China, and eventually, most of the Earth. His offspring, our culture, is hell bent on growing more food to produce more people, giving us more power over our neighbors, a process repeated *ad infinitum* right up to our day. Our Ring is not the construction of some god or devil, though one might argue that the spirit behind it is in balance with such beings.

In our world, there have been numerous evil or mad scientist types—a few Nazis come to mind—though none so evil as the one who came up with the idea that the *world was made for us, and we were meant to rule it*, in other words, the scientist, philosopher, or king—or all of the above—that originally managed to sell this idea to our ancestors, now lost to us in the mists of time, some 5000 years ago. While he is the root of our culture's ills, there have been others who have tried to profit through his craft, even to supplant him. Some modern corporations certainly act Sauron-icly and seem to be hell-bent on destruction. But Sauron was not the only wizard vying for power in Middle Earth; there was also the White Wizard of Isengard, the former head of the White Council, whose Greed and lust for power ultimately became the ruin of the Shire: Saruman.

## Saruman: CEO of Greed Incorporated

There was a time when he was always walking about my woods. He was polite in those days, always asking my leave (at least when he met me); and always eager to listen. I told him many things that he would never have found out by himself; but he never repaid me in like kind... I think that I now understand what he is up to. He is plotting to become a **Power**. He has a mind of *metal and wheels*; and he does not care for growing things, except as far as they *serve him for the moment*. And now it is clear that he is a black traitor. He has taken up with foul folk, with the Orcs. Brm, hoom! Worse than that: he has been doing something to them; something dangerous. For these Isengarders are more like wicked Men. It is a mark of evil things that came in the Great Darkness that they cannot abide the Sun; but Saruman's Orcs can endure it, even if they hate it. I wonder what he has done? Are they Men he has ruined, or has he *blended the races*

*of Orcs and Men*? That would be a black evil!
[italics/bold mine] — *LOTR*: II, *Treebeard*

I do not see Sauron, but I see that Saruman has many
descendants... —J.R.R. Tolkien, *Speach in 1958*

Saruman, once the wisest of the race of wizards, and head of the
White Council, became obsessed with obtaining the Ring so that
he might rule over Middle Earth in place of Sauron. For me,
Saruman is an excellent example of the kind of mentality that
has for centuries driven the elite: royalty, the aristocracy and the
modern equivalent, the corporate oligarchy that currently runs
our planet as if it were one big factory, designed to extract every
last nickel of wealth from it before moving on to greater profits
somewhere in the Universe. In their minds, the *sky's the limit*,
literally. Saruman is the combination of corporate Greed meets
mad scientist. Those scientists, philosophers and CEOs, much
like the wizard Saruman, who at first set out on the side of good
against the powers of Sauron—much as some American
corporations did during WWII against Hitler—have been
enticed by the lure of Power and Greed, the power that the One
Ring affords them.

Not all scientists, philosophers and business people are
Sarumans, of course. Many still play by the rules, look out for
their employees, and try to respect the environment. But even
the best intentioned of them make mistakes or miscalculate the
true costs of doing business. They forget to include the impacts
of their drive for profit on the environment, and the lives of
their employees, and their customers. Some companies,
however, are so focused on the here and now, the short-term
profitability of their companies, that they fit nicely in the tower
of Orthanc and with the title of Saruman. Some of them are
doing such willful harm that it is difficult to see their actions as
anything else but evil.

Saruman was certainly a wizard of great power and a
scientist as well! He dabbled in genetic engineering by cross-
breeding the races of orcs and men to create a new race of orcs,
the Uruk-Hai, who did not fear daylight and were much more
intelligent. I like to call them GMOs, *Genetically Modified Orcs*!

Saruman sent these new monsters against the people of Rohan at Helms Deep, where they revealed another of his new creations: explosives! These he crafted in the bowels of his cave-like factories at Isengard, fueled by the burning trees of Fangorn Forest! Can there be a better example of the industrial revolution than that? How many forests, mountains and lives has our culture sacrificed in the name of cheaper goods, faster transportation, and creature comforts for us all, but especially for the comfort and luxuries of the Sarumans of our world. How much more shall we poison our air, water and food with the products of greedy, corporate wizards? Is there a limit? Surely there must be another way to provide those things that we need.

Like Saruman, a great number of the elitist, greedy, unchecked, corporate capitalists of today believe that they alone possess the wisdom to run this planet, that they can manipulate the power of human 'nature', i.e. our collective desire to consume, to dominate everything! In many ways, they have been miraculously successful. They have, for millennia, used our own greed and self interests against us to feed their own. In the modern age, with the help of propaganda-public relations-advertising wizards they have played upon our fears and desires, employing modern psychology and their Saruman-ic voices to soothe us, to manipulate our minds into believing that *more* is *better*, that if we could only possess one more pair of shoes, one more car, a bigger house, two televisions for every person, and cellphones for our toddlers we would finally walk into our own golden, Garden of Eden and live happy ever after.

To supply our demand for all of this, they have raped the planet to produce, ship, and sell us the keys to a mythical paradise, while simultaneously chainsawing the very trees that might make up such a place. As Don Henley once sang in the Eagles' song *The Last Resort,"* "Call someplace Paradise, kiss it goodbye." Mr. Henley was addressing the very situation that we are discussing here, namely, the out-of-control expansion of the *Taker* ideal of happiness at the expense of the very things that might have provided it and at the expense of the indigenous peoples, the *Leaver* cultures, who can help us realize our folly by showing us the way to live as *part* of the Earth, and not as the wannabe *rulers*. But if we do not wake up from our stupor soon, the *Leavers* will be gone, leaving us not with a Garden of Eden, Rivendell, Shire, or Lothlorien, but with the reeking, smoking ruins of Mordor and the flotsam and jetsam of Isengard.

When the evil wizard Saruman, dragging his tail between his legs after his summit with Gandalf and Theoden and the destruction of Isengard, escaped north and westward, he ended up in the precious untouched lands of the Shire. Here he wreaked havoc, destruction, desolation, and death. With his golden, corporate voice he easily swayed the unsuspecting and innocent Hobbits to join in on his program of industrialization. He also brought assistance from Breeland in the form of Bill Ferny, and found ready allies in people like Ted Sandyman and the Sackville-Bagginses. He built a smoking factory on the river, pumping pollution into the once pristine waters. He cut down the Party Tree and many others to fuel his avarice and Greed.

The Scouring of the Shire is an excellent example of what happens when *Taker* culture moves into *Leaver* territory, especially when the latter has very little warning of invasion and no real knowledge of the former's destructive nature. This story has played out thousands of times over the last five to ten thousand years, from Mesopotamia, to Europe, to the Americas, as well as all over the Far East, Africa, Asia, the entire planet. There are few if any places left untouched by our corrosive culture. Indeed, it is very difficult if not impossible for *Leaver* cultures to resist or repel a *Taker* culture once they come into contact with it.

When *Takers* move in, if they don't bring fire and destruction immediately they lure the natives in with promises of wealth, of trade. It was Saruman's desire for the Shire's number one cash crop, pipe weed, that brought the Hobbits to his attention and gave him economic connections there which he later exploited to take control of the entire area. This is reminiscent of the Dutch and their trade with the unsuspecting Natives of what is now New York who were dazzled by beads and blankets, and duped into selling their homeland to the Europeans. It was even easier for the Dutch, than for Saruman, because the Native Americans of what would be called, New Amsterdam, had no concept of *selling land*. How does one own or sell something like land? The foreign concepts gave *Takers* the advantage in the transactions.

*Taker* culture has so many unfair advantages over *Leaver* culture, especially when it comes to expansion, population, and technology. The irony is that in order for *Leaver* cultures to resist *Taker* invasion they are forced to adopt *Taker* culture: total war, new weapons, more centralized organization, new transportation (horses). In other words, to 'beat' the *Takers*, you had to *become* a *Taker*; if you can't beat'em, join'em to beat'em? It was a Catch 22 situation for certain, and it still is. The only other option was to surrender the land to the invader and run like hell. Most chose to fight, and even when they *won*, which was rare indeed, they lost in the end by abandoning their culture and adopting *Taker* mentality.

Luckily for us, there are still a few indigenous peoples in the world living in a *Leaver* way but they are disappearing quickly. Much like the Shire under Saruman's rule, if we Hobbits do not return soon from our quest for Mt. Doom, the Saruman CEOs of our world will finish the despoliation of our backyards, cities, farms, lakes, rivers and oceans; and the *Leavers* will be gone. There will be no boat sailing into the West for Valinor, or spacemen beckoning us to "Come Sail Away" to some planet in the solar system of Betelgeuse We will have gone the way of the Dodo Bird. What we need is a new breed of scientist-philosophers to design sustainable alternatives to the orcish products produced in Saruman's labs. We need some Radagasts!

# Radagast the Brown: Post-hole Scientist of the Forest

> Indeed, of all the Istari, one only remained faithful, and he was the last-comer. For Radagast, the fourth, became enamoured of the many beasts and birds that dwelt in Middle-earth, and forsook Elves and Men, and spent his days among the wild creatures. —J.R.R. Tolkien, *The Unfinished Tales*, 390

Most readers are probably unsure why the brown wizard of the forest was included in *LOTR*. He, also of the Istari, seems to be content to spend all his time wandering the wild places, communing with animals and plants, instead of assisting Humans, Elves, and Hobbits. It's interesting that Tolkien, in the quote above, suggests that Radagast seems to have forsaken his purpose for an exhaustive study of the flora and fauna of Mirkwood. Before re-reading that passage in *The Unfinished Tales*, I had always assumed that he was just *supposed* to be some kind of Steve Irwin, Crocodile Hunter of Middle Earth.

Radagast reminds me of some modern scientists and scholars who seem to shun society to concentrate on their highly focused subjects with what seems little care or regard for how their knowledge might be used for good, or ill, in the world. I've read work by scholars in history, as well as other subjects, that remind me of ole' Radagast, wandering around in his own little space oblivious to what is going on in the greater world. I am being overly harsh probably. Most of them aren't as oblivious as they look, I'm sure, but I have talked with some of them who really are that way. One of my professors referred to these scholars as *post hole diggers* because they found a narrow topic in a particular field of study and just started digging downward, as if to dig to the very bottom in order to know everything there was to know about *X*.

There's nothing inherently wrong with scholars who dig post-holes. We need scholars and scientists who dig deep, because that's where you find very interesting things. What's sad is that many post-holers discover wonderful things and ideas that might be useful to the rest of mankind but because they rarely come up from their hole, microscope, or archive, they never see how their hole might connect with many others to help solve some of the world's biggest problems. Some do occasionally make the effort to place their highly focused work in a greater perspective, but many never do, and in many cases their work goes un-noticed. While we need their work and expertise, we desperately need others to connect all those post holes into a broader picture, to back out and view things from wider, even global perspective.

My own training is in history. However, I am not a post-hole historian. I would never have the patience to do that. I'm always glad when others do though because I can grab all the data from their holes and try to draw a picture with it. In a very real sense, that is what I am doing with this book. I've spent most of my adult life wondering what the heck is wrong with our planet, and why. I've read hundreds and hundreds of books on many subjects—many written by post-holers—and only now, after about 20 years of reading and studying have I been able to make any sense out of it all.

It is my hope, that after reading this, that you, or someone that you know will be inspired to connect other post holes in other subjects. What are your special talents and knowledge? How might you apply them to help save our Earth? Can you be a wizard? Are you a scientist? A philosopher? An historian? A writer? Give this a lot of thought, because while we are all in a sense *Hobbits* in that we must all destroy our Ring, we also need wizards to dream up innovative new technologies, ways of thinking, ways of organizing, and new ways of looking at our history. We need everyone's talents, but first, we need yours! This is a call to action. Get up, get walking and get to thinking about how you can make a difference, in small ways, and in larger ones. Start small like a Hobbit, but always be working towards bigger changes, like a wizard. If you are a post-hole digger, dig deep, but come up occasionally and let the rest of us know what you've discovered. You never know how important what you have found may turn out to be.

As tangential as the character of Radagast may seem, it is his talent for listening to Nature and her creatures that saved his fellow wizard, Gandalf. Radagast had been deceived by Saruman into delivering Gandalf into the clutches of the White Wizard but he had not been corrupted himself, and so followed Gandalf's request to send word and news to Isengard to inform Gandalf of goings on and news of the Nazgul. It is Radagast's talent and expertise in communication with the wild creatures of Middle Earth that allows Gandalf to escape the tower. Radagast sent the great Eagle to bring news to Gandalf, only to find him perched at the top of Orthanc, the great tower of Orthanc. If not for this assistance what might have been the fate of Middle Earth? So if you're a Radagast make sure to send an eagle to Gandalf once in a while, preferably before the Black Riders reach the Shire. Better yet, come out of the forest occasionally to let the rest of us know what amazing things you are finding there!

Radagasts are great. They provide us with the details, but what we need desperately these days, are global-thinkers and global-connectors. Scientists, scholars, philosophers, and leaders with enough expertise and breadth of vision to connect all those post holes into a map to a sustainable future for our Earth. What we need, is Gandalf the Grey!

## Gandalf Stormcrow: Wise Pilgrim and Global 'Dot-connector'

> A lord of wisdom throned he sat,
> swift in anger, quick to laugh;
> an old man in a battered hat
> who leaned upon a thorny staff.
>
> He stood upon the bridge alone
> and Fire and Shadow both defied;
> his staff was broken on the stone,
> in Khazad-dum his wisdom died.

To make sense of all the amazingly detailed work of scholars, scientists and philosophers that is being produced at a lightning pace, we need global thinkers, and global connectors, scholars who can quickly process all this information, parse out what is important and useful, and then design a plan to use these ideas to help clean up our Earth and help us all to live more sustainably. At the same time, some of these *connectors* need to be adept at diplomacy, writing, and rhetoric in order to get their messages out to the public, and to those who are in power to make major changes. But it's not only the major changes that we need.

That is of course the purpose of this book: to bring the message to ordinary, average people that they can make changes too, small ones, like carrying Rings to mountains, and cleaning up their Hobbit-holes. What we need is a Gandalf Stormcrow, as he was called by Wormtongue, for always bringing ill news. While his news was sometimes not what people wanted to hear, it was necessary. And he didn't just bring news; he also brought his expertise and experience as well as the expertise of his friends: warriors, burglars, and gardeneners!

## Wisdom and Prudence

Unlike his counterpart, Saruman, who was consumed with desire to obtain Isildur's Bane, Gandalf retains his virtue and wisdom and vehemently refuses to take the Ring, even when it is offered to him freely by Frodo. The great sage knew that to entertain such an idea was fraught with the most severe danger, for himself and for all of Middle Earth. For someone of his power to wield Sauron's Ring, would be tantamount to becoming another Sauron, something that Middle Earth would not survive. Even though he might take such a thing with the intention to do good with its power, he fears that he would be quickly corrupted by its evil. Gandalf is wise enough to know that not even he could bend the Ring to his own will but would eventually become one with it, if not be consumed by it entirely.

Gandalf was sent to help Middle Earth but stays his course and is not swayed from the path of good for the sake of Greed and Power, like Sauron and Saruman. Nor does he choose to become a post-hole digger like Radagast. He is more philosopher and diplomat than CEO or scientist, though he wields great power with his Ring of Fire. Unlike his evil counterparts he uses this power with good intentions and usually to good effect to protect the innocent and vulnerable creatures of Middle Earth. Sometimes that power has unintended consequences too, as all new scientific or philosophic ideas do. It was Gandalf's fiery pine cones that set the forest on fire in *The Hobbit*. While his intentions were noble—he was attempting to drive away the wolves at his and his companions's feet—once released the fire escaped his control and spread to the very trees they were sheltering in. It was only his good luck, and the keen eyes of the great Eagles that saved them all from the *frying pan*.

This is a caution to all scientists, scholars, and diplomats. Be careful what you create, or say; you never know where your discoveries or words will travel or what repercussions they might have later. That's not to say that we should not use science and technology or that we should not philosophize, but only to say that we must be ever cognizant that our ideas and creations have lives of their own and we should give a great deal of thought as to what the possible ramifications of our creations might be before we release them on the world. This is why Gandalf rarely uses his magical powers, and relies more often on his wisdom and his personal philosophy. He is always aware that actions carry unintended consequences that can never be predicted with any accuracy; so it is prudent to think before acting.

## Dot-connector and Nose-follower

Unlike the other wizards, Gandalf seems able to detach himself from his immediate situation, to view it from an objective perspective, from a distance. Gandalf has a rare talent that Daniel Quinn calls a *Martian Anthropologist* perspective. What Quinn means by *Martian*, is the ability to examine human culture from an imagined, alien viewpoint, to suspend one's own human perspective. From this perspective, one is able to analyze the messages of Mother Culture hidden within *Taker* Culture.

Gandalf, as a *Martian*, or *Valinorean* — he's not from Middle Earth, he's from Valinor — is able to connect post-holes, or connect the disparate dots of a great puzzle, to see an outline of what needs to be done to save Middle Earth. He is able to cut to the point and examine things differently than any of the other characters in the books. It is his keen eye that first discerns that there is *more to* Bilbo than meets they eye, after Bilbo miraculously escapes the Misty Mountains and Gollum. He senses that Bilbo might have found a magic ring, though it is not until later that he knows for sure. Once his senses are confirmed, he begins to wonder about the nature of the Ring though it takes him many years to discover its true nature. Even after he is sure that it is the One Ring he still puts it to its last test, in the fires of Frodo's hearth. Then he swings into action. He devises travel plans for Frodo and Sam, then rushes off to seek the advice of his allies, Aragorn and Saruman. It is in his haste to talk to the latter that he makes a crucial miscalculation, as do many *dot-connectors*. He does not know that Orthanc is now a second tower dedicated to domination until it is too late. Luckily, that Eagle came to his aid, or the quest to destroy the Ring might have failed before it even began. Though rescued, Gandalf is too late to help Frodo and his friends to reach Rivendell. Without his guidance they run into dark dangers, barely escaping the clutches of the Black Riders of Mordor.

## The Nazgûl: Slaves to Fear

> The Nazgûl came again, and as their Dark Lord now grew and put forth his strength, so their voices, which uttered only his will and his malice, were filled with evil and horror. Ever they circled above the City, like vultures that expect their fill of doomed men's flesh. Out of sight and shot they flew, and yet were ever present, and their deadly voices rent the air. More unbearable they became, not less, at each new cry. At length even the stout-hearted would fling themselves to the ground as the hidden menace passed over them, or they would stand, letting their weapons fall from nerveless hands while into their minds a blackness came, and they thought no more of war, but only of hiding and of crawling, and of death. — *LOTR*: III, *The Siege of Gondor*

> The apples turn to brown and black,
> The tyrant's face is red.
> Oh war is the common cry,
> Pick up your swords and fly.
> The sky is filled with good
> and bad that mortals never know…
> The pain of war cannot exceed
> the woe of aftermath,
> The drums will shake the castle wall,
> the Ringwraiths ride in black, Ride on.
> — Led Zeppelin, *Battle of Evermore*

The Black Riders of Mordor are the most unsettling and terrifying of all the creatures we meet in *LOTR*. Their very presence is palpable. They are the symbol of Fear. Fear runs rampant when they approach, even from a distance. Men, Hobbits, and animals lose control of their minds in abject fear. They exude the malice and evil of their master Sauron, everywhere they go, relentlessly searching for the One Ring. They were once great kings of men, who Sauron gave rings of power and lured with promises of ever more dominion. What they did not know was that the real power behind their rings, was another ring — one forged in secret by Sauron — the One Ring, designed to dominate all of Middle Earth. Slowly enslaved by their desire the Nine came under the power of the One Ring. Their lives, minds, and bodies were corrupted, twisted and drained of real life. They became wraiths, ghost-like creatures of Fear, and the chief servants to the One Ring and its master, the Dark Lord of Mordor. Of all the rings fashioned by Sauron, only the nine he gave to men could he wholly dominate. Men, it seemed, were susceptible to corruption.

**Modern Wraiths?**

I'm sorry to say, since it is self-damning, that the Black Riders, the nasty, corrupted servants of Mordor are for the purpose of our comparison, symbolic of the truest converts of *Taker* culture, those of us who have succumbed to the lust for more and still more in spite of the fact that it brings us less and less satisfaction. The original Nazgul of our culture were those who, millennia ago, accepted the idea that the *"world belongs to us and we are meant to rule it."* It is this mentality that has created our culture, one built on the desire for nothing, but more, more, more. This mentality is best seen in the modern world in the materialistic, corporate greed for greater profits at any costs.

The Black Riders of our culture have been so long addicted to the power of the Ring, that they have lost their humanity, it seems. How is it that the elite of our world — the corporate 1% and their servants in the political aren — seem to be so out of touch with reality? It is as if they are unable to see in the light of day, much as the Nazgul, instead choosing to live in a foggy, shadowy, darkness, of half-light, unable to focus on anything but their drive for more, advancing the cause of Totalitarianism. It seems that they have lost their core being to the lust for power and wealth. They have lost their souls, and are wandering as malevolent spirits, Ringwraiths, leaving Fear, waste, destruction, poverty and death in their wake.

We all know a few Black Riders, people that have been nearly consumed by our Taker mentality, have *drunk the Kool-Aid*, so to speak, of corporate and political power. Most of us are probably guilty of drinking the waters of Mordor on occasion; I know I am. In many ways it is understandable. We were born into *Taker* culture; how else *would* we think? Have you ever felt like a wraith, even for a moment, a day or during some period of your life? I have experienced that *soul-sucking* feeling while working some wage-slave job or another. I think a lot of people feel that way these days, and have for a long time. It's a desperate feeling, one that should demand action, a struggle to *do* something positive or negative to affect change. But the feeling of soullessness oftentimes leads to paralysis, not action. It is very much the same paralysis that inflicted those who confronted the Black Riders. On occasion, some members of modern society are spurred to do something, anything, to right the wrongs they see around them. Most cowered in Fear. Only a few were able to keep their heads in the presence of the dark force of the Ringwraiths.

## The Path to Wraithishness

How does one become a Modern Ringwraith? Many modern wraiths have inherited their attachment to the Ring from their ancestors. In a sense, we all have, but some—the financially wealthiest—have never been in touch with reality, growing up in homes filled with all the luxuries that money can buy. What is the purpose in such a life? There is none. But they fear losing it, which leads to a driving Greed that drains them of what soul they possessed. Fear—ever the source of a myriad of evils— leads towards Wraithishness. Other Wraiths are created by extreme poverty, or violence. Some poor manage to gain wealth through hard work, or luck, and then the fear of losing it sets in and the soul-sucking begins. Some people lash out in revenge or hatred due to violence they have encountered, or a fear of violence. Always on the horizon, Fear drains them of their life-force, leaving them as wraiths.

What are the effects of the Ring on us, on our culture? The most insidious symptom of the Ring, of our drive to *rule the Earth*, is that we become disconnected from all that is *real*. We have been for millennia now, walking around in that shadowy, half-light, or darkness: the Great Forgetting that Daniel Quinn talks about. It is a kind of *invisibility*. We have forgotten what it was like to be truly *part* of our Earth. In the process we have become estranged from all that is important to us: our food — especially those who produce it, our neighbors — we are increasingly isolated, our government — *Taker* culture is dependent on centralized authority, not Shireness, our environment — we are destroying it, our true purpose — to build communities and gardens, our true nature — to be in harmony with the Earth, and as a result, our lives have little meaning, scant *purpose*. This leads to a sense of hopelessness. We've all felt it, as if we were invisible to all those around us, as if we didn't matter anymore. Our jobs have lost meaning. Even our families, our friends, and neighbors seem strangers to us.

It was these feelings of hopelessness, disconnectedness, and invisibility, I believe, that led the *hippie* revolution of the 1960s to lash out and walk away from normal society. Many felt that something was seriously wrong with our culture and tried desperately to find a way out, though as a group, they failed to do it, even if some individuals did escape. Quinn compares this situation to what he calls the *boiling frog* experiment. In short, if you put a frog in a pot of water and slowly bring the temperature up he will remain in the water even after he realizes it is getting too warm. By the time he realizes that it's too late, he lacks the strength to clamber out of the pot to safety. Our *Taker* culture is the frog; the water was boiling decades ago, in the 60s to be exact. Many tried to get out of the pot, maybe a few made it, but most remained. *Taker* culture is dead and souless, slowly, inexorably drained of it's life-force, like the frog, much as it was for those nine kings of Middle Earth who accepted the power of the One Ring, and ended up Ringwraiths.

Contact with our Ring, the poisonous philosophy that *the world belongs to us* – while unavoidable, is a corrupting force in every life. The *Taker* mentality is killing not only Nature but draining our souls and lives. It's poisoning us from within, just as sure as the Nine Rings of the Nazgul did for those unsuspecting kings of old. If we do not destroy our Ring we might just destroy the Earth, or it might destroy us.

## Bombadil and Goldberry: Mother Nature Laughs at Us

> Don't you know my name yet? That's the only answer. Tell me, who are you, alone, yourself and nameless? But you are young and I am old. Eldest, that's what I am. Mark my words, my friends: Tom was here before the river and the trees; Tom remembers the first raindrop and the first acorn. He made paths before the Big People, and saw the little People arriving. He was here before the Kings and the graves and the Barrow-wights. When the Elves passed westward, Tom was here already, before the seas were bent. He knew the dark under the stars when it was fearless – before the Dark Lord came from Outside. – *LOTR*: I, *In the House of Tom Bombadil*

> Do you see the slightest evidence anywhere in the universe that creation came to an end with the birth of man? Do you see the slightest evidence anywhere out there that man was the climax toward which creation had been straining from the beginning? ...Very far from it. The universe went on as before, the planet went on as before. Man's appearance caused no more stir than the appearance of jellyfish. –Daniel Quinn, *Ishmael: An Adventure of the Mind and Spirit*

"We could destroy the Earth." Growing up during the Cold War in the 1970s and 80s, I remember hearing that phrase a lot. It scared the crap out of me, of course. I remember waking up sometimes in the middle of the night from a recurring nightmare. In this frightening dream, I was always standing outside of my house looking up at the sky where I could see the ice-trails of inter-continental ballistic missiles streaking across the cold blue like some kind of sinister, tic tac toe game; then there was a flash. That's usually when I would wake up in a cold sweat.

I don't have those nightmares anymore, thanks to the collapse of the Soviet Union in 1989, though nuclear war is still a threat, of sorts. Instead, I worry about other threats these days, ones that are very much as real, and already happening. When it comes to global climate change, the loss of safe drinking water, and several other major environmental crises, the missiles are in the air, the x's are lined up 3 in a row, and we're waiting for the shock wave.

But we cannot destroy the Earth any more than Sauron could destroy Middle Earth, in Tokien's timeless stories. I've always thought that was the most arrogant thing I've ever heard a human say. The Earth, and life, was here billions of years before we ever dropped down out of the trees and started walking upright, and it will be here for a very long time after we've ceased to exist, I suspect.

## To Bombadil, or Not...

In *The Lord of the Rings*, the ancient-ness or permanence of Middle Earth is embodied in two characters, a man and wife: Tom Bombadil and Goldberry. Bombadil's character is probably the most enigmatic one in all of Tolkien's stories. He is controversial as well, mostly because fans are divided on a couple of points. One, is his character necessary to the story? And two, just who the heck *is he*, or more accurately, *what* is he?

To the first question, there is only one answer: yes. Tolkien certainly felt he was necessary to the story, or he wouldn't have included him. At the very least, he serves a couple of plot advancing purposes. He gives the Hobbits a well deserved break from adventures, not to mention the fact that he rescues them from the clutches of a pissed-off willow tree. Up to this point the Hobbits have been pursued by Dark Riders, lost in the Old Forest, and nearly swallowed by Old Man Willow! They needed a break. Two, and most importantly I think, Tom

Bombadil demonstrates that the Ring is not the most ancient power in Middle Earth, nor is its true master, Sauron.

There are things and beings that are far older and immune to Sauron's evil. Tom is unaffected by the Ring; he sees it as an interesting trinket, at best. That's not to say he doesn't understand that it's evil; he does advise Frodo that the Ring is unsuited for his fair fingers. But the Ring has no hold whatsoever on Tom. He plays with it, puts it on his finger, flips it into the air, makes it disappear, but shows no sign that it affects any lasting hold on his mind and had no effect on him or his senses. Tom can even see Frodo while the Hobbit is wearing the Ring! Gandalf points out, at the Council of Elrond, that to send the Ring to Bombadil—as some suggested—might seem prudent from the standpoint that it had no power over Tom, but that's because it held no fascination to him; he might easily toss it aside or forget where he had stored it, only for it to resurface in the hands of someone less worthy than Frodo.

### Who or What are the Bombadils?

There have been numerous attempts to answer that question. In an essay, almost twenty years ago, Professor Gene Hargrove suggested that Tom was an earthly embodiment of the Valar, Aule the Smith, and for many years I was convinced that he was correct. But lately I've given it more thought and after reading an article by Steuard Jensen, "What is Tom Bombadil?: A Nature Spirit? and Conclusions," awhile back, I tend to mostly agree with him that old Tom and his wife, Goldberry, are more likely the embodiment of the spirit of Arda or Middle Earth itself, the equivalent of our Mother Earth.

When the Hobbits ask him to come along with them after their adventure in the Barrow Downs, Tom basically admits that to leave his forest is not something that he is interested in doing. While this seems to suggest that Tom is a localized spirit, Gandalf later reveals that Tom was not always tied to the Old Forest and Barrow Downs, "now he is withdrawn into a little land, within bounds that he has set, though none can see them, waiting perhaps for a change of days, and he will not step beyond them. —*LOTR*: I, *The Council of Elrond*

Jensen argued that Tom seems to have chosen to remain there, because it was an area that was still wild, and closer to the natural state that all Middle Earth had known. Tom certainly has great power, especially over his domain, the Old Forest and Barrow Downs. He calms Old Man Willow and the barrow-wight by singing magical songs. When he sings, things listen. Goldberry seems to have power or influence over everything watery and the birds, plants and animals.

We will probably never solve the mystery of Bombadil and his wife, Goldberry, but whatever they were intended to be, they are symbols of the natural world, or are closely allied to it. Bombadil, in our world, as far as I'm concerned anyway, symbolizes the power of nature and of certain places in nature: forests especially. His wife, Goldberry, is running water and rain. They are for us like Mother Nature, who is much older than our corrupted, evil Ring—the idea that the Earth belongs to us. As bad as we humans abuse Mother Nature, I personally don't think we can *kill* her. She does not belong to us, we belong to her, and she can kick us to the curb in an instant if ever she's of a mind to do so. She is laughing at us and our arrogance and could squash us like a bug at any moment. Our trinkets and technologies are curiosities to her, nothing more. They are like flashes of light: here and gone in an instant, like Sauron's Ring in the hands of Bombadil.

Ancient, indigenous cultures have long worshiped such Nature spirits. They learned to *listen* to the spirit of a place, a forest, a river, a tree, and to communicate with them in a very real sense. Don't think for a moment that Mother Nature isn't talking to us. Just because we have *selective hearing*,—like mother Bivans has always said of my father, and me—doesn't mean she isn't whispering in our ear. Sometimes, like my mom, it's a bit louder than a whisper. Sometimes she's roaring and calling us by first, middle, and last name, "Stephen John Bivans!!!" That was never good news. And you couldn't run away. There is no *away* from Linda Bivans. There's also no away from Mother Nature, or Tom, or Goldberry.

Humans—even if we included our primate ancestors—have existed for only the tiniest fraction of the Earth's immense history—about 3 million years roughly—and within that time period our destructive *Taker* culture has existed for even less time, about 10,000 years—a comparative blink of an eye, the time it took Bombadil to *wink* the Ring out of sight, and back again.

So while *we* are not permanent, the Earth is comparatively so. Sure, we can destroy and have destroyed much of the life on this planet. We continue to do that every day. But long before we destroy it all we will cease to exist, since, you know, we kind of need that life to sustain our own. The Earth will still be here laughing at us for a brief second, then forget we ever existed. Yes, at some point, billions of years from now, the Earth itself will be destroyed by the sun or bombarded into a rock by asteroids or a comet, but I suspect that we will be long gone by then if we haven't figured out how to live more harmoniously and found a way to blast ourselves into the Milky Way to find a new home. Hopefully, we'll learn our lesson before we do, or ole Tom Bombadilo will just be laughing at us again, on a different rock, spinning around a different sun, watching us play with our magic techno-ring-trinkets.

If we want to survive to land on the planet Vulcan, we better take some advice from the *Leavers* and more enlightened beings among us; it's time to approach the Elves for advice.

## Elrond, Galadriel, and Legolas: Wisdom of the Leavers

### Galadriel

In contrast to the corruption represented by Sauron, Saruman, and the Nazgul, stands Elrond, Galadriel, and Legolas of the Elven race. Other than Gandalf, only one other character of comparable power is ever offered the Ring, also by Frodo: Galadriel. The great and powerful queen of Lothlórien—and one of the few left of the Elves of the First Age—is tempted by the Ring when Frodo offers to give it to her, much as he did to Gandalf. The scene is worth quoting in full, I think, as it is one of the most illuminating passages in the story to demonstrate the insidious, magnetic, and corruptive power of the Ring:

Galadriel laughed with a sudden clear laugh. 'Wise the Lady Galadriel may be,' she said, 'yet here she has met her match in courtesy...I do not deny that my heart has greatly desired to ask what you offer. For many long years I had pondered what I might do, should the Great Ring come into my hands, and behold! it was brought within my grasp. The evil that was devised long ago works on in many ways, whether Sauron himself stands or falls. Would not that have been a noble deed to the credit of his Ring, if I had taken it by force or fear from my guest?

And now at last it comes. You will give me the Ring freely! In place of the Dark Lord you will set up a Queen. And I shall not be dark, but beautiful and terrible as the Morning and the Night! Fair as the Sea and the Sun and the Snow upon the Mountain! Dreadful as the Storm and the Lightning! Stronger than the foundations of the earth. All shall love me and despair!

She lifted up her hand and from the ring that she wore there issued a great light...She stood before Frodo seeming now tall beyond measurement, and beautiful beyond enduring, terrible and worshipful. Then she let her hand fall, and the light faded, and suddenly she laughed again, and lo! she was shrunken: a slender elf-woman, clad in simple white, whose gentle voice was soft and sad.

'I pass the test,' she said. 'I will diminish, and go into the West, and remain Galadriel. —LOTR: I, *The Mirror of Galadriel*

Can there be a more powerful indictment of the evil of this trinket? If it can so easily tempt the great, the wise, and the good then there can be only one solution: destroy it. What is amazing in the cases of Gandalf and Galadriel is that they are both characters of immense power who refuse the offer of more. Either one could have easily, as she pointed out, seized the Ring from Frodo and put it to whatever use they wished, or at least they could have attempted to do so. However, both resist such temptation, even when the Ring was freely offered to them.

Galadriel seems to have spent some time daydreaming about what she might do if such an opportunity came to her, but when the Ring came within her grasp, into her very kingdom and domain, she refused to take the Ring by force, as she most certainly had the power to do. There would be none with sufficient force to resist her if she had. Gandalf had fallen in Moria. Aragorn and Boromir might have put up a fight, but they would have had no chance against the most powerful Elven queen in Middle Earth, especially since she herself was a Ring-bearer. Thankfully, she and Gandalf, were in the possession of something far more powerful, in that Age, or any since: an ancient wisdom and experience that stayed their hand. They knew all too well that to wield the Ring would be to become a Dark Lord themselves. Both chose to forebear.

## Elrond

The great Elrond also resisted such temptations. Though Tolkien does not draw attention to Elrond's forbearance in this matter he certainly possessed the power to wrest the Ring from Frodo if he had truly desired to do so. At Rivendell, of course, there were others who might try to prevent him but if he managed to get ahold of it, who knows whether Gandalf and all the other Elves, Men, Dwarves and Hobbits would have been able to dislodge it from his finger! He made no such attempt, however; he was also wise enough to pass on such temptations.

## Legolas

Frodo also had one Elven companion in the Fellowship of the Ring: Legolas, the Prince of Mirkwood, son of King Thranduil of the Sindarin Elves. Legolas proves to be an invaluable companion to the Fellowship, especially his talent for killing orcs from great distances. He also seems to have possessed the same natural resistance to the Ring, as Elrond, because Tolkien never suggests that he was tempted by its power, even though he spent months in close proximity to the evil talisman.

# Wisdom of the *Leavers*

These three Elves possessed an ancient wisdom, one issuing from an Age long before the Ring, indeed, long before the rise of Sauron. Their wisdom is similar, in many ways, to that of the indigenous peoples, the *Leaver* cultures of our world: Native Americans, the Aborigines of Australia, the Yanomami of the Amazon, to name a few. How many native cultures tried to pass their wisdom and way of life to *Taker* culture over the centuries? Many of them, or at least many of their leaders knew that to accept the offer of *Taker* culture — Totalitarian Agriculture and the myth that man is meant to rule the earth — would be the ruin of their own way of life. Many tried to warn their own people and many times to warn Europeans, as well. Tolkien's Elves are akin to those *Leavers* who came into contact with our *Taker* culture, adopted what tools from us they needed, yet refused to become like us. But as we see in *LOTR*, the Elves are in decline; the undoing of the One Ring brought about the diminishing of the Three Rings of the Elves. Their power waned, and instead of living in Middle Earth where they would have to watch its magic and beauty slowly fade, many, including Elrond and Galadriel, and eventually Legolas, sailed into the West never to return.

Unfortunately for us, there are very few indigenous, *Elven* peoples left on our Earth, especially those who have come into contact with our culture. However, there do seem to be some people *within* our culture who have a natural resistance to the Ring. I know of a handful personally, and others by their messages. People like the late Pete Seger, Arlo Guthrie, the Dali Lama comes to mind, as do some of my truly *hippie*, liberal friends. I'm sure you probably know a few? You know, those *tree-hugger, pinko-commie* types, bleeding heart liberals who need to *get a hair-cut and get a real job*. You know, the hard-core Democrats on your Facebook list. I'm not talking about politicians, either. I'm talking about *real* liberals, who actually believe in the goodness of human nature, who you can't *help* but love because they refuse to be ruffled by anything. For me anyway, they're a walking reminder of the Elves of Lothlórien.

One my good friends, Kitty West, is such a person. She is one of the most amazing souls you could ever meet. She has always been a glowing light of positivity in the face of the world's insanity. Her daily, weekly posts on Facebook are like falling Mallorn leaves reflecting sunlight to illuminate the darkness. She reminds me of Galadriel, though without the sense of underlying, crushing power. Maybe she's what you might get if you crossed Galadriel, Goldberry, and Samwise Gamgee, a kind of ancient, almost naive wisdom that comes from eons of walking in the forests and fields and talking with the animals and trees. Here's a sample of her approach to life and its insanity:

> Got to the Courthouse and asked to speak with a policeman. Three policemen appeared on the spot.
>
> I began to tell my car-car ticket-code problem story, and within seconds two of the policemen vanished, and the third probably would have vanished except he was the last one standing and had to stay. Number 3 Policeman's eyes kept getting bigger and bigger and he finally told me he had no earthly idea about an answer. He then sent me to the DA's office. The DA and assistant DA and I talked about the situation-at length—and the bottom line is that they rescheduled the court date for January 10th, 2014. Then they told me to do what I had to do to get my tags. I pointed out to them that it meant I'd have to drive illegally and I might very well get more tickets. They said to drive anyway and if I get more tickets, they will dismiss them all, AFTER I get tags & registration taken care of. SO, it's unanimous. State Troopers, Sheriff, District Attorney & Assistant DA all agree that I am officially on a secret criminal mission. In order to over ride the computer's glitch I must drive illegally to get legal car status. Home now. I intend to thoroughly enjoy my next 100 miles worth of crime. But now, it's time to get ready to give some Halloween candy away. I think for a costume I'll just write "ESCAPED CRIMINAL" on my forehead. Signed, Kitty West, Softened Criminal

Kitty is well aware that Mordor is at the Door but resists it with humor in a seemingly effortless way. Maybe she, and the others like her are the last remaining Elves on our Middle Earth? I like to think of it that way. We should take the time to listen to them; they have much to tell us about how we ought to live, in harmony with the trees, and all living things, not to mention with each other.

The Elves in Middle Earth weren't quite as liberal as my friend, Kitty, however. For modern comparison, I think that we can look to more moderate liberals, those friends of ours who believe we should give a helping hand to the less fortunate among us and to safe-guard Mother Nature against the ravages of corporate Sarumans but hold grudges with their conservative counterparts. They are the liberals you find in political arguments with their conservative friends on Facebook. Legolas, carries certain prejudices as do some of the other Elves in the story. They have a deep love of Nature but they are none too fond of Dwarves. Legolas clashes with Gimli more than once early on in the story. Elves and Dwarves had long standing differences, had even fought wars with each other, though at times managed to put those aside in the interest of preserving peace in Middle Earth and resisting the forces of Evil. Legolas and his new friend, Gimli son of Gloin, forge such a friendship in spite of inherent differences.

## Gimli: Enlightened Conservative, Defender of Middle Earth

> The only power over them [the Dwarves] that the Rings wielded was to inflame their hearts with a greed of gold and precious things, so that if they lacked them all other good things seemed profitless, and they were filled with wrath and desire for vengeance on all who deprived them. But they were made from their beginning of a kind to resist most steadfastly any domination. Though they could be slain or broken, they could not be reduced to shadows enslaved to another will; and for the same reason their lives were not affected by any Ring, to live either longer or shorter because of it. All the more did Sauron hate the

possessors and desire to dispossess them. *LOTR: Appendix A*

But when King Elessar gave up his life Legolas followed at last the desire of his heart and sailed over the Sea…We have heard tell that Legolas took Gimli Gloin's son with him because of their great friendship, greater than any that has been between Elf and Dwarf. *LOTR: Appendix A*

We made a promise we swore we'd always remember
No retreat no surrender
Like soldiers in the winter's night with a vow to defend
No retreat no surrender. —Bruce Springsteen, *No Surrender*

The race of Dwarves, we are told, were brought to life by one of the Valar, Aulë the Smith. He created them out of the very rock of Middle Earth, and for that reason they were drawn to the mountains, stone, and things *from* the earth, in particular, precious metals and jewels. They were staunchly conservative, slow to make friends, slower to forget trespasses, quick to anger, and prone to revenge. We get a taste of this in *The Hobbit*. Thorin and company are on a mission to wreak vengeance upon Smaug for the death of their kinfolk and the destruction of their Kingdom Under the Mountain. On the positive side, they were also great miners, smiths, and craftsmen. They were also loyal allies who were loathe to break oaths. Though susceptible to Greed they were resistant to external corruption. Though their rings of power were forged by Sauron they could not be fully corrupted or twisted into Wraiths like the kings of Men.

Gimli is, I think, a prime example of the ideal Dwarf. He is wrathful towards his enemies, but compassionate towards his friends. He appreciates the beauty of the hard things of the earth, of gold, silver, gems but is not possessed by them. He is supremely loyal to his companions, especially to his Elven friend, Legolas. As tough, and stoney as Gimli seems to be, he is not a stereotyped character. Possibly because of his father's friendship with Bilbo, he seems to have a *Hobbity* side. He loves pipe-weed, for instance, and forms an unbreakable bond with the four Hobbits. He seems to have an innate tolerance for those of different viewpoints. Though he's prone to stand his ground, he shows deference to the wisdom of his friends, especially Aragorn, Gandalf, and Legolas. In the beginning of the story, Gimli is suspicious of Legolas — old prejudices die hard — but as he and the Elf struggle as part of a team to protect the Ringbearer, his tough, conservative, preconceptions fall away. His admittance to the Golden Wood of Lothlórien was an eyeopener for sure, and his meeting with the Queen of Elvendom, Galadriel, changes his viewpoint on Elves forever. In the end, he and Legolas are the strongest of friends. So much so, that Gimli becomes the first and *only* Dwarf to ever be allowed to sail to Valinor with his friend, Legolas.

If Elves are an example of a guarded *liberal* mentality, the Dwarves are certainly their *conservative* counterparts. Before I go any further, I want to state, categorically, that I am NOT putting a value judgment on either way of thinking, not really. I believe that both conservatives and liberals can be Hobbits. Absolutely they can. That being said, many on both sides of that divide have some distance to travel to meet in the middle somewhere, much as Legolas and Gimli managed to do. We will talk more about their relationship in Part III.

The race of Dwarves are for us symbolic of the modern conservative mentality. And I'm not talking about the extremist, hate-preaching, conservatives like the Westboro Baptists freaks, that we all see everyday on Facebook. I'm talking about moderate, reasonable, tolerant people who happen to see the world from a more conservative viewpoint. Gimli reminds me of some of my conservative friends and of an earlier version of myself. You know the type, I'm sure. They will defend their families, friends, and neighbors against all comers, even if they frequently disagree with them. They have strong core values based on things like the Golden Rule. They believe the world works in a certain way, but will not go to blows, or destroy a friendship to defend an opinion. They are often suspicious of strangers and newcomers, but keep and open mind. They are tight with their money, yet generous and compassionate in times of crisis.

As I mentioned in the introduction to the book, I'm more Dwarvish than Hobbity, certainly more of both, than I am Elvish. I've spent a good deal of time with Elves like Kitty, and Bombadils like Monk, and I've learned a lot from their perspectives. I've become, over the years, more and more like a Hobbit, which is good because smashing stuff isn't always the prudent response—though it might be fun. There's a place for Dwarvish conservatives in the Shire, for sure. Their loyalty and willingness to defend their friends and neighbors is a quality worth having around, as it was for the Fellowship. Defenders of all kinds will be needed in the War with the Sarumans of our Earth.

## The Humans of Middle Earth: Bravery, Honor, and Susceptibility

Tolkien's story, in *LOTR* is about the rise of the Age of Men, though we'll call it the Age of Humans—I don't want to leave out the girls. It is very much a story about mankind, even if its focus is about Hobbits' role in that transformation. It is the time when mankind asserts its place as the ruling elite in Middle Earth, while the other races, Elves and Dwarves, and Hobbits begin to fade.

Humans in *LOTR* are complex characters probably because they are in real life. They can be capable of great evil and treachery, as in Wormtongue and Bill Ferny. But of the men who came into direct contact with the One Ring, they seem to fall into two categories: those who successfully resisted the power of the Ring, and those who succumbed to its allure. There is also one human, a woman, who faced a Ringwraith and lived to tell the tale. We've already discussed the nine kings who were seduced by Sauron and turned into Wraiths but not all those who came into contact with its power were *Wraithified*. Some were more stout, especially the men from Gondor. But even they could be tempted to use its power, even if to do good. The Ring was too powerful for the two who chose to possess it. In the end, it destroyed them, long before they lost their humanity. Two of them were more successful at resisting the lure of the Ring. We'll begin with Isildur and Boromir.

# Isildur and Boromir: Defend at All Cost

> True-hearted Men, they will not be corrupted. We of Minas Tirith have been staunch through long years of trial. We do not desire the power of wizard-lords, only strength to defend ourselves, strength in a just cause. And behold! in our need chance brings to light the Ring of Power. It is a *gift*, I say; a gift to the foes of Mordor. It is mad not to use it. to use the power of the Enemy against him. The *fearless*, the *ruthless*, *these alone will achieve victory*. What could not a warrior do in this hour, a great leader? What could not Aragorn do? Or if he refuses, why not Boromir? The Ring would give me power of *Command*. How I would drive the hosts of Mordor, and all men would flock to my banner! [italics mine] — *LOTR*: I, *The Breaking of the Fellowship*

### Isildur, King of Gondor: Bravery to a Fault

Before we criticize Isildur, we should first remember that it was he who hacked the Ring from Sauron's evil hand at the end of the Second Age of Middle Earth, defeating the Dark Lord, face to face. This was no mean feat. He is the only character in any of the books able to face down Sauron which is particularly amazing considering that Sauron was wearing the One Ring at the time. Brave as he was, Isildur stands as a warning to all those who would try to use Sauron's Ring, that ultimately it will corrupt your mind and lead to your downfall. At the foot of Mt. Doom he had the opportunity to destroy the Ring and banish Sauron's power forever, but entrapped by its power, he could not bring himself to part with it even when counseled by Elrond to do just that. Even the strong are susceptible to its power.

In some ways it was Isildur's strength of character that was his undoing and which left the earth in peril for another age. We are not told that Isildur had any particular streak of evil or weakness that made him unable to destroy the Ring. Possibly it was not weakness or evil at all that drove him to claim it but a fear that Sauron would return and that he would need its power to defend his people. Fear, again, leads to a downfall and to further evil and destruction. If this was Isildur's motivation we should forgive him his weakness. Who among us is without Fear? If it *was* Fear that drove him to keep the Ring, he was essentially no different than Boromir, an Age later. Both wished to defend Gondor from the threat of Sauron's armies, and believed, firmly, that any and all means should be employed to do so.

## Boromir, Prince of Gondor: Desperate Defender

Boromir is one of my favorite characters in *LOTR*. The reason I love Boromir is that he is not that different from myself. I suppose I don't identify as much with Isildur because his *redemption* – if you will – came *before* his contact with the Ring, by standing up to Sauron, face to face, and cutting the Ring from the Dark Lord's finger. Indeed, Isildur's strength must have been exceedingly great, because he was able to do this while Sauron was wearing the Ring! I doubt Boromir could have accomplished that, though Boromir reads as a much more sympathetic character, because he attempts to wrest the Ring, immediately realizes his folly, then sacrifices his life doing what he does best, fighting to the death to defend the defenseless: Merry and Pippin.

I see these two characters, Boromir and Isildur as examples of what I might call the Desperate Defender mentality. In our time, we might find them as members of the Earth Liberation Front (ELF), the amorphous movement, Anonymous, Greenpeace, or any other number of such activist, protest groups who firmly believe that their cause is right, and in many cases are. These groups, while attempting to promote laudable causes – protecting the environment, promoting freedom of speech, resisting greed and corruption – tend to use any means necessary to accomplish their goals. That's not to say that the leadership – if they indeed *have* leaders – of these groups sanction all of the efforts of their followers, all the time. But the spirit of these types of groups is to save parts of our planet and to do so using time honored, face-to-face, battle it out in the street tactics, even if some of them employ modern communications technology to do it. In this way, they are very much like Boromir and Isildur. For them, direct conflict is not only necessary to achieve their noble goals, it is the only possible way. I'm over simplifying it a bit but that is the essence of their methods.

What they haven't realized is that to save the Earth, a more direct, yet subtle tactic must be employed, one they seem not to have considered. The Ring must be *destroyed*, not *employed*. We cannot win the war, so to speak, *simply* by using the age old tactics of political lobbying, or popular protest, and certainly not violence and destruction of property. While lobbying and peaceful protest have their place, violence and destruction are negative responses that lead to push back from not only those who they oppose, but from the public at large, and damage the reputation of those who work on the grass-roots level to find peaceful solutions to the world's problems. We cannot defeat wanton Greed and violence, with violence and destruction. Our enemies, the Saurons and Sarumans of the world, are just to powerful on that front. They have too much money, influence, and military might to ever win head to head.

That doesn't mean that some of us shouldn't continue to butt heads with them, of course. And it doesn't mean that the efforts of resistance groups are completely futile. The problem with such tactics aren't necessarily in the tactics themselves, but in the mind set that they are *the only way* to win the war. Such tactics — as long as they are restricted to peaceful modes — would be more effective if we realize that the goal of such efforts is mainly to keep the enemy engaged in a traditional conflict, a more public, obvious conflict, so that Hobbits can slip under the Nazgul Radar to bring them down by destroying the very essence of their power. The other two examples of strong human characters, Aragorn and Faramir, represent this new mindset.

## Aragorn and Faramir: Peaceful Warriors

> War must be, while we defend our lives against a
> destroyer who would devour all; but I do not love the
> bright sword for its sharpness, nor the arrow for its
> swiftness, nor the warrior for his glory. I love only
> that which they defend. *LOTR*: II, *The Window on the
> West*

In contrast to Boromir and Isildur, was Boromir's brother,
Faramir, and Isildur's descendant, the returning king, Aragorn.
Here were two heroic characters willing to sacrifice their lives to
defend their people, much as Boromir and Isildur. The
difference being that Aragorn and Faramir both know that it
was not their mission to destroy Sauron's power, only to resist
it, to protect their people through force of arms, keeping the
Dark Lord's gaze and malice directed upon themselves while
Frodo and Sam inched their way towards Mt. Doom.

Aragorn knew at the beginning of the story—from his
discussions with Gandalf—that Frodo carried the most
powerful trinket in Middle Earth. If he had been tempted and
unable to resist such temptation the story would have turned
out much different indeed. Aragorn, or Strider—as he's known
when Frodo first meets him in the darkened room in the
Prancing Pony—could easily have seized the Ring from four
little Hobbits, and pointed this out to them:

> ...my only answer to you, Sam Gamgee, is this. If I
> had killed the real Strider, I could kill *you*. And I
> should have killed you already without so much talk.
> If I was after the Ring, I could have it—NOW! —
> *LOTR*: I, *Strider*

In fact, at any point up until the Falls of Rauros, Aragorn
could have taken the Ring and become a new Dark Lord, or
servant thereof. He did not. Nor did he seem to be tempted to
do so. Aragorn knew that to touch the thing would be to risk
corruption and the destruction of all he had sworn to defend,
not just Gondor—Boromir's primary Fear—but all of Middle

Earth. That was his life's mission, not only to defend it, nay, but to restore it to a semblance of its former glory.

Dentheor's younger son, Faramir also rejected the Ring, even when he could easily have seized it. Faramir, the son of Denethor and brother of Boromir, apparently lacked his family's penchant for rashness. He was not attracted to the Ring's power. Faramir proved his *"quality,"* and a strength of forbearance lacking in his older brother, by resisting the temptation to take the Ring from Frodo. Indeed, he told the Hobbit:

> But fear no more! I would not take this thing, if it lay by the highway. Not were Minas Tirith falling in ruin and I alone could save her, so using the weapon of the Dark Lord for her good and my glory. No, I do not wish for such triumphs. — *LOTR*: II, *The Window on the West*

The difference between Aragorn/Faramir and Boromir/Isildur seems stark. But what seems an ocean is in fact just a drop of rain.

All four men were noble warriors. They were drawn to the fight. They were highly trained fighters, indeed from birth. The difference is that Boromir and Isildur firmly believed that fighting alone could carry the day, that in fact *their* solution *was* the *only* solution, the means and end. It was this belief that destroyed them both, Isildur in the great river Anduin — shot through by orcish arrows while the evil Ring slipped from his fingers to the bottom — and Boromir, desperately trying to salvage his soul and reputation after being overcome by the Ring — also shot through with orcish arrows, near the banks of the very same River — while the Ring slipped away over the waters into the East towards the smoke of Mt. Doom.

Aragorn and Faramir, also warriors and fighters, *knew* that their tactics could not destroy Sauron's power. Only the destruction of the Ring could accomplish that goal. Their job, as they clearly saw it, was merely to keep Sauron's lidless, flaming eye diverted elsewhere, to resist and destroy what evil forces they could, while the real threat to his dominion slipped in the backdoor. Sauron never saw it coming, in large part because of the noble sacrifices of so many warrior types who accepted the blow of the Dark Lord's armies, at Helm's Deep, the Pelennor

Fields, and at the Black Gates. Aragorn and Faramir knew that what they were doing was not the true means to the end, it was only a part—an important part no doubt—but only a part of that end. To achieve victory the Ring had to be destroyed, not employed. If distracting Sauron could help achieve that end, then they were willing to risk everything to do it. Luckily for them, there was also one woman, a human woman, who defied the traditional role of "shield-maiden," and rode into history in defense of Middle Earth: Éowyn of Rohan!

## Éowyn of Rohan: the Slayer of Fear

> "Hinder me? Thou fool. No living man may hinder me!"
>
> Then Merry heard of all sounds in that hour the strangest. It seemed that Dernhelm laughed, and the clear voice was like the ring of steel. "But no living man am I! You look upon a woman. Éowyn I am, Éomund's daughter. You stand between me and my lord and kin. Begone, if you be not deathless! For living or dark undead, I will smite you, if you touch him." —*LOTR*: III, *The Battle of the Pelennor Fields*

> From now on, every girl in the world who *might* be a slayer...*will* be a slayer. Every girl who *could* have the power...*will* have the power...*can* stand up, *will* stand up. ...every one of us. Make your choice. Are you ready to be strong? —*Buffy the Vampire Slayer*, Season 7, Episode 22, *Chosen*

The scene between Éowyn and the Captain of the Nazgûl during the epic Battle of the Pelennor, is possibly my favorite moment in all the books that Tolkien wrote. The lead up to it is gripping. The *Ride of the Rohirrim*, and the subsequent charge of the horsemen into the fray before the walls of Minas Tirith are in my opinion, some of the best written prose in all of literature. By the time we get to Éowyn's stand against the Witch King of Angmar the tension is at its highest. And her fierceness is infectious. I never read that section or watch the movie version without the blood boiling in my veins. If a portal were to open up in the wall that would allow me to walk into that battle, I would do it. There's absolutely no question about that in my mind. What a strong character she is. I f'n LOVE HER!

What's funny is that many scholars and fans criticize Tolkien for not featuring women more prominently in his works. It's true that there are comparatively few women mentioned. But those who are, are remarkably strong characters. Does anyone really question that Galadriel could kick some serious ass? I think not. In fact, she's probably the most powerful Elf in all of Middle Earth. Arwen, in the books at least, comes across as a marginal character, though if you read the appendices you'll see that she really was a motivating factor in all that Aragorn did. But of all the women, Éowyn is the strongest, quite frankly, because of her weakness: she's only human. She has no special powers, no immortality, only her innate grit and drive to be something more than just a shield-maiden. And nothing whatsoever will stay her on her course. In the end, she, and her faithful companion Merry, take down the Witch King *HIMSELF!* She kills the one servant of Sauron that no man can kill; she kills Fear itself in what is arguably the most dramatic moment in the books. I think it is significant that the embodiment of Fear in *The Lord of the Rings* is slain by a woman. In fact, only a woman is capable of doing so.

What I don't want to do here is to make some kind of lame, feminist argument that women have some kind of special powers they can employ to save the Earth. I'm not sure that's true. Every person has special gifts, and that includes women. Unfortunately, for the human species, women have been relegated to secondary roles throughout much of our history and are still under-represented in leadership positions even in the so-called, free-world. Tolkien did not forget about them; that's why he had characters like Galadriel and Éowyn. Suffice it to say that women, whether they be Rohan Princesses, or Hobbit Mamas, are essential to the goal of saving the Earth, and not just in their capacities as mothers and home-makers.

I don't know a single man on this Earth—myself included—who is as emotionally and mentally strong as the women in my family. My mom, certainly of the Rohan persuasion—though she's not a fan of the books—would stand up to anyone or anything that threatened her family, and woe be unto them. Much of my strength, and fire, I got from my mother, as well as my ability to see through B.S. My daughter, Samantha, a huge Tolkien—and Buffy—fan, has never been afraid to speak her mind, especially in the defense of the vulnerable, and against injustice. Patience has overcome trials that would kill the average man. Physical strength has been over emphasized for too long. And the assumption—among some stupid men—that men are naturally more intelligent or logical than women, should be buried and forgotten. The world needs the perspective that women can provide. Personally, I think that most women are far braver than men. Think about it for a minute. Women are on average physically weaker, and always have been. They've been living in a *man's world* for a very long time, a world that can physically dominate them, but they have resisted that and continue to do so. They stare Fear in the face every day, and keep on going. Situations that we men see as ordinary, they see potential danger, and for good reason. But they don't stop going. And they keep us in line and moving, too.

Women have for millennia been the caretakers of the family, but they are more than that. Most of the modern Hobbits that I see pushing the ideas in this book are women and girls. They are overwhelmingly the ones in the lead for the organic food movement. They are predominantly the ones working for social justice and human rights of all kinds, not to mention animal rights. But women need to be better represented in politics and business if we expect our civilization to survive. We need more Éowyns leading us into a new world, facing the Sarumans and Ringwraiths and taking them down!

We—those who wish to *save the Earth*—need brave and noble men *and* women who will sacrifice their time, even their lives to keep the attention of those who would destroy the Earth, distracted, and to resist those Wraiths, wizards, and orcs on every field of battle, whether that be in the street, on the farm, in court, or in congress. But in the end, the only way we can truly save our planet is to destroy the Ring, to change our minds, to realize that we were **not put here to rule** but to be a

**part of our earth.** We must, in that way, be more like Hobbits, and less like Humans. It is our Hobbit nature that will save the Earth, or nothing will.

# Hobbits: Small Steps, Shaking the Towers

> Such is oft the course of deeds that move the wheels of the world: small hands do them because they must, while the eyes of the great are elsewhere. —*LOTR*: I, *The Council of Elrond*

> I think that this task is appointed for you, Frodo; and that if you do not find a way, no one will. This is the hour of the Shire-folk, when they arise from their quiet fields to *shake the towers* and counsels of the Great. [italics/bold, mine]—*LOTR*: I, *The Council of Elrond*

> When I despair, I remember that all through history the way of truth and love have always won. There have been tyrants and murderers, and for a time, they can seem invincible, but in the end, they always fall. Think of it—*always*. [italics/bold mine] —Mahatma Gandhi

The most amazing characters in *LOTR* are the Hobbits. While the book is about the coming Age of *Men*, or humans, it is still in fact a book *about* Hobbits, as was, of course, *The Hobbit*. The reason they are so amazing—besides the fact that they love to eat, drink and be merry—is that they are the *most* resistant to the power of the Ring. No less than four Hobbits carried the Ring for a period of time, and only one of them was consumed by its power.

## Bilbo Baggins: the Incorruptible

It was Bilbo Baggins, an unlikely, reluctant candidate for greatness—if ever there was one—who stumbled upon the Ring in the dark of the Misty Mountains and thanks to its power of invisibility, stumbled out again into daylight on the other side. Bilbo possessed the Ring for longer than anyone else—except for Gollum and of course, Sauron. But for some reason he was not twisted or destroyed by it. That's not to say that he did not suffer consequences. He did admit to feeling, "stretched, like butter scraped over too much bread," one of my favorite quotes from the entire book. I've never buttered bread since, without thinking about Bilbo and then making sure I had plenty of butter on my biscuit. The dairy industry, and my elevated cholesterol can thank Tolkien and Bilbo for the many extra tons of butter that I have consumed as a result. What Bilbo was describing was the process of degradation that the Ring brings to its bearer, slowly turning them into a Wraith, like the Nazgul. Bilbo held onto the Ring for 60 years while managing, somehow, to hang on to his soul. He then passed the Ring to Frodo, his cousin. The fact that he was able to part with it so easily is one of the most amazing things about his character, indeed, as we'll see, about Hobbits in general.

## Frodo of the Nine Fingers: Ring-bearer, Savior of Middle Earth

Frodo, while possessing the Ring for less time than his uncle, or Gollum, bore it in the most extreme of circumstances, slowly trudging from the Shire to the burning steps of Mt. Doom, all the while hunted and harried by the servants of Mordor. The burden took an enormous toll on him, physically, but most importantly, emotionally and *spiritually*. Even though he reached his goal, Mt. Doom, the power of the Ring had taken such control on his mind that he could not muster the strength to throw it into the fire. It was only the overwhelming, consuming desire of Gollum to possess the Ring that eventually destroyed it when Gollum bit it off of Frodo's finger and fell to his death, affecting the redemption of Middle Earth in the bubbling magma of the Cracks of Doom.

Frodo never fully recovered from his ordeal. I've always thought that the major issue he had with reintegrating into Hobbit society was akin to PTSD and it probably was, though there were probably several reasons. First, the physical toll, the lost finger, would have been a constant reminder of the terrors he'd seen and experienced. Second, the memories of the struggle to get to Mordor would have exhausted his mind. The weight of the Ring itself, the proximity to such evil took its toll on him, too. But I think the thing that bothered him the most was his failure at the end of the mission. Frodo did not destroy the Ring; Gollum did. This is something he would always be reminded of, especially since the very finger that bore the Ring was missing. In the end Frodo had failed. His will was not strong enough to complete the deed. However, it is doubtful if anyone else could have completed it either. The great King Isildur had failed in the same spot at the Cracks of Doom. No one else had even attempted it, nor were they willing to try; only Frodo had the courage to carry the burden to the fire. For lacking the strength to throw it in we should forgive him. It is amazing that he even made it to Mordor in the first place and that would have never happened without his most faithful friend and companion.

## Samwise the Brave

Sam Gamgee is arguably the most heroic character in all of Tolkien's writings, and Tolkien might just agree with me on that point. Heroism does not require great skill in war, lack of fear in the face of danger, or super powers. <u>Heroism is simply doing what must be done, in *spite* of Fear, while overcoming all the obstacles blocking one's way</u>. Sam was one of the most fearful of the group of Hobbits but he never let his fear prevent him from doing what he believed needed to be done, especially when it came to assisting Frodo on his journey. He refused to be left behind at the Falls of Rauros, and even though he could not swim and had a normal Hobbity fear of water he plunged into the racing river to reach Frodo's boat before his friend could paddle away. Sam had made a promise to Gandalf, and more importantly to himself, that he would not leave his master and he never did, at least not while he believed Frodo to still be alive.

It is in fact Sam's quick thinking in an extreme situation, that saves all of Middle Earth from certain destruction. After the attack from the great spider, Shelob, with Frodo's limp and deathly body before him, Sam—in extreme agony and sorrow— managed to pull his thoughts together enough to realize the danger of the situation, not just to himself but to all of Middle

Earth. If he left the Ring on Frodo's body it would be taken by orcs and delivered swiftly to the Dark Lord himself; then all would be lost. In this moment of clarity, Sam sucked up his courage—of which he seemed to have no shortage—took the Ring and Frodo's sword and continued the quest for the smoking mountain. Sam was a ring-bearer, if only for a short time. The amazing thing about him is that when he found Frodo alive he returned the Ring to Frodo with only the slightest of pauses, then continued his job of getting Frodo and the Ring to its destination. There can be no greater example to live by than that of Samwise Gamgee. <u>Always be loyal, do what is right, and just keep going</u>. It also helps to have youth and a sense of humor on your side as well.

## Merry and Pippin: the Unyielding Spirit of Youth

> It was not in vain that the young Hobbits came with us, if only for Boromir's sake. But that is not the only part they have to play. They were brought to Fangorn, and their coming was like the *falling of small stones that starts an avalanche in the mountains*. Even as we talk here, I hear the first rumblings. Saruman had best not be caught away from home when the dam bursts! [italics mine] —*LOTR*: II, *The White Rider*

The two youngest Hobbits, Merriodoc Brandybuck and Peregrin Took should be mentioned because they were in close proximity to the Ring for years, being friends of the Baggins family and friends of Samwise Gamgee. They had known of the existence of the Ring some time before they were swept up in the war surrounding it—as they reveal in the chapter, 'The Conspiracy Unmasked." Merry had seen Bilbo suddenly disappear on the road once to avoid the Sackville-Bagginses, and then reappear slipping something into his pocket. Though these two mischievous Hobbits were close enough to the Ring to steal it from Frodo if they were so inclined, they never seem tempted to do so. It might have been their love and loyalty to Frodo that stayed them. They certainly got into plenty of trouble in other ways. Pippin definitely had a curious streak and a bit of larceny when he slipped the Palantir from Gandalf while the wizard was sleeping, but he never seems to have considered taking the Ring, or if he did, Tolkien did not tell us.

What these two symbolize, for us, is the powerful optimism of youth. The relative young age of these two Hobbits shielded them, somewhat, from the despair and negativity that plagued other characters in the story. There were certainly times when their youthful optimism was challenged, but somehow, they managed to keep their exuberant spirit in the face of increasing darkness. It was their friendliness and playfulness that captured Treebeard's affection which in turn led to the downfall of Isengard, where they celebrated, as young victors will, with beer and pipe weed. Their spirits won over King Theoden and even crusty, ole Denethor found Pippin to be a small ray of sunshine in a very dark moment. They are a reminder that ANYONE, no matter their age, can change the world. Children are not exempt from Hobbit-hood! In fact they can be, and are, a source of joy: the embodiment of everything *Hobbity*. We should all work to be more like them, as often as we can manage it. Never give up your youth, not entirely. Indeed, I think it is the purpose of life to hold onto it, while simultaneously giving it away in bundles.

### Hobbity Natural Resistance

Why were the Hobbits so resistant to the pull of the Ring? Bilbo, who held it the longest of the Shire Hobbits suffered little from it, other than the *butter-stretching* he mentioned. Frodo, while permanently damaged from his prolonged exposure managed to live among society for some time afterwards, and was not entirely consumed by the Ring's power. Sam seems to have suffered no ill effects at all. Merry and Pippin seem mostly oblivious to the trinket. It seems that something within Hobbits themselves, their DNA if you will, gave them an internal shield against evil, at least the four Hobbits that the Ring was entrusted to.

The Hobbits of the Shire, most of them at least, have much in common with modern Leaver peoples, like the Bushmen of Africa, who while surrounded by *Taker* culture, seem oblivious to it. There are few left of these cultures, the Bushmen included. The best example of interaction between modern *Takers* and

*Leavers*, is the movie *The Gods Must Be Crazy*. In the film, the pilot of a small plane drops a Coke bottle onto the African plain from on high where it is discovered by Xi, a Bushman. Thinking it a gift from the gods, Xi brings it back to his people, where they put it to multiple uses, to grind grain, as a rolling pin, etc. Eventually, the bottle becomes so prized that the tribesmen begin to quarrel over whose turn it is to use it. Predictably, one of them uses it as a weapon against another tribe member. At this point, Xi decides that the thing must be returned to the gods and sets out to find them to give it back. He goes through many adventures and meets many other modern peoples before finally reaching the ocean where he tosses it back to the gods. Hmmm. Sounds kind of familiar doesn't it?

While the Hobbits are similar to the Bushmen, in the sense that they are somewhat naive of the outside world, they are not entirely isolated, and do have a sense that there are other places, races, events going on out *there*, but they are unconcerned with them. The Hobbits are not hunter-gatherers living in the Bush of Africa or the jungles of South America. They are agriculturalists, settled down in their comfy holes but they are also, most emphatically, not *Takers*. Hobbits are uninterested in expansion, domination, war, politics, in short, anything that *Takers* regard as essential. Hobbits would much rather be left alone to follow the cycles of nature, from Spring to Summer to Autumn to Winter to Spring again, with little concern for the things that seem to consume the Big Folk. That's not to say that everything is hunky-dory in Shireland. There are still the Sackville-Bagginses and Ted Sandymans to deal with. We all have a few of those in our neighborhoods don't we?

## Who are the Modern Hobbits?

For me, *Hobbitness* is a state of mind, an ideal, an archetype, not a measurement of stature, a place, a time in history, or just a fictional race of beings in the greatest books ever written. The ideal of *Hobbitness* is something that many of us—even non-Tolkien fans—aspire to when we are being true to our nature. Most of us, myself included, rarely *live* as a Hobbit but we aspire to do so. We would love nothing better than to simplify our lives and to bring them more in balance with our environment, and Shires. So a Modern Hobbit is anyone who WANTS to be one, even if they aren't currently living as one. I am a Hobbit, like I said at the beginning of the book. That doesn't mean that at times, many times, I wasn't a Dwarf, an Orc, even a bit Gollum-ish or Wraith-ish. But deep down, what I want to be is a Hobbit. Do you? I reckon you'd never have reached this point in the book, if you didn't.

## To Be a Hobbit, That is the Suggestion

Those of us who reject the Ring of *Taker* culture can become modern Hobbits. The path to this transformation is, in fact, the path through Mordor, much as Frodo trod. Once we realize that we possess the Ring it is a simple thing of discarding it and changing our view on the world, but it is not a foregone conclusion; it is not an easy mission. We may also choose to retain our *Taker* mentality. I know this. I've been guilty of holding on to my *precioussss* for nearly 15 years since I became aware of the Ring.

*Taker* mentality is a very hard thing to shake. We were born with it. It has been passed down to us over hundreds and thousands of generations. The rejection of our culture is a simple thing in concept but a difficult one to achieve in practice. If, however, we can muster the courage to destroy our personal Ring we can learn to live in harmony with the land and with each other. We must reject the idea that **the Earth belongs to us and we were meant to rule it**, or perish with it. If we continue to cling to our *precious* it will slowly destroy us, from within. It has nearly accomplished our destruction already. As we know, not all Hobbits were resistant to the evils of Sauron's Ring. One Hobbit, centuries before, and far far away from the Shire stumbled upon it, claimed it for his own, then sequestered it away in the bowels of the Misty Mountains where it slowly consumed him, twisting him into a monster. The Ring was not content to sleep in the dark forever; one day it abandoned him, in favor of Bilbo.

## Gollum: the Danger of Attachment

> In the darkest depths of Mordor
> I met a girl so fair.

But Gollum and the Evil One
crept up and slipped away with her. —Led Zepeplin,
*Ramble On*

We know that Gollum was once a Hobbit or a cousin of the race at least, living on the banks of the Anduin River near the Gladden Fields some 500 years before Bilbo stumbled into him in the dark. Smeagal, as he was known then, was instantly corrupted to the core by the Ring. His friend, while fishing, found the Ring in the river. Smeagal was so taken by the thing that in a fit of desire he throttled his companion to death. Thus begins his transformation into the wraith-like creature, Gollum.

Why did the Ring have such an effect on this particular Hobbit and not on the five from the Shire? Tolkien does not tell us but it seems certain that Smeagal's character was flawed from the beginning. It's not clear why. Possibly it's because his community of Hobbits had been living in an area exposed to danger and evil? After all, the Gladden Fields are where Isildur was attacked by orcs and lost the Ring to begin with. Maybe Smeagal's Hobbits were not as innocent and naive as those who had lived for hundreds of years in the Shire, sheltered from the influences of the outside world. Whatever the reason, Smeagal must have had some *issues* long before he came into contact with the Ring. He was more akin to the men who were given the Nine Rings and were consumed by the power of the Dark Lord. But unlike the Ringwraiths, Gollum was never completely consumed. Even after 500 years of exposure to the Ring he never became a wraith, not completely. He had faded, for certain, but never became completely invisible like the great, kings of men. Maybe, just maybe, his inner Hobbit was still resisting the power of the Ring.

This is both an encouraging and a cautionary thought for those of us who aspire to be Hobbits. No matter how *resistant* we think we may be, the Ring is pure evil. It should not be used, but carried far, far away, like Xi's Coke bottle, like Sauron's Ring and tossed back into the fiery chasm whence it came. To court the Ring is to become invisible, a wraith, or wraith-like. We become separated and disconnected from all that is true and good in the World. **We cannot *rule* the Earth.** We need to rewrite our culture's story; we are *part* of Nature, not Nature's *masters.* <u>We need to return to harmony *with* Nature and with each other, to become what humans were destined to be, builders of gardens and Shires, Hobbits, not Masters over creatures great and small.</u>

The job does not end there, however. One of the great things about Tolkien's story, is that the climax, the destruction of the Ring, wasn't the end of the book. There was still work to do, as the Hobbits discovered when they returned home to find their Shire in ruins, thanks to the CEO of Greed Incorporated, Saruman, who had set up shop in their backyard. We modern Hobbits must clean up our Shire too, even after destroying the Ring. Our Shire is also in flames, and in fact, cleaning it up, and Saving the Earth is the biggest part of the job.

# PART III

## SAVING THE EARTH THROUGH SUSTAINABLE SHIRE LIVING

# 16

# THE SCOURING OF THE SHIRE

The travelers trotted on, and as the sun began to sink towards the White Downs far away on the western horizon they came to Bywater by its wide pool; and there they had their first really painful shock. This was Frodo and Sam's own country, and they found out now that they cared about it more than any other place in the world. Many of the houses that they had known were missing. Some seemed to be have been burned down. The pleasant row of old Hobbit-holes in the bank on the north side of the Pool were deserted, and their little gardens that used to run down right to the water's edge were rank with weeds. Worse, there was a whole line of the ugly new houses all along Pool Side, where the Hobbiton Road ran close to the bank. An avenue of trees had stood there. They were all gone. And looking with dismay up the road towards Bag End they saw a tall chimney of brick in the distance. It was pouring out black smoke into the evening air. —*LOTR*: III, *The Scouring of the Shire*

Even though Frodo and Sam, with Gollum's assistance, destroyed the Ring, when they returned home to the Shire the sight that greeted them was appalling. Their homeland had been largely destroyed and polluted by the work of Saruman. This is one of the things that Peter Jackson cut from the movies that I really wish he hadn't. I understand why he did it but it really changes the nature of the story. If you have not read the books, you should, but for the time being you'll have to make do with my brief summary.

When the four friends returned alone to the Shire they found it under guard by henchmen of some guy named 'Sharky', who turned out to be Saruman. He had escaped Isengard along with Wormtongue and made his way to the Shire whence he had secretly been purchasing pipe-weed for years. Once there, he used his golden tongue to convince many Hobbits and Men to join him in his bid for power. While the four heroes had been off saving Middle Earth from the Dark Lord, the tricky Saruman was in their backyards mucking things up. He put up factories, tore down trees, including the famous Party Tree. Some Hobbits and Men had been killed and more pressed into slave labor in the smoke-belching factories.

This was our heroes' welcome home, no ticker tape parade, no kisses from the girls. But instead of turning around and going back to Gondor or somewhere else, they directed their ire at the source of the problem, Saruman. In short order they organized a rebellion of Men and Hobbits and kicked the evil wizard out on his ass along with Wormtongue, who promptly murdered his boss in a fit of rage just before being transfixed by a Hobbit arrow bringing the two of them to a fitting end.

Our Shire is also burning with the smoke of Saruman's factories. As pointed out earlier, we have quite a mess to clean up. It can be done, even if it can never be returned to what it once was. But what was it anyway? What '*was*' are we aiming for? The '*was*' before the 20th Century? Or maybe a time before indigenous peoples were wiped out? Before humans? The Earth has always been changing, so instead of thinking about returning it to some mythical state of being we should concentrate on cleaning up what we have and working from there. Nature is very resilient, and as I've said, I doubt that humans really have the power to eradicate life on this planet, not all of it. Mother Nature may kick US off if we don't *clean up our rooms*. That is a distinct possibility, maybe even probability. Let's not let that happen. Let's become *part* of the Earth again instead of trying to rule it. But the first thing to do, is to start that revolution, like the Hobbits did when they got home to the smoking ruins of their beloved Shire. The first step in that revolution, is to create one in our own minds, and homes. We must rewrite our *personal stories*. The second involves blowing our collective Horns of Rohan, to see who else will join us. Then we can rewrite our *collective story*.

# 17

# FIRE, A NEW SHIRE, AND A FORGOTTEN RING

But I suppose it's often that way. The brave things in the old tales and songs, Mr. Frodo: adventures, as I used to call them. I used to think that they were things the wonderful folk of the stories went out and looked for, because they wanted them, because they were exciting and life was a bit dull, a kind of sport, as you might say. But that's not the way of it with the tales that really mattered, or the ones that stay in the mind. Folk seem to have been just landed in them, usually — their paths were laid that way, as you put it. But I expect they had lots of chances, like us, of turning back, only they didn't. And if they had, we shouldn't know, because they'd have been forgotten. — *LOTR*: II, *The Stairs of Cirith Ungol*

She had a dream
And boy it was a good one
So she chased after her dream
With much desire
But when she got too close
To her expectations
Well the dream burned up
Like paper in fire — John Mellencamp, *Paper and Fire*

Don't be satisfied with stories, how things have gone with others. Unfold your own myth. —Rumi, the Sufi Mystic

The key wouldn't turn.

The key to my house still fit the lock but it would no longer turn.

I was standing on the front porch of what used to be mine, what was supposed to still be mine—if only temporarily—but I could not enter. There were new locks on my house. MY house. There was a realtor's lockbox on the door handle, and there was a note.

The note simply read, "For questions, call..." and there was a name and a number.

I'm pretty sure my head exploded in the next few seconds. If the unfortunate realtor that had put new locks on my house had been standing there, I would have killed him. I'm pretty sure about that, and I'm not joking. I'm not sure if I've ever been that enraged in my life. But he wasn't. Luckily for him, and for me, he was sitting behind a desk somewhere awaiting the inevitable ring of the phone.

All I could think, was "How did my life come to such a pass?"

## From Moria to Mordor

My now ex-wife and I moved to Minnesota in 2007. We transferred from North Carolina to Minneapolis so I could go to graduate school at the U, the University of Minnesota, part of my longterm journey from the roach-infested kitchen floor to wannabe rocker, to something-useful scholar. Instead of renting a house or apartment for the next 5 years—which I argued was just throwing money away—we decided to buy another house, in South Minneapolis. That was my first mistake. And it was MY mistake—or at least my miscalculation—one for which I kick myself to this day. I was the one who argued that we should *buy* instead of rent.

You see, the real estate market had already begun to slip in N.C. I knew this because we had recently sold our old house back home. It took almost a year to sell it because the market went cold right about the time we put it on, in 2005. But the prices in Minneapolis were still at, or near their peak in 2007. That's when we bought our house in South Minneapolis.

It was a two story, 1900 square foot, 1903 Victorian home, on a corner of Park Ave—which used to be *the* street in town, back in the day when people lived in town and not in the suburbs— in other words, a hundred years ago. It was a nice neighborhood, for the most part. There was some trouble a couple of streets in either direction and that came to our doorstep a couple of times while we lived there. But on Park Ave the neighbors all seemed nice and respectable, so the purchase seemed reasonably solid.

But before the ink dried on the 100 pages of the closing papers we had to sign, the market crashed, nationwide. Some places were worse than where we lived but it was pretty bad in the Twin Cities of Minneapolis and St. Paul. That would not have been a problem for us, except for the fact that our marriage also crashed about the same time. That's a story that I will not be telling. Suffice it to say that the marriage dissolved. She wanted to go back to North Carolina, understandably, and I chose to stay in Minnesota to finish grad school, and to look after the house as we put it on the market.

The next couple of years are now a blurry, haze of half-memory. There were months of renting out rooms, there was waiting for the bank to decide on a short-sale that they eventually turned down, there was the depression of divorce and separation by 1500 miles from one's homeland, family and friends. There was a lot of Jimmy Beam, late nights, and expletives. There were days I just wanted to die. But I was too stubborn for that—probably the Dwarf in me. It was about that time that the house caught on fire.

## Frying Pan to Fire

One week before Christmas, 18 December, 2011, the closet in one of the bedrooms caught fire thanks to badly wired lighting and old costumes, including my Rohan cloak. Luckily, my roommate at the time, Patience, her son, and I were home at the time or the entire structure would have burned down. The funny thing—if there is anything funny about a house fire—is that there was a scheduled realtor showing of the house that afternoon but the prospective buyers drove by while the firetrucks were outside pumping hundreds of gallons of water into the upstairs bedroom, while smoke poured out the window. Nice. Believe it or not, they waited for a month, came back, loved the place and made a fair offer on it. The bank sat on the offer for five months, then turned it down. The house promptly went into foreclosure. Patience and Duke found another place, and offered to let me come with them. We moved. One afternoon, a week later, I went back to pick up the last few items, only to discover the bank had changed the locks on the house. So there I was, standing on my front porch, key in hand, wondering what the hell had happened to my life. 2011 was the worst year of my life, and that's saying something— remember the futon?

## The Hobbit Mama to the Rescue

Things were at an all time low. My self esteem, once rock solid, was nearly destroyed that year, and 2012 wasn't much better. My graduate appointment at the university ran out in May, so I spent the next year unemployed trying to find suitable work for someone with too *much* education. I looked all over the country, even interviewed for a position at a community college back home where my brother and sister-in-law teach, but didn't get the job. I moved home to North Carolina for about four months in 2012. I enjoyed seeing my family, especially my daughter, but I had left something behind in Minnesota that I could not live without: Patience.

Patience came into my life as I hit the deepest dark of Moria. She was also struggling through divorce at the time. What began as two people sharing negative stories of misery, became a fast friendship, then more. I won't go into it all, because this isn't a love story book, but without her, at that moment in time, things might have turned very dark for me indeed. They were dark enough as it was. But we both got through it, and then we found a place we could call *our* Shire: Westside, Saint Paul.

# A New Shire

After a year or more in a crappy rental house in South Minneapolis, Patience found and purchased a home in Saint Paul. Our new Shire, the Westside Neighborhood, is a storied section of the city. It has always been a melting pot for immigrants coming to America to start at new life, with new possibilities, and so it is with me and Patience. After all, I'm an immigrant of sorts; I'm from the South. Yet St. Paul feels like *home* to me. Yeah, they still talk *funny*, and they aren't as likely to stop you on the street and say, "How Y'all doin'?' or tell you their life story, but the city is friendly and unpretentious.

When I first drove up the driveway to the house—the day we found it—I immediately knew this was the place. There was a garden gate covered with an arch and Virginia Creeper vines. The backyard was full of landscaping and it was very quiet. At night we can hear crickets in the middle of the city! St. Matthew's Church is just down the street, and their bell—a real bell—rings on the hour, one of the most amazing sounds ever. It's our favorite thing about the neighborhood, which is very friendly, too. There's a small local farmer's market, parks, and an amazing view from the bluffs overlooking the Mississippi River onto downtown St. Paul. There are ethnic restaurants, and soon, a brewery opening up just a couple blocks from me. So we moved into a great neighborhood, but my negative story was still gnawing away at me. I couldn't seem to shake my negative attitude. I didn't seem to yet have a *purpose*.

Yes, I was supposed to be working on my dissertation on Viking military history, but I had come to question the utility of doing it, since the state of higher education is in such disrepair and disarray. I finally found a job in St. Paul working for a charter K-12 school, working with special education students. Like most jobs, the job had its positives and negatives. I enjoyed the people I worked with and most of the students, but it just didn't feel like it was really my *purpose*. I was dissatisfied with the work. I didn't feel I was really helping the kids that much, with a couple of exceptions, so I found myself wondering just what the hell to do? Then I stumbled upon another book. This time it was historical fiction, sort of.

# Inferno: the Fires of Mt. Doom

Thanks to the 8th grade literature class at work I had been reading books out loud to Patience for about two or three months, when last December she downloaded Dan Brown's book, *Inferno*. I won't go into a lengthy critique of the book. You can read my review on Goodreads if you want. I've been a fan of Mr. Brown in the past. I really liked *DaVinci Code*, and to a lesser degree, *Angels & Demons*. While I like *Inferno* much less, for several reasons, what I *did* like was the premise of the plot. Not to give away too much but the premise—that the world's population was headed for disaster if something radical wasn't done to curb its exponential growth—was thought provoking. And it rang a bell for me, though it was more like a *tinkerbell* and not the big church bell at St. Matt's down the street. Not yet.

In *Inferno*, the antagonist's solution to the problem of overpopulation was radical, to say the least, but the idea set my mental wheels spinning for a few days. "Is there some other way to slow down and reverse population growth and the damaging effects it has on the Earth?" Now, I'm aware that there are experts who argue that population growth is slowing, and that it will peak out somewhere around 10 billion or so, and then decline. Unfortunately, experts have been predicting peaks for a very long time, and it has yet to happen. However, the new experts might be right. Population might just peak, finally, not because of any new influence but because we might actually reach the limit the planet can sustain.

I spent several days rolling all that stuff around in my brain, and then one day I was on Facebook—wasting time as usual— browsing through my home page feed of the normal kinds of things you find there, mostly negative stuff about how the government sucks—which is true, Monsanto is evil—also true, how it's all the Republicans's fault, and how it's all the Democrats's fault, or the President's fault, *ad nauseum*, when I hit on a positive post by a friend of mine, Michele.

She had posted a link to "30 Questions you should answer before you die." You know, it's the kind of questionnaire that's supposed to help you *find yourself*, or the Holy Grail, the Golden Fleece, your missing socks and cigarette lighters. I'm sure you've probably seen this kind of fluff on your Facebook feed all the time, too. Maybe you actually read them. I don't, not usually. But for some reason I clicked on this one and began to read. It's not an exaggeration to say that as a direct result, I'm writing a book to quote, "Save the Earth."

### Riddles in the Dark

As it turned out, the 30 questions really *were* questions that everyone should ask themselves before they die, in fact, before they can really *live*. I won't list them all here but there were questions like "How much have you loved?" "What do you love doing that you're not doing?" Stuff like that. But the big one was **"If you could add something to humanity, what would your contribution be?"** That was a tough one. Because, as I mentioned, I was already struggling with that one. I mean, who really *cares* why the Vikings attacked Paris in 885 A.D.? What difference does it make in the grand scheme of history? How does that knowledge contribute in any way to the survival and well being of my fellow humans who are still alive today? Hell, how does it contribute to my own?

I still don't have a compelling answer to that and a person *should* have an answer to that question. I mean, I'm a pretty smart guy. I'm in grad school right? I managed to get through under graduate studies with a high grade point average, passed all my classes and exams in graduate school, got a master's degree in the process, almost a Ph.D. But what am I doing to make the world a better place? That question was a real kick in the nuts, I won't lie. I'm not capable of passing up hard questions so I gave it a lot of thought, for like two or three weeks, and here's the answer I came up with:

**I would like to find practical, positive solutions to the following problems:**

- Over population, without killing people.

- Unchecked greed, corruption and power-mongering, worldwide.

- Clean energy, worldwide: break the grip of fossil fuels on the world economy/ political system.

- Hunger, Poverty, Fear, and Ignorance.

- The poisoning of our food supply by GMO food, chemicals and pesticides.

- Save the Bees.

- Rectify the plight of women worldwide: human trafficking, equal rights, body image/fashion standards.

- Stop religious-driven violence; appeal to the moderates to suppress the radicals.

Simple, right? Nooooo pressure there! Basically, all I want to do is *save the world*.

Yeah, I know, I laughed at *myself* so it's ok if you laugh. You should. Even Patience, who probably believes that I *could* save it, laughed, until she saw I wasn't laughing anymore. I was dead serious, and I am. I believe that if we are alive for any reason, it is to make the world a better place than when we came into it. If we're not doing that, what the hell are we doing? Of course, it's one thing to say, "I'm going to Save the Earth." It's quite another to figure out how to do it.

# Where the Hell Do I Start?

After all, I'm not the first person to attempt to solve the problems I listed above. There's a lot of very smart people working on them already, have been for a very long time. But where have they gotten? The world seems just as screwed up as it ever was. And I should know, I'm an historian after all.

All I saw and read, every day it seemed, was how the world was messed up and how there's nothing we can do about it. "That's just the way it is" or "It is what it is," has become the cop out answer for every problem the world faces. Hell, I've said both of them so many times I can't count. Negative, negative, negative, blah, blah, blah. I was sick of seeing it, hearing it, and reading it. I'm still sick of it. So I turned off the computer for a few days, and I just sat, thinking, or *cogitatin'* as I like to say. I started writing notes on a legal pad.

I wrote down all of those problems I listed above, and then searched for connections, "What is linking all of these things?" What drives these problems? Is it overpopulation? Is it Greed? What drives Greed? Is it hate? What drives that? Fear? Fear of what? Death? Starvation? Annihilation? So all this stuff was spinning around in my head like a Waring Blender of dog-shit and crackers, when I woke up one morning about 2 AM and decided that I would form my own think tank of smart people, my friends, and we would come up with a way to save the planet and solve all those damned problems.

## The Return of the Ring

A few nights later we had a couple of friends, Sharon and Cameron, over for dinner. I was talking with Sharon, who used to practice poverty law—and is super smart and not one of those lawyers that should be at the bottom of the ocean—about the state of the world.

"I want to save the Earth." I said, matter of factly. "You wanna help?"

Strangely enough she didn't laugh. She knows how I am when I set my mind on something, kind of like a dwarf in a room full of orcs, if you know what I mean.

"Sure, let's do it." she said. Then she asked if I had ever read Daniel Quinn's *Ishmael*? My brain exploded, and the church bell started ringing, the one at St. Matt's, the ones in the Cathedral downtown, like at the end of A Christmas Carol kind of ringing.

There comes a moment in the birth of any idea, whether the idea is *great*, or just *good*, where two things come together in an instant that had not previously slammed into one another. You know, the proverbial *light bulb* moment. It was that moment, when Sharon asked me about Quinn that the idea for *Be a Hobbit, Save the Earth* began to formulate, or at least it was the seed that led to it. As you already know, I *had* read Quinn's stuff, like 15 years ago, or so, and it had hit me like a sledge hammer. But I had put the ideas down, on the shelf, now literally in boxes somewhere in my dusty garage and they were out of sight, out of mind. They were so secret and safe, that I had nearly forgotten I had ever read them. Sharon was for me, as Gandalf was for Frodo. "Remember Bilbo's old ring? How about pulling it out and let's have a look at it."

So, the next night—since I was too lazy to dig through my entire garage for one book in a box buried in a *Radiers of the Lost Ark-y* warehouse *full* of boxes—I downloaded Quinn's first book, *Ishmael* onto my Kindle and read it out loud to Patience and the back of *her* head disappeared, too. So then I was left with a heightened sense that I needed to *DO SOMETHING* about the problems on the earth, and I had a starting point. I had the answer to all of those questions because Quinn had already figured it out. I now knew the root to all our culture's problems: the ancient myth that **the Earth belongs to us and we were meant to rule it**. But I still didn't know what to *do* about it.

As I've mentioned, the problem—if there is one with Quinn's books—is that they explain how and why the world is the way the world is but they stop short of telling you what to do about it, just *how* to 'save the earth.' Basically, he says that all you need to do, is to *think differently*. And he's right, sort of. To save the planet, we do have to change the way we look at it, and ourselves. It's quite simple really and the answer to all those nagging, Earth-shattering questions, really is so damned simple it's comical.

But thinking differently is only the *FIRST* step, the most important one, for certain, but only the first. Then you must *DO SOMETHING* different. Lots of things. For if you don't *act* differently then nothing really changes. In my case, and for many others who had read Quinn, I knew—in an intellectual way at least—that our Ring was evil, destructive, and needed to be destroyed but I didn't know how to do it, so it sat, on the shelf, continuing to influence my every thought and deed. "Of *course* I don't *rule* the Earth!" I'd say to myself, but then continue to act as if I did. I bought bottled water, drove my big Dodge Ram truck, sprayed RoundUp on my yard, sprinkled artificial fertilizer on the grass, and more or less *ruled* my Earth. Nothing really changed, other than my underlying knowledge that the world was messed up, and why. And as years went by, I forgot *that*, as well.

It's kind of like Gollum hanging onto the Ring, long after he knows it's evil as hell. It was *precious* to him; it gave him a sort of security. But it was not *precious*; it was evil. There's nothing *precious* about our Ring either. Far from it. I had been holding on to my *precious* for 15 years or more! It had been on a shelf, in a box; I had packed it up and brought it with me over 1500 miles to a new home where it helped to destroy that life, and was nagging me in my present one.

### Homecoming to a Shire on Fire

After re-reading Quinn's books this year I went *binge reading*. I mean, I read like 40 books in about three months, maybe more. I swallowed books about population, the environment, global warming, pollution, economics and greed, violence, poverty, famine, and chased them down with numerous web articles, and blog posts, and stiff bourbon whiskey.

When I was done, I was thoroughly depressed, and not a little hung-over. I won't lie, reading so much negativity in any span of time probably isn't the healthiest thing to do. I don't recommend it, at **all**. I won't do it again I can assure you. I was very discouraged during the process. "What the hell can one person do against so much greed, avarice, and apathy?" I asked myself. And I had no answer.

I was at an impasse. I was Denethor, if you will. I was there, alone in the Tower of Ecthelion, staring into the Palantir. I could see all the evil that Sauron and Saruman were up to. I could see their legions of orcs, trolls, men, and Oliphants. I could see the Nazgûl on their winged, serpent steeds, and I sank into despair. I was catatonic, frozen. It seemed that the forces of darkness in our world were just too daunting to fend off. How could any one resist, let alone defeat, such overwhelming force? And that's when I heard, in the distance, the Horn of Helm Hammerhand, and remembered *Hobbits*. The book that had pulled me off of that sticky, kitchen floor in 1991, returned to show me the path to *Save the Earth*.

# The Hour of the Shire!

I had glimpsed in the Palantir—all those books, and articles—the desperate plight of the Earth, and thanks to *Ishmael*, I knew *why* it was that way, The One Ring. But that left me in despair. "What can one person do, to change all of that?" Cue Beethoven's 5th. Dun dun dun dunnnn! And then it hit me, it's all about Hobbits and rings and Dark Lords and Ring Wraiths and wizards! If a handful of Hobbits, with a little help from some Men—and Women, a wizard, an Elf, and a Dwarf could save Middle Earth then a whole bunch of *modern* Hobbits could save *OUR EARTH*! One person can't save the Earth but a surely a whole lot of persons, *CAN*!

I had hit on the most positive solution to the world's most negative problems. What we needed were a bunch of little, hairy Hobbits! Not large armies of Gondoreans and Rohirrim, just beer drinking, song-singing, riddle-solving, barrel-riding, pipe-weed-smokin', second-breakfast-eatin', long-walkin' Hobbits! You see, Frodo and Sam didn't walk up to the Black Gates of Mordor and slap Sauron in the face! If they had, things would have turned out differently for Middle Earth, indeed. In fact, that's what Sauron expected his enemies to do. He fully expected that someone like Boromir—who tried, or Gandalf and Aragorn—who refused, would seize the Ring and attempt to use it against him, and that would have been their undoing. No, Frodo and Sam slipped in the backdoor to Mordor and brought down Sauron's Empire in one fell stroke, and Sauron never saw it coming. In a similar way, Merry and Pippin slipped from Saruman's grasp, into the darkness of Fangorn, made some friends, and marched to the destruction of Isengard. They did not use the Ring; they employed their wit, their humor, their tenacity, a wee bit of sneakiness, and their genuine love for what is good and right, to defeat the evil will of Barad-dûr and Isengard.

The Ring could be mastered by no one, except Sauron—and one might argue that not even *he* could, since it managed to escape his hand as it did Isildur's, Gollum's, Bilbo's, and eventually, Frodo's. It was wholly evil and destructive. We can destroy *our* Ring too; it's really just as simple as thinking differently. We've been living and writing a very dark story for millennia. We need to *change* our story. We need to rewrite our story, to tell a different one. If we do, then we can get to work cleaning up the mess that Sauron, Saruman, the Black Riders and all the nasty orcs have been making of our planet. We don't have to slap Sauron, bank CEOs, or unlucky real-estate agents, either. We just have to toss the Ring into the abyss whence it came, and break out the brooms and dustpans.

# 18

# Don't Despair Denethor; Be a Hobbit!

"Pride and despair!" he cried. "Didst thou think that the eyes of the White Tower were blind? nay, I have seen more than thou knowest, Grey Fool. For their hope is but ignorance. Go then and labour in healing! Go forth and fight! Vanity. For a little space you may triumph on the field, for a day. But against the Power that now arises there is no victory. To this City only the first finger of its hand has yet been stretched. All the East is moving. And even now the wind of thy hope cheats thee and wafts up Anduin a fleet with black sails. The West has failed. It is time for all to depart who would not be slaves. —*LOTR*: III, *The Pyre of Denethor*

It is perilous to study too deeply the arts of the Enemy, for good or for ill. —*LOTR*: I, *The Council of Elrond*

Where there is ruin, there is hope for a treasure." — Rumi, the Sufi Mystic

It is easy to despair, like Denethor, when confronted with the enormous task of cleaning up our planet. There are so many problems, and so much to undo and rebuild. But we should not despair. Why? Because it will not help. Despair did Denethor no good, nor did his despair help those under him who were trying to resist the evils of Sauron. His attempt to commit suicide, taking Faramir with him, distracted Gandalf at a key moment during the siege of Minas Tirith. The Wizard's efforts were needed on the fields of the Pelennor—where Theoden, Eomer and Merry were confronting the Black King of Angmar—but instead he had to leave the gates of the city to rescue Faramir from his father's insanity.

When Denethor discovered that the two little Hobbits were carrying the ring towards Mt. Doom, his despair deepened, more so because Faramir had not tried to prevent it, had not brought the Ring to him to be "kept, hidden, hidden dark and deep." It is well that Farmair was wiser than his father, because Denethor surely would have employed the Ring's power in defense of his city. This is certainly what Sauron expected his enemies to do with the Ring, as Gandalf pointed out:

> He [Sauron] supposes that we were all going to Minas Tirith; for that is what he would himself have done in our place. And according to his wisdom it would have been a heavy stroke against his power. Indeed he is in great *fear*, not knowing what mighty one may suddenly appear, wielding the Ring, and assailing him with war, seeking to cast him down and take his place. That we should wish to cast him down and have *no* one in his place is not a thought that occurs to his mind. *That we should try to destroy the Ring itself has not yet entered into his darkest dream*. In which no doubt you will see our good fortune and our hope. For imagining war he has let loose war, believing that he has no time to waste; for he that strikes the first blow, if he strikes it hard enough, may need to strike no more. [italics mine] —*LOTR*: II, *The White Rider*

Denethor also could not see past war or conflict as a solution. But we know that war was not the ultimate solution to the problems of Middle Earth; only the destruction of the Ring could do that. So it is in our time. Only by destroying our personal Rings can we achieve the ends we want, but that is difficult because it seems so small a thing, much like Sauron's Ring: a small thing with massive power.

# A Heavy Weight

Knowing that our civilization faces destruction is a heavy burden. As Frodo stood there in Rivendell, holding the One Ring in his tiny hand, feeling its evil weighing on his mind, he probably felt helpless. I'm certain he thought, "Great. Now I know what this thing really is, and it's mine to bear, but what the hell do I do with it? Destroy it? Mt. Doom? That doesn't sound like fun. Ugh. But if I don't do it, who will? But how does one get there? Is there a map? Do I have to go alone? Maybe I should! The burden shouldn't drag my friends down too! But I don't know how to get there, and if I fail, the Earth is doomed." The weight of Middle Earth was on his narrow shoulders and he could feel it pressing his body down into the dirt, through his hairy feet. I've had that feeling more than once in my life. For a very long time I have known that the world was a brutish place and that corruptions and conspiracies abounded, and the knowledge paralyzed me. I felt just as Frodo probably did. King Theoden put it best, "How shall any tower withstand such numbers and such reckless hate?" — *LOTR*: II, *Helm's Deep*

The Greek philosopher, Plato, explained this paralysis in his famous *cave* analogy. He proposed that what most people regarded as *reality* was analogous to shadow puppets on a cave wall, created by the limited sunlight coming from above and reflecting on the wall. People, Plato argued, could be expected to believe nothing less than that the shadows were reality, since they had no knowledge of what created them. They would not believe those from outside the cave if they attempted to explain it and they would be resistant to any efforts to be dragged into the sunlight. But if it *could* be accomplished, and they were to see the sun and the hands of the puppeteers there could be no returning to the cave, no matter how much one might *want* to return to the illusion; once it is shattered by reality, it cannot be remade.

This is how many of us feel, and maybe you are feeling it for the first time or coming to a new understanding of it. That's okay, and it's perfectly normal. Gandalf had to practically drag both Bilbo and Frodo out of their comfy hole. If he had not, where would Middle Earth have been? Doomed? I think so. So like Plato, and Gandalf, I am knocking on your Hobbit-door to say, "Come out friend! The sun is shining; there are dragons to slay, adventures to experience, and a Ring to destroy!"

## Destroying Our Ring

Never fear, however. Reality, as bleak as it may sound and look, can be changed, and it can be changed by little Hobbits, like you and me. Luckily for us the sheer knowledge of the Ring is the end of the journey to Mt Doom. All that is left is to destroy our individual part in it, by rejecting the idea that, '**the earth was created for us, and we were meant to rule it.**' Hopefully, I have convinced you that the idea is false, dangerous and quite frankly, deadly. It's also stupid and insane. If we want to be free of its power we cannot continue to use the Ring. That is to say that we must reject the idea, and then begin to *act* differently, and *think* differently. I knew about this Ring many years ago, but I continued to live as if the world still *belonged to me*. Nothing in my life changed that much. Like Isildur, and like Frodo, I could not find the strength to toss the Ring into the fire, and walk away, even though I knew I should. There are many other people in that predicament. Many of us have known, in some form or another, academically, or spiritually, that the Earth isn't just our *resource*, but we continue to do things, every day, that reflect that mentality.

It may be that the time has come, for all of us to destroy it and walk away but it may take a Gollum to do it. Possibly it is the sheer terror of being confronted by our future selves, as Gollums, as Ringwraiths, that will allow us to be free of this poisonous mentality? Maybe we can sacrifice a metaphorical finger — or at least *raise* our middle one — to those who would possess the Ring, and let them fall into the abyss with it? If the Sarumans, Saurons, Ringwraiths, and Gollums of our world want their illusion that badly, they can have it. But we don't have to go down with them into the Crack of Doom. Let them fall away and then let's run like hell, and pray for Eagles!

# The Power of Fellowship

It is understandable to be overwhelmed by the problems confronting our Earth. But remember, Frodo did not allow his fear to keep him from his goal. As Winston Churchill once said, "If you're walking through hell, keep walking." And, Frodo was not alone. Neither are we.

Frodo had a group of companions along side him. Closest was Sam of course, walking step by step with him, the entire way. Disregard the film version where the two friends were divided by Gollum as they climbed their way into Mordor. It never happened. Though I'm a big fan of the movies, that scene is one of my few critiques of the film version of the story. **Nothing** ever got between Frodo and Sam, and we all need a Sam in our lives. If you haven't found yours, keep looking. We have other companions though: Merrys and Pippins. There are also lots of Aragorns, Boromirs, Faramirs, Eowyns, Theodens, Gandalfs, Gimlis and Legolases out there fighting on our behalf and for the protection of the Earth. I stress this again, you are not alone. There are also many Hobbits and wizards already working on it! We will run into them along the path. Hopefully their efforts will be an inspiration to keep on walkin'! Just keep in mind that we don't have to clean up everything at once! One step at a time is all it takes. And start those steps in your own home, and your own Shire. But the journey truly begins even closer to home than your *home*, it begins in your own mind. That is where Hobbit-ness must be cultivated first. To destroy the Ring we have to *be* Hobbits. And those who would hold *on* to their precious Ring would never think that we would choose to destroy ours. Therein lay our greatest weapon: surprise. Once again it pays to listen to the wisdom of our greatest guide, Gandalf the Grey:

> "Despair, or folly?" said Gandalf. "It is not despair, for despair is only for those who see the end beyond all doubt. We do not. It is wisdom to recognize necessity, when all other courses have been weighed, though as folly it may appear to those who cling to false hope. Well, let folly be our cloak, a veil before the eyes of the Enemy! For he is very wise, and weighs all

things to a nicety in the scales of his malice. But the only measure that he knows is desire, desire for power; and so he judges all hearts. Into his heart the thought will not enter that any will refuse it, that having the Ring we may seek to destroy it. If we seek this, we shall put him out of reckoning." —*LOTR*: I, *The Council of Elrond*

# 19

## BEING A HOBBIT:
## THE INNER JOURNEY

**What has been well planted cannot be uprooted;**
What is embraced tightly will not escape one's grasp;
And with one's children and grandchildren
performing the customary rites
The autumnal sacrifice will never be interrupted.
**Cultivate it in your person,**
And the character you develop will be genuine;
**Cultivate it in your family,**
And its character will be abundant;
**Cultivate it in your village,**
And its character will be enduring;
**Cultivate it in the state,**
And it's character will flourish;
**Cultivate it in the world,**
And its character will be all-pervading. [bold, mine] —
*Dao De Jing*: Chapter 54

I set out months ago, to write a book. I set out, like Frodo, to
*Save the Earth*. But I can't do it. I'm just one person, one Hobbit,
insignificant in the larger scheme of things. Hell, I'm more
Dwarf than Hobbit. Most of the time I'd rather smash the
destroyers of our Earth than to work with them to save it. The
problems facing our world, and the Ring seem like missions too
large for ordinary people to tackle. We have all faced the

question at some point or another, "What can we do?" In this final part of the book, I will outline a plan of action that can lead to a change in your life, change that can eventually be exported to your communities, towns, and countries. It cannot happen overnight, even if we are certain that it needs to. Frodo would have loved to take an Eagle Airline flight to Mordor to get the job over with, I'm sure, but just like him, we cannot rush the process. All journeys begin with the first step, which you have already taken by reading this book. Let's draw a map, a plan for fixing our Shire and returning it to its natural, green, Party Tree atmosphere.

That plan follows a basic pattern, one from the inner to the outer, in concentric *rings*, if you will, much as the *Dao De Jing* suggests above. We must begin the *cultivation* of our *inner* Hobbit, our Hobbit-*mind*, before we can build our Hobbit-*hole*, then our Shire.

# From *Homo Sapiens* to *Homo Hobbitla*: Sowing Shireness in the Mind

> There is a *seed of courage* hidden (often deeply, it is true) in the heart of the fattest and most timid Hobbit, waiting for some final and desperate danger to make it grow. Frodo was neither very fat nor very timid; indeed, though he did not know it, Bilbo (and Gandalf) had thought him the best Hobbit in the Shire. He thought he had come to the end of his adventure, and a terrible end, but the thought hardened him. He found himself stiffening, as if for a final spring; he no longer felt limp like a helpless prey. [italics/bold, mine] — *LOTR*: I, *Fog on the Barrow-downs*

> "Do what you can, with what you have, where you are." President Theodore Roosevelt

### Destruction of the Ring, and the Birth of a Hobbit

The first step to *being a Hobbit,* is to begin thinking in a new way. We cannot change the world, if we don't first change ourselves. That doesn't mean that you have to *perfect* your mind before you start changing outward stuff, like turning off lights, recycling, and eating better food. In fact you should start working on the practical stuff immediately, but don't neglect the internal transformation while reaching for your cloth shopping bags, and putting on your organic, cotton T-shirt. Because the change of *mind* is the most important part, and it's easy to forget it.

Focusing on the *external* problems is a mistake made many times in the past, and by almost everyone today, myself included. The problems of the world aren't the *cause*, they are the *symptoms*; the cause is our flawed mentality, the Ring. For example, the *hippie* movement of the 1960s, in many ways was focused outwards on what was *wrong* with society and civilization. Their main question was "how can we fix society?" They had figured out what to fight *against*, but not the root cause or exactly what to fight *for*. They had a pretty good handle on what was *wrong*, but not exactly what to *do right*. I'm oversimplifying and generalizing, of course. There were some who had a very good handle on what needed to be done and did work on their own inner turmoil first. But the majority of the movement tended to drift because they were reacting to outside forces instead of focusing on the chaos within. Most only had a vague idea of what kind of world they really *wanted*. Vagueness never leads to anything. You cannot expect to hit a target that you haven't chosen to hit. But the first target should always be ourselves. <u>We need to focus on the Shire we *want*, not the Mordor we *don't*.</u>

In order to Save the Earth, we need to start at home *where you are*, like Teddy Roosevelt said above. And *home* means in your *noggin*, your head, your mind, your skull. If you've read the previous section on the Ring then you are probably well on your way already. If it hasn't sunk in, give it some time. Roll the ideas around in your head. What would the *Leaver* mentality feel like? Read to the end of this book, and I think you'll have a better idea of the practical side of it, though what drives it, or should, is your new mentality, your new worldview: a Hobbit, *Leaver* one. So what does *thinking differently* mean? Start by thinking small, like Hobbit small.

### The First Step Out the Door

To think small means to reevaluate our <u>needs versus our wants</u>. This idea is almost cliché these days, but it's extremely important. We have to turn off the noise for a while and look at the things around us in a more objective way. While I'm speaking metaphorically, *physically* turning it off is the best way to accomplish it. Turn off the TV, the computer screen, commercial radio, and toss the weekly newspaper ads, too, for a few days.

A change in thinking involves many other things, but the biggest message that I want to get across is rethinking our needs. What do we really need? Are they just *wants?* Wants and desires are not evil, in and of themselves but our *attachment* to them screws up our priorities. Do we really need more stuff? Is that what a Hobbit would want? Is that what life is about? More stuff means more space to store it and that means more money to purchase or rent that space, which means more time working for Saruman and less time building our Shire, eating second breakfasts, and blowing smoke rings in the garden. And isn't leisure time with our families and friends, engaging experiences, meaningful work, and good health what we all really want out of life? Down deep?

It might be helpful to break down this inner transformation into smaller parts, too. Think of it this way. We first need to work on the *mind*, our psychological health. What can we do to lower stress, increase our focus, and be more productive and happy? As part of that, we need to work on our *body*, our physical health. What can we do to improve the way we feel and function? And lastly, we'll look at what *actions* we should take to change our personal lives to make them more Hobbity. So, *mind, body, action*.

# Healthy Hobbit Minds: Shire Mental Health

> "Yesterday I was clever, so I wanted to change the world. Today I am wise, so I am changing myself." — Rumi, the Sufi Mystic

Everything in the Universe is created in the mind. No, that doesn't mean that chairs, tables, and walls don't exist, so I'm not suggesting that you ram your head into the wall in your room to see if it's just a projection of your mind. That would be painful and probably make the reading of this book, pointless. Walls, chairs, and planets exist in a real physical sense. But their *form* is a projection of our mind. We decide what they look like and more importantly, what they *mean*. *THAT* is completely under our control. The same goes for our own thoughts, which is where that projection begins. If we can learn to control our thoughts, or at least to guide them or keep them in check, we can be Hobbits in a very real sense. Hell, if we can do that, we can be Gandalf! The reason this is important, and why so many ancient philosophers, and modern ones are interested in it, is because our perception of reality, *IS* reality. And our perception of ourselves, our lives, our jobs, our families, our Shires, and even our bodies, controls how those things work.

An aspect of modern medicine that has traditionally been slighted, if not entirely ignored, is the psychological health of the patient. While this seems to be changing, some, there's still a long way to go. Let's just look at it logically for a moment. The body is a system—not a machine as some scientists would like to imagine—but a system. It's very complex, for sure, and modern medicine, for all it's scientific claims is really a long way from understanding it. However, since the body is a system it has a control center and guess where that is? The brain, the home of your mind, of course. So if the brain won't function properly, due to physical or emotional damage, then guess what? Neither will the mind or the body. The mind controls every single function in the body, except possibly cell division, and it might even control that. It is imperative that we make sure our mental health is in order if we want to be healthy in general. What are the best ways to do that?

# Meditation

Possibly the oldest form of mental therapy is some form of meditation. There are many health benefits from meditation, most of them related to the relief of stress. Meditation can be anything from prayer, to sitting in a lotus position for hours focusing on your breath, to walking in your favorite park—a favorite of the late Professor Tolkien. Now, before I begin, I will give another disclaimer:

> I am not a yogi master, or zen master, or a saint, especially the last one. I have tried meditation many times in my adulthood, with little success at making it stick. Maybe you have too? I suck at it.

Though I suspect that if I were to meet a real Zen master, he would tell me that, "there is no suck, there is only *DO*," or some other Yoda-esque thing like that. I'm sure Gandalf would have something similar to say. He's the only one in *LOTR* who seems like he might spend hours or days contemplating something without stirring to make toast. Tom Bombadil is another possibility though he always struck me as one of those masters who didn't need to meditate anymore; he has *BECOME* meditation, like one of those laughing Buddhas, or Chevy Chase in *Caddyshack*, "Be the ball..."

For the rest of us hasty Hobbits, I guess we have to keep struggling on to focus our spinning brains and learn to calm down. Lately, I've begun to include ten minutes of meditation in my early morning ritual before I sit down to write. I figure if I can keep it up for thirty days, like the writing that it will become an ingrained habit. I still suck at it though. If you've ever tried to meditate you know what I mean. You sit down with your little candle burning, or counting breaths, or focusing on a flower, or trying to do that Tibetan monkish 'two tone' chanting thing—forgetaboutit.

"Today," you think, "I will master this!" But two-seconds into it your mind starts to wander around, "What's for breakfast?" "Hey, why are those socks on the floor?" "Check out that cup ring on my new coffee table!" or "Hey, I'm pretty good at this!" And then you realize that your mind is spinning all over the place and you say, "Damn it! Focus!" But you can't seem to stop the mind from racing so you mentally flog yourself thinking that *THAT* will help, and then realize that floggings, fun as they are—I mean, who doesn't love a good spanking—

really isn't going to bring your mind back to focus, and then you remember from the book you read on meditation that you're supposed to *gently* refocus, so you try that and then your spouse, girlfriend, boyfriend, walks into the room and you surrender to the fact that you're never going to be a Buddha after all, and get up to go make coffee or mix another margarita. This Zen master stuff is too hard!

But if Gandalf, or Myagi from *The Karate Kid* was there with you, he would tell you to just "Wax on, wax off." And that is the trick to it, if there is a trick. It has nothing—any Zen master will tell you—to do with being *good at it*, only with *doing it*. So, try it again. Try to give yourself credit just for sitting there for ten minutes, and it doesn't have to be in a lotus position—if I sat that way, hell, if I *could* sit that way with my old stiff, creaky bones, I'd never get up again. Sit where ever you want, how ever you want. Find something to focus on. Forget about things like, "Am I doing this right?" The answer is *yes*, if you're doing it at all and not flogging yourself every time your mind wanders. Just laugh for a second at the absurdity that is the human brain, and then refocus it. It doesn't matter what you focus on, as long as it's not too complex, especially for us beginners. Don't pick out a painting by Salvador Dali, for instance. Focus on the flame from a tea light, or the feeling of your breath as it comes out your nose. The more specific, the better. Just remember, where the mind goes, so goes the body. I'm still waiting for my body to sit on a beach in Jamaica with a piña colada and some jerk pork; my mind has been there for months.

## Religion and Spirituality

> Christian, Jew, Muslim, shaman, Zoroastrian, stone, ground, mountain, river, each has a secret way of being with the mystery, unique and not to be judged.
> —Rumi, the Sufi Mystic

> The legitimate powers of government extend to such acts only as are injurious to others. It does me no injury for my neighbor to say there are twenty gods or

no god. It neither picks my pocket nor breaks my leg.
— Thomas Jefferson

Many people turn to religion or spirituality and find solace in their beliefs. In that respect, religion can be a positive force in the World. When beliefs are intolerant, however, they become destructive forces and will bring *no* peace of mind no matter how much your preacher, priest, rabbi, or Imam might tell you it will. Before I go any further, let me say, first off, that I am not an atheist, nor an agnostic. I have been both in the past, even though I was raised as a church-going Protestant, by wonderful, compassionate, parents who were both ministers, though now retired. I do believe in a higher power but I'm not here to convert you to my way of thinking. I used to tell my college students when I was teaching as a grad-student, while giving my obligatory — *we're studying religion as an historical phenomenon only* — speech, that I didn't care what their beliefs were, and that I wasn't going to share mine with them, because quite frankly, I didn't *want* anyone else to believe what I believed, and hell, I was probably wrong anyway. So you won't get a sermon from me. Not today, I promise. But your religion — if it's a useful one — is compatible with the ideas in this book.

There will be a few of you that object to some of the ideas in this book on religious grounds. Others who have managed to read this far, will at least *know* someone who will object to the ideas in this book. That's unfortunate, and unnecessary. While an entire book could be written on the how religion and spirituality might actually help to *solve* the problems of the Earth instead of contributing to them, I will not be writing that book, at least not today.

I'm not going to go into a dissertation on the major religions and how they mesh with Tolkien's books, or the Hobbit lifestyle; I'm just going to ask a few questions that you can answer in your own way and in your own time.

### Does your religion, faith, or philosophy,

- allow for tolerance of other beliefs, religions, and faiths?

- allow for peaceful coexistence with people of other beliefs, religions, and faiths?

- allow for love and compassion towards people of other religions and faiths?

- allow for cooperation with those of other religions, faiths and beliefs?

- allow for a love and respect for all of creation?

If you can answer all of these with a *yes*, congratulations! You can be a Hobbit. If not, then you should ask yourself, "Why not?" Are you really following a religion, or holding on to a personal belief that requires you to feel intolerance towards other human beings, simply because they believe differently than you? If so, then you are part of the problem, and have chosen to join the ranks of Saruman and Sauron. You can of course change your way of thinking but to convince you would be beyond the scope of this book, and perhaps, any book. Such intolerance is usually rooted in Fear. What do you fear? Is your Fear based in reality or just a perception you gained from experience, or learned from others? Fear is at the root of all the Earth's problems. Always work towards minimizing your own, and that of others. Fear is the enemy of Shireness, and all things peaceful. Love, understanding, and compassion are the building blocks of Shires.

## Cultivating Shireness

Personally, I think the biggest issue with mental health, especially in America, is the loss and breakdown of community. We have all just become entirely too tied down to our gadgets: TVs, computers, pads, phones, which, oddly enough, disconnect us from the actual living, breathing people around us. At the same time we've been persuaded—thanks to the instantaneous news we get from those sources—that the world outside our door, i.e., our own neighborhood, is to be feared! In some cases this is probably true. But why is it true? I think it's because we allow it to be so. I'm going to go off on one of those,

"Back in my day, things were so awesome" speeches here, so hang on.

When I was young, I remember the time when you could leave your house unlocked, even though we probably shouldn't have even then, considering that we lived for a while in Wichita, Kansas when the BTK Strangler was active. I also remember neighborhood *welcome wagons*—local neighborhood women—invariably women—who would come by after you moved in and bring food to your door to welcome you to the neighborhood. I used to know most of my neighbors on the street. I played with their kids, in their houses on occasion, and we all kind of looked out for each other. It is unfortunately not that way in a lot of places these days. It's time we got out and got to know our neighbors again. The best way to do that, is to get off your little Hobbit butts, stretch your Hobbit legs, and go for a walk, also a panacea for mental stress, and crappy moods.

## Walk-about: Hobbit Exercise

I know, you're thinking that *exercise* should be in the *body* section, and it is. But one of the benefits of exercise is that it releases endorphins that fight depression and give you a sense of well being, so not only is it good for the body but good for the mind. Walking is one of the best for this. Walk around your neighborhood, talk to the neighbors, focus on the beauty of your neighbors' gardens. Then you will be accomplishing three of the things I've just been talking about: meditation, Shire-building, and exercise at the same time! One of Tolkien's favorite things was to go on walks, sometimes with his friends, C.S. Lewis and the other Inklings. It was a form of meditation for the group.

Hobbits were natural walkers. Bilbo had a collection of walking sticks in his hole. He walked all the way to the Lonely Mountain, and his nephew walked even further! Some of the best ideas, revolutionary ideas have come from a good walk. It was during a walk that the Industrial Revolution came into being. Well, maybe that's exaggerating a bit, but not much. The inventor, James Watt, was on a walk when the idea for a two-chambered steam engine popped into his mind and the world has never been the same, for good or ill. Of course he had spent years trying to improve on an older design but it was during a walk that the final inspiration came to him. So get out there and walk! You might consider wearing shoes though, unless you have leathery Hobbit feet.

# The Hobbit Family

Neighborhoods are awesome—and for many of us, myself especially, since I'm a Southern boy living in Yankeeland, is very important because my family lives far, far away—but spending time with your family, and here I'm talking about the extended family, is very important to mental health. Trust me, I know that families can often be the *source* of stress. For some people, cutting ties with their family is the best option to *keep* their sanity. We all have a few Sackville-Bagginses related to us. Some of us may *be* Sackville-Bagginses and are stuck with what we have. That's unfortunate, because we all actually crave a connection with our blood kin.

After all, even though Bilbo was an old bachelor, he had his cousin, Frodo, to keep him company, and visa versa. Frodo had Merry, Pippin, and Sam. Sam had his father, the Gaffer. We need ours too. If you can do it without choking them, make time to spend with your families. If they live close by make sure to schedule events every so often, once a month, or every two months at least. Get together to talk, eat, drink and be merry. My family, blood kin that is, lives very far away, some 1500 miles so I don't get to see them very often, though I am sitting right now in my mom's sunroom in North Carolina writing this section of the book, which is apropos. It is important to keep those connections, so make an effort to do so. I know I'm probably not the best at this, and need to work on it more. I have been lucky that Patience's family has taken me in and accepted me as part of their family, and that has been a big help, especially at holidays. Nothing really replaces being with your blood family though so do it as often as you can and make sure to schedule time to do it. It will help your mental, and therefore, overall health.

# Advice from the Gaffer: Professional Counseling

Sometimes, all the zen-master meditation, walking, community building, friends and family just aren't enough to ease your troubled mind. If so, then it is time to find a professional to help you. I have spent many hours talking with one, and if you can afford it I highly recommend it. Though there are programs for people who can't. Check with your local health department. Most of them have a mental health division that offers counseling for those who can't afford it otherwise. Ask around for references from friends and family. Do you know someone who sees a therapist? Ask them if they have any recommendations.

All of these things are important to relieving stress, and adding quality to our lives and the lives of those around us. But there's one thing that stresses most of us out more than anything else: work. We all have to do it, but does it have to be a source of weariness and dread? Not really.

# Hobbit Work: for Love or for Fear?

You could spend your whole life imagining ghosts, worrying about the pathway to the future, but all there will ever be is what's happening here and the decisions we make in this moment which are based in either *love or fear*. So many of us choose our path out of fear disguised as practicality. What we really want seems impossibly out of reach...ridiculous to expect. So we never dare to ask the Universe for it. I'm saying I'm the proof that you can ask the Universe for it.

My father could have been a great comedian but he didn't believe that was possible for him. So he made a conservative choice. Instead he got a safe job as an accountant. When I was 12 years old, he was let go from that safe job and our family had to do whatever we could to survive.

I learned many great lessons from my father, not the least of which was that *you could fail at what you don't want, so you might as well take a chance at doing what you love.* [italics/bold, mine] —Jim Carrey

Well, all I can do is a shake my head
You might not believe that its true

For workin' at this end of niagara falls
Is an undiscovered Howard Hughes
So baby, don't expect to see me
With no double martini in any
high-brow society news
Cause I got them steadily depressin',
low down mind messin'
Workin' at the car wash blues.
    —Jim Croce, *Workin' at the Car Wash Blues*

This is the chapter where I'll probably stir up the most inner turmoil, and get the most push-back. I'm going to talk about your job. I know, a subject we all love to hate to discuss. Most of us hate our jobs or at least we hate a good portion of what we have to do there, or some*one* we have to work *with*. Most of us don't think we are compensated enough for what we do—and based on statistics, that's probably true. The median wage hasn't really gone up since the 60s if compared to cost of living which has risen steadily. All this while those at the top, our bosses, seem to be rolling in the dough.

So many of us are stressed out, burned out, and disillusioned by the work we do. Why do we do it? A paycheck? Security? What if, like Jim Carrey's father, that secure job disappears? What then? A scarier thought, what if it *doesn't?* and we spend our entire adult life working a soul-sucking job slowly turning us into Wraiths, or Gollums? Is that what we want out of life? What greater *purpose* does it serve? Is there any meaning to our work?

## Meaningful Work

Maybe you're one of the lucky people, and you love your job. If so, then this section isn't really for you, but for the rest of us, whose work seems to fall somewhere between Mirkwood Spider-slayer and Mordor Sanitation Engineer. Most of us would rather be doing something different, but circumstances and necessity seem to have pushed us into doing something just to make a living, something *safe*. And are our jobs really safe?

Not if the financial collapse in 2007-8 tells us anything. There are no safe jobs. Any one of us could be out of a job tomorrow. But we cling to our jobs as if our very life depended upon them. We cling to them out of *Fear*.

This is an unfortunate thing and one of the big problems with the modern world, especially in the United States. Fear is everywhere. We fear losing our jobs, because we fear losing our homes — like many of us have. We fear not being able to feed our families, losing our social status. We fear being inadequate at work, at home, the list goes on. Even when we have a job the majority of us feel like wage-slaves to Saruman, chopping down forests, digging holes, or banging out swords in his smoky, hot forge for his army of Uruk Hai. Do you sometimes feel like a Ringwraith? Are you being paid what you're worth? Is your job helping to heal the planet, even in some small way? These are things worth considering, though they can be tough ones to deal with mentally. I know.

You're not alone. I've asked them of myself many, many times over the years, but in a very big way the last few months which is the main reason I decided to write this book, instead of working on my dissertation in medieval history — something I know my family wishes I would get back to. But the problems of our Earth were just too compelling for me. I came to the conclusion that I could use my writing talents for something more meaningful, and began to brainstorm on how I would approach the subject of *saving the Earth*.

If you're unhappy with your work or career, I recommend you watch Jim Carrey's full graduation speech, and then answer the "30 Questions you should answer before you die," the same questions that set me on the path to write this book. If you're afraid to do it, then you need to do it more than anyone. Hobbits cannot be ruled by *Fear*. Rings are not destroyed in that way. Courage and *Love* is the only way to defeat Sauron, and the only way to realize your dreams. Once you're finished with the 30 Questions, really give some thought to your answers. Spend a couple of weeks pondering over them. What are the common themes? What are your strengths? What is it that really makes you feel alive? What do you *LOVE TO DO*? Figure *THAT* out, and you're on your way to really living your life as a

Hobbit. Figure out how you might do it for a living or incorporate more of it into your current job or business, and you WILL save the Earth! If you're unhappy with what you're doing now, come up with a plan—actually write it down—to transition from your current job to one that you would be happy doing, even if it means less money. This is not an easy thing to do but there is nothing more important to your mental health and physical health, than to shed the major source of stress and unhappiness from your life: your unhappy, unfulfilling work.

What should you do for a living? I can't answer that, other than to say that you should find something you really *love*, and then find a way to make money doing it. It is possible, trust me. It's not just something that highly talented people like Jim Carrey can do. You know why Mr. Carrey was successful? Because he believed he could be. The man has made a mega-career out of falling down and acting like an idiot. How? Because he had faith in himself and believed that success was possible.

You need to think outside the little box that society, your family, and your own mind keep telling you exists. You do not have to have a traditional *job* to make money. In fact, very few people ever acquire real wealth from a traditional job as a wage-slave working for someone else. Real wealth is rarely found in that direction. It is usually created by entrepreneurs who take risks and start businesses. This can be as small as one woman and a laptop, writing books, to hundreds or thousands of employees designing sustainable products for mass consumption. Don't restrict your mind to thinking like a slave of Mordor. Become a Hobbit, or an Aragorn; strike out and do something new. Stop believing the lies that the Sarumans keep telling us. They want us to conform, to stop dreaming, to keep working, for **them**. But that is draining us of our mental health and as a result, our physical health, as well.

# Healthy Hobbit Bodies: Preparing for Uncomfortable Adventures

Thereupon the herb-master entered. "Your lordship asked for *kingsfoil*, as the rustics name it," he said; "or *athelas* in the noble tongue, or to those who know somewhat of the Valinorean..."

"I do so," said Aragorn, "and I care not whether you say now *asëa aranion* or *kingsfoil*, so long as you have some."

"Your pardon lord!" said the man. "I see you are a lore-master, not merely a captain of war. But alas! sir, we do not keep this thing in the Houses of Healing, where only the gravely hurt or sick are tended. For it has no virtue that we know of, save perhaps to sweeten a fouled air, or to drive away some passing heaviness. Unless, of course, you give heed to rhymes of old days which women such as our good Ioreth still repeat without understanding.

> When the black breath blows
> and death's shadow grows
> and all lights pass,
> come athelas! come athelas!
> Life to the dying
> In the king's hand lying!

It is but a doggrel, I fear, garbled in the memory of old wives. Its meaning I leave to your judgment, if indeed it has any. But old folk still use an infusion of the herb for headaches."

"Then in the name of the king, go and find some old man of less lore and more wisdom who keeps some in his house!" cried Gandalf. —*LOTR*: III, *The Houses of Healing*

The doctor of the future will give no medication, but will interest his patients in the care of the human frame, diet and in the cause and prevention of disease. — Thomas A. Edison

Be careful about reading health books. You may die of a misprint. —Mark Twain

This is the most dangerous of all sections of the book to write. I will start off with the following disclaimer:

> I am not a medical doctor. Before making any changes to your diet, medicines, or medical treatment, you should consult a real medical doctor.

As I mentioned in Part I, I'm not a fan of doctors, or their offices, and especially the hospital. I'm quite certain that I am not alone in that sentiment. That's not to say that I hate doctors. Doctors are people too, unlike politicians and lawyers—just kidding, sort of. I have friends who are doctors and even lawyers and I love them dearly. I give them hell of course, but I still love them. So before you take any of my advice, consult your doctor. If you don't like your doctor, find another one, then consult *THEM*.

The problems with the health care system, at least in the U.S., appear quagmire-y, kind of like the Dead Marshes on the way to Mordor. But in some ways the problems are fairly simple. As mentioned earlier in the *Mordor* section, big corporations—the chemical, pharmaceutical ones—have exploited Americans' penchant for the quick and easy solution to everything and made billions upon billions trying to sell us the newest panacea to everything from the common cold to the Black Death. If a child gets a hang-nail these days we pump him full of petro-drugs just to see what happens. Maybe some of these drugs actually do what they say, but I'm skeptical.

I am not suggesting that you go throw your prescriptions in the garbage and stop taking them. This can be as harmful, or more so, than taking them in the first place. What I *am* suggesting is that you do some research on the drugs you're taking, and ask your doctors all kinds of uncomfortable questions—uncomfortable for *them*—before continuing to take medicines long term or before accepting any new prescriptions. Ask them about natural alternatives. Many doctors are reluctant to discuss alternatives due to legal constraints, or their own philosophy of medicine. Hopefully yours is not. In the end, it is *your* health that's on the line, so don't take it lightly. Do your research.

## The Return of the Kingsfoil: Alternative Medicines

There are a lot of alternatives to the modern health system out there. Many of them can be dangerous, especially if they advocate breaking entirely with modern medicine. Some of the proponents are quacks, or snake-oil salesmen though the pharmaceutical companies also qualify for that title more often than not. As with modern medicine and drugs, do your research before you start taking herbal or *natural* remedies. If possible, consult an actual MD that is conversant with herbal and alternative medicines. Definitely do your research before you pick an herbalist. Make sure they really know what they're talking about. Ask questions, double check their answers with online advice. You can start here, the government site for the United Kingdom. They have advice about herbal medicines. A mistake that a lot of people make, and I've been guilty of this as well, is that we assume that just because something is *natural* it is therefore *safe*, and *ergo, good for us*. I like to point out that cobras are natural too, but I don't want to kiss one. Some people might, and do I'm sure—the late great Steve Irwin comes to mind, but then again, he was killed quite *naturally* by a sting ray—but *making out* with a king cobra isn't my idea of a fun date. My point is, Mother Nature can kick your ass quite *naturally* so do your research.

The argument that the chemical and drug companies often make, to counter the growing movement of natural or alternative medicine is similar to my warning about kissing cobras. They will say things like, "Not all things natural are good for you" and "Even walking to the bathroom in the morning carries risks!" They then trot out extreme, obvious examples like drinking hemlock, or kissing cobras, people falling down stairs in their house, and the like. Okay Mr. Chemicalman, some natural things can kill you, like CEOs of chemical companies who poison almost everything they touch with their products? That's assuming of course that CEOs are natural. Their counterarguments are just a rhetorical attempt to divert attention away from the fact that what **they** make is almost always dangerous and unhealthy for us, and most of the time, unnecessary.

That's not to say that *all* manmade medicines or chemicals are bad for us, but it *is* to argue that they are severely overused and overprescribed. People constantly wonder why kids turn to drugs to solve their problems, especially in the U.S., but the answer is so glaringly obvious that few can see it. The addiction to drugs starts at birth, if not before! Our mothers are usually on one drug or several before they give birth to us. From the day we learn to look at TV, or listen to the radio, or read billboards, one drug company or another is smacking us upside the head with ads touting the miraculous healing properties of their new pharmaceutical wonder-drug.

The message is clear, "Drugs solve your problems! Have some more!" So by the time we grow up it's second nature to look for a chemical solution to every problem we have. I'm depressed, give me some booze, or pills. Allergies? Have this pill. Distracted at work? Our drug will give you focus! Come on people. This is out of control. Most of us know it too, but every year the drug companies and chemical companies rake in record profits and the money goes—after buying new yachts and world cruises for the CEOs and stockholders—to purchasing politicians to write new laws that protect their hegemony over us, and them from our wrath.

## An Ounce of Prevention, a Pound of Lembas: Food and Health

> Let food be thy medicine and medicine be thy food. —
> Hippocrates

This topic is one that even doctors will tell you about. You know the spill, "Eat your veggies, exercise 30 minutes a day, blah blah blah." My last doctor, who weighed about 90 pounds soaking wet—and due to her ethnicity and religion had never eaten an ounce of animal based cholesterol—would ask me, every time I went in, if I wanted to talk to the nutritionist about eating better.

"No," I said, "I already *know* what I'm *supposed* to eat. I just have no intention of eating that way."

As patients go, I'm kind of a pain in the ass. If you're a doctor, I'm the patient you run from or at least shake your head while laughing. She also wanted to put me on this and that drug, a couple of which I agreed to, but others I simply put my foot down and said, "Hell No." But she did bring up an important topic and that is prevention goes a long way to avoiding the doctor to begin with: the old adage, "An apple a day, keeps the doctor away." Or maybe for us Tolkien fans, "Some Aethelas Tea makes the doctor flee!" or "Eat your Lembas bread, or you'll soon be dead!?" Nothing like positivity to sell an idea.

## Better Food: Healthier Hobbits, Duh

The best thing we can do for our health, and most doctors would agree with me on this one, is to eat better food and for most of us, less of it. I'm all on board with the first part and like many others, struggling up the slopes of Mt. Doom on the second. In my opinion many of the health problems we suffer are probably due to the un-natural way our food has been produced in the last 50-60 years, especially the last 15, since GMOs were introduced into our diet. As I've said, the root of many of the world's problems, is food. The solutions are almost all related to food as well.

We'll discuss food in more depth when we get to the *Bilbo's Larder* chapter but most people who have cut out GMOs and transitioned to a diet rich with organic food have noticed marked changes in their health. I'm still in the early stages of transitioning but I can tell a difference already, though only slightly. I'm still a bit sluggish but most of that is probably because I live in a place with so little sunlight for five months out of the year, and it's currently still winter, no matter what the calendar says. Once spring actually arrives, I suspect I'll feel a great deal better when I can get outside more and get back to walking around the neighborhood and cleaning up my garden which leads us to the second most important preventative: exercise.

## Active Hobbits: a Walk a Day, Keeps the Gollums at Bay

This one is a tough one for me. I know—academically—that exercise is like the Silver Bullet for good health but I have never been successful at keeping an exercise routine, like many people I'm sure. I suspect that if I could manage to do a routine 30 days in a row that it might stick, but I hate most exercise. I don't mind walking, but in Minnesnowta, in winter, it's not that much fun; something about a 25 mph wind in your face when the air temperature is -20 Fahrenheit just takes the *zippity doo dah* right outta your step. I'll keep working at it till I find something that sticks, because it is important. My suggestion, and this is *NOT* my professional opinion since I have been an abject failure when it comes to this subject, is to find something you like to do: walking, bike riding, swimming, dancing, or working in the garden, and create a plan to make it a habit.

For some great advice on creating positive routines, read S.J. Scott's *23 Anti-Procrastination Habits: How to Stop Being Lazy and Get Results in Your Life*; he has some simple, straightforward advice on how to form longterm habits. Following his advice I was able to form the habit of writing for 1 hour per day, at minimum, and achieving an average of about 1500 words per hour. I'm planning to apply the same process to exercise and see if I can't work that into my daily schedule as well. Time will tell I reckon. However you do it, try to get some exercise into your daily, or weekly routine. The more, the better of course. It will keep you out of the doctor's office and help to curb the number of drugs you may be taking currently. Once you get the mind and body in shape, and moving, then it's time to get to work saving the Earth. It's time for action.

# 20

# Hobbits in Action: Get Movin'

While getting out minds and bodies in shape are crucial steps in the transformation from modern human to modern Hobbit, those changes are a life-long process. As such, it is imperative that we also start getting to work changing our lifestyle, cleaning up our homes, our gardens, and our Shires. Simultaneously, we can begin to think about ways to be more Hobbity in our actions. There are infinite, concrete ways to change the way we do everyday things that will impact the world around us, and help to clean up the Shire. The great thing is that these actions have a secondary effect: they help to reinforce the internal changes in our minds, and our bodies. So don't neglect outward action and become some sort of contemplative *monk* off in the forest somewhere. Not that's there's anything wrong with monks who meditate in the woods but what the world needs right now, are Hobbits who live in the Shire. So let's get to work!

## But I'm Only One Hobbit!

> Stop acting so small. You are the universe in ecstatic motion. —Rumi, the Sufi Mystic

The biggest stumbling block I come up against when discussing the world's problems with friends, coworkers and strangers, is that while they all know something should be done they expect that real change only comes from the top, i.e., political means. There are many who argue that traditional, head-on politics is the most effective way to deal with the enormous problems facing our world today. As I argued earlier, this makes sense on paper, but in reality, the weight of corporate wealth blocks most efforts in that direction. The argument over whether individual efforts — like cutting back on one's carbon footprint via multiple means has any real effect on global issue — is ongoing.

To my mind, the argument is almost identical to the one that erupted in Rivendell, at the Council of Elrond between those, like Elrond and Gandalf, who realized that the Ring must be destroyed, and Boromir, who championed the idea that it could be employed as a weapon against Sauron. For Boromir, direct confrontation, *war*, was the only option he could envision. He was at his very core, a warrior, noble yes, but a warrior still. He could not grasp the negative power of the Ring until he nearly lost his soul trying to wrest it from Frodo. To his credit, he immediately realized his insanity then went back to work as a warrior in defense of Merry and Pippin.

## A Few Hobbits=Big Change

I'm not saying that we shouldn't attempt to make changes via the political system, but rather that the more effective and long lasting changes will only come from a mental shift on the part of ordinary people, modern Hobbits, who then begin to change their way of doing things. Naysayers will respond to that I'm sure, with the argument that the problems are just too big, too complex for individuals to make a real difference. Certainly, one, or a handful of individuals would only be a drop in the bucket, or a drop in the sea, and would go virtually un-noticed in the grand scheme of things. But a million drops in that bucket makes a river, and rivers run together into oceans! Small deeds have ripple effects that can end up shaking mountains and sweeping millions of people into revolutions. But we don't need *everyone* to change their minds in order to make the world more

Shire-like. This is something that most people don't know about how movements and revolutions actually work.

## Tipping Points: Blowing the Horn of Rohan

Author Malcolm Gladwell, in his book, *Tipping Point: How Little Things Can Make a Big Difference,* has demonstrated that it really takes a small percentage of people to start thinking and acting differently before a *tipping point* is reached where the majority suddenly join in. Marketing experts know this. What they hope to achieve via advertising is to attract enough adventurous, icebreakers, to get the ball rolling. At some point, usually about 15-20%, things start to swing in favor of the idea or product. By the time 30% is reached, it has *tipped*. This is because most people don't want to be *first* at anything. They're not leaders, they are followers. That's not to put a judgment on either type of person; there plenty of examples of bad leaders, and good followers, or visa versa. It's just a fact of human nature. I'm sure most us have seen this in action many times in microcosm if not on a large scale.

## The First Hobbits on the Dance Floor

I remember in high school, sometime during the 1st Age of Middle Earth, going to the local Ramada Inn on Friday nights after football games for the weekly teen dance night. My best friend, Chris, and I would show up fashionably late due to the fact that we had to change from our marching band uniforms into something more *with it* before we drove over for the dance. We'd stroll into the club full of our peers. A live band called Zippers was usually pumping out current dance and rock tunes. But when we rounded the corner past the bar, and looked to our right we invariably noticed that there was no one on the dance floor. This always struck me as odd. It was as if everyone in my high school was waiting for Chris and I to arrive to start dancing.

So every Friday we obliged. We both grabbed a girl and headed for the floor. By the middle of the first song, there would be at least 8 or 10 others who had screwed up the courage to be in the second group. By the end of the song, the floor was full. True, Chris and I were totally badass, and the coolest things goin' but the point I'm trying to make is that in order to get a movement to be, well, a movement, it only takes a leader or two, then it takes that second group who say to themselves, "Hey, if they can look foolish, why can't I?" And if you've ever seen me dance, you know what I'm talking about. This second group joins in and all of a sudden, most of the crowd decides that if they don't join in too, they'll be the ones looking foolish or different. Like I said, and Gladwell points out, marketing executives have been aware of this phenomenon for some time, and it's their goal to find that *second* wave of consumers to bring legitimacy to their product.

There is growing evidence that the movement towards a more sustainable earth is well under way already. Those second groupers have already joined and now we are closing in quickly on the tipping point when it will become less socially acceptable to be outside the movement than to be inside. So get off your ass and dance already!

"But I don't know *how* to dance!"

"So what!" That never stopped *me*.

Keep reading, I'll give you some pointers on how to dance like Hobbits. Even better than that, I'll tell you a couple of stories of Hobbits and how they are dancing on Saruman's Grave.

## A Short but Meaningful Life: a Modern Hobbit Hero

> "When I get out of the hospital, I want to have a lemonade stand." — Alexandra Scott

Alexandra Scott was born in 1997, and was diagnosed with cancer before her 1st birthday. Doctors told her parents that even if she managed to beat the cancer she would probably never walk. They were wrong. She beat the cancer back, and she did walk, but the cancer returned. She spent many days and weeks in the hospital during her first 4 years of life undergoing various treatments, but she braved them like a trooper. While she was in the hospital she started to tell her mom that she wanted to run a lemonade stand when she got out. Her mom told her, "Ok, sure," thinking that the idea was kind of cute, and not sure what prompted it in the first place. Well Alex continued to bring it up, more and more often, till one day her mom—wondering what she wanted the money for—asked her. She told her mom that she wanted to open a lemonade stand, so that she could raise money for *her* hospital since they had helped her. So she, and her older brother did just that. They raised over $2000 that first summer! But she didn't stop there. That would have been stopping on the edge of her Shire. She kept on going.

She soon realized that the problem of cancer was much larger than just *her hospital* so she decided to raise money to fight childhood cancer, everywhere. She continued to run her stand, and her fight with cancer and for a cure, caught on. People learned of her brave struggle and began running their own lemonade stands, in her name, and donating their proceeds to her cause. Now she was marching across Middle Earth carrying her own Ring, but she kept going.

As if to take the fight all the way to *Mordor*, she set a goal of raising 1 million dollars, and with the help of thousands of other kids and parents around the country, she did it! Alex achieved her goal even while losing her personal fight with cancer. At the age of 8, cancer finally claimed young Alex's life, but not her legacy. She died knowing that her cause had raised over $1 Million towards cancer research, and is still raising it today! In fact, Alex's Lemonade Stand Foundation has raised over $80 Million. Her bravery is a lesson to modern Hobbits everywhere, that *anyone*, can Save the Earth, or at least a small part of it, no matter how old, how small, or what handicaps or obstacles they may face.

# Dancing on Saruman's Grave: a New Model for Revolution

> Put your money where your mouth is. —Traditional Wisdom

We all want a revolution. I'm going to assume that if you've made it this far into the book, you do want to save the Earth. We want to bring down Saruman and Sauron's towers of Greed and Fear, but what would this movement or revolution look like? How can we counter all the money spent by corporations to corrupt the system? Which foot goes first in this Hobbit Hoe-Down? I admit, the situation seems dire and impossible but that's because we tend to look at the so-callled effectiveness of corporate efforts and not to the *source* of their power. I was discussing this with one of my best friends, Monk—remember him? So one day recently, on the phone, I asked him, "Ok, so corporations are corrupting our system?"

Monk, "Yes!"

Me, "How do they do this?"

Monk, "They bribe politicians and pay lobbyists to argue for laws that benefit them and not us."

"What do they use to bribe these politicians and pay lobbyists?"

"Millions of dollars, of course!"

"Where do all these millions of dollars come from?"

With the irritated voice of a Socratic student, "The corporations!"

"No, I mean, where do the corporations *get* the money? Does it fall out of the sky?"

Monk replied, after a short pause, "They get it from selling their products!"

"Yes, and who *buys* those products?"

Monk, with the *ohhh yeahhh* voice one gets when realization hits you like a ton of bricks, "US! WE buy those products, with OUR MONEY!"

"Yes, exactly. We are, in essence, bribing politicians to vote against our best interests so that corporations can accumulate more profits, unbalance the distribution of wealth, corrupt our politics, pollute our environment, poison our food, water, and air."

So then I posed the obvious question, "So how do we stop this insanity?"

"Damn. I guess we should stop buying their products."

"I reckon so."

The solution sounds too simple, right? Einstein once said that if he ever found the illusive Unified Field Theory, that it would be a very simple equation, you know, something like E=MC2. Well, I am arguing, as others have, that the actual solution to corporate greed is simply to take their money away, not via taxes—though I'm not opposed to employing that strategy as well—but via an even simpler method: stop giving them our money to start with!

Me, to Monk, "What happens when we stop buying their products?"

"Hmmm? I guess they go out of business?"

"Jellybeans! That's exactly what happens. And how many politicians can a bankrupt company bribe, with no money?"

Monk, "Not a damned one!"

## But Where Would We Shop?

That sounds great on the phone, but then of course most of my friends bring up the problem of finding all the stuff we need without spending money with the very corporations that are destroying our planet. This does seem to be a difficult problem, mainly because we are so brainwashed into thinking that the only place to find those things we need, and I emphasize, *need*, is to shop at Walmart or any of the other huge corporate entities. This is due to their advertising, propagandizing, public relations juggernaut. They have convinced us that they are the only place to shop for everything we need, meanwhile pushing out local businesses who were there all along to supply those needs.

But there is a resurgence of locally owned businesses thanks in large part to the financial crises in 2007-8. Many people started to look around and realize that their money was leaching out of their communities and into the pockets of Wall Street and the big banks, where it mysteriously went up in a puff of smoke. So in response to that they started finding alternative places to spend their money: local restaurants, co-op grocery stores, local farmers markets, Craigslist and many others.

## What about Lost Jobs?

Yes, big corporations do employ lots of people, but not nearly as many as they like to take credit for. Most jobs in this country are still in small businesses. If the big box stores disappeared tomorrow, by some Gandalf-ian stroke of magic — wouldn't that be nice — there would be a lot of unemployed people. But aren't there already loads of unemployed people? Where are all the great jobs that the corporations and the ultra rich keep telling us that they create? Hmmmm.

I'm going to postulate something. If the Sarumans disappeared, there would be a momentary slump in employment, yes, but very soon after, within a year or two, local businesses would flourish once again without the unfair advantages that huge corporations bring to the competition — subsidies, tax breaks, etc. — and then those unemployed people would be able to find jobs working for better employers, or at least, *local* employers. And yes, I am suggesting that *local* is *superior* to corporate, or non-local. Is every local business owner a good businessman and a compassionate, wonderful employer? No. They are not, but what they are is immediately accountable for their actions because they are *LOCAL*. You don't have to go through tons of corporate bureaucratic B.S. to contact them with complaints. Many of them are actually working, *on the floor* in their business, interacting with customers on a one-to-one basis, every day. This is how Hobbits should do business.

# Is Shireness *Anti-Captilist*?

Not really. There is nothing *inherently* wrong with commerce, or capitalism. There's loads wrong with many commercial *ventures*, and *capitalists*, however. And there's a lot wrong with the way *corporate capitalism* has been allowed to run rampant and unchecked; it's out of control. It's not commerce that's the problem; it's the corporate mindset that *profit* is synonymous with *value*. It isn't, but that's for a later chapter. I want everyone reading this book to know that I am not advocating *communism*, though many of the ideas in the book are compatible with that philosophy. I believe that well-regulated commerce can be a positive force in the World, and *IS*, in many instances already that way. Wealth, in and of itself, is not evil, or destabilizing. What are destabilizing, however, are Greed, and Fear. I believe that Hobbits *should* be rich: rich in experiences, friendships, food, security, peace, and hell, money. Why not? As long as you're generous with it I wish you all the dragon's gold you can find.

## The Rich and Generous Hobbit: How to Employ Smaug's Gold to Save the Earth

> Bilbo was very rich and very peculiar, and had been the wonder of the Shire for sixty years...The riches he had brought back from his travels had now become a local legend, and it was popularly believed, whatever the old folk might say, that the Hill at Bag end was full of tunnels stuffed with treasure...There were some that shook their heads and thought this was too much of a good thing; it seemed unfair that anyone should possess (apparently) perpetual youth as well as (reputedly) inexhaustible wealth.
>
> "It will have to be paid for," they said. "It isn't natural and trouble will come of it!"
>
> But so far trouble had not come; and as Mr. Baggins was *generous with his money*, most people were willing to forgive him his oddities and his good fortune. – *LOTR*: I, *A Long Expected Party*

> When I give food to the poor, they call me a saint. When I ask why the poor have no food, they call me a communist. —Hélder Câmara, *Dom Helder Camara: Essential Writings*

> The man who dies rich, dies disgraced. —Andrew Carnegie

In 1917, the Westside Neighborhood of St. Paul, Minnesota got a gift from a very wealthy man, one of the richest men on Earth at the time: the former *robber-baron* turned philanthropist, Andrew

Carnegie. Thanks to funds that the steel baron had set aside, Westside got a new library on the corner of George and Humboldt Streets. It's a beautiful, if small library. It's one of three such Carnegie libraries in St. Paul, and one of thousands built all over America.

This outpouring of generosity sits at odds with much of Carnegie's life and work. He was, by all accounts, a ruthless businessman, responsible for the poverty and even death of hundreds of his workers. During a strike at his Homestead mill in 1892, ten workers were gunned down by Pinkerton detectives hired by Carnegie's manager to break the strike. Carnegie, of course, was not there, nor did he directly *order* the violence, but his greed drove it. And his greed knew few bounds. Like a modern Saruman, and like his counterparts, the Rockefellers, the Vanderbuilts, and St. Paul's own James J. Hill, Carnegie clawed his way to the top of the business heap and carved a place for himself among the elite of the new American aristocracy, built on 'boot-strap' entrepreneurship, unparalleled drive, and an unrelenting work ethic. These were not lazy men. Not like many of their descendants, that is, who have slipped into an entirely different mentality altogether. No, John D., Andrew, and James J. were hardworking, men of steel. But their accumulation of wealth came at a great cost to themselves, their consciences, their families, their workers, the environment, and society at large.

Towards the end of his life, Carnegie came to realize just how much he owed to the country that he helped to drive into the 20th century. It was not only *his* work that created the great railroads and shipping he was famous for. The bulk of that labor was on the backs of his employees who suffered a great deal in the process. As an older man, he reflected on this and came up with a new philosophy on wealth. What was it for? Why had he been so successful? What good is accumulated wealth? He sat down and began to write. The following is an excerpt from his *Gospel of Wealth*:

> The problem of our age is the proper administration of wealth, so that the ties of brotherhood may still bind together the rich and poor in harmonious relationship. The conditions of human life have not only been

changed, but revolutionized, within the past few hundred years. In former days there was little difference between the dwelling, dress, food, and environment of the chief and those of his retainers. The Indians are to-day where civilized man then was. When visiting the Sioux, I was led to the wigwam of the chief. It was just like the others in external appearance, and even within the difference was trifling between it and those of the poorest of his braves. The contrast between the palace of the millionaire and the cottage of the laborer with us to-day measures the change which has come with civilization.

Of course, Andrew concluded that this was not necessarily a bad thing, as long as those with wealth realized their true purpose in life: to give back to society. He reasoned that it was his superior intellect, drive, and talent for organization that allowed him and others to succeed, and as such, it was their duty to accumulate wealth for the purpose of redistribution under their enlightened guidance. In other words, they were rich because they had the talent and ability to make money and therefore the talent and ability to reallocate those funds for the good of those with less talent to do so: everyone else in society. It was an elitist bent on a decent idea. That's not to take away from the generous things he did with his money. At least he did give away the vast majority of his wealth before his death. But I think that the wealthy of today can do a might better.

### Give Like a Hobbit or an Elf

The richest person in the Shire was Bilbo Baggins. He was also renowned for his generosity and hospitality. His 111th birthday party was an event unparalleled in Hobbit history. Everyone was invited, even those who he disliked. All were included and welcomed warmly. All received birthday gifts, a Hobbit custom that we should all take up, and not cheap re-gifts either—though there's nothing wrong with re-gifting—especially fruit cakes. Bilbo gave rare and interesting gifts, if not overly expensive.

If we want to find other rich characters we have to leave the Shire and visit with the Elves of Rivendell and Lothlórien.

Elrond's house was known as the 'Last Homely House' and renowned for its hospitality, food, music, and healing. All peaceful beings were welcome. There is no mention of money exchanging hands. Elrond was certainly wealthy, in every sense of the word. So was his mother-in-law, Galadriel of Lothlórien, the oldest Elf in Middle Earth. She also showed great hospitality to the Fellowship, including kingly gifts to each member on their parting from the fair land. Gimli, a Dwarf no less, sailed away down the Anduin with a gift beyond price: three of the great lady's hairs, and a mended relationship between Dwarves and Elves that had been strained for centuries.

There is nothing wrong with wealth, with making money, with capitalism, or commerce, not inherently anyway. What is wrong with money, capitalism, and commerce, isn't the ideas, it's the *attachment* to them that most of us have. We believe that they are the solution to our problems; they are not. They are merely tools that humans invented to help recirculate wealth. But if that wealth doesn't circulate, if it all accumulates at the top then money no longer holds any value for those at the bottom, who will then invent a new way to trade goods. When that happens the entire system will come crashing down. Don't believe it can happen? Do an internet search for images of German 'marks' in the 1920s. The U.S. is no more immune from this scenario than Germany was, and if the haves and have-nots in America continue to separate, if some of that wealth—nay, a *lot* of it—isn't recirculated, there will soon be pictures of American Dollars on the internet, stacked to the ceiling like toy blocks, blowing down Wall Street, or burning in American wood-stoves to boil water.

### Be a Bilbo: Recirculate It

We don't own money. If anything, it owns us. It is just a tool, and it's completely useless sitting in an offshore bank piling up on itself. That's a Smaug mentality. What good did all that Dwarfish gold do the dragon? Did it keep him warm? Personally, I don't think dragons need central heating. Could he eat it? No. Accumulating wealth for wealth's sake is Greed, greed based on some underlying *FEAR*. What do you fear? Figure it out, and dispel it. Aspire to be more like Bilbo, or

Elrond; spend that money, and spend it on someone other than yourself and your children. The world is aching, and not because they're lazy. It's because 85 people on Earth, own more wealth than the bottom 3.5 billion. Fact. Can that be justified? No.

Accumulating wealth for the sake of accumulation is insanity; it's killing the planet and those living on it. I know I'm probably preaching to the choir at this point since you made it this far into the book, so I'll not beat a dead horse. Our children do not need millions of dollars to live on. They just don't. It's the worse possible thing we could do for them. If you don't believe me, just take a look at what that kind of money has done for the elite families of inherited wealth. It's an ugly picture. The robber barons left us an example of the mentality that such wealth engenders. We don't need any more of that in the world. What we need are generous Hobbits who give back to the Shire that enabled them to be successful. What we need is a new model for business. A new guide for Hobbit Business People. We'll return to that in the last section, since it has more to do with our interaction with people in the Shire and beyond. To round out this section on Being a Hobbit, let's talk about something everyone loves: *saving* money.

## Frugal Hobbits: Saving the World, While Saving Money

> A penny saved is a penny earned. —Benjamin Franklin

> Annual income twenty pounds, annual expenditure nineteen six, result happiness. Annual income twenty pounds, annual expenditure twenty pound ought and six, result misery.
> —Charles Dickens, *David Copperfield*

The one thing that keeps most of us from implementing more green changes into our lives is the cost of doing so or at least the perception that it is more expensive. I was discussing the *corporate* problem with an associate at work the other day, and trying to make the argument that we need to spend our money with local businesses, buy better food, etc.

"But our what choices do we have? There are no alternatives!"

"Sure there are!" "Look across the street." I said, pointing to my co-op grocery store, Mississippi Market, "There's one example right there!"

"Yeah, but who can afford to shop there all the time? I sure can't."

His point was a valid one, and one I'm sure many of you are thinking right this moment, if you haven't already. True, organic produce and meats are more expensive, up front. Sometimes shopping for other things from a local supplier will cost you a few extra dollars. The cost of *not* buying them locally, however, is far more expensive in the long run, as I pointed out earlier. But there is always the dilemma of feeding, clothing, and sheltering our families *TODAY*!

It is a Catch 22 situation for many people at the lower end of the economic scale, and trust me, I've been there most of my life, and for years I wanted to change my diet to more natural stuff but just couldn't persuade my family to make the sacrifices necessary to do it. The good news is that once you start to implement some of the changes that I lay out in this last part of the book you will begin to save money. Most Hobbit ideas are frugal. There are endless ways to shave money from your family budget, as you'll see. The author of the book, *Zero Waste Home: The Ultimate Guide to Simplifying Your Life by Reducing Your Waste*, Bea Johsnon, and her family, shaved as much as 40% from their monthly budget by eliminating waste in their house and lives. If you want to see how she did it, read *her* book after you finish this one. It's a great read, and there are tons of good ideas in it. Don't stop reading this book though because each of the following sections will in some way address the central question, "How can I afford to do this?"

## Take it Slow Hobbits: One Step at a Time

One way to *afford* it is to reevaluate our needs and wants but the best way to reclaim our wealth from those at the top, is to start spending it with our neighbors, people just like us, who are more likely to be concerned about more than just maximizing profits at the expense of the local environment, both the physical and political environment. Money spent locally tends to stay local which means there's a better chance that it will return to you, directly, if not indirectly.

But where should we start? We buy so many things, everyday. It would be a mistake to try to change our buying habits all at once. **Don't do it!** It will lead to confusion and frustration, which leads to failure. **Start small, and start in your own home/Hobbit-hole first.** And that is the goal of the next section of Part III: how we can make our houses *homes*, or better yet, Hobbit-holes!

# 21

# MAKING YOUR HOUSE A HOLE

Before we can save the Earth we must first save ourselves and the best place to begin, after we've decided to embark on this adventure, is in our own homes. In this section of the book we're going to be looking at all the *stuff* in your house, room to room, to see where we can eliminate clutter and poisons, and minimize the amount of waste, trash-wise, energy-wise, and time-wise. After all, a good system of living should leave us with plenty of time to enjoy eating, drinking and hanging out with the Hobbits we love, as well as those we "like less than half as well as they deserve." To begin cleaning up our homes there are some key wasteful, poisonous things that we'll look for in all rooms of your house, though some rooms contain more waste than others.

# 22

# WORMS AND OOZY SMELLS: AGENTS OF MORDOR IN YOUR HOBBIT-HOLE

In a hole in the ground there lived a Hobbit. Not a nasty, dirty, wet hole, filled with the ends of worms and an oozy smell, nor yet a dry, bare, sandy hole with nothing in it to sit down on or to eat: it was a Hobbit-hole, and that means comfort. — *The Hobbit, An Unexpected Party*

## Saruman's Synthetics: Purging Plastics from the Hobbit-hole

We've already talked in some length about the nasty orcishness of plastic so I won't go into another long diatribe here. I will caution you that once you start taking notice of how much you have in your life, it will astonish you, even though most us are aware that plastic is a big part of modern civilization. As for general strategies for minimizing plastic use, it's good to follow these basic guidelines from Beth Terry's book, *Plastic-Free: How I Kicked the Plastic Habit and How You Can Too*, what she calls the *Five Rs*:

- **Refuse** to buy it or take it to begin with. Refuse to buy more things made of plastic, if at all possible. Don't become a plastic NAZI though, that will just lead to despair. Do what you can, one step at a time. Refusing to buy new plastics is the most important strategy because when we buy new plastic, especially brand new products, we generate a market to make more of them which the planet does not need.

- **Reuse** any plastics you already have.

- **Reduce** the amount in your house over time.

- **Redistribute** it by giving it to someone that can reuse it.

- **Recycle** This should be the last option.

If you have to buy plastic, try to buy used items first then recycled plastic items second. Always ask yourself if what you're buying is something you really need. Recycling of plastic should be the last option, as many can't be recycled, and the process of recycling takes a good deal of energy as well as the fact that most plastics aren't recycled into a version of their former use. Instead they are *down-cycled* into something else which creates a market to replace the original item. For example, the orcish water bottle. When a water bottle is recycled it is rarely reformed into another water bottle but usually into something else. So the water bottle manufacturer has to create a new one, from new oil, to replace the one that was just downcycled. In 2006 alone, the plastics industry consumed **17 million barrels of oil**, just to produce bottles for *WATER!* Not for all the other uses, or other drinks, like sodas, *JUST WATER.* If you want to help put a stop to that, get a reusable water bottle and stop buying plastic encased water.

Recycling is important but more important is to create a market where plastics aren't consumed anymore, because we — the Hobbits of the world — no longer purchase them. When you purchase a product, any product, it creates the demand to replace it with another one, and so on and so on. Stop the cycle. Avoid buying plastic. This can't be achieved over night. Take your time and eliminate it one item at a time, until you get rid of all of it from your Hobbit-hole — except those items that can be used indefinitely—and that aren't in direct contact with your food or your person.

As we move through your Hobbit-hole from room to room we'll focus on individual items that are probably made of plastic and how you can find alternatives to them, but some general ideas are good to cover right here at the beginning of this section. As you work to eliminate them from each room, remember that it's not just the *hard* plastics you need to look for but also the *fabric* or soft ones. These are hidden in your clothes, bedding and other places. One place you will find them is in your *cloth* grocery bags. Now, as long as the bag, or item, is still functional and not directly affecting the health of your family, continue to use it. To store cleaners, for example, is an acceptable use for plastics that you already have. After all, as long as you keep using them they are not in a landfill or being down-cycled into something else, which will also end up in a landfill eventually. However, do eliminate them from your kitchen when possible. More on that later when we get to the kitchen chapter.

### "What do I replace plastics with?"

There are many options actually. I am old enough to actually remember when plastic became a huge thing in the 1960s-70s, and hearing my parents and other *old* people complaining about all the new products made of *plastic* with a note of disdain that I haven't forgotten. Back then, lots of products were still contained in glass, cardboard boxes, and tin cans though they were losing ground to plastic containers at an alarming rate. Here are some old school and some new fangled alternatives to orcish plastic.

### Glass

If you're storing food, probably the first option is glass. The beauty of glass, is that you can see what's in it. I love Mason jars. I'm from the South, and down there, they are used for everything, including drinking glasses. When we recently moved to St Paul, we got rid of—recycled or gave away—most of our drinking glasses, especially the plastic ones and I replaced them with a bunch of quart-sized Mason jars. There's no better way to drink sweet iced tea than out of a big 'ole Mason jar! What's great about them, too, is that they come with lids, so I can take my tea to work by just screwing on a metal lid, and head out the door!

There are numerous other glass containers out there that are great for packing lunches, storing food in the fridge and freezer. Yes, you can freeze some glass containers—like Mason jars—as long as you leave some air space at the top so that the liquid in the food can expand. You can also use them for their original purpose, of course: preserving or *canning* food to store it for winter or longer. This is particularly useful if you have your own garden, which you should work to create if you do not have one. More on that later. You may have a canning expert in your family already that you can call up for tips, otherwise, Google it. There's plenty of help out there. I'm going to do it for the first time this year, probably in the fall when the tomato season is about over. I love 'maters.

**Stainless Steel**

Stainless steel is also a good option. It's effective, stainless, which is always good, and unlike glass it doesn't break when dropped, though you can dent it to the point where it may not be effective. There are more and more stainless options these days. I see them in my co-op grocery store, and elsewhere. Try to find ones that have little or no plastics involved, in particular make sure they are not *lined* with plastic. Check the labels, as with everything.

**Cloth**

Cloth is a good substitute for plastic in some situations. It is a decent thing to use to store fresh bread, for instance. You can store bread, baked fresh and un-bagged from the bakery, for a few days in an old pillow case. You can freeze it in the case too, but it won't keep that way forever, but who wants to keep bread forever anyway? It's too good fresh! Cloth is also used in shopping bags which is one of the first things you should start using to eliminate those nasty, orcish, plastic ones that you get at the store. I hate those things anyway. Half the time they just rip on you, spilling your beer bottles on the sidewalk! Use cloth bags, tell the grocery store — in your best Gollum-esque voice — to "keep nasty plastic." Also remember to take them into department stores, too! I usually think of them as my *grocery* bags, but they can carry anything, so take them into every store!

Before you buy new bags you should know that not all cloth bags are made equal. Most of the cheap ones you get from the store are actually made with synthetic materials, i.e., plastic, and they don't last very long. If you have some already, and most of us do, keep using them until they finally fail. Then recycle them. Find good cloth bags made from organic cotton, or other materials. When possible buy organic cotton materials, as opposed to cotton that is not organic. The cotton plant is one of the most heavily sprayed crops when it comes to pesticides. Not only will these pesticides be in the cotton — where most of them will be washed out — but much of those chemicals will be washed off the fields where it will run off into our rivers and oceans. What doesn't run off then will be washed off in your washing machine at home and end up in our drinking water, or the rivers. Don't go out and throw away all of your non-organic cotton. Just be mindful when you buy new stuff to look for organic options.

## Wood

For many items, wood is an age-old option, and what can be more beautiful than wood? Not much. I love wooden stuff. Of course most of us think of it in terms of furniture, or building materials, but it can also hold food and be employed to make many other items around the house: boxes, bowls, plates, spoons, etc. Use your imagination and then keep your eye open for new-old ideas to incorporate wood into your hole. We've found lots of wooden plates and bowls on Craigslist.

## Pottery

Good ole' clay! Where would the human species be without clay pots? Answer, probably still living in a *Leaver* lifestyle. Without pots to store all that extra grain that the first Totalitarian, *Taker* Agriculturalists were growing it would have spoiled and the experiment would have failed. They did have clay, however, and the experiment did not fail, or at least not yet. Pottery was the storage option for most civilizations on Earth, since before civilization and until the 20th century when cheaper glass and then plastics were introduced. It is still an excellent choice for most storage needs. You can find it on Craigslist, in antique stores, garage sales, etc. The really old stuff is usually expensive, but not always. Keep your eye out for it and grab it when you can find it at a reasonable price. There are many potters still at work these days though. Make sure to look for local potters, who probably make some really cool stuff. Also you can look for stuff online at Etsy.com, where there are numerous potters, as well as other craftsmen/artists making all kinds of things with sustainable materials, as well as recycling plastics and other materials.

**Skin and Bone**

Leather was, for millennia, a staple storage and clothing option and still is for some things, especially shoes. It can be made into many different things, however. Yes, animals must be killed in order to make it but they are being killed for food every day. If you're a vegan, or vegetarian, you probably won't opt for leather but it can serve many useful functions. Also, on that note, bone or horn make excellent materials for many things. Before the invention of plastics, the *horner* — someone who worked with and created stuff out of bone/horn—was an important craftsman. Almost anything you can imagine plastic doing, horn can do, and did do for tens, if not hundreds of thousands of years. Of course, there aren't many horners left, a few still exist but you may find horn options for some items. You can usually find a horner at larger Renaissance Fairs and historical reenactment events. They almost always have something for sale. You can always search for them online, too.

**New Materials**

There are some new materials being introduced these days too: mushroom packaging and cellulose-poly. Basically, scientists have come up with ways of using bio-degradable materials, plants essentially, to make things that we normally would use plastic for. We'll discuss this in more depth towards the end of the book. There are also links in the Resource section at the end of the book. This is the way of the future. Look for these items in the near future, and do buy some to support the new industry. Better yet, contact the manufacturers of some of your favorite things and ask them to start a line of products made with these new materials or to replace all of their lines with the new stuff! They can be the leader of the new wave of sustainable manufacturing! Why be the last one on the wagon? Ask them if they wouldn't rather be first? Make sure to give them websites to check out so that they can read about the materials for themselves. In fact, make their job as easy as you can. Do some of the research yourself but don't get preachy. Just tell them how you've always been a loyal customer but that you're concerned about plastics and looking for non-plastic options to their products. If there are other competitors that are using alternatives, you might gently point that out. Some things that might be made from these new materials:

- **Computers/phones/electronics**: This is something that definitely needs to be done. Our discarded electronics are filling landfills at an alarming rate.

- **Foam/cushions/pillows**: Natural materials need to be used for these, especially styrofoam for packing. The new mushroom product is the way to go.

- **Furniture/kitchen ware/housewares**: The new cellulose material can be molded into anything!

- **Vehicles/transportation**: Again, the cellulose material can be used to make nearly all of the harder surfaces for any application, including cars. No more fiberglass and plastic.

## Paper: Saving the Old Forest

Paper, while made of natural fibers is not environmentally friendly because it takes a great deal of energy and, in particular water, to make it. On top of that is the fact that trees must be cut down to make it. Most paper is processed and bleached using nasty orcish chemicals that pollute the very water used to produce it. The use of paper will probably never be eliminated but we need to find alternatives to tree pulp to make it. Luckily those already exist. Probably the most sustainable of them is hemp. Hemp, long used for a myriad of useful things, has been outlawed in the U.S. for a very long time. This is mainly due to the fact that the oil from the seeds can be used for many things: fuel, medicine, and food, to name a few. This made it a target for the pharmaceutical and chemical companies—not to mention their buddies in the fossil fuel industry—who lobbied to make it illegal. The fact that hemp is the male of the *marijuana* plant helped them make a case, though there's nothing really damaging about marijuana either—but that's a debate for another day. Hemp can make excellent, stronger paper than wood pulp and do it with less energy and time. And it's a renewable crop. Trees really aren't. They don't grow fast enough. Not only is hemp renewable it also helps to replenish the soil with nutrients often sapped by other crops.

Walgreens Pharmacy—a company that I'm not fond of due to their thwarted corporate inversion plan to avoid paying U.S. taxes—has come out with an entire line of Earth-friendly products, called *Ology*. One of the products is toilet paper which uses no trees at all. Instead, they make it from discarded sugar-cane husks and bamboo and are whitened with Hydrogen Peroxide, far less damaging to the environment than chlorine bleach, which is horrible stuff. Hopefully other companies will follow suit and start making more paper products from alternatives. Until then we need to stretch the paper resources we already have.

Since wood paper is nearly unavoidable at present we need to make sure that we are using it to its full capacity before we discard it. Here are some things to think about before you toss paper into the can.

- **Use it All:** I've started trying to keep all scrap pieces of paper, including misprints from the printer, mailing envelopes, and other scraps in a bottom drawer of my home desk. I reach for them anytime I need a Post-It Note. No, they don't have the convenient glue on the back, but so what. Our grandparents didn't have that crap and they lived. Hobbits can live without them, too. Use the paper up before you get rid of it.

- **Keep Scrap to Burn:** We grill a lot at our house, and I use paper to start the charcoal instead of lighter fluid. I have a paper shredder for sensitive stuff, but stuff like grocery ads I put out in the garage for starting charcoal or fires in our fire pit.

- **Recycle It:** Did you know that it takes 30 to 50% less energy to recycle paper than it does to make it from new pulp? It also saves trees at the same time, which makes Treebeard happy and allows us all to keep breathing. Recycling paper reduces pollution by more than 90% compared to making new. So it pays to recycle paper. Don't throw it in the trash. Put it in your recycling bin once you've written little loves notes and shopping lists on both sides of it.

## Orcish Chemicals

Most modern houses are chock full of poisonous chemicals and it's amazing that we rarely think about the effects they might have on our health and the health of our families. They come in many different forms too: cleaners—the most obvious, perfumes and colognes—many have toxic chemicals in them, storage containers—plastic leaches chemicals into stuff, automotive stuff, yard chemicals—like orcish RoundUp, dust or particles from our poly blend clothing—more on that later. None of these chemicals are needed in the home, or at least very few are. There are more natural substitutes for almost all of them. We'll look at some of those when we come to them during our tour of the Hobbit-hole.

# Energy

We will look for ways to lower our energy usage, which at the same time will of course reduce your energy bills! And who doesn't want to save money?

# Water

As mentioned earlier, clean water is becoming a scarce resource on our planet. Many of us in the Western world especially are oblivious to just how scarce it is but if we don't start conserving it, we will soon discover that the River Isengard is running with poison that we cannot drink. So we will discuss ways to conserve this.

### Water filtration

If you don't already have some sort of water filtration system, or if it's antiquated and doesn't filter out stuff like fluoride— most don't, then you should consider upgrading, or buying a system to do it, especially for the water you drink and cook with. The best systems are *reverse osmosis* systems, because they can remove fluoride and most other contaminants in your water. If you're unsure about what's in your water visit the EPA's website and do some research. If you don't trust them look for local water suppliers and find one to come out and test your water. You might want to get a couple of them to do it so you can compare their results.

If you can't afford to put in a reverse osmosis system there are cheaper alternatives but most of them have filters made of plastic, which are expensive to replace. We had a Zero Water filter for a while, but the expense of constantly replacing plastic filters that were going to end up in a landfill, drove us to look for an alternative. We decided to purchase filtered water from our co-op grocery store. Their system, called Natural Pure, is a reverse osmosis process that removes fluoride and most everything else. Many grocery stores now have them. What's really cool is that you bring your own bottles or jugs and refill them so you keep them out of the landfill. I want to go to using all glass or ceramic jugs, but they're so heavy that I haven't made the change. I really should though, so I can stop using plastic jugs. It's a process transitioning away from the so-called *normal* way of doing things back to what was once *normal* and hopefully will be again. We're really not doing anything *new*; it's actually quite old.

## Waste

Most of us throw away entirely too much stuff. We used to fill our rolling trash can to overflowing, every week. But now that we're more conscious of what we toss and how we toss it, we barely fill it to the half way mark. There are ways to minimize the trash we generate. We'll focus on this in each chapter but do keep it in your mind as you throw things *away* in your daily routine. Think to yourself, "Could that be disposed of differently? Could it be recycled or reused? Or is there an alternative for it, like buying the product in bulk instead of in a one-use container?" For many creative ideas, read Bea Johnson's *Zero Waste Home: The Ultimate Guid to Simplifying Your Life by Reducing Your Waste.*

## Clutter

Related to trash, is just general clutter. We could all probably pare down the stuff in our homes. Most of it creates what the great Buddha called *attachment*. It's not the stuff that's the problem—well sometimes it is—but rather our attachment to it. Less is more, is a big part of the mind shift that is required to save the planet so keep that question on a back burner as you go through your day. If you see *stuff* lying around or stored in a closet, or basement, or garage that you haven't paid attention to in some time, maybe it's time to reevaluate whether it is of any practical use to you anymore?

I have lots of crap like that, and the ridiculous thing is, we just *MOVED* recently so that means that I did look at it and decided that I should keep it, pack it up, move it, and then store it again! Sometimes I think I need my head examined. I'm sure my mother would agree. Now I'm rethinking some of that crap. Don't just throw it out, however. You should first attempt to sell it or give it away to someone that might just be looking for that neon Christmas necktie. A rule to use: If it's not a seasonal holiday item, and you haven't used it in six months, put it on Craigslist, or donate it to the Salvation Army or Goodwill. If it's just broken, worn out crap, then by all means, toss it, or put it in the recycling bin. Don't keep a lot of stuff around just *in case* you might need it 50 years from now. I can hear my mom's voice in my head as I write this paragraph, "Just git rid of it!"

### Christmas Trees, Bailing Wire, and

So I have to tell this story about my mom. Love you mom, in case you're reading this. A couple years ago I was living back home with my parents for a few months, and just before Thanksgiving I agreed to help my dad put up Christmas decorations. My dad loves Christmas, like, a LOT. In some ways the inside of the house is always decorated for that time of year since he has like four gazillion collector, Department 56 houses all over the place, most of them sitting on that fake, foam, rollout, snow stuff. They drive my mom nuts, though secretly I think she kind of likes them. *Don't tell her I said that by the way.*

Anyway, so my mom went to get her hair done that morning, it must have been a Wednesday I reckon, so my dad and I took the time to start putting up the fake, plastic, Christmas tree in their sun-porch. I hate plastic Christmas trees, but my dad gave in years ago and started buying them. Anyway, as we were putting it up the top section broke right where it slips together. The plastic broke, of course, because it's crappy plastic from Taiwan or some place that doesn't even celebrate Christmas. So we decided to *fix* the tree, instead of tossing it. We're men. We're cheap by nature. "Suuuure, no problem! Just put some duct tape on it, or some bailin' war'— that's bailing wire, for you non-Southerners—It'll be good as new!" So we went to the garage, and found no *war*, or wire, to fix it with.

Now, my father is a grandpa, so my obvious question to him was, "Dad, why do you not have tons of *war* and crap hanging all over your garage like your dad used to have? You're not holding up the time-honored traditions of grandfather-hood!" Both of us knew very well why he didn't have any: my mother. Mom has an extreme aversion to clutter, or *mess*, as she calls it. I have more or less inherited that attitude from her though as I mentioned above, I sometimes fall short of the mark.

Anyway, my dad and I rushed out to the store to buy some bailing *war* so we could fix the tree before my mom returned to stop us. The reason we were worried has to do with 1975. Yes, I know, that was a rather abrupt seque, but we're now in the 70s, the glorious era of disco and bellbottoms. My dad had gone to pick out the Bivans Family Christmas Tree without my mother's help and wisdom, and came home with the Charlie Brown version. To be fair, it looked more Christmas Tree-y than Chuck's did, until you put a string of lights on it. That's when the problem became apparent. Every limb on that pitiful tree drooped to the floor under the enormous weight of 1970s, hot and heavy Christmas lights. I'm not exaggerating, trust me.

My mom went into a critical frenzy on the tree, my dad's ability to choose trees, why did we need one anyway, "I can't believe you couldn't find a better tree than that..." You might as well have added, "You're such a blockhead, Charlie Brown" to the end of that, though to be fair, she didn't say that. Not exactly. It was certainly implied. To all this my dad, the eternal optimist, just said, "Oh, no problem, I can just *war* the branches up and it'll be like new!" like Linus and his magic blanket. And he did. He proceeded, much to my mother's consternation and verbal critique, to *war* every single branch of that tree to the trunk. It was the most ridiculous thing I'd ever seen, and maybe the best thing my father ever did because it has provided us with an annual belly laugh ever since. Not ONE Christmas has gone by that we haven't talked about that tree from 1975 and laughed till we cried. I long since moved away, started my own family, put up 30 plus trees of my own, but I never look at one without thinking about that *war'd* up tree from 1975.

So we rushed back home, to *war* up the plastic tree in the sun porch, hopefully before the boss returned from her hair appointment. We pulled up to the house, and her van was in the driveway. Damn! Well, that's what I thought. My dad doesn't curse, well, not exactly. He says, 'Shoot!' when the rest of us would just change the vowel to express the same sentiment and he may well have said it when he saw that van. I'm pretty sure he was thinking it. He looked at me, and said, "Put that *war* in your pocket. Maybe she won't see the tree until after we've had a chance to fix it?" There was a question mark on the end of that statement. That's because my mother sees *EVERYTHING*!

I just looked at him with the *really?* face. You know the one. REEEally? But I had no choice at this point but to hope she had walked through the sun porch, right past the tree and not seen the top hanging over like a chicken with its head partially cut off. Suuure. Once more into the breech as they say. So as we pulled up the long driveway I noticed that mom was sitting on her sun porch—it's her favorite spot, indeed, the reason she bought the house to start with—and she was staring at the chicken, I mean tree. Great. So here we come, dad and I, quietly sneaking in the door, right in front of her, waiting for the hammer to fall. Here's how the *conversation* went—*inquisition* would be more accurate:

Mom: "Where have y'all been?" In a tone that suggested she had already surmised the answer.

Dad, "Oh, (pause), up to the store to get a few things."

Mom, "Like what?" At this point, I *knew* she knew. She was just toying with us. It was uncomfortable. Kind of like what Mary, Queen of Scots must have felt like with her neck on the block, or a mouse backed into a corner by our cat, Squishy Kitty—she's a real killer.

Dad said, "Just a couple things from the Dollar Tree," —we were in a hurry so we didn't go all the way to Lowe's hardware.

"You bought some *war* didn't you!?" Silence and a pause.

"Well, if you think, you're gonna *war* that tree back together you best just DRAG IT TO THE STREET RIGHT NOW! I don't know why you even thought about it!" She got up and walked into the kitchen, much like The Duke, John Wayne, used to do in his movies when he would throw down his half-smoked cigarette and walk away with a parting shot. Translation, "The conversation is OVER."

She left my dad and I looking back and forth at each other with the look of two idiots who've been shot between the eyes but haven't bothered to fall down dead yet. Then we got out the *war* and tried to fix the tree. Well, we couldn't let mom win! Though admittedly, I'd known it was a fool thing to try to begin with, but if it worked in 1975, surely it would work now! It did not. So we quietly admitted defeat and dragged it to the street.

So the lesson is, if it's useless, worthless, or just cluttering up your Hobbit-hole, follow Mama Bivans's advice. JUST DRAG IT TO THE STREET RIGHT NOW! Or you can reuse, recycle, or pass it along, unless it's a headless chicken, Christmas tree. If you don't, I'll send mom over to tell you in person, and you don't want that!

Speaking of cleaning out clutter, let's start our tour through the house in the pantry, where I'm sure there are some orcish things lurking.

# 23

# BILBO'S LARDER: BETTER FOOD, BETTER LIFE

"And raspberry jam and apple-tart," said Bifur.

"And mince-pies and cheese," said Bofur.

"And pork-pie and salad," said Bombur.

"And more cakes, and ale, and coffee, if you don't mind," called the other dwarfs through the door.

"Put on a few eggs, there's a good fellow!" Gandalf called after him, as the Hobbit stumped off to the pantries. "And just bring out the cold chicken and pickles!"

"Seems to know as much about the inside of my larders as I do myself!" thought Mr Baggins, who was feeling positively flummoxed, and was beginning to wonder whether a most wretched adventure had not come right into his house.

Humor keeps us alive. Humor and food. Don't forget food. You can go a week without laughing.
— Joss Whedon

Luckily for Bilbo, when all those hungry, sweaty Dwarves showed up uninvited he was well prepared for his unexpected party, with plenty of food supplies. We should all be so lucky and, if not so lucky, then at least prepared. The most impactful thing we can probably do to change the world for the better is to eat better food. This may sound a bit weird, or overly simple, but it is probably the most important thing we can do. At the root of the world's problems—as we've enumerated in Part I—is food. It was the Agricultural Revolution that kicked off civilization and the idea that the *world belongs to us, and we were meant to rule it*. Modern, corporate agriculture is the biggest polluter and waster of our water supplies while at the same time burning up fossil fuels and spraying them on the very food we eat. Corporations like Monsanto are attempting to dominate the food supply of the World by engineering the staple crops and eliminating their competitors while simultaneously corrupting the governments and legal systems of the Earth.

All this can be changed simply by changing *what we eat, how we raise it*, and *who we buy it from*. Hobbits can do this, and really, no one else can. We cannot depend on our governments or business leaders to lead on this. It would be nice if they would but as a group they have proven, time and again, that they are incapable or unwilling to do so. It is up to us my gentle Hobbits, to Save the Earth. And we should begin with our food. Because other than sleeping and relieving ourselves in the bathroom, the one thing most of us do **every single day**, is eat.

Yeah, I know some people, usually super skinny people, who occasionally say things like, "You know, I plumb forgot to eat yesterday!" What? Huh? Run that by me again? You *forgot* to eat? How does one do that? Hell if I know. I'm sure no self respecting Hobbit would ever consider such a thing, much less do it. Well, I can tell you from my own experience that I have never forgotten to eat. Ok, maybe occasionally I'll get totally involved in some cool project, working my butt off during the middle of the day and mentally forget to eat, or not think about food for a while but let me tell you something, my **stomach** ain't ever forgotten to eat! It reminds me in no uncertain terms, "Hey you! I'm **hungry down here! Feed me!**" No, this Hobbit doesn't skip too many meals, trust me. If you're reading this book, I doubt you do either. In fact, I can't read Tolkien without snacking my ass off. The professor should have developed his own line of potato chips or something. He would have made an even bigger killin'.

Since we eat every day, and it's the fuel that keeps us alive and moving, I'm sure we all think a lot about what we eat, right? Unfortunately, if you're like me you're just too busy to give it much thought. Though I think a lot of us these days are really starting to wonder just what the heck is in our food. Sometimes I'm afraid to look too closely. Health problems are out of control, especially in the U.S. Food allergies are ubiquitous. I'm 48 years old, so I grew up in the 70s and 80s. I don't remember a single child in school with me in the 70s, heck even in the 80s, being allergic to any foods. Now that's not to say there weren't any but I don't remember it. Part of that might be the way I chose to live my 'Tweens' of course; I spent a few too many days in the Green Dragon, if you know what I mean, so my memory might be foggy on the whole 70s decade, but I don't think so.

No, I don't think it's just me, or my nights in the pub. When I bring this topic up to my friends I get the same reaction. It seems that the allergy thing really didn't come into focus until sometime in the 90s. This is roughly about the time that the big food corporations, like Monsanto and others, started tinkering with the genetic codes of the food supply, especially the big cash crops like corn, soybean, and cotton. Why is cotton important to food crops? Because guess what crop gets rotated with cotton regularly? Peanuts! So all of a sudden, in the 90s, you started to hear about kids dying of anaphylactic shock from eating a peanut-butter sandwich or being in the same room as someone else eating it. Turns out, peanuts planted in cotton fields are absorbing the glysophate pesticides used on the GMO cotton crops — RoundUp being the number one culprit. As covered earlier, GMOs are everywhere now, mainly because corn and its derivatives are in all of our packaged and preserved foods! Try finding something in a box, bottle, or can that doesn't have high fructose corn syrup in it. I dare ya. And good luck with that unless you're already shopping in Whole Foods or a local co-op.

Ok, GMOs are bad. I'm just gonna go out on a limb there and say it. You can argue with me if you want but I will just concede that we disagree and let you keep eating them. So, I'm sure you're asking, "If we don't buy our groceries from the big chains and the corporations that sell to them, then where do we get them? It's too inconvenient to have to drive around to ten different stores, looking for organic stuff that costs twice as much as the regular stuff!" To this I would reply that there are various options of places to shop, depending on where you live. For instance, stores like Whole Foods and Fresh Market are expanding all over the U.S. Grocery Cooperatives, Co-ops, are also expanding all over the U.S., and in other countries.

Whole Foods is moving to make all their products certified organic in the next couple years. While not all the food at Fresh Market is organic, lots of it is. Some foods, that are not yet or do not want to go through the process of certification as organic, are certifying that they are at least GMO free. Also, a lot of local farmers in the U.S. and around the world are actually farming and producing meats, eggs, and cheese organically, but aren't certified as organic, which is an expensive process. In such cases, it is worth taking some time to research their practices. Look them up online, or call them up and ask them how they raise their crops or animals. Ask such questions as, "Do you use any artificial fertilizers, pesticides, herbicides?" For meat producers ask "How are your animals treated? Are they allowed to roam free in pastures, as opposed to being cooped up in a barn with little sunlight, air, or space to move? What do they eat? Are they given any hormones or antibiotics?" Hormones and antibiotic use in livestock production is common in non-organic operations. What these things do to our meat, dairy and eggs, is hotly debated but there is growing consensus that there are myriad negative effects on human health.

## Price vs. Costs

The other problem brought up by most people, myself included, is the price of organics in comparison to non-organic, or as I call it, Orcish Food. The average American family spends between $150 and $300 per week on food, most of that being of the Sarumanic variety. What people don't take into consideration are the *hidden* costs of Orcish foods. Most food is shipped on average, about 1200 miles before it arrives in your supermarket!

All this shipping takes time, time in which the produce is losing nutrients, beginning to spoil and probably absorbing chemicals from the plastic bag it's in.

That's not to mention the chemicals sprayed on it to keep the bugs off of it in the field, the weeds from choking the life out of it, and the chemical fertilizers pumped into the depleted soil in order to allow the poor plant to grow in the first place. All of that is headed to your table, after tons and tons of fossil fuels were consumed to grow it, harvest it, package it, cool it, and ship it to your big box grocery store. It boggles the mind when you actually look at all the waste that goes into shipping food. Most of this waste could be eliminated simply by buying food grown near your home, by farmers who care about their customers, because, in many cases, they get to know them personally.

Yes, the effort to eat real food takes more time and effort. We're all busy, but if we don't have time to make sure we're not eating poisons, what do we have time for? How long will that time last if we sacrifice our health? As mentioned above, most of our produce loses nutrients during it's 1200 mile journey to our table and that is subtracted from the original total of nutrients — much lower than local, organic produce to start with — because most of it is picked *before* it's ripe so that it won't spoil before it makes it to market. Much of it is also sprayed with other chemicals to make it ripen just about the time it hits the shelf. All these chemicals are part of our meal, every time we sit down to eat.

So, if the food has lower nutrients to start with then shouldn't *that* be figured into the true *costs* of our food? I mean, when you buy food aren't you buying *nutrients* and *calories*? That is what we need from food, after all. And if Orcish food is lower in both, and it usually is, then you have to buy more of it to get the same amount of the essentials that you get from a slightly higher priced, local, organic equivalent. That should make you go 'hmmmmm,' I reckon. All of this *convenience* ads up to a lot of garbage, if you ask me. As Mother Bivans used to tell me, and I'm sure yours did too, "Haste, makes waste!" Or as Pippen told his companions who wanted to cut through the Old Forest to save time and avoid the Black Riders, "Short cuts, make long delays." It's simply not true that the big stores are more convenient, or cheaper, not when you add up *ALL* the costs.

The beauty of buying your food from local producers is manifold. For one, your money stays in your local community, supports a farmer, co-op or farmer's market that is selling quality produce, not overly processed, orcish food. That money is more likely to be reinvested in the local economy, not shipped off to some corporate bank in New York, or to suppliers on the other side of the earth. If we want to make a difference, not only for the planet but for our own health, eating better food is the best place to start.

# Tips to Improve and de-Orcify Your Panty

### Organic is King

Or the Return of the King, if you will. Also make sure it is *NON-GMO*. This is a goal we should aim for, for all our food. If it is certified organic then you're headed in the right direction. But unfortunately, the USDA is lowering the bar for what is considered organic, so it pays to do a little more research. Once you've found an organic version of a particular product, then examine it further. What do other customers say about the product? Is it truly organic, or are they cheating somehow? Is it packaged in a sustainable way? Over-packaging means waste that will either have to be composted, reused/recycled, or will end up in a landfill, or in the ocean like our plastic milk jug. Unfortunately, many organic products are still being offered in plastic containers. This is probably due to convenience. It is our job to contact these suppliers and ask them, as their loyal customers, to please try to find sustainable alternatives. Many of them, maybe all of them, know that this is an issue and are working to find solutions. There are companies already doing it, so the scales are tipping but there's a long way to go still

### Natural Practices

If there is not an organic version of what you want, look for alternatives that are at least grown in a natural way. The term *natural* is so overused when it comes to food that you cannot trust the label on the box to determine whether or not it is natural. Essentially it means nothing. Companies have been using it for years to flat out lie to us. When I see the word *natural* on a product I assume that there's nothing natural about it and that in fact, they are trying to dazzle me with bull-hockey. You have to do some research. Google the product and see what the company website has to say about the source of their products. This does take time, but remember, you don't have to change everything all at once though the urge to do so will be strong. I know it has been for us. Patience and I are really in the beginning stages of doing this ourselves so we have to resist this urge because it can lead to despair and that never ends well, just ask Denethor.

Some *naturally* grown products are actually organic but for whatever reasons, usually the cost, the producer hasn't gone through the process of certification. The best research, of course is to meet the producer and talk to her about their farming practices. Maybe you can even go see the farm! That's best, and it's fun, as well as educational. This is something that kids usually love, after you get through the whining stage that inevitably comes when prying them away from their video games. Of course, to talk to the farmer, she needs to be nearby unless you're independently wealthy and can just jump on a jet to Ireland or France or Italy, which isn't particularly Hobbity.

## Shop in the Shire

After finding organic or natural products, the next thing to look at on the label is the *where* section. Where was your product produced? The closer the better. I don't expect you to have a map of Middle Earth in your pocket all the time so you can plot out the locations of all the farmer Maggot's—and I've always thought that was an odd name for a farmer—in your state, but if the producer is, in fact, *in* your state that's a good start. Or maybe, like me, you live close to a border—for us that's Wisconsin, think *cheese*—then you can extend the boundaries over those borders. Don't carry the local thing too far.

Sometimes what you want/need just doesn't come from your area. There are three things you can do when this is the case. One, <u>do without</u> until the item is in season where you live. This is after all, how our parents or at least our grandparents and great grandparents used to live. Two, buy an organic, sustainable product from far away. I do this, at least now I do, especially when it comes to cherry tomatoes—I have a weakness. Three, you can grow your own, which for me means building and maintaining a green house since I live in what I call Freezin'-Yankeeland, or Minne*snow*ta. More on growing your own a bit later.

### Beef

Beef is a *tough* one—sorry, I couldn't resist a cheesy pun about chewing. The first thing to avoid—and I hope this has already become obvious—is fast food chains. You will *NOT* find organic, natural, or sustainable beef or any other kind of *real* food in McDonald's. At least not yet. If they want to survive the Hobbit Revolution, then they better start cleaning up their act quickly. Most beef in fast food restaurants comes from South America where ranchers—locals trying to survive in an altered world—are encouraged, nay, pressured into clearing rain-forests at an alarming rate to make room for raising cattle for the U.S. fast food market. Their practices are completely destructive. In fact, it is beef that is clearing the most rainforest every year, more so than coffee or other crops—though they are destructive as well.

One of the biggest impacts you can have on the environment, global warming, and animal habitat, not to mention your family's health is to refuse to eat fast food beef. While you're at it, refuse eating anything from fast food joints. Instead, join the Slow Food movement! The Slow Food movement is dedicated to local, sustainable farming and eating practices. If you choose to eat beef, and hey, I do sometimes— even though the price is exorbitant these days—then follow the basic guidelines when you buy it: organic, natural, local. Most co-op grocery stores carry organic or at least naturally produced beef, as well as other cuts of meat, and you won't believe the quality. There is just no comparison.

## Coffee and Tea

In the Western World, Europe and the U.S. in particular, we love our tea and coffee. So did the Hobbits, and why not? It gives us a lift when we need it and what could be better with roasted pork or Hobbit fried chicken on a Sunday afternoon, than an ice cold glass of South Farthing Sweet Iced Tea? Nothing I reckon. I drink it constantly. It's one of my vices I guess. I'm not a coffee drinker though Patience, is. I never acquired a taste for it. I usually tell people that I love the smell but fortunately not the taste, as I have enough vices already to keep me busy. Unfortunately, most of what we consume is produced in very unsustainable ways and has done irreversible damage to ecosystems around the world, especially in South and Central America, India, and China where a great deal of the coffee and tea is grown.

In order to maximize production, coffee plantations in the Americas clear cut huge sections of rainforest so they can grow the coffee in the sun. The topsoil in the rainforest is not deep, so the coffee crop quickly depletes the soil in a season or two. Then they have to cut down more forest to grow more coffee. As mentioned earlier, the rain-forests of the world used to produce most of our oxygen and at the same time remove CO2, a greenhouse gas, from the atmosphere. The rain-forests are also home to uncountable species of animals and birds.

Many of the beautiful songbirds that we enjoy in North America spend their winters in the rain-forests of Central and South America. Thanks to clear cutting over decades, some species, like the cute little, Hobbity hummingbirds are declining in number because they are losing their winter habitat, as well as many of the food sources and shelters that lie along their migration routes. Luckily, coffee doesn't have to be grown in the sun. There are an increasing number of producers, growing organic, shade-grown coffee. Please, please, please, if you drink coffee, make sure it is shade-grown. Ask your coffee shop, do your research. This simple change, if everyone did it, or a least a lot of people, could swing the coffee industry into more sustainable practices.

Tea production is a similar situation. Most of it is grown in Asia, or India, and for a long time has been destructive to the ecosystems there, in particular because of the use of chemical fertilizers, pesticides, and herbicides. Also, pretty much all of the popular brands of tea, ship their product in little mesh bags that are coated in nothing other than plastic, to hold the bag together. So every time you brew a cup or gallon of tea, you're drinking plastic. Yuck. I stopped buying my old brand a couple of months ago when I discovered this fact and went looking for other options. It is really this situation that got me back on the organic, sustainable trail, though I had been thinking about it for a long time. There are organic tea options out there and most co-ops, or organic food stores, carry them. If not, you can ask them to, or look for a local specialty tea shop. Call them and ask them if they have organic teas. You can also order it online.

### Brewing coffee and tea

I've been giving this one some thought lately since I'm trying to slowly eliminate the plastics in my house, starting in the kitchen. We have a drip coffee machine which works fine, but most of it is plastic, including the part that comes into contact with the coffee most: the filter cup. I would like to find another option. One is a French press, which is usually made of glass, and metal, though most of them have some plastic on them: handles and lid. Patience doesn't seem to like the coffee it makes, so we're still with the drip one for now.

As for tea, I shamefully have an ice tea maker which my mom thinks is kind of silly. It is I reckon. It's entirely plastic and I'm really considering parting with it. My mom used to make tea in a pot on the stove when I was growing up. Of course, she then poured it into an empty, plastic milk jug, ahhh the good ole 70s. Plastic all around. What I need to do is just find a kettle, maybe cast iron, and steep it either in the kettle or in a pyrex glass measuring cup or something. I'm working on it. If you want to read more about South Farthing Sweet Iced Tea, read about it on my blog, the link to the recipe and instructions is in the *recipe* section. Of course, once you brew it, you have to sweeten it, because it's not tea if you don't. I'm from the South, remember. Trust me.

## Corn syrup, NO

Avoid any product with high fructose corn syrup in it. These are almost all made from non-organic, GMO corn. There may be some organic versions out there but unless it's certified, I wouldn't eat it. Use organic sugar, stevia, or local, raw honey. Unfortunately almost all sweetened drinks these days use orcish corn syrup, not to mention pretty much any processed food in a box, bag, can or bottle.

# Flour

Wheat is one of the biggest GMO crops, next to corn. There is some new evidence that suggests that a lot of the wheat/gluten allergies that have sprung up in the last 20 years or so, are linked to the tinkering that companies like Monsanto have done to our wheat supply. Even before they began screwing around with it, scientists had been cross-breeding wheat for over 60 years. Dr. William Davis, a cardiologist and author of *Wheat Belly: Lose the Wheat, Lose the Weight and Find Your Way Back to Health,* argues that what we use as flour for our bread, pancakes, pasta, biscuits, and dumplins has been so altered genetically, it barely resembles wheat at all anymore. I am currently working on switching over to organic, GMO free, non-wheat flours, because I love biscuits! And I'm not talking about those dry, cookie things that they make in England, I'm talking about big ole fluffy, Southern biscuits with loads of butter dripping out of them: no scraping butter on my biscuits, man. Organic alternatives to wheat, like spelt, and barley are available in most grocery stores and certainly in co-ops and places like Whole Foods. I've even seen spelt pasta in our co-op. Recently they even began carrying a new pasta made from Einkorn, an ancient grain, like spelt, that hasn't been hybridized to oblivion. If I figure out how to make fluffy biscuits with one of these alternatives, I'll make sure to put the recipe up on my website: www.stevebivans.com.

# Beer, Wine and Spirits

Most of us Hobbits love to drink and socialize, so a few words on booze is appropriate. Many of the beers brewed in the U.S. use GMO ingredients, especially corn derivatives. In general, if you don't know, assume they are probably GMO and do your research. Many European beers do not use GMOs but are not certified organic. There are a growing number of breweries producing organic and non-GMO beers. Look for them, and ask your supplier to carry them. There are also a growing number of organic wines available. Hard liquor, especially my favorite, bourbon, are many times made with corn which more often than not is of the GMO variety these days. Many of the chemicals in the corn would probably be boiled off during the distillation process but purchasing them means putting money into the pockets of Monsanto. I'm still working on a solution to this one.

### Brew Your Own!

Of course, brewing your own beer or making your own wine is an option, if a bit labor intensive. I've done it in the past but it does require some specialized gear. It's not overly expensive stuff but there is a good deal of work in making beer. Wine is easier, or so I'm told. There is also mead. Mead, made famous by the Vikings, is basically a brewed, honey wine, which can be combined with fruits and allowed to ferment and mellow over a period of months. If you're interested in making your own subscribe to my blog where I post recipes for lots of things. I will be posting one for mead soon, if it's not already up by the time this book goes to print.

# Where to Find Good Food

If you don't already know where to find good food, do a search online for organic grocers, farmer's markets, and co-op grocery stores, there's probably one closer than you think. Also check out the resources section at the end of the book for more help on that.

## Hobbits Co-operate!

Co-op grocery stores are member owned. Most of them will allow anyone to walk in off the street and shop, however, so just walk into one and check it out! The one where Patience and I shop, Mississippi Market, is super friendly and helpful, and totally non-orcish. In fact, it's quite Shire-like. I'm lucky. The one where I shop is literally right across the street from the school that Duke attends so I can pick him up in the afternoon, pop in there, grab the things I need in my cloth shopping bag, and before you know it I'm back in my Hobbit-hole ready to cook dinner.

I shopped there for a few months before I finally said to myself, "Self, uhhh why don't you just join already? You shop here 3-4 times a week for cryin' out loud!" So I did. You pay a membership fee—mine was under $100 for life—and you're a stockholder in a local grocery store! You get member discounts and specials, and you're doing something to help save the Earth! And they have great organic choices for food. My favorite is the chocolate milk from Castle Rock Dairies. It even comes in old fashioned glass bottles, which are returnable! Imagine that! In fact, one day, I came back with about 5 or 6 of them, turned them in, bought some bread, and maybe some tea—which is sold in bulk—and the cashier guy said something like, "That will be minus $8.56. Would you like that on your card or in cash?" To which I gave a double take before it set in. After a few seconds, or years, I realized that he was trying to pay ME back! I said, "Uhhhh cash I reckon! THAT'S never happened before!" as I laughed, and walked out with more money than I came in with.

## Request it

If your grocery store, or co-op, doesn't have what you're looking for, just ask them if they will consider stocking it! To make the process quicker and easier for them, do the research ahead of time. Find a source for the product, preferable local, and give the store the information. If they care about your business, they'll take your request seriously. If they don't, stop giving them your money!

## CSAs: Buy it from the Farmer

Community Supported Agriculture groups, or SSAs — Shire Supported Agriculture groups, as they should be called — are another way to find great produce. CSAs allow farmers to sell products directly to customers who get together and place bulk orders. The produce is delivered to one of the customers' houses or picked up at the farm and then distributed from a prearranged central location. This cuts out middle men all together and is a good option to save money, especially if you don't have a co-op grocery store or local farmer's market. Do an internet search for CSA — you might want to add *food* to that search, or you'll end up with stuff about the Civil War — and see how many there are near you! I'm guessing you're gonna be surprised.

## Farmer Maggot's Market

Now, I don't know about you, but I've often wondered what the heck ole Tolkien was thinking when he named the nice, helpful farmer who's mushrooms were a magnet to little Hobbits? Really J.R.R.? Maggot? What an unfortunate name to be born with, especially if you're going to be a farmer. But apparently, he was a hell of a farmer and a friendly one to boot, so we'll overlook his name. One of the best places to find organic produce is a local farmer's market. There are now 8,144 farmer's markets in the U.S. alone, and they are even more popular in most European countries where it's been a tradition since at least the Middle Ages, and probably long, long before.

The markets in the Twin Cities where I live are amazing and there are so many I can't count them. We even have one like three blocks from our new house, which was one reason we chose the neighborhood. Make sure to take cash, as many do not take credit/debit cards, though some do. Some of the larger ones have ATMs installed. Some are also issuing their own *tokens* which helps to raise funds to keep the market going. Don't forget! Take your cloth shopping bags, non-plastic containers for bulk items — more on that later — and an appetite, because many markets also sell cooked food!

One of my favorite places anywhere is the Minneapolis Farmer's Market. When I first moved up to Yankeeland, from

North Carolina, about seven years ago I discovered it thanks to a friend of mine. The first time I went it was early in the morning in the spring, which means June up here and I was overwhelmed by the sights, sounds, and smells. I had a hard time holding back tears of joy as a strolled through the aisles jammed with people. There was fresh corn roasting, sweet rolls, hot mini doughnuts, cheeses, and salsas to sample, flowers for sale but my favorite spot of all is at the very end of the market, on the very end of the last row, next to the street: the Tollefson Pork stand. They have some of the best, naturally-raised pork I've ever had, especially their Italian Sausage—I know, a friendly, blonde-haired, blue-eyed Norwegian family making Italian sausage—the irony is not lost on me either. And they cook it on the grill *RIGHT THERE*! Not only do they make the sausage, bacon, ham steaks, and several other pork products, but they raise the pigs on their own farm, feed them a natural diet free from hormones and allow their pigs to roam around.

These are the kinds of jewels you can find at your local farmer's market. The other benefit of a farmer's market is that you meet other people there, talk to the actual producers of the food you will be eating and through this join a real Shire, something seriously lacking in the modern world, especially in the U.S. Too often we rush from work or rush out on Saturday morning to get the shopping done because it's such a chore, and it is if you shop at large grocery stores where you have to walk half a mile to get from one decent product to the next past aisles full of processed orc food.

Just a few blocks from our new house in St Paul, is the Westside Farmer's Market which opened last year. It's tiny, I mean so tiny it's cute. But the people there are so nice that it's one of the reasons we decided on the house we bought. We managed to shop there a couple of times before they shut down for the winter, and we've totally enjoyed this second season, getting to know the vendors, listening to local musicians, and meeting our neighbors. In fact, I will be making a community soup for the Harvest Festival this year. Many of the customers and vendors all bring vegetables and one vendor is bringing chickens, and we make two huge pots of soup for everyone! There's music, face-painting, a garlic-growing class, and I'm going to read some of this book in public for the first time! Shopping for food should be fun and engaging, not like walking the Mines of Moria.

### Hunting and Fishing: Kill it Strider!

My best friend back home in NC, Keith, is one of those East-Coast-Yankees-turned-Southern-Redneck types. When I first met him he was a wild, bullet-proof, hippy, shot out of a cannon from somewhere in Connecticut or New York. Since then—that was a long time ago—he's become a mellowed-out, horse-ridin', chicken-raisin', organic farmer, and avid hunter. He's Strider, all day long. He can kill a deer with a bow, a gun, probably a club, and can clean it, cook it, and live off of it. Just don't let him drag you through a snowy wood at Christmastime carrying a 20 pound flashlight and a 12 foot spear tracking wild boar through Br'r Rabbit's Briar Patch—but that's a story for another day. Entire books have been written on hunting and fishing and I'm neither qualified nor inclined to reinvent those wheels. Maybe one day I'll help Keith write one. Suffice it to say that if you have the training, talent, and gear to hunt and fish, there are few better ways to feed a family, and while Hobbits didn't seem to emphasize wild game, their companion Strider, kept them alive in the wild on his talents with a bow and his trusty knife. So if you're a Strider, like Keith, go kill a wild boar. Just don't call me until it's time to barbeque it! I'm an expert at that! I'll even bring the beer.

# Eating Out: Dinner at the Green Dragon

"Well," you say, "All that is fine and good, eating at home but what if we want to go out to eat?" A very good question indeed, and a tougher one to tackle. To some extent, if we want to eat away from home, and Patience, Duke—that's Patience's son—and I love to eat out, we have to take into consideration that most people are not yet on the bandwagon when it comes to organic, sustainable food, especially the restaurant industry but that is changing, and I think it will change a great deal more in the next few years.

My first advice is to forget about fast food, as I've already mentioned. It pretty much sucks anyway, and it's orcish. Slow down and enjoy your food when you decide to go out. My basic philosophy when it comes to eating out is, locally owned first, then sit down chains second. Avoid fast food unless actual starvation is a risk and there is no other option. The main reason for eating at local establishments is that you can get to know the owners and the employees and make connections with them. Find places that have good food that you like, good, friendly service and then make them a standard place to go.

We have one a place like that in St Paul: Bennett's Chop and Railhouse. I have enjoyed everything I've ever had there. We go there often, in fact, one day last December, I went in there after work — it's just a couple blocks away — to hit their happy hour, left to go pick up Patience, who decided she wasn't ready to go so I went back IN for another drink, then later, after picking up Duke we decided to go back AGAIN, for dinner. So the owners know us quite well now. This is the kind of relationship you want to have with the places you shop and eat; it's like Cheers, if you're old enough to remember that TV show from the 80s. You know, a place where "everybody knows your name." Once you've established a relationship then you can subtly plant seeds in the owner's ear to make little changes that will improve the quality of their food — organic/sustainable produce, reduce costs — get rid of disposables/plastics/one use items like straws and paper napkins, and make them a model of what a modern restaurant can be.

Restaurants employing these practices can turn it into profits by promoting the quality of the food and the positive impact it has on the local farming community and economy, not to mention the health of its customers. I hope that one day I can get Bennett's on that track. Their food is excellent but moving to more organic and local produce would improve it and boost their image, while returning money to the local economy. You can do the same with your favorite restaurants. Show your loyalty, then gradually ask them about changes to their menus, or other practices that would help make them more sustainable.

**Some things restaurants can do to improve their sustainability:**

- Serve more organic, natural, sustainable meat and produce, especially from local producers.

- Donate leftovers to local soup kitchens and homeless shelters.

- Cut down on *one use* items, especially plastic ones: tableware, napkins, straws, cups, plates, paper towels. Instead buy and reuse real stuff. It's okay to carry straws but make it part of the waitstaff's training to *ask* before they hand out straws. That also goes for water at the table. Water is a precious, waning resource on our planet and too much of it goes to waste in restaurants. Staff should ask first before pouring water. Explain why you do it to your customers.

- Use cloth towels, aprons, table-cloths, and napkins. Rent them from a laundry service.

- Extra mile things: Cut down on power usage by buying more efficient equipment, air conditioners, heating systems. Hey, why not go solar or wind? There are some restaurants doing just that. Izzy's, a local ice cream store here in St. Paul is one of them. To date, about 1/3 of their power comes from solar!

Be gentle, subtle if possible, and always tactful when suggesting changes to a business owner. They have lots of things to worry about, so try to anticipate the things that will be a stumbling block for them when implementing new ideas, and suggest ways to smooth that out. Remember to point out how it will save them money and make their establishment an even more enjoyable place to eat.

### Hobbit Dine-Out Bag:

Sometimes, especially when traveling, or eating at new places, we have little control over the practices of the places we choose to eat. In those instances it's best to be prepared. I'm thinking about putting together a Dine-out Bag to keep in the car, or to take on long trips that would help to mitigate some of the waste generated in restaurants. Here are some ideas of what to put in one:

- **Glass jars or take home/storage containers for leftovers.** This is a big one. How many plastic/styrofoam containers have we thrown away in our lifetimes? Ugh! I don't even like to think about it, or where they are now. Half the time the food goest to waste before we eat it anyway. So, either refuse the leftovers or bring your own container. I've done it recently and had no problems with it. Most of the time, the waitstaff think it's the coolest thing they've ever seen.

- **Flatware.** Keep some stainless knives, forks, and spoons with you in your bag just in case all the restaurant has is plastic stuff.

- **Glass, or Stainless Straws:** Beth Terry, in her book, *Plastic-Free,* talks about her glass straw that she ordered from a company called GlassDharma. I don't really use straws unless I'm drinking a frozen piña colada on the beach. So when my drink comes with a straw it ends up on the table then in the garbage, then Gandalf only knows where after that, hopefully not floating around the Atlantic somewhere. Try to remember to tell the waiter that you don't want straws. After all, there's a big hole in the top of the glass to drink from. I know some people have teeth that are sensitive to cold, so in that case maybe one of those glass straws? I actually found stainless steel straws in my local co-op grocery store, so there are options.

- **Cloth napkins:** Bring enough for everyone to save on the paper ones at the table. We have a bunch of second-hand wash cloths we got from a thrift store that we use at home and sometimes pack to take with us.

- **Mugs/Bottles/Cups:** Keep coffee mugs and stainless steel/glass water bottles in the bag too, to avoid the paper/styrofoam cups in many places.

- **Plates?:** I would suggest plates too but that might be pushing it a bit too far, unless the restaurant is one of those redneck BBQ joints where the only good BBQ comes from, then you might need to bring everything because they almost always use disposables.

## Picnicking in the Shire

One of the best places to eat, is outdoors. Who doesn't love a picnic? Well, there are the pesky bugs, and wind, and sometimes heat, and maybe the occasional grain of sand in your turkey sandwich Get it? SANDwich? But seriously, not enough people do this anymore. Drag the kids away from their Xbox, leash the puppy, leave the kitties to rule over the *hole*—you know, like they do 24/7, pack up some *vittles*, throw'em in the trunk with the Frisbee and head out!

Do try to follow the basic rules you follow at home, though. Take your Hobbit Dine-out Bag; don't leave a bunch of waste in the can at the park, much of which seems to blow out all over the place anyway. If you bring it with you, take it away with you. Enjoy being outdoors. Soak up some sun and fresh air. The air in most houses, are 10-50% more toxic than the air outside! Get outside and *BREATHE*!

And in glorious conclusion, if you want to be a good Hobbit you have to eat good food, and drink good drinks. If you follow the, buy-organic-sustainable-local, motto then you'll also be striking a blow against Saruman's evil food corporations trying to poison us and our environment! Food and drink should be enjoyable and good for you. Slow down and savor life as a Hobbit would and always remember what Thorin Oakenshield said on his deathbed, "If more of us valued food and cheer and song above hoarded gold, it would be a merrier world." — *The Hobbit, The Return Journey*

If you choose only *one* chapter of this book to follow, I hope it's this one. Work on the quality and source of your food. It will strike a blow against the corporate farms and chemical companies who want to monopolize the World's food supply. More importantly than that, food is who you are. You are a Hobbit, and Hobbits are made of food. Shouldn't you be made of the best food you can find? Cost is an issue for many of us, myself included. But that should not deter you from your ultimate goal of eating fresh, healthy, non-toxic food. If buying good organic produce is too expensive, consider growing some of your own! That's what Sam Gamgee would do. We'll return to that topic later, after we've finished our tour of the inside of our Hobbit-hole.

Are you overwhelmed now? Maybe you're feeling a bit anxious, even angry, after discovering what's in your food? Do you feel like you've been lied to by the companies you trusted? The companies you thought were wholesome? Join the club. So did I. It's time to break up with them.

# 24

# Breaking Up with Grandma: Saying Goodbye to the Brands We Love

Théoden opened his mouth as if to speak, but he said nothing He looked up at the face of Saruman with its dark solemn eyes bent down upon him, and then to Gandalf at his side; and he seemed to hesitate. Gandalf made no sign... The Riders stirred at first, murmuring with approval of the words of Saruman; and then they too were silent, as men **spell-bound**. It seemed to them that Gandalf had never spoken so fair and fittingly to their lord. Rough and proud now seemed all his dealing with Théoden. And **over their hearts crept a shadow, the fear of a great danger**: the end of the Mark in a darkness to which Gandalf was driving them, while Saruman stood beside a door of escape, holding it half open so that a ray of light came through. [italics/bold, mine] —*LOTR*: II, *The Voice of Saruman*

If we understand the mechanism and motives of the group mind, is it not possible to control and regiment the masses according to our will without their knowing about it? The recent practice of propaganda has proved that it is possible, at least up to a certain point and within certain limits. —Edward Bernays, *Propaganda,* p.47 [excerpt from Wikipedia]

You can thank Patience for this chapter. When I began that binge-reading period of research to write this book she caught the tsunami of angst, fear, anger, frustration, depression, and grief that I set into motion by plunging into the ocean of negativity that threatens to overwhelm our world. Like I said in the beginning of this tome, I was thoroughly depressed by the process. And so was Patience. Yet there was one thing in the process that didn't affect me to the same degree that it did her and so it never occurred to me to discuss it in the book. But thankfully, Patience hit me with it one day not long ago when she was reading through the book, proofreading and marking through my commas—you can thank her for that, too. We were both sitting in the office one afternoon when she just blurted out, "You need to write a chapter about the emotions that arise when people discover that the food they eat is full of poisons and isn't really good for them like they always thought!"

"Hmmm," I said, "I guess you're right. I never thought about it that much."

"Yeahhh! You totally need to write about that!" she said. "When you first started all of this, I remember just being, pissed off! I was like, 'what do you *mean* Betty Crocker isn't good for me!? My *mom* fed us Betty Crocker! My *grandma* used it! How can this be right? They've been lying to us all this time? All these companies that my grandmother, my mom, and I put our faith in? I *trusted them!*'"

"Wow, I guess it never really dawned on me that people would have such a powerful reaction." I said.

"Well, I was pissed off! Then depressed, and sad! It was like someone in the family had died. It was actual *grief!* Over the break up with a brand! You need to talk about that, and about how we're all taken in by the psychology of advertising and how that's been going on for decades, almost a hundred years, and how it's like Saruman and his silver tongue spewing silken lies to lull us into a spell!"

"Damn. That's a great idea!" I said.

So you can thank Patience for what I'm about to say. Thanks to her, I am writing the final chapter of the book, at least the final one to *write*, not of course the final chapter in sequence.

# The Pain of Truth

All of those emotions that Patience brought up are natural and to be expected. If you've made it this far into the book you're probably already feeling them. I'm sorry for that. The reason I never thought about writing this chapter is that I guess I experienced those feelings so long ago that I barely remember it anymore. I've been looking at the world and its problems most of my adult life so I've become somewhat anesthetized to the angst and pain, especially the grief that it causes in others when they discover the negative things going on around them. It *is* painful, however. I do remember it even if it is a distant memory.

### Pain, Anger, and Trust: the Loss of Identity

In some ways this realization is a shattering of reality itself. The things you once trusted are now suspect. We've been lied to. Trust has been broken. We feel ignorant, even stupid. "How did we not *know*!?" We feed our children these brands! Our mother fed *us* with them! Our grandmothers fed *our moms* with them! If we can't trust Coke, Pepsi, McDonald's, Kellogg's, General Mills, Betty Crocker, Hershey's, Nestlés, and Jimmy Dean— who *can we trust*? In fact, who *are we*? And that is where the rubber meets the road, and at the heart of the matter. We *identify* with the brands we use, especially the brands we *EAT*! Our very sense of self is tied up in the products we purchase and feed our families every day. They are *part of us* in a very real way. Patience told me that the feeling you have when you first find out is not unlike the feeling an abused spouse goes through. "But he still loves me. He said he was sorry. He won't do it again." To walk away from that relationship is a very difficult thing to do. It's painful because we've believed the lies for so long. Saruman is a very sly fox. He is a very smooth talker. Meanwhile he's chopping down Fangorn, burning villages, and poisoning rivers. Why are we so emotionally attached to the brands we use? If you stand back for a moment and think about it, it doesn't seem logical. But we *are* attached; there's no denying that. There's a reason, and the story of how that came to be takes us back to the period between the two world wars, almost 100 years ago.

## The Voice of Saruman: the Birth of Advertising and the Power of Brands

We have all been put under a spell, a spell not unlike that cast by Saruman on those who came to parley with him on the stairs of Orthanc—his dark, stone tower. As they approached, Gandalf warned them to be wary:

> "What's the danger?" asked Pippin. "Will he shoot at us, and pour fire out of the windows; or *can he put a spell on us from a distance?*"
> "The last is more likely, if you ride to his door with a light heart," said Gandalf. "But there is no knowing what he can do, or may choose to try. A wild beast cornered is not safe to approach. And Saruman has powers you do not guess. *Beware of his voice!*" [italics/bold, mine] —*LOTR*: II, *The Voice of Saruman*

Beware of his voice, indeed! The power of words to deceive is a danger far exceeding any we might encounter from physical weapons. Sticks and stones *can* break bones! But words can lead worlds into ruin!

Following the close of the First World War, Edward Bernays moved to New York City. "Who the hell is Edward Bernays?" you ask. Well, he had spent the latter period of his twenties working for the *Committee of Public Information*, an independent government agency in charge of writing and designing propaganda for the war effort. The agency was responsible for galvanizing public opinion behind the war by plastering the country with posters demonizing the Huns—otherwise known as the Germans—and glorifying American democracy. Edward had a singular talent for the job. He is credited with coining the phrase, "Making the world safe for Democracy!" which became

President Woodrow Wilson's *go to* line. When Bernays arrived in New York after the war he set up a new firm as a *Public Relations* consultant. He invented this new term as a substitute for *propaganda* which had negative connotations thanks to its use by the *Huns* during the war. He quickly became the new rising star in the up and coming field of advertising. He decided that the talents he had employed to "Stop the Hun" during the war could also be employed to sell products and make money doing it. He was very successful. He made lots of money and sold lots of products.

Then one day not long after setting up shop in the Big Apple, he got a letter from his uncle living in Germany. His uncle—a neurologist from Austria working on a book about *group mentality*—had fallen on financial hard times and asked if his nephew might consider extending him a loan. Edward promptly sent his uncle a check and a box of Cuban cigars—his uncle's favorite. Some time later Edward received a package from Germany which included a thank-you letter and a copy of the book his uncle had written. The book was *Group Psychology and the Analysis of the Ego*. Edward's uncle was none other than Sigmund Freud, the father of modern psychology. Bernays now had the proof that what he long suspected was in fact, true: the human mind could be manipulated by playing on the latent fears and desires that reside in everyone's psyche. It was this moment in history, when two new ideas came together—advertising and the emerging field of psychology—that the idea of *branding* really came into being. Think of this as a Reese's, "Hey! You got your chocolate in my peanut-butter! You got your peanut-butter on my chocolate!" moment. And Edward ran with it! He consumed his uncle's ideas, combined them with his natural talent for propaganda and revolutionized the field of marketing, issuing in the Age of Consumerism that threatens to consume the planet.

Of Bernays' many claims to fame, he helped the American Tobacco Company to convince American women that smoking Lucky Strikes cigarettes was a *liberating* and defiant thing to do, calling them "torches of freedom." Thanks Ed. My grandmother and grandfather—on my mom's side—both smoked themselves to death. May your bones be exhumed and ground into dust.

Edward Bernays was the first true Saruman of advertising, and he has "many descendants" as Tolkien pointed out. Bernays went on to write his own book, *Propaganda*. Here's an excerpt in which you can see the birth of modern advertising, and it's twisted goal:

> The conscious and intelligent manipulation of the organized habits and opinions of the masses is an important element in *democratic society*. Those who manipulate this unseen mechanism of society constitute an <u>invisible government</u> <u>which is the true ruling power of our country</u>. ...We are governed, our minds are molded, our tastes formed, our ideas suggested, largely by men we have never heard of. <u>This is a logical result of the way in which our democratic society is organized</u>. Vast numbers of human beings must cooperate in this manner if they are to live together as a smoothly functioning society. ...In almost every act of our daily lives, whether in the sphere of politics or business, in our social conduct or our ethical thinking, <u>we are dominated by the relatively small number of persons</u>...who understand the mental processes and social patterns of the masses. It is they who pull the wires which control the public mind. — *Propaganda*, 9-10 [excerpt from Wikipedia]

This Saruman also helped the aluminum industry to push for the fluoridation of our water supply as a way to increase their profits and dispose of a nasty orcish byproduct at the same time. In the 1930s he ran a campaign for Dixie Cup to convince Americans that only disposable cups were sanitary. Thanks to Bernays we now drink poisoned water from cups made from trees that once provided us with oxygen, coated in plastic which will sit in our landfills for millennia or be washed into our oceans to poison our shrimp dinner. Thanks asshole.

This, my fellow Hobbits, is why we are fearful, angry, and depressed about breaking up with our favorite brands. We have been manipulated for at least a century by elite Sarumans with silver tongues. There's nothing *democratic* about what Bernays is describing in the above passage! It is a facade of democracy, overlaying a reality of elitist, Oligarchism and this was written almost 90 years ago!

Thanks to the *marriage* of modern psychology and propaganda we have been manipulated into consuming poisons, polluting our environment, and smoking ourselves into oblivion. Down deep, most of us sense this though we don't think about it that much. I've been thinking about it for so long that advertising isn't that effective on me anymore; it just pisses me off because I know what they're trying to accomplish and how they're doing it. You will become the same way. I don't listen to or watch commercials anymore. I hate them.

It's time for us to wake up from this dream, like those present at Saruman's speech. Like the scene above, let's make it his *last* speech. Let's stop being lulled into the lies. Turn it off! Do we really *need* someone to tell us what's good for us? What to buy? How to live? What's important? The answer is "HELL NO!" I don't. Neither do you, or anyone who wishes to live *free*! The first step to freedom is to realize that the world isn't *ours*! The second step is to tell Saruman to "shut the hell up!" We don't need *brands* to live. Not if they wish to deceive us. Make it a new rule to clean out your pantries, closets, and garages of the products of Saruman. If that means breaking up with Grandmother? So be it. Take your time if you need to. You can't do it all in one day, anyway. But do it. Find new brands, Hobbit brands, that are working to clean up the Shire and care about the health of your family and the Earth. Load up the shopping cart with them! Pack them into your cloth shopping bags, bring them home, store them in your glass jars, and then get to cookin'! It's time for second breakfast, already! Let's head for my favorite room: Frodo's Kitchen!

[Note]: For a fairly extensive list of GMO laden labels, especially those that have funded *anti-labeling* initiatives in recent years, read this article at GMO Awareness.com.

# 25

# FRODO'S KITCHEN: FEEDING UNEXPECTED DWARVES

All Hobbits can cook, for they begin to learn the art before their letters. —*LOTR*: II, *Of Herbs and Stewed Rabbit*

Am I tough? Am I strong? Am I hard-core? Absolutely.
Did I whimper with pathetic delight when I sank my teeth into my hot fried-chicken sandwich? You betcha.
—James Patterson

While obtaining food is important to a Hobbit we also have to store it and cook it. So we will continue our clean-up tour in the most important room of the modern Hobbit-hole, the kitchen. How many of us, even those who do not cook much, have found ourselves drawn to the kitchen when company are over, especially when they are rowdy, noisy Dwarves? I know *this* modern Hobbit spends the majority of time at home, in or around the kitchen. Of all the rooms in the house the kitchen is where we can make the most impact in our struggle to save the Earth, so we will continue our tour there, and since we started with the food, let's look at how Hobbits should store it.

# Food storage

How we store our food is almost as important as where the food comes from. I touched on this in the last section where I mentioned my puzzlement over organic food producers who packaged their certified products in plastic containers. Plastics leach chemicals into whatever they are containing. They especially do this when they are heated or cooled in a microwave or refrigerator/freezer. While many food container makers have removed the harmful BPA chemical from their products, the replacements—that they rarely reveal to the public—have been tested no more than BPAs were when they were introduced many years ago, and sold to us as perfectly safe! So, until plastic companies can *PROVE* to us that they are safe through verifiable, independent tests, we should work to eliminate them entirely from our kitchens.

To do this we need to look for alternatives. The obvious ones are glass, ceramic, and stainless steel. There are many products out there made with these materials. You can certainly purchase new ones in stores, and online but don't forget to also look for used ones on Craigslist and other online sites, as well as garage sales, second-hand stores, and flea markets. Canning jars, or Mason jars as we call'em back home are a great storage option even if you're not canning. You can put bulk food in them, like coffee, tea, nuts, anything you can think of that will fit. You can even take them to the butcher counter and have them put your ground meat in them! You can freeze foods in glass containers as long as you leave space at the top for expansion so that the jars won't crack or break in your freezer.

You can use repurposed pillow cases to put bread in at the store. Try to buy bread that has not already been packaged in plastic bags which is difficult sometimes, though most high-end groceries have some that aren't already bagged. You may need to order it that way from your grocery store, or co-op, or find a local bakery that will hold some for you. If it's uncut, it keeps quite well un-refrigerated—bread drys out in the fridge, so don't keep it there—and in the freezer. Freezing bread is okay but it only keeps that way for a few days. Better yet, make your own bread! Either do it the old school way or get a used bread machine—there are hundreds of them on Craigslist—and start making it at home. Nothing beats fresh bread out of the oven!

For much more information on food storage ideas read Bea Johnson's *Zero Waste Home*, and Beth Terry's book, *Plastic-Free*, who both have gazillions of ideas on how to store stuff without plastic. You can also read my article "Hobbit Shopping #1: How to Buy in Bulk and Reduce Plastic," for more instructions on bulk shopping.

## Cooking the Hobbit Way

Now that we have our food purchased and stored neatly in our Hobbit-pantry we can focus on the hardware of the kitchen as well as practices that could help alleviate waste and toxins around your food preparation. Our focus will be on the following: saving energy, eliminating toxins, preparing/cooking food, and disposing of waste.

If you are like me, or a Hobbit like Bilbo, cooking is not only a necessity but a delight. If you are not of the culinary persuasion, that's okay, though I would suggest you might want to open your mind to the enjoyment that cooking your own food can add to your life. In fact, it will be very difficult to make substantial headway in cutting waste from your lifestyle without learning to cook the basics that you eat every day. Eating out, or buying pre-cooked, frozen, microwave dinners, isn't particularly good for you and they are packed in loads of waste. Plus, the food sucks and it's expensive as hell. Cooking your own food saves loads of money over eating out or buying pre-cooked, frozen, orc food.

Cooking really isn't mysterious, or difficult. It's not rocket science however much Alton Brown might make it look that way on his shows. It's pretty simple really, if you follow these two maxims:

- Buy quality food.
- Don't screw it up

How easy is that! I know, it sounds like I'm being sarcastic— and I probably am—but really, it is that simple. Quality food already tastes good. The problem that most people make when cooking — and this goes for people who supposedly know how to cook as well as everyone else — is that they try to get *cute* with their recipes. That's when they break the second maxim. Have you ever thought to yourself, as you're cooking some new dish, "I wonder if I add 10 more ingredients if it will be a *masterpiece?*" It will not. Stop right there! If you don't you will probably turn your Shire-surprise into Mordor-mash!

Keep it simple and don't over cook it. That doesn't mean that you can't have 40 different spices and herbs in your kitchen — I do — but just because you have them doesn't mean they all go into every dish. Like I said in my introduction to the book this isn't a cookbook, but I think I need to write one soon. Anyway, if you aren't a great cook take some lessons! Can't afford those? Watch the Food Network or the plethora of other cooking shows on other networks, or Google your ingredients and see what comes up! There are millions of websites and Youtube videos that will show you how to make basic dishes. Start by reading the recipes on my website and watching the videos there. I promise I'll keep adding to them.

## Kitchen tools

So what kinds of tools should every good Hobbit have, and which ones can he/she do without in their kitchen? I will give you a few suggestions below but follow some basic rules and you will cook better and, healthier, food by avoiding toxins that come along with some modern cooking methods and tools. If it's plastic, phase it out. I know I'm beating this orc to oblivion but plastics really do suck. It's okay if you still have them in your kitchen. I have plastic in my kitchen right now but not a day goes by that I don't look at it now and think, "How can I replace this orcish crap?" Most of it isn't that difficult to replace, especially the spatulas, tongs, containers, etc. It may seem difficult at first glance, but there are alternatives for all of it. Plastics, as mentioned earlier, can and, do leech chemicals into our food, during storage, but even more when we cook/reheat the food IN the plastic container. If you do nothing else with your kitchen plastics, avoid, or just stop microwaving food in them. Even if plastics were *safe*, the production of plastics cannot be sustained, as already discussed, so let's eliminate them as much as possible where ever we find them. Find other uses for the containers: to store non-food items, clothing, office supplies, tools, batteries. Anything but food.

Next, avoid non-stick pans and pots with Teflon coatings. Teflon—a product by Dupont—emits a toxic chemical when overheated that can cause flu-like symptoms, and kills pet birds. It also chips off into your food over time. Dupont, and some tests, argue that the solid Teflon is inert and therefore safe to consume, but call me old fashioned; I don't want to eat it. Not only do I not want to consume Dupont chemicals, I'd rather not give them my money, either. The company has a checkered history when it comes to the environment and they recently spent millions of dollars to oppose a bill in California that would require food manufacturers to disclose the use of GMOs in their products. Dupont's subsidiary, Pioneer Hi-Bred produces GMO seeds.

## Cast Iron: Dwarvish Strong

Personally, there is no cookware substance that I would recommend more highly than cast iron. First off, it lasts forever if given the proper care and nothing cooks as well. Many people avoid it because it *rusts* or their food sticks to the pan. These are symptoms that your cast iron that has not been properly seasoned. The basics of seasoning aren't that complicated. Rub your pan down with a food oil. I have been using olive oil for years to season pans. Rub a very light coating of oil on all surfaces then bake it in a very hot oven—500 degrees if you can get it that hot—for an hour. This best done when it's not cold outside because you will want to open a few windows and/or turn on your oven hood to pull the smoke from the kitchen. It will come out with a hardened sheen. Your pan is now seasoned. If you want an even better seasoning, with a very hard non-stick surface, try flax seed oil. I haven't tried this yet, but I plan to. Check out Sheryl's Blog for full instructions.

A word on cleaning cast iron: You can find conflicting information on this, but I'm going to tell you here, DO NOT use dish soap or any kind of cleaner on your cast iron cookware, unless you intend to re-season it before using it again. Cast iron, like all metals, is porous and will absorb soap into the pores where it will sit until you cook again, then guess where the soap ends up? Yep. In your food. Soap in your food equals extra time on the toilet, which is no fun. If you season a pan correctly and keep it lightly oiled after cleaning then you won't need soap to clean it. Run hot water into the pan, and if you need to—for burnt or crusty food particles—lightly rub it with a wire scrubby till it's clean. Dry it immediately and rub a little oil on it, if it needs it. This is usually only necessary if you had to scrub extra hard to remove baked on cheese or egg or something. Whatever you do do not put your cast iron into the dishwasher!

## Stainless Steel

Stainless steel is the next best option for cookware. I like stainless. It's easier to clean, you can use soaps, as it's not as porous as cast iron, and you can put it in the dishwasher. It is a good option for stock pots and pots in general, though a big cast iron Dutch Oven is hard to beat for a lot of things. I have some stainless pans that I like, though I haven't had much luck with cooking over-easy eggs in them. I usually do that on my little cast iron, pancake pan, and flip them with a spatula.

## Glass

Glass cookware is another option though other than a couple of casserole dishes, I don't have many in my kitchen. I suspect I will be adding more. We have lots of other items made of glass: measuring cups/bowlls, mixing bowls, and pie pans, though. Earthenware, or pottery is a great option, too, or addition I should say. We have a big, earthenware roasting dish that you can put an entire chicken into, with rice, etc. It's awesome for making rice, or chicken, or baking one pot meals. And it's very Hobbity.

# Saving energy in the kitchen

A lot of energy and water is consumed in kitchens. While this is certainly true of any kitchen, there are a couple of things that should be considered. One is the amount of energy you are saving by cooking your own, organic, locally — maybe even home — grown, bulk-bought, food. If you bought or grew your food organically, you've already saved energy because as mentioned earlier, non-organic foods burn an inordinate amount of fossil fuels and that is only in the production stage. If the food is locally grown, then you've saved on the fuel costs it took to bring it to market, especially if you grew it in your back yard! If you bought it from a bulk-bin, then you've saved on the energy to package it individually, usually in plastics made from fossil fuels. So, you're already ahead of the game, so give your self a pat on the back! Now we can save a little more energy in the preparation, cooling, cooking, and cleaning up of our food and our kitchen.

# Water Conservation: Saving the Anduin, Saving Girls

Going was easy.

Going, the big plastic container held only air...Nya could switch the handle from one hand to the other, swing the container by her side, or cradle it in both arms...There was little weight, going. There was only heat, the sun already baking the air, even though it was long before noon. It would take her half the morning if she didn't stop on the way...

Nya took the hollowed gourd that was tied to the handle of the plastic container. She untied it, scooped up the brown muddy water, and drank. It took two gourdfuls before she felt a little cooler inside.

Nya filled the container all the way to the top. Then she tied the gourd back in place and took the padded cloth doughnut from her pocket. The doughnut went on her head first, followed by the heavy container of water, which she would hold in place with one hand...she might reach home by noon, if all went well. —Linda Sue Park, *A Long Walk to Water: Based on a True Story*

Nya's story is a common one for nearly 1 billion people on Earth, every day. Most of the time young girls perform this essential labor, especially in Africa. On average, these children walk 3 to 5 miles to get water that isn't even safe to drink in the first place, and they do it 2 or 3 times a day. Every return trip the girls must balance a 5 gallon, 40 pound can of water on their heads. The situation is dire and devastating to the lives of girls and women in these places. As a result, most girls never get to go to school, even in places where there is one because they are too busy carrying water and working on house-hold chores. Thankfully, there are Hobbity organizations working to change that, and they are having increasing success but lots more needs to be done. Keep Nya's story in mind as we talk about conserving water in our homes, starting with the kitchen.

## Water in the Hobbit Kitchen

One of the most used things in our houses, and especially in our kitchens, is water. In the developed world we rarely stop to think about how much water we consume every day. It is worth considering, since fresh, clean, safe water is quickly becoming a scarce resource. Most of us who live in the West have yet to experience this scarcity but a large part of the world has been suffering from it for some time. In the U.S., for example, the average family consumes about 300 gallons of water, per day. 70% of that is indoors. That's a lot. Much of the bottled water that we all drink, and need to stop drinking, comes from other countries who are struggling to supply their own people with water! Bottled water companies, like Nestle, lay claim to water rights in these countries, extract inordinate amounts of water, and ship it to the Western World where we pay a ridiculous price for the *convenience*. There is nothing right about the process. At the same time the oil industry is poisoning our fresh water supply through fracking. We simply must consider other fellow humans and Hobbits, not to mention our children and ourselves, when we turn on our faucets. Be mindful when you turn the water on. Don't just let it run. Think to yourself, "Do I need this much water to do this job?" That one thought alone will save hundreds of gallons of water over a year's time. It doesn't take that much more effort to turn off the faucet while scrubbing your hands with soap, for instance. Think about the effort it takes to carry water for miles over scorched desert.

## Washing dishes

We use a lot of water to clean our dishes. While there is no avoiding cleaning them—unless of course we resort to all throw-away dishes coated in plastics—and that of course is a big no-no, we can work to minimize our water usage as much as possible. After some research online I've come to the conclusion that dishwashers usually use less water than hand washing, especially if run on economy or short-wash mode. A normal sink faucet can run out 2 gallons of water in a minute, at full volume. Unless you are a really fast dishwasher then it's hard to beat the average of 4 gallons of water used by most automatic dishwashers. Now, of course, there is the electricity burned to run the machine. If you have a machine use it on a econo-mode. If yours is broken and you're thinking of replacing it, get the most efficient one you can afford. If you're a minimalist, or don't have room for a machine, then it's best to fill the sink with warm/hot water, wash them and quickly rinse them before either letting them drip dry or drying off with a cloth towel.

## Recycling Water

If you really want to conserve water you can recycle the water that you've already used for one job and use it to do another one. There are gray-water systems that can be installed under your sinks, and for that matter, your tub and shower as well that will send the waste water to a tank in your yard or garden. You need to check with local regulations however because many places have restrictions on gray-water usage. I've even seen a sink/toilet design, where the sink sits on top of the toilet and drains into the toilet tank to be used when flushing. For most of us changing out our entire plumbing set up isn't feasible, but if you are designing a new house, or Hobbit-hole, or remodeling your kitchen or bathroom these are things you can think about that will conserve water, save you money every day, and at the same time save the Earth. I hope to one day install such systems in my house.

# Solid Wastes

Another place in the kitchen, and the entire house for that matter, where we can cut our environmental impact is in the garbage and trash cans. I would recommend watching the documentary, *Garbage: the Revolution Starts at Home*, to get an idea of just how much an average family produces in a short amount of time and to see just where all of it goes when we push it to the curb. You can rent it on Netflix and Amazon. It's easy to leave garbage for the garbage man and forget that it must actually GO somewhere, usually a landfill that's already overflowing with your neighbors' garbage. If you really want to cut your solid waste, and waste in general, don't forget Bea Johnson's *Zero Waste*, where you will get very detailed information about how to cut your waste down to almost nothing, literally, if you choose to take it that far. I don't know that I will ever achieve quite what Bea's family did, but I hope to cut it a great deal in the next couple years.

There are a few things you can do to minimize waste. Bea suggests a system of 6 Rs, 5 of which we've covered already, as suggested by Beth Terry, in the plastics section. To that, Bea Johnson adds one more: *Rot*.

### Composting

If you want to cut your kitchen waste down a butt-ton, start composting your vegetable waste. One of the best and easiest ways to improve the soil in your garden is by adding compost to it. You can either buy compost which usually means large plastic bags, which are a no-no or you can make your own. Buying compost is a waste of money, especially when you already have the ingredients to make it sitting in your garbage can. It's also a waste of money because you are paying someone else to carry those ingredients away! Making compost is really quite simple. Most experts will say that any plant material is acceptable to compost so you can throw in all your vegetable waste from the kitchen, hair from human/pet brushes, dust from your floors, plus all the leaves, grass-clippings, small sticks, etc from your yard.

Keep a large compost jar — we have a glass cookie jar we got cheap at a second-hand store under the counter — to collect any and all vegetable and egg shell waste in your kitchen. Most experts will tell you to avoid animal products, meat and bones, because they don't usually break down quickly enough in a backyard compost pile. The heat generated in a small pile just isn't enough to break them down in a timely manner, usually before critters, like raccoons and the like get to it.

Make sure the jar has a lid on it. It doesn't really smell like you would think but a lid is preferable, especially if you have Viking Pirate Kitties living in your house, like we do. If they smelled our compost jar it would be tantamount to waving rum and gold Doubloons in the face of Captain Jack Sparrow or Blackbeard. So keep yours covered. It will fill up quickly so you will need to empty it at least once a week, if not more. Put the kids to work. Tell them they're *making dirt*, if you have to. If they're *real Hobbits* they have to like dirt. Tell them that and it will probably work. All they have to do is take it out and sprinkle it on top of your compost pile. We'll discuss the compost pile itself when we get to the Gamgee's Victory Garden chapter.

## Cleaning Chemicals

Most kitchens are packed with toxic chemicals, usually under the sink where we put all our cleaning solutions. Why do we need so many? Do we really need 5, 10, 15 different formulas to clean one kitchen? Hell, one house? The answer is an emphatic NO. We do not. Our grandparents or great-grandparents didn't use all of those or have them *to* use. Most of them are very toxic; some of them are linked to numerous physical disorders. They poison us just be being in our homes, and if our children or pets get hold of them, some of them can even kill. They aren't needed.

Americans in particular have an abiding fear of germs, viruses, and bacteria, mostly due to the advertising campaigns of the *soap*, and cleaning product industry. They have convinced us that the way to better health is to kill all the bacteria and germs in our homes. But science and medicine are now coming to a realization that this is not necessarily a good thing to do. Many bacteria are actually *beneficial* to us, our digestive system, and the environment in general. Even those that make us sick help to build our immune systems to fight off deadlier diseases. By killing all of the germs in our homes, it seems, we are inviting disaster in the future. Heather Flores, in her book *Food Not Lawns*, says, "Show me a house full of cleaning supplies and I will show you a medicine cabinet full of pharmaceutical drugs." Let's stop this. Get rid of the poisonous chemicals in your kitchen and home. Take them to the local *hazardous waste* drop off. Find alternatives to them. There are many online, but here is an all-purpose cleaner that will clean any and all surfaces in your Hobbit-hole, and if not for the soap that's in it, you could put it on your 'tater chips and eat it! So it's non-toxic, and it works!

## Hobbit Mama's All-Purpose 'Shire-Cleaner'

- You need a 1 quart spray bottle, in which you mix the following ingredients:
- 3/4 cup of water
- 1/4 cup of vodka or other clear alcohol
- 1 tablespoon of liquid Castille soap. You can get it unscented, or with scents.
- 3 cups of distilled white vinegar

Shake it up and spray anywhere you would normally use a spray cleaner. Don't actually put it on your chips, though. Unless of course you want to spend a lot of time on the toilet, which just happens to be where we're heading next.

# 26

# The Bath at Crickhollow: Washing Weary Hobbit Parts

Sing hey! for the bath at close of day
that washes the weary mud away!
A loon is he that will not sing:
O! Water Hot is a noble thing!
— *LOTR*: I, *A Conspiracy Unmasked*

I could tell that my parents hated me. My bath toys
were a toaster and a radio.
— Rodney Dangerfield

While the kitchen may be the central room of any self-respecting Hobbit-hole, eating and drinking lead to other essential bodily functions, like brushing teeth, scrubbing Hobbit feet, and other things we do in there. All of these things require water. Much like Pippin, who splashed water all over the bathroom in Crickhollow, we Hobbits waste a lot of water in our bathrooms too. We use it to flush our toilets, wash our faces and hands, brush our teeth, and bath our bodies, and sometimes the bodies of our pets, though I wouldn't advise on washing Viking Pirate Kitties in your tub, unless you like bleeding, seeping lacerations. As mentioned in the kitchen section, there are new innovations out there to help save water in the bathroom, like the toilet/sink combination.

There are also ways to divert the *gray* water from your sink and tub so that it can be filtered and reused in other places, like your clothes washer, or your garden. If you're doing a major renovation of your bathroom please look into these options because they will save a great deal of water which the planet can't afford to waste, and at the same time, save you a great deal of dragon gold.

If you can't afford to do all that right now — I know I can't — then the next best thing is to keep in mind how much water you are using. Do what you can to conserve it. Do you have a dripping faucet in the house or bathroom? Have it fixed. It's very wasteful, and expensive too. I say this while my tub faucet is dripping; it's been that way since we moved in a year ago, and if I ever finish writing this book, I'm gonna call up Patience's dad and we're gonna finally fix it. So *do as I say...* Another way to save water is to install shower heads that have flow restrictors. Opt for good ones that also increase the pressure, instead of a cheap version that will just break down sooner anyway.

One simple idea to conserve grey water for other uses, is to keep a small bucket or garden watering can in your bathroom to catch the water that escapes while you're waiting for the bath water to heat up. You could save a gallon or two of water there every time you bathe! After your shower, take that bucket out to your garden and water your plants with it! Or water your indoor plants with it! If you have a vanity sink you could also detach the trap and run sink water into a 5 gallon bucket under the sink, and use that water to flush your toilet. I know, it sounds radical — I haven't employed this trick myself — but that's just because we're so used to convenience. People in most parts of the world wouldn't think a second about doing such a thing. In fact, they'd be happy to have a toilet at all.

When washing your hands or face in the sink don't just let the faucet run while you're lathering up. Turn it off while you lather, then turn it on to quickly rinse. Remind yourself when you are doing this, that you have saved enough water to allow another person — maybe on the other side of the planet — to wash the hands of their entire family for a day. It's true. In many places, they simply don't have clean, safe water to wash, or drink. It's one of the biggest problems we face on our planet, as mentioned at the beginning of this section of the book.

Another source of water waste in the bathroom is towels. We'll come back to this subject a little later, but in brief, the more towels you use the more water you waste washing them. Come up with a system to limit the number of towels each Hobbit gets per week—two is probably plenty. You could color code them for each person or tag them in some other way so everyone knows which towel is theirs. This is a problem in my Hobbit-hole too. I try to reuse the same towel a few days in a row but Patience ends up stealing it—probably to wrap her hair in—and so I have to pick up a new one. So mark your towels, and save water. It will also save electricity when it comes to drying them.

## Paper Waste

Ahhh toilet paper. In some parts of the world, people never shake hands with their left hand. You know why? Because that's traditionally the hand used to wipe one's ass, sans toilet paper. Am I suggesting you do the same? Uh, no. I'm not going to either, and I'm pretty sure Patience would kibosh it anyway. Toilet paper is definitely considered an essential in most parts of the world but we should keep in mind that it is also waste. Any form of waste is a break in a loop, that we should work to try to mend.

Of course there are toilets made that have *bidets*—that's the French style toilet with the water jet for cleaning your crack. Some of those also have dryers integrated into their design. I haven't personally tried them so I can't really endorse their drying ability, but if Dyson came up with one I'm quite sure it would work though I'm not sure if it wouldn't be a bit painful, especially for us guys.

For most of us, toilet paper is the only reasonable option, for the time being anyway. But we can do our best to close the loop of waste by purchasing the stuff made from recycled paper and without bleach which is a horrible orcish pollutant to the water supply. Walgreens's *Ology* line includes toilet paper. So if you shop there, look for it, or look for products like it in your favorite stores, or ask for them.

## Plastics in the Bath

Look around your bathroom. How many plastic things do you see? Yeah, that's what I thought. If it's anything like mine there's a butt-load of them. It's amazing how little we think about it these days. Keep in mind, however, that some of these plastics are performing a duty, at least at present, so don't freak out and start chucking plastic shampoo bottles out the window. Calm down. Everything will be fine. Put Rubber Ducky back in the tub! It's ok if you have plastic shampoo bottles, and one Rubber Ducky. They are what economists would call a *sunk cost*, in other words, you've already purchased them. What you do next is the important thing.

First off, don't just throw them out, not yet anyway. As I've mentioned more than once, it's best to use and reuse things before getting rid of them entirely, and even then, if you can lend them to someone else who might use it, do that first. Just avoid, as much as possible, buying NEW plastics, in any room for any purpose. You will do it, because if your hair is dripping with oil because you've forgotten to bring your plastic bottle into the co-op to refill it with bulk shampoo you're going to buy that new bottle of shampoo. It's okay. Just try to plan ahead next time and you can avoid those situations more often than not.

Refill bottles of shampoo and hand-soap. Most co-op stores will have large bottles of both that you can use to refill yours. And don't fall for all the advertising crap that says you must have *such and such* label of shampoo or soap because it will save your marriage, sex life, and bring about world peace. That's just Saruman-Bernays talking. It won't do any of those things, in fact, it might just accomplish the opposite, while killing the environment with nasty, orcish chemicals.

## Beards, Legs, and Teeth

Probably the biggest source of plastic waste in the bathroom is disposable razors and toothbrushes. For us men, we could opt for an old fashioned straight razor. Yeah, I know, "those things are dangerous!" But is there a more *manly* way to shave? I think not. Actually, they are not that hard to use. I've been shaving with one for over 10 years and I've nicked myself less with it than I ever did with a so-called *safety* razor. I wouldn't dance naked around the bathroom singing Bohemian Rapsody with a straight razor in my hand while shaving my throat—unless I had a death wish or something—but as long as you pay attention to what you're doing they're as safe as a good kitchen knife, or the Shards of Narsil. If raw blades on your neck is intimidating then find a solid, non-plastic razor handle and buy replacement heads for it. They make the handles in various materials. I used to have a nice brass one. Look for these options in your co-op, or grocery store or do a quick internet search.

Toothbrushes also come in different materials. Brush with Bamboo makes a toothbrush with a bamboo handle. The bristles are plastic but can be removed with needle-nosed pliers and recycled. The handle can be composted, or reused for other things. They have a good deal of information on their website. Check it out! There are other options, which you can find in stores, especially co-ops. Some of them are made from recycled plastics with replaceable heads, so you can switch out heads when they wear out. There are also versions with bristles made from boar's hair, which would be biodegradable.

**Our Chemical Bath**

Most of our bathrooms are full of orcish chemicals: toilet/tub cleaners, perfumes and colognes, antiperspirants, hair sprays and products, shampoos and soaps. So many of the things we use to clean ourselves and our houses just aren't good for us or the environment. Most of the ones in the bathroom are going to end up on our bodies or in the waste water running out in gallons through the pipes which in turn pollutes our rivers, lakes and oceans. This is unnecessary, and avoidable.

There are more sustainable alternatives for all of these orcish products. Spend some time and effort to phase out these things from your bathroom. I've already mentioned the bulk shampoo and soap. Most co-ops have them and they are usually poison free versions. But there are many other options for cleaning products. The best are really the old ones that your grandparents, or great-grandparents used. Things like Castille soap, a great general purpose soap, baking soda, lemon juice, and simple vinegar and water. You can make your own vinegar and water cleaner and it's super cheap! Hobbit Mama's All Purpose Shire-cleaner is great in bathrooms, too.

## Bye, Bye Fluoride

One of the most insidious things we have done to our water is to add fluoride to it. Fluoride is a poison, a byproduct of the aluminum industry. Look it up. Heck, just read the back of your toothpaste tube and see what it says. I'll save you the time, but do read it later. It says that if you swallow toothpaste, enough of it at one time that is, you should call the poison control center immediately. It also tells you to keep it out of reach of children. Yes, it says that. Does your child brush her teeth? Probably, but only after you threaten her with a quick trip to Mordor. Seriously? So this chemical, added to our toothpaste, is a deadly poison and we're giving it to our kids? Most *children's* toothpastes are actually fluoride free. So why is it in the adult version? If kids' teeth would benefit from its use, why not put it in their paste, as well? Why? Because it's freakin' POISON! Of course, most of us just give our children the adult version anyway because we've been told that it works wonders for tooth enamel. But recent studies have linked fluoride to many maladies, but the worst may be that it is a neuro-toxin. It poisons brains. This is just insane.

And if it wasn't bad enough that they put it in our toothpaste, most municipalities in the United States and many other places around the world put this poison in our *WATER SUPPLY*! In other words, it's in every drop we drink, every drop we bath in, and every drop with cook with. Now that is *really* insane.

"But isn't fluoride good for our teeth?" you ask.

Well, maybe, and maybe not. There are studies that attempt to demonstrate the benefits of fluoridated water in the fight against tooth decay by purportedly showing a correlation between countries that have introduced fluoride into the drinking water and signs of improved tooth enamel, lower rates of tooth decay, etc. This may be true, but the correlation does not prove that fluoride was the *cause* of this improvement. All it really demonstrates is that *some* improvements were recorded during the same time that fluoride was introduced. Correlation and cause are not the same thing. In most areas where fluoride was introduced—I remember this as a child—they were also pushing us to brush our teeth and visit the dentist more often. So what can we really attribute the improvement of teeth to? Is it brushing more and more frequent dentist visits? Or is it the poison introduced to our water supply because the aluminum industry had a bunch of surplus chemicals lying around that they created a market for? Hmmmm.

In point of fact, fluoride is only effective at strengthening tooth enamel—if at all—if it is applied directly to the teeth, topically! In other words, it only works if you put it directly on your teeth. It does absolutely *NOTHING* to improve your teeth if you swallow it in your drinking water. Nothing that is, except slowly poison you and your family. We stopped using fluoridated toothpaste months ago and started filtering our water. A good alternative toothpaste is the fluoride free versions by *Tom's*. You can also make an old fashioned toothpaste with baking soda. See the Recipe/Resource section at the end of the book.

With some ingenuity and mindfulness—the latter more important than the former—we can work to lesson our impact in the bathroom by saving water, cutting paper waste, eliminating or cutting down on plastics, as well as orcish chemicals. All these are good things to do, but don't forget, when you leave the bathroom to turn off the lights! Saving on energy use is our next chapter.

# 27

# SAVING POWER
# IN THE HOBBIT-HOLE

Saving on electricity usage is a big way to help the environment and one most of us are conscious of, though it seems that there is so much conflicting information about how to do it and what it's actual impact is on the Earth, that most of us just throw up our hands and surrender. Most electricity in the U.S., at least, comes from burning fossil fuels, either petroleum products, natural gas, or coal. Petroleum and coal, as we have already discussed, are extremely dirty ways to generate power and before long will either run out entirely or become so expensive to extract that the industry will close up shop. Unfortunately, they may complete the process of ruining and poisoning the environment beyond the limits of human sustainability *long* before they quit burning it, drilling and mining for it. So it's imperative that we find ways to curb our need for them, and begin to find alternatives, now! We'll start first with ways of curbing need which is much more important. Our future on this planet depends in large part on the realization that the way we currently do things is an aberration and cannot be sustained any longer. The future must be very different and we must use less power if we want to have any at all. After discussing ways to cut power use we'll look at alternative ways of generating power that may be applicable to your personal situation.

# Light in Dark Places

The first thing most people think about when it comes to burning electricity, thanks to Mr. Edison's most famous invention, is probably light. It is certainly the most visible use of electric power and a constant reminder for those who are aware of environmental issues, that we need to find ways to limit our use. The easiest thing to do to save power for lighting, not to mention money on your electric bill, is to turn off lights when they are not absolutely needed. Americans especially, have become accustomed to turning on big overhead lights and leaving them on for hours on end. This is wasteful, so we should go back to the way our grandparents, and great-grandparents used to light their homes: area lighting. They did not turn on halogens to illuminate every nook and cranny of the house. They turned on a lamp over their reading chair or on their bedside table. Consider making your electric light setup more sustainable. Install more efficient bulbs.

Motion sensitive light switches are great, if in a room where you always want light if occupied; for most rooms this is not necessary. Newly designed dimmer switches can help to save energy too. The old designs relied on resistance and as such, created heat, which was a waste of energy. The new designs actually turn your lights off and on rapidly, so fast you can't see it, and do cut power use, saving money and electricity. However, they only work with incandescent bulbs, NOT the new fluorescent ones! It can be dangerous to use the fluorescent bulbs with dimmers. Keep these things in mind as you evaluate your Hobbit-hole.

### Natural Light

Natural light, you know, the **sun**, is the most efficient way to light your house and the best kind of light anyway! Consider opening up window blinds more often, or installing more windows in the new house you're building. Maybe even put in a skylight? Sunlight has other benefits too, like heat in the winter. Indoor plants love it, and best of all, it's free! At least until Duke Power finds a way to corner the market. That was a joke, mostly.

**Firelight**

My favorite source of light is just plain ole' fire, in all forms. There can be no substitute for candles, lanterns, etc when it comes to setting a Hobbit-hole mood. Big torches on the walls of your castle would be preferable but probably not as practical as other options. Candles are my favorite, though you do have to be careful with them, especially if you have children or Viking Pirate Kitties running around the house. Place them up higher and make sure they are secure. Big, wide candles are the best, because they are far less likely to turn over. Keep them away from hanging drapes, curtains or clothing. Hurricane lamps are great if you just need a little light in a room, and a bit safer, since the flame is contained behind glass, but they can be knocked over too so placement is key. It's best if you do not leave them unattended, especially with children and pets around.

# Appliances

Modern homes, especially in the U.S., are full of energy sucking appliances. In Europe, you see less of them and they are usually smaller in comparison to anything you see in America. Reevaluate each appliance in your home. What is its efficiency rating? How old is it, and are you considering replacing it soon? If you are going to replace it consider whether you really need one as big as what you already have, or if a smaller, more efficient one would do the job.

**Kitchen Gadgets n Machines**

This is especially true for refrigerators. I know that sometimes mine seems entirely too big, like right now since I'm leaving on a trip today, but sometimes it seems too small—when I throw parties. If you are eating more fresh, organic foods, you might need less storage space. As you change your food buying habits keep an eye on how much space you use in your fridge. It may be that you could do with a smaller one. This goes for your other kitchen appliances too.

If you have a dishwasher, is it working properly? Is it efficient? How many dishes do you wash a day, per week? Could you accomplish it just as quickly by hand? What about your microwave? There's a lot of energy sucked up in them. I have one too, so I'm not preaching, just thinking out loud. I don't actually *cook* in it since microwave *cooking* sucks. It's great for quickly heating things up but there's growing evidence that they destroy a lot of the nutrients in our food. Maybe it would be best to slow down a bit? That goes for other tools in the kitchen too.

Do I need all of the kitchen gadgets I have? Are there alternatives for them? The answers are no, and yes, because our grandparents didn't have all of the so-called time-saving gadgets we have in our homes these days. Are they really time-saving? When you consider how long it takes to find it— sometimes I spend ten minutes trying to find the damned blender—and the time it takes to clean it after you use it, maybe it's not really saving time? All this depends on your own style of cooking, working, etc.

For instance, I'm probably going to get rid of my iced-tea maker. First off, it's plastic—yuck—and secondly, my mom made tea for decades, and still does, in a pot on the stove. What about the food processor? I'm pretty certain that in the time it takes me to find mine, hook it up, use it, and clean it, I could have accomplish the same task with a chef's knife. Learn to use one well. Take a class on it. You'll thank me later. Oh yeah, buy a good one: Henkel and Wusthof are really the best, though there are some really goods ones coming out of Japan these days, too. As for the blender—I love my *piña coladas* man—I've seen manual, hand-cranked ones online. I love my old-fashioned egg-beater! That thing whips eggs up like mad! But it can be accomplished with a simple wisk, too. Check out Cottage Craft Works; they have a bunch of hand-cranked kitchen gadgets and can even convert KitchenAid mixers to be manual!

# Laundry: Washing the Hobbit Walkin' Clothes

Even weary Hobbits have to eventually wash their traveling clothes unless they want to start smelling like Gollum, yuck. I'm not much into raw fish — sorry sushi lovers — so I prefer to clean the duds, often. But we could probably do it more efficiently than we do.

Washing clothes uses not only electricity, but also a lot of water, accounting for between 15 and 40% of the water used in your house depending on size of household, and efficiency of the machine. That's not to mention the polluting impact of the nasty chemicals that are in most of our detergents and softeners. We all have to have clean things to wear and sleep under and on but there are ways to minimize the impact.

First, when you go to replace your machine next time make sure it has a Low Water Factor (WF) Rating. In the past, machines could use around 45 gallons per load! Newer models, both top-loading and front-loading, can get that number down as low as 15-20 gallons. Look for one of those; it will save you money in the long run, and save water, which we've already discussed as one of the crucial crises facing humans on the planet. I've read that units in Europe are even more efficient but that because they aren't popular in the U.S., they're very expensive. Maybe if more of us were demanding them the prices would come down.

Something you can do immediately is to find alternatives for the orchish detergents we all use. You can make your own, eco-friendly washing detergent, cheaply quickly with a bar of Castille soap, some borax and washing soda. Check out the recipe in the resource section at the end of the book.

## Drying Hobbit Undies, and Other Items

Maybe you're old enough to remember your mother hanging out laundry in the backyard on a clothesline? I do, but only vaguely. There are people going back to it. Drying clothes does burn a lot of electricity and there is almost no better smell than that of sun-dried sheets! Patience and I are definitely installing a line this spring. Of course, line-drying in the great outdoors is not really an option up here in Minnesnowta, at least for about 6 months of the year unless you like sleeping on a block of ice, and while I'm *hot natured*, thank you no, and I'm pretty sure Patience wouldn't be too happy about it either. If you have a basement and your washer is down there already, like mine is, consider putting up a line down there. What's more Hobbit-like than drying clothes under ground? If your basement isn't too stinky and musty, it's an option to consider. If they aren't drying fast enough, try running a small fan on them to help speed up the process. Make sure the fan is an efficient one.

Probably the best way to save on washing, as well as other things is to re-evaluate your wardrobes, which we will talk about in a bit, in the bedroom chapter. Also, as mentioned in the bathroom section limit the number of towels each person uses per week — two is a good number. Mark towels, either with monograms or separate colors so everyone knows which towels are theirs, and dole them out 2 at the beginning of the week, or on washing day, whenever that is. Wash and dry less often. This is especially true of running the dryer. If you do all your laundry on one day of the week, drying the loads back to back, you can take advantage of the residual heat stored up in the dryer, instead of letting that heat go to waste in between loads. As with the washer buy the most efficient dryer you can afford; it will help to save the Earth.

## Training Little Hobbits

If you have young Hobbits in your hole — especially preteen boys — you'll need to give them a lecture on putting their clean clothes away, and not just throwing their dirties on top of the freshly cleaned clothes in that hamper that you put on their bed so that you have to clean the already cleaned clothes, again! Seriously, it happens. Just remind them, that when they do this that they are not only wasting energy and *killing Mother Nature* in the process — which is very orcish — they are also wasting TIME, your time and theirs by doing a job twice. Time is something we all wish we had more of and doing things inefficiently is just a time suck.

# Heating the Hole

One of the big drains on power is of course the attempt to control temperature within our homes. Those of us in the West, and in particular, the U.S., are fairly intolerant of temperatures outside our comfort zone. Personally, if the outside temperature never went over about 75 degrees Fahrenheit I'd be as happy as Bilbo in a barrel of beer. I don't mind cold weather, but five to six months of *polar vortexes* and tons of snow — especially when it comes in March, April, and MAY — is pushing the limits of my tolerance. But I chose to live in Minnesnowta, so I can't complain much, though I do, and probably will. There are some ways to enhance climate control in the Hobbit-hole that will save both power, and money.

## Clothing

What we wear is really the primary climate moderator. After all, how many of us agree with our significant other about the temperature in our homes? Not many of us, I'd be willing to bet. That being said, and agreed upon, the only way to settle the question, or the quickest way, is to set the temperature so that the person with the hottest nature is comfortable in summer, with a minimum amount of clothing, while the other person wears more clothes! The same goes for winter. For instance, my house has been set on about 64 all winter because I'm very hot natured. Patience, on the other hand wears about 5 tons of garments in the house to keep warmer. In the summer, since we don't have central air-conditioning, we put in two window units in the bedrooms which managed to keep the temperature to around 75 or so. I walked around in nothing but boxer shorts while she wore her wool lined parka! Sorry, sometimes I suffer from *hyperbolia*.

## Efficient Systems

Have your heating and cooling systems checked for efficiency. Many power companies will come out and give a free inspection and offer other sound advice on saving energy in the home while they're at it. Take advantage of this advice. If your system is out of date, and inefficient, consider upgrading it, if you can afford the upfront costs. In the long run it will save energy, and of course, money.

## Insulation

One of the things you can do is to make sure your home is well insulated. Much of the energy we spend on heating and cooling is wasted as it seeps out drafty windows and doors, or up through the ceiling. When I was a bachelor Dwarf, many moons ago, my brother, Tim, and I lived in a peach of an apartment that had been carved out of an old house in New Bern, NC. We had one gas heater in the living room—that was all we had—and it either burned hot-as-hell, or cold-as-ice; there was no happy medium. When I say that the windows in that place were drafty, I'm being generous. In fact, it was *WINDY*; you could see the curtains billowing inwards every time the wind blew outside. At times I wondered if there was any glass in them at all! That's an extreme example of course, but illustrates my point well enough I reckon. If your windows are drafty—the power company can check that too—then you can use weather stripping to seal them up better, or put up storm windows outside. If you can afford it install new more efficient windows. The same goes for doors as well.

Make sure to insulate all the ductwork in your house, if you have any. Much heated and cooled air is lost due to dissipation through the metal in your duct work. And if some of it is in your basement, where your plumbing is, make sure to wrap the hot water pipes while you're at it, and get an insulating blanket to wrap your hot water heater, too! If you have an attic, make sure it has the maximum amount of insulation. Heat rises. Don't give it anywhere to go.

## Think about Spaces

In the *olden* days, people did not heat their entire homes all winter, or have the luxury of central air conditioning in the summer. They heated and cooled the rooms they spent time in, and many times shut off rooms and sometimes entire sections of a house during the extreme seasons of the year. Now most of us probably have no desire to return to the olden days but it's worth considering these things, if for no other reason than to remind ourselves of just how pampered we have become.

I remember my dad telling me about how his mother grew up in rural Georgia back in the early days of the 20th Century. My great-grandfather was a musician which means he was probably broke most of the time. Trust me, I've been one myself. So his family of nine or ten lived in a little shack-of-a-house with a dirt floor and holes in the roof. My grandmother remembered at least once when they got a fairly rare snow one winter, waking up to see her father brushing snow off of her blanket because it was coming through the holes in the roof! So suck it up little Hobbit! Things aren't that uncomfortable in your hole! If you have options to shut off rooms or add a little space heating to the rooms you spend most of your time in, do it. If you make sure the space heaters are highly efficient, and use them in small rooms when you're actually *in* there, it will save money and energy. And don't forget the blankets! If nothing else, they'll keep the snow off your hairy toes!

## Sunlight

Don't forget the power of the sun. In fact, all power and energy on Earth originates in the sun. If you have sun-facing windows make sure your blinds are open during the day to capture as much of that free heating as possible, or in the summer, keep them shut during the times when you're getting direct sun through them. Have you considered installing a skylight? However you do it, find ways to bring more free light and heat into your home.

## Windows, Doors and Screens

In the summer, on milder days, but especially in the spring and fall, take advantage of natural cooling that occurs during the night by opening up your windows and letting fresh cool air circulate through your house. You can enhance this with the smart placement of a couple of fans. Most of the time, the most efficient way is to place the fans—box fans work best—in a south-facing window, blowing OUT of the window. Then open one window per room and the fans will pull hot air out and the cooler night air in through the open windows. In the morning, before it heats up outside, close them to trap the cool night air in the house. Just watch the temperatures on the thermostat, outdoor thermometer, or via the Weather Channel to gauge when it's best to close the windows and seal in the cool air you gained during the night. If you remember to turn off your cooling system at night this little technique can maximize your results and save energy. This can also be run during the day to heat the house up as well, depending on the balance of temperatures between outside and inside.

## Breezes and Shade Trees

Open windows and doors to take advantage of breezy days. If you already have shade trees on your property, as I do, then you are lucky. If you're looking to buy a home, make sure it has some shade falling on the house during the middle of the day. This will help keep your house cooler in summer, and if the shade is hardwood, then in winter the leaves will not be there and you can take advantage of sunlight beaming down on your roof and in through your windows to heat your house. Unless you live in Minnesnowta, of course, where the winter sun is an ancient myth, like the Loch Ness Monster, the Yeti, or honest politicians.

The point is, that we should not think that just because it's our home that we can set the thermostat to a magical number and be comfortable, nor that we should. We need to be mindful of the energy it takes to run the system. How comfortable is the temperature in your home when in the back of your mind you're thinking, "How much pollution is this pumping into the air?" or "How much money am I giving away to the fossil fuel industry?" That's the one that sends me to the thermostat to turn it down, up, or off. Always keep in mind that saving energy is not just saving the Earth from pollution but also keeping our dragon gold out of the pockets of Saruman's corporations, where he will certainly use it to hire more Wormtongues to pollute our political systems. Keep your dragon gold by turning down the heat and air. Spend it on something else, like food or beer.

# Sundry Power Sucks...

## Computers

I love my little Macbook. Without it I would probably not be writing this book. However, it's a power drain when it's plugged in to charge. I don't want to overstate the amount of power that gadgets, like our computers, use. In reality, they make a small dent in our power usage but if there are easy fixes, it pays in the long run to do them. There's no way around that power suck when it's charging but when it's not charging, it should be disconnected from the power strip and run on it's batteries.

A tip on laptop batteries, or rechargeable batteries in general, which includes your cell phone, Kindle, iPad, etc. Rechargeable batteries are like muscles, sort of. When you first get them, before you charge it up fully you should <u>run the battery all the way down to zero the first time you use the device</u>. This calibrates the battery. It will function much better, last longer each time and for life. Run it down to zero often. This seems counter intuitive, I know, but trust me, if you Google the issue that is the advice most experts will give. There's no need to waste power from the wall when you have a battery powered tool.

"But what about my desktop computer?" you ask. Most of us have probably heard that all of our little chargers and computers drain power from the wall, even when the device is off. This is true. So, either unplug chargers when they are not being used or put them all on a central power strip somewhere in your home, and hook that up to a timer set to go off at a certain time when you won't be using it. There are also power strips that will automatically shut down all the peripheral units plugged into it when the central thing is shut down. This would be useful for the strip your desktop computer is plugged into. All you have to do is to power down your computer completely when you're not going to use it, like at night when you're asleep, and the strip will shut off all the other things plugged into it, i.e., speakers, monitor, etc.

The first step in solving the energy crisis on this planet is for us Hobbits to cut back on the amount of power we use, via the methods above. There are many other power saving tips out there. Take some time to look for them. Also subscribe to my blog at www.stevebivans.com, the *Be a Hobbit* Facebook page, or follow me on Twitter, for updates and news about new and exciting things happening in the world of science and technology, some of which has to do with saving energy, but some of it with how we can generate our own!

# Generating Power for the Hobbit-hole

The best way to save energy and to contribute to the future health of our planet is to generate cleaner, renewable energy. Many people are starting to find ways to generate their own power, at home. There are a couple of viable options available to us these days: solar and wind. Water driven power is another one that people talk about, but because it requires damming up rivers, I'm going to leave it out. Dams create lots of other environmental problems, so for now we'll stick with wind and solar.

**Solar Power**

In reality, all forms of energy on Earth originate with the sun. Light energy from our nearest star is turned into life energy in plants, which is then stored in their cells in the carbon which is concentrated over millions of years into coal, oil and natural gas. But those forms of "ancient sunlight," as Thom Hartmann refers to fossil fuels in his book, *The Last Hours of Ancient Sunlight: The Fate of the World and What We Can Do Before It's Too Late*, are finite. There is only X amount of it on the Earth, as mentioned earlier in the book, and when we burn all of that we will have to find another source of energy, or get used to freezing.

But why should we keep burning ancient sunlight when we have an essentially infinite amount of *current* sunlight to use? Yes, eventually the sun will burn out, like all stars do, and if we don't find a way to colonize other solar systems before then, we will die with it. But that is a very long time in the future. We are more likely to kill ourselves off by continuing to burn ancient sunlight, eating RoundUp, or rioting over the World Cup.

Solar power is one of the best options going to replace our dependence on fossil fuels. And you don't have to wait around for your local, state or federal governments to get in on the action, though some of them are, already. You can install solar panels on your own house or property and start reaping the benefits of the most renewable energy source there is. Yes, solar panels can be expensive to purchase, though if you have the money up front, it might be the best option. There is good news for those of us who can't afford to drop thousands of dollars up front, however. There are a couple of companies now offering lease options to home owners. If you own your home, you can rent solar panels!

Companies like SolarCity will come out, assess your situation to see if solar is viable for your property — you do need a lot of sun for it to work — and then if you decide to go with it, they will install the panels, hook up your system, and you're ready to roll! You pay a monthly rent, they own the equipment, and they repair it when there are issues. Check them out, or search for similar programs where you live.

One of the problems with solar, is that you need, well, lots of sun on your property for it to work and they require the mining of loads of rare metals which can have other environmental effects. Luckily, there are some wizards out there working on improving the efficiency of solar panels, by a LOT! We're talking by like 100 times more efficient. And these new panels are smaller and therefore use way less rare metals. If you want to know more about the new technologies, see the *Resource* section, or my website.

If solar power is an option for you, it pays to look into it. If you own your own panels, any surplus energy you create can be sold to the local power company, which means dragon coins in *your* pocket, not theirs! How awesome would that be? It's worth a look, at the very least. I don't know about you, but I'd love to tell the power company to stick their bills where the *sun don't shine.*

But maybe you have a shady yard, or you live somewhere like me, in the frigid, wastelands of the great white north, where the sun never seems to shine, or at least for like six months of the year. Solar isn't really an option for my house, I don't think, but the wind blows almost all the time, especially in the winter.

## Wind Power

If you live on an open plain out in the country, you should really consider putting up a windmill or two, or more, and generate your own power. There are far less restrictions out in the countryside than in urban areas, but check on the laws before you install them. In the city, there are almost always more restrictions so it definitely pays to do your research first. If your city allows private windmills and you have enough average wind speed, you can think about putting up a windmill too! There are companies that will inspect your wind speeds, set up the permits with the city/county and the power company, and install them. Unitedwind has a leasing program, similar to the SolarCity deal. Or if you're the handy, engineer type, you can build your own. See the Resource section for links.

## Combination

If you have a good bit of sun and live on a *Weather Top* where there's lots of wind, then why not install wind *and* solar options! It's good to have more than one source of power. Think about it for a minute. When is it usually windiest? When it's sunny, or cloudy? Usually when clouds are rolling in, just the time when solar panels would be useless. Wind tends to die down when weather is nice and sunny. Not always, but usually. If you have both options set up then you can take advantage of the strengths of both and minimize the weaknesses.

Don't feel like you have to run out and put up solar panels and windmills just yet, or over night. Like everything else in this book, it takes time to implement the ideas and incorporate them into your life. The Hobbits did not race to Mount Doom after all. It was a long journey. Take your time and celebrate the changes you make, as you make them. Occasionally sit back and take notice of the things you have already done to clean up the Shire. Sit back on your Hobbit chair, kick your hairy feet up on a stump, smoke your pipe, have a drink and say, "Ahhhhh." You deserve it.

# 28

# FURNISHING THE HOBBIT HOLE: COMFY CHAIRS, AND CUSHY BEDS

"Now let us take our ease here for a little!" said
Aragorn. "we will sit on the edge of ruin and talk...I
feel a weariness such as I have seldom felt before." He
wrapped his grey cloak about him, hiding his mail-
shirt, and stretched out his long legs. Then he lay back
and sent from his lips a thin stream of smoke.

"Look!" said Pippin. "Strider the Ranger has come
back!"

"He has never been away," said Aragorn. —*LOTR:*
II, *Flotsam and Jetsam*

Aragorn was happy to sit on the ruins of Isengard, but I'm quite
certain that Merry and Pippin would rather have been lounging
in Frodo's parlor on some comfy chairs, next to a warm fire.
Every Hobbit-hole has to have a place to sit, to eat, to sleep,
somewhere to kick up those hairy Hobbit feat and say, "Ahhh."
Most of us are not accustomed to doing these things on the floor
though it is important to remember that many people in the
world DO in fact spend most of their *home time* on the floor. I'm
certainly not going to start doing this at my age. I was never
limber enough to do the *indian* style sitting. I tell people all the

time that if something is below waist level, forget it, it's staying there. Most of us will want furniture to get us off the floor but there are no requirements as to where Hobbits are to acquire these furniture items.

Most westerners, at least, have too much furniture and pretty much all of us pay too much for it and end up buying low quality stuff because it's so expensive to buy the so-called *high quality* furniture. I worked in the furniture industry when I was a young man. Even the *high quality* is just factory, mass-produced garbage. So my first advice is to STOP BUYING NEW. You are wasting your money, and getting low quality for every dollar spent. If you want good furniture that will last a lifetime, take your time, and buy used stuff. Or if you have plenty to spend, find a true artisan and craftsman, and have them make it from reclaimed materials.

## Buy Proven Quality: Used Furniture

Case in point: When we moved to our new hole last year, we wanted a new desk. When I say *new* desk, I actually mean a *real* desk. The *desk* that we had been working on was purchased by Patience two years ago from Target or somewhere like that. It was one of those pressed-board pieces-of-crap that you can pick up in any mega-store, take home and assemble yourself. It was nearly falling apart from the beginning. You couldn't type on the computer without the entire thing swinging to and fro, like a cork in a hurricane. So when we were getting ready to move we went shopping at a local antique store to find a replacement.

One of my favorite antique stores is a shabby-chic place in Minneapolis, called *The Cottage House*. They only open for about five days each month, they sell like mad then close the doors, go searching for new stuff, repaint large sections of the store—which really is an old house—then reopen the next month, largely with a lot of *new* stuff. How they keep things turning over so quickly is by pricing it low. So you can always find a deal as long as you don't go in looking for something specific, like we were. We got lucky and they had a big, wooden, office desk sitting right there on the floor just waiting for us. It was all solid hardwood construction, even the drawers, which were dove-tail jointed. In contrast to our old *desk*, which could barely hold up a cup of coffee, our new one is sturdy enough for me to get up on top of it and jump up and down, and I am NOT a little Hobbit, trust me. I weigh around 300 pounds, closer to Cave Troll than halfling! I have not *actually* done said dance—because I pretty much suck at dancing—but I *could*, if I could dance. How much did I pay for this fine specimen of craftsmanship? $100. Yes, you read that correctly, and I did not forget a zero.

Such deals are out there if you take the time to look and if you're not in a hurry to buy something. That is the problem with *Taker* culture: we are always in a hurry to own something *right now*. It's the consumer mentality. We already had a *desk*, and quite frankly the day we went in to the Cottage House I really didn't want to buy anything yet because we were packing to move to our new house, so what was the point of buying *more* stuff to pack? But the deal on the desk was just too good to pass up so we snatched it, stuck it in the garage, where it was ready to go straight on the moving truck a week or so later.

## Slow Down and Breathe

Take your time acquiring furniture. If you don't have anything to sit on, borrow a few pieces from someone, or buy some used stuff at a thrift store. You can always donate them back later when you find better things. New furniture, stuff made in the last 50 years or so, is made to break down after a few years. It's factory made with cheap materials. Like I said, when I was a young lad, in my tweens I worked in a couple of furniture stores in North Carolina. These were not the low end, sell-to-the-masses, furniture outlets either. They were the uber-expensive, sell-to-the-Sarumans, type. The mark up on furniture, any kind, was about 500%. That was largely because the stuff that came in through the back door, was at least half of the time, damaged before it ever reached the customer or the showroom floor.

We had a full time furniture repair man on site and he was busy as hell, every day, fixing defects in the stuff that came through the door. So the furniture that rich people were buying, was already repaired. And they paid full price for it. A hefty percentage of what did make it into homes was returned shortly thereafter due to other defects found by picky consumers who, rightly so, did not want flawed merchandise when paying premium prices for it. So, when I say don't buy new furniture, I mean it. I NEVER do, and I never will again. There is simply too much used furniture out there for super low prices. If you buy new you are getting ripped off and you're creating a market for more new, crappy furniture which takes a enormous amount of material—much of it fossil fuel based—and water to create. One of the hidden wastes of water is the enormous amounts used and polluted by industry. So instead of buying new junk, buy solid, old furniture with proven, time-tested quality.

### Craigslist is Hobbit-Mart

Craigslist—one of the simplest, but greatest, inventions ever known to ma—is the Hobbit's super store, or Hobbit-Mart! I've bought numerous things on CL, and sold quite a few, too. I've found furniture, sold furniture, rented out rooms, found rooms to rent, and met some really nice people in the process. Some of you are probably wary of safety concerns when it comes to shopping on CL but the stories are overblown and sensational. Yes, there have been horror stories but if you really compared the number to the number of non-Craigslist stories, there are very few. Use common sense, take a friend, and meet other Hobbits in your Shire. We have become disconnected with each other. Let's reconnect, and take advantage of resources like CL. If you can't afford to buy furniture, another thing you can find on CL is construction material, like wood, many times, for free.

## Hone Your Inner Dwarf: Build Your Own

If you're handy with tools, why not build your own furniture? There are loads of plans and ideas out there on the internet for those with a little woodworking talent. Maybe you have a family member with a shop? Dads and grandfathers are great for this! Hit them up. Tell them you need a new dining table, but don't want to pay premium prices for a piece of junk.

Look for reclaimed lumber! If you do decide to build try to find reclaimed lumber to use. There are a few reasons why this is the best way to go. For one, it's cheaper, and that should be enough to convince most of you. Any lumber you can find will help save the planet. It saves trees, which is probably the most important reason to use reclaimed lumber. Did you know that 60% of the lumber produced in the U.S., ends up in a landfill? Neither did I, but it's true. 60%! A substantial portion of that — in the U.S., about 40% — is in the form of shipping pallets. The shipping industry, worldwide, uses up these things by the gazillions. In the U.S., one third of them are only used once and then discarded into landfills.

This is a huge waste of trees. Innovative people are finding thousands of ways to reuse these things by modifying them in numerous ways. Just search online for *pallet* and any combination of project, furniture, shelving, etc., and see what you find! Some of the things people have come up with are simply stunning, and beautiful! Step outside the box and allow yourself to see 'junk' in a different light. There is even a plan for building your own 'tiny house' with mostly shipping pallets! By using reclaimed lumber in all its forms you can save money and the Earth at the same time.

### Shop at Hobbit-Mart for Lumber Too!

Every time you buy new wood at Home Depot or any other hardware store you contribute to the death of a tree somewhere in the world. So only buy it new if you simply cannot find it used, and can't do without it. As mentioned above, you can find quality wood, including hard to find, hard woods, on Craigslist every day. Search for it just for kicks. Look under *materials* or just *for sale*, but don't forget to look under the *free* section. Yes, there is a large section on CL that is dedicated to giving away stuff for free! I bet you didn't know that. I didn't until recently and I've used CL for years. I just didn't read all the categories until a few months ago!

### Reuse, Rebuild, Refashion

Reuse furniture or remake it into something else. If you have otherwise solid furniture don't just discard it when a part breaks. Especially if you are talented with woodworking or know someone who is. Fix it, or disassemble the wooden parts, and keep them to make something new. Some people have created a business out of doing just that! And it's not a new idea, in fact, it's a very old one. Again, your best source for ideas is the internet. Look up *broken chair*, and other combinations and see what comes up. Do it! It's fun to see all the creative ideas that people come up with.

### Grandma Bivans's Piano

The only thing handed down to me from my grandparents, on my dad's side — besides DNA — is their old piano. Yes, there are many times in my life, since my dad inherited it, that I wish my grand-parents had just passed along a pocket watch instead of a 500 pound upright piano. Alas, the piano is what I got. It's not pretty, not anymore anyway, thanks to three boys banging on it and running their matchbox cars over the keys, not to mention battles between 'Kung Fu Grip" G.I. Joes, Batman and Steve Austin, on the top of it. It's been moved so many times and the strings are so rusty that it can't be repaired or restored back to working condition. But I can't seem to part with it since it's the one heirloom I have left. So, I'm considering ways to use the parts to make something new with it that will be useful as well as attractive, instead of consigning it to an already bulging landfill somewhere in Minnesota. There are a lot of ideas online, but I haven't yet decided what to do with it, but I will. Keep an eye out on my website, and Facebook page, and I promise I'll post pictures once I figure it out.

# Rugs and Carpet

Most carpet and rugs that are made today are made with synthetic materials, mainly fossil fuels. If you must have carpet try to find more sustainable stuff — see GreenAmerica's article on it — otherwise you are adding more plastics to your house, which will be sucked up by your vacuum cleaner and wafted around in the air where you and your family will breath in microscopic particles of it. Not to mention that carpets are homes for allergens and dust. Area rugs are generally a better option, as long as the materials are natural, and most are not. Do some research online for more natural options.

### Sustainable Shampooing

Carpet and rugs get dirty—ours definitely do with the Viking Pirate Kitties and our old dog, Bubble sleeping on them, rolling around on them, leaving their fur, hair and dander everywhere. Not to mention that Bubble only likes to eat her T-R-E-A-T-S *on* the rug in the office so there are microscopic dog treat crumbs along with dried dog spit worked into the fibers. Yay. Recently Patience has been suffering from seasonal allergies, so we decided to do a deep cleaning of the house, including the rugs. The only significant one we have is the one in the office so we dragged it out onto the driveway on top of a tarp. I went to the grocery store and rented a Rug Doctor carpet cleaner but I didn't really trust—or want to pay for—the chemicals they sell for it so we mixed up our own cleaning formula with hot water, vinegar, dish soap, and super washing soda. See the recipe in the *Resource* section.

## Comfy, Sustainable Hobbit Beds

One of the things that many of us overlook when it comes to furniture is the quality of our mattresses, pillows, sheets and blankets. The bedding industry, like many, is fraught with negative environmental impacts. They have been heavily dependent on fossil fuels, especially oil, to make foam mattresses, pillows, as well as the covers for both. Mattresses are rarely recycled so they go to fill up landfills with essentially more plastics. The more important and immediate problem is that which it may inflict upon our health, as we sleep.

Because most of the foam we sleep on is made from oil, it *off-gasses* chemicals used in the process of manufacturing and we breathe those in. Some people seem to suffer no obvious effects from this, but many do, and are looking for more natural alternatives. A select few companies in the industry have been working to clean up their act and to produce more sustainable, non-toxic options, but they have a long way to go. Some of the so-called *green* companies have been caught *green-washing* their image, more than actually producing *green* products. TripplePundit has a very good article on this topic. It pays to do one's research before purchasing new bedding.

There's not enough time and space to cover all the options that are out there when it comes to mattresses, pillows, and other bedding but here are some general thoughts.

- **Read the labels:** If you can't pronounce the ingredients in your pillow or mattress, it's not a good sign.

- **Research online:** There are numerous articles and websites dedicated to natural, organic bedding.

- **Buy natural/organic materials when possible:** Buy only organic cotton/wool textiles, or other natural, organic options, like hemp. The cotton industry in particular, is a very damaging one.

Materials are also important when it comes to the garments we wear, which is where we're going next: into the closet.

# 29

# LOBELIA'S CLOSET:
# THE HOBBIT'S WARDROBE

"You won't find your clothes again," said Tom, bounding down from the mound, and laughing as he danced round them in the sunlight...

"What you mean? asked Pippin, looking at him, half puzzled and half amused, "Why not?"

But Tom shook his head, saying: "You've found yourselves again out of the deep water. Clothes are of but little loss, if you escape from drowning. Be glad, my merry friends, and let the warm sunlight heat now heart and limb! Cast off these cold rags! Run naked on the grass while Tom goes a-hunting!" —*LOTR*: I, *Fog on the Barrow-downs*

Clothes make the man. Naked people have little or no influence on society. —Mark Twain

Normal is getting dressed in clothes that you buy for work and driving through traffic in a car that you are still paying for—in order to get to the job you need to pay for the clothes and the car, and the house you leave vacant all day so you can afford to live in it. — Ellen DeGeneres

This is a touchy subject, especially for some of my readers, and for Patience—she doesn't really have that many garments, I just

like to give her crap. However, most of us in the West—
especially in the U.S,—have entirely too many clothes in our
closets. Obviously, we all need clothes to wear, as Mr. Twain
pointed out above, but how many is enough? Speaking for
myself—even after weeding out clothes before we moved last
year—I still have a bunch that I never wear, for whatever
reason: I just don't like a particular item, it doesn't actually fit
me, it shrunk or I expanded—I prefer to use the first excuse,
otherwise I might have to start skipping second breakfast—or
any combination of those, or other reasons. I'm getting ready to
dive into my closet again soon to really take a tough look at
what's in there and get rid of most of it. I'm sure my mom will
be whispering in my ear the entire time, "Oh, if you don't *wear*
it, just get rid of it!"

## Weeding Out

Bea Johnson, author of *Zero Waste*, weeded her closet down to
what would fit into one suitcase, along with everything else she
needed for international travel. I'm not suggesting that you do
that; I'm pretty sure I'm not, but cutting our wardrobes down to
what we really need can free up time as well as money. Think
about how much money we spend on clothing. According to
U.S. government statistics, in 2013, on average, men spent over
$300 and women over $700, for clothing and that doesn't
include what we spend on our children's clothes! And of course,
that is just the initial costs of our clothing. There is also the cost
of cleaning all of it. The more you have, the more you have to
wash, and there's a lot of costs involved in that, not just the
obvious ones either. Time is money, right? How much time do
you spend washing clothes? Too much, I'm betting. At the very
least, go through your wardrobe, and give each piece an
interrogation.

- **Do I ever wear this?** If so, how often? Don't keep
  garments just because you think you might need them
  sometime down the road, especially if they are too small,
  or too large.

- **Does it fit?** Most of us are guilty of the excuse, "I'm on a
  diet; I'll probably be able to fit into it in a couple of

months." Or, "I might get fat again, maybe I should keep those old sweatpants with holes in them." Think positive; you probably will lose the weight, but if so, buy some *new* clothes. If you gain weight, you'll look better in something that fits, not holey sweatpants. No one looks good in those. Okay, maybe a couple of people on Earth can pull it off, but I'm not one of them.

- **Is it comfortable?** If you don't like wearing it, you probably don't wear it. Get rid of it. Give them away, use them for rags, sell them, or recycle them—some cities will accept them in your regular recycling bin.

- **Do I have duplicates?** If you have two or more of the same item, in the same color, rethink them.

Personally, I have some items that I don't wear very often, but I will keep. For example, I have a full Scottish black tie outfit: kilt, jacket, shirt, shoes, bowtie, etc. Do I ever wear it? Yeah, rarely, but I do wear it on occasion, so it stays. I also make allowances for costumes, but not too many. I used to have a lot of them in boxes, or trunks, but now I'm trying to put together one good Middle Earthy one for parties.

If a particular article doesn't pass the interrogation put it in the recycling bin! If it's in good usable shape donate it to the Salvation Army, or Goodwill so someone else can benefit from it. If it's too worn out for that cut it up and use it as a cleaning rag, napkins, handkerchiefs, or patches for jeans. Old T-shirts, as long as they're not falling apart can be made into a cloth shopping bag, with only one seam. Basically, you cut off the sleeves, on the outside of the seam, cut a larger neck hole— much larger, this will be the top of the bag—and then sew the bottom of the shirt together with a strong stitch, and voila! You have a bag! Check out the instructions here, or see the link in the Resource section.

### Buying Clothes

Buy used. It's time we got over the stigma of doing so. Trust me, I know it's not as easy to find all sizes in thrift stores. Some second hand stores are more organized than others but if you adopt the maxim that you only replace one item for one discarded and keep a small wardrobe to begin with then you won't have to shop very often and you can go with a specific purpose when you shop. Too many times I have been dragged shopping for clothing—kicking and screaming mind you, I'm a man—with the intention of only buying a pair of jeans, or shorts, and walked out an hour later having purchased two pair of jeans, two shorts, five shirts, some socks and a couple of belts and my bank account was drained! You must do better than I, and I have to do better than that! We simply don't need that many clothes, and there are lots of good clothing in thrift stores. (Note: Patience—when she read the *dragging, kicking* comment, pointed out that I used to like going shopping with her, so let me be clear. I *love* shopping with her, for *her* wardrobe, but I hate shopping for my clothes. Peace is restored).

When shopping, especially for new stuff if you must have it, avoid polyester and any other man-made fibers. You'll be wearing oil, literally. It's orc skin. It's not healthy, and it's not even comfortable. It doesn't breathe so you sweat more. I hate the stuff, always have. Most of us do. I remember back in the early 90s I was out of work for a while, with a young daughter to feed, so I went out one day with the intent of finding a job, any job, or not coming home till I did. I found one but it was working at Burger King—remember? Wading in hot grease? Back in the 90s, fast food workers didn't have the snazzy cotton uniforms they do today; it was all polyester. They simply could not have chosen a hotter, more uncomfortable fabric to put on wage-slaves than that. It made a miserable job even more miserable. So avoid that stuff, and while you're at it don't forget to avoid the fast food too.

Instead, choose real food, natural fibers, and if possible, organically grown ones: cotton, wool, silk, etc. This is especially true when it comes to cotton. Most cotton is sprayed with chemical pesticides and herbicides, like Roundup, and is one of the main crops, behind corn and soybeans, that contributes to the pollution of our water. And cotton, even organic, consumes an enormous amount of water. To produce one t-shirt and a pair of jeans the industry requires <u>20,000 litres, or over 5200 gallons of water</u>! Organic growers do try to limit that somewhat, so, if you're buying new garments, buy ones made of organic materials, better yet, buy used. The organic ones will be more expensive, but if you're buying fewer items, it will wash out—sorry, couldn't avoid that pun; it was just lying there.

## Shoes

I once read somewhere—so long ago that I don't remember where—some advice given to a young man looking to go into business. The advisor, whoever it was, told the man to get into selling food, or shoes, because everyone had to eat and the average American woman had about 10 pair of shoes at any given time. That number has probably increased since then. A survey in Britain suggests that women there have an average of 19 pair.

I know I'm going to get into trouble on this topic as well, but since I'm usually into trouble anyway, I'm just gonna charge right in, like Theoden on Snowmane! We simply don't need 10-20 pair of shoes. If we were true Hobbits, we wouldn't need shoes at all! Remember, Bilbo and Frodo walked all the way to the Lonely Mountain and Mordor—respectively—and back again, barefoot! Maybe 10 should be the upper limit—if you include snow-boots and those Gene Simmons, K.I.S.S., platform boots you have hidden in the corner of your closet—you know who you are. But no one should need more than that, unless they're a performer or something—or Imelda Marcos (If you don't know who she is, look it up and include *shoes* in the search).

I have too many, and I probably own about 6: snow boots—no way around those in MN, hiking boots, tennis shoes, sandals and two pair of worn out *dress* shoes. I only wear one of the dress pair now because the brown ones are so worn out that they don't keep out the dew on the grass, much less if I step on wet pavement. Yuck. I'm getting ready to get rid of those and probably buy some new dress shoes, though I'll be kicking and screaming then as well. There's nothing I hate much more than shopping for shoes—*my* shoes, that is; I *love* shopping for Patience's shoes. She just informed me that she only has 10 pair, so I guess she's a below average American shopper, which isn't the same thing as a below average American woman—which she's definitely not.

If you must shop try to find used shoes that are still in good condition. If you can't, buy quality shoes that offer repair instead of just throwing them out when they're worn down. Also, there is some progress being made in the industry to make shoes that are more sustainable for the environment. Much of them are made with poly-rubber soles, of course, which are going to end up in a landfill where they will sit for eternity. Timberland is one of the leading companies trying to change the way shoe manufacturers do business. They have initiated shoe labeling that gives the consumer information about the materials being used, where it was made, its carbon footprint — another pun — if you will. Hopefully, the other major manufacturers will join them before long. So, I would recommend you check out their brand when you go shoe shopping next time. Also see if anyone else is copying them with the labeling idea. If so, support them, too.

**Recycle and Donate**

When your shoes wear out or you're tired of storing them don't just throw them into the landfill. Some 20 billion pairs of shoes are produced every year in the world and 300 million are tossed into landfills. This is a waste of materials, and many times just a waste of shoes that someone else could use! Pass them on. Give them to Goodwill or the Salvation Army or some other charity that accepts them.

Shore are important if you don't have leathery-soled feet to walk on. After all we have to get around from the market to the Ivy Bush Pub somehow right? The cleanest way to do that is by walking, but when it's too far to walk and you don't have a year to get here and back, like Bilbo and Frodo, then you need faster transport, and guess what? That's the destination of our next chapter!

# 30

# GETTING THERE AND BACK AGAIN: HOBBIT TRANSPORTATION

The Road goes ever on and on
Down from the door where it began.
Now far ahead the Road has gone,
And I must follow, if I can.
—*LOTR*: I, *Three is Company*

Ramble On, And now's the time, the time is now,
to sing my song.
I'm goin' 'round the world, I got to find my girl,
on my way.
I've been this way ten years to the day, Ramble On,
Gotta find the queen of all my dreams.
Got no time to for spreadin' roots,
The time has come to be gone.
And to' our health we drank a thousand times, it's
time to Ramble On. —Led Zeppelin, *Ramble On*

If we want to make a huge personal impact on the environment of our Shires, the best place to start, after our food and household energy consumption is to examine how we get around from the Shire to Bree and beyond. One of the biggest contributors to pollution and waste is, of course, our motor vehicles. We burn a ridiculous amount of fossil fuels—not to mention the amount consumed in the manufacturing process— all to get us around to the places we need or want to go. While there are public transportation options in most big cities in the U.S., most of us cling to our personal cars as if they were our final lifeline or something.

I'm not preaching, I do it too. I have a car in the driveway, though we only have one for the household. Still, I'd love to get rid of it most days. The expense of owning a car is huge. How much do you spend on yours every month, every year? Don't forget to include insurance, gas, and maintenance in that figure. Families in the U.S. spend on average about $5000 per year on just the gas and maintenance of their vehicles. They spend another $3000 on a car payment. All of this expense we incur while on average most of us only drive our vehicles about 1 hour per day! That's right. That's the average for a household in the U.S. Do the math. Does it make sense to keep doing this? Patience and I have been discussing what we're going to do once we pay off our car. We haven't decided yet, but we are both leaning toward either parking it most of the time, or getting rid of it entirely. While most of us are still clinging to the independence that our cars supposedly give us—or that Bernays-Sarumans have told us they give us—many of the millennial generation of drivers are opting out in large numbers, instead choosing to use public transportation or to share cars with friends. They are also joining the *cooperative consumption* movement.

## Cooperative Cars: Shared Ownership

There are alternatives for those who need a car to drive on occasion, or even daily, without the expenses and hassle of buying and maintaining a personally owned vehicle. Zipcar, is one option. Instead of owning a car or leasing it month to month, you only rent and pay for the time you actually use it. If, like most Americans, you only drive one hour per day, then that's what you pay for. Once you sign up to be a Zipcar customer you get a card with an imbedded chip which becomes your key to unlock the car you've rented. When you set up a rental online the card is activated and will unlock the vehicle you chose, parked somewhere near where you live. At Zipcar you pay for the actual time you drive it: an hour, a day, or however long you may need it. They even include the price of insurance and GAS! There's a gas card in the car to refill it when you're done. According to surveys they've done with their customers the average house-hold saves around $400 per month by switching! That's a lot of dragon gold, Frodo.

What Zipcar does differently than any other car rental company is to personalize the transaction; their cars have names for a start. Maybe the new Shire-Nation could start suggesting Tolkien themed names for Zipcars!? I'll have to check into that.

There are other companies getting in on this new model of transportation. Some metro areas are getting into the business. In St. Paul, we have HOURCAR, which works in a similar way to Zipcar. The main difference is the HourCars are tiny, compacts, really only good for short trips with two people and groceries or two parents and a small child or so. The upside is that you can park them anywhere when you're done, even in the street in front of your Hobbit-hole! Most of these new companies also pay closer attention to their customers' usage patterns: where they live, how often they rent, how far they drive, etc., so they can better plan to serve their customer base. The business has exploded in the last few years and is continuing to expand. Some have trial periods with discounted rates. Keep an eye out for that. But even if they don't run a trial period maybe your family will want to try it out? I think we're going to do it this summer sometime. We'll pick one month; park our car, and use Zipcar for those times we need a vehicle, just to see how well it works for us.

### Rent Your Car

Even if you decide to keep your vehicle, and Zipcar doesn't fit your lifestyle, there are other options to save money and lower the carbon footprint of your vehicle. You can even *make money*! Many Eco-conscious people are now renting out their personal cars when they're not being used. As mentioned, most people only drive their vehicles an average of 1 hour per day, so for 23 hours every day, it just sits there *costing* you money. Why not make yours available for other responsible people to use, when you're not? RelayRides is a fairly new company that arranges for car rentals between people, kind of like Craigslist, but with safeguards to protect your vehicle. Much like Zipcar, drivers who want to rent vehicles through RelayRides are vetted for a clean driving record — they have to go through an application process which includes their driver's license #. RelayRides then checks their record and if they're in good standing they can then rent cars through their service.

Maybe you have a second or third vehicle that you don't drive very much? It's just sitting there costing you money. Put it to work for you when you're not using it. Someone else might just need a pickup truck to haul organic mulch for their garden. I know I do. Many times I wish I still had my old Dodge Ram truck with it's primer gray paint job, huge dent in the rusty, front right panel, the broken right taillight hanging on with duct tape and a bungee cord. The steering was so loose that you had to counter-steer to keep it on the road. And forget about what speed you're traveling; the speedometer didn't work, so I just guest-imated. But alas, it died many years ago, and I sold it off as junk. But there are days I sure could use it. Though paying for the gas in that thing is not something I miss. Maybe you have a truck I could rent? If so, put it on RelayRides and I'll check it out!

## "But I Love My Car"

I'm not twisting your arm to sell your car, or rent it for that matter, but it's worth considering. Patience was very, very reluctant to even consider the idea when I first discovered these options but after rolling it around in her noggin' for a few days, she started to think, "You know, that car is really expensive to keep. Maybe I should rethink it?" And so now we're going to try Zipcar or RelayRides soon, for a short period, to see how it works out. When we aren't renting a car we'll ride public transportation.

## Public Transport

If you live in an urban area, you probably have public transportation options available to you. If so, take advantage of them. Buses, trains, subways, light-rails save tons of carbon by moving lots of people at a time. If you opt to try one of the many shared-ownership options mentioned above then public transportation might be the quickest way to get to that car you rented. We have a pretty good system in the Twin Cities. I used to ride the buses and Light-Rail a lot when I lived in Minneapolis and had to go to campus every day. These days I rarely ride public transport but I'm going to start doing it again. Some cities have discounts if you buy a monthly pass that lets you ride unlimited times. Some of them are basically a debit card that subtracts from a prepaid amount. Some cities offer unlimited passes at a reduced rate to college students through the college website. If you're a student, check on this! I used to have an unlimited pass through the University of Minnesota. If you ride a lot it's worth the cost, which was only about $100 per semester a couple years ago.

**Share with a Neighbor**

If you rarely drive anyway, and you're close friends with your neighbor, a neighbor that does have a car, maybe you could borrow theirs every once in a while? Maybe work out a deal where you help pay for some of the expenses in exchange for X amount of driving time? You never know, they might just be interested in saving some money. Most people are. If they don't drive a lot either then the arrangement might be even more attractive to both parties! Maybe set up a *Shire-Ride* exchange website, or do it through the neighborhood Facebook page? You never know; there might be more people interested than you think.

# Ride Your Bike

Bikes are probably the cleanest form of non-Hobbit-foot transportation. Yes, there is the carbon footprint created in the manufacturing process and the replacement of tires occasionally, but other than that it's pretty much carbon free. If you have a bike, pump up the tires, straighten the handlebars, and get moving! I need to get a new bike myself. I used to ride a good bit from the house to school a few years ago. I could actually get from my driveway to my desk on campus *faster* on a bike than in my car. That's because I could park my bike right outside the building, literally next to it, whereas I had to park the car two blocks away and walk. It would take me close to 20-25 minutes via car while only 17 on my bike. So cars are not always the faster means, at least for short trips. And of course, there are the health benefits from the exercise you'll get pedaling from Bag End to Frogmorton.

## Scooters

I've been considering buying a scooter to drive to work and other places where I don't need a big car to carry a bunch of crap. This is another option if you aren't as athletic as some people who would rather pedal their bike up and down hills. If you are considering buying one, that is, if you don't already have one then consider getting an electric one. Gas-powered scooters do save money, over all, on gasoline, and so at the same time consume less fossil fuels but they are more pollutive than cars, emission wise anyway. Electric ones can be plugged in, which of course means that fossil fuels are usually being consumed somewhere to charge it but less than if you burn it in your scooter tank directly. Also, you could consider setting up a small solar panel on top of your garage just to charge the scooter! Then you would avoid burning oil altogether.

## Pat 'n Charlie: Hairy Hobbit Feet

The cleanest way to get from one place to another, of course, is by foot. Hobbits had an aversion to most types of transport anyway, unless it was via cart, and then only a slow one. They could ride a pony, and would of course do so if chance or need arose. But most of the time they preferred to walk. Bilbo loved walking. He had several maps of the Shire hanging in his house, with all his favorite walking paths marked out, and a small collection of his favorite walking sticks close at hand. There's nothing quite like a good walking stick. I personally think that the best ones are found while walking in the woods. Or maybe I should say that the best walking sticks find *you*, while walking in the woods. I used to carve walking sticks as a hobby, years ago. I carved several with dragon heads, and at least one with a wizard's head. I gave them all away, as Hobbit gifts, to friends of mine. I don't have one for myself, though I've lately been wishing I had. I will have to spend more time in the woods this spring and summer and see if one finds me.

Walking is one of the best things we can do to live as a Hobbit. It's therapeutic in many ways. It slows us down, which most of us need to do; I certainly do. I tell people all the time that there's this clock in my head, just tick-tocking, tick-tocking away, all the time. I wish I could shut it off sometimes. Maybe you're the same way? Get outside and walk. See what's in your neighborhood, your Shire. Meet people, as I said earlier in the book. Take time to look at the beautiful things growing around you. Maybe start your walk in your own garden, the topic of the next chapter.

# 31

# GAMGEE'S VICTORY GARDEN: HOME-GROWN GRUB

No one had a more attentive audience than old Ham Gamgee, commonly known as the Gaffer...and he spoke with some authority, for he had tended the garden at Bag End for forty years, and had helped old Holman in the same job before that. Now that he was himself growing old and stiff in the joints, the job was mainly carried on by his youngest son, Sam Gamgee...

With perfect truth: for Bilbo was very polite to him, calling him 'Master Hamfast', and consulting him constantly upon the growing of vegetables — in the matter of 'roots', especially potatoes, the Gaffer was recognized as the leading authority by all in the neighbourhood (including himself). — *LOTR*: I, *A Long Expected Party*

Gardening is the most therapeutic and defiant act you can do, especially in the inner city. Plus, you get strawberries. — Ron Finley

We've covered in some detail most of the stuff inside the Hobbit-hole. Now it's time to walk outside and see what we can do *around* the hole to save the Earth and bring spring again to the trees. As we did inside, when we started with the food in our kitchens we'll begin with growing food in our gardens. The surest way to take control of what we eat is to grow it ourselves. By doing so, we save money, which also takes money out of the hands of evil corporations. We also eat better food because we know what went into it. By sharing with our neighbors, our Shire, we build community and resilience against disasters, no matter what form they come in.

## Plant a Hobbit Victory Garden

During both World Wars, Americans were asked to start Victory Gardens in their backyards to help with the war effort. They were told it was the sure fire way to "Save the World for Democracy." Sound familiar? Yeah, it should. It's a product of Edward Bernays' work for the Committee of Public Information during the first war. It's interesting that the idea has resurfaced in the 21st Century, in large part a response to ever increasing food prices, the fear of corporate, engineered foods and the economic crash of 2007-8. What can be more democratic than growing some of, if not all of, your own food? I'm sure any Hobbit would say, "Who *ELSE* would grow it?" All Hobbits know how to grow things, especially fruits and veggies. On top of being democratic, it's the perfect way to stick our finger in Bernays' empty eye sockets! "Great idea Ed! Thanks! We'll take it, and use it to bring down all those corporate Sarumans you helped to set up!" Now *there's* some poetic justice for ya.

In *LOTR*, Sam Gamgee is the master gardener at Bag End having taken over that duty from his father, the Gaffer. He looks after Bilbo's and then Frodo's gardens and lawns. Of all the members of the Fellowship, it is to Sam that Galadriel gives a cultivator's dream: earth, and a Mallorn seed from Lothlorien! It is fortunate that she did because when the Hobbits returned to the Shire they found it devastated by the evil work of Saruman. Not only was the place a mess, Saruman had the great Party Tree cut down! Of all the acts in the *LOTR* this is the one that pisses me off the most! It makes me quite homicidal, actually. I can't watch documentaries about the rainforest without thinking about it. We could use some Mallorn seeds today, for sure.

## Why can't we all be Gamgees?

Answer: There's no good reason why not! Now, just so you know, I am *not* a master gardener. My thumb is closer to black than green though I have had some luck with a few plants in my life, I've had very little luck since moving to Minnesota, especially with tomatoes, my favorite. This summer we had a little more luck with 'maters, but our 'tater patch in the backyard was, well, pathetic. We planted like twelve potatoes, and reaped six or seven: not very Gamwise, I'm afraid. This spring, I'm going to get up with a local gardening group and find a master gardener to come to my house to help me out. Maybe I'll trade them something in return. You can do the same! There are millions of pages of advice online as well. I'll include some as we go along, and also at the end of the book in the *Resources* section.

## Ask Gamgee: Do Some Research

One thing a master gardener will tell you to do is to have your soil checked for nutrients by the local agricultural extension or the equivalent for your country. Even if you don't have a Sam Gamgee living in your neighborhood there are lots of good books on organic gardening. Also, check out Facebook for gardening clubs or organizations in your neighborhood. A lot of neighborhood organizations have pages on Facebook. Join yours, or search to find their website, and join. They will be happy to have you and many of them have links to gardening organizations in the area. If not, go to a locally owned garden center near you—preferably one that emphasizes organic gardening—and get to know the owner or some of the people working there and just pester them with questions till they 'shoo' you away. You can always come back another day with more questions. Most of them love to talk about plants anyway so it's probably you who will do the shoo'ing.

## Safer, Better, Cheaper Food

For me, the main reasons for growing my own food are controlling what goes into it and keeping my money in the local economy, and in my own pocket! As far as what goes into it, I plan to use no man-made chemicals. What I want is 100%

organic produce and to reduce the carbon footprint, i.e., how much power and resources I use. Also, I want to, as much as possible avoid using plastics in my garden or green house except when no other viable option is available. If I must use them, I will try to reuse existing plastics instead of buying new which just fuels further production of more plastics. At least if we keep using plastics that are already made we keep them out of the landfill, if only for a few more years.

**So the goals are:**

- organic
- low energy footprint
- used or no plastics.

# Planning Your Gamgee Victory Garden

### Foodscaping

A new idea, or I should say newly *rediscovered* idea, that's gaining ground lately is the idea of foodscaping. Instead of planting a bunch of ornamental plants and lawns around your house, plant food instead! Fruit trees, veggies, you name it! Who needs a bunch of grass anyway? It takes too much water and work—more on that later. The idea behind foodscaping is to reclaim our food independence by planting food on our own properties. It is very much the same kind of idea as the WWII Victory Gardens that our grandparents, and great-grandparents grew to support the war effort. Think of your garden as supporting the war effort too! Instead of supporting some war for oil supremacy—like some of the wars we are still engaged in—think of it as supporting the War against the Ring. Your foodscape is a blow against the forces of darkness: the Saurons and Saruman's of our world. And don't think for a moment that it isn't a blow. Every fruit tree and carrot grown in a backyard, takes dollars out of the pockets of the likes of Monsanto.

**"What would I do with all the extra produce that might occur?"**

Well, you could grow some of it on the boulevard next to your street and let your neighbors harvest food from it, for one. There are efforts in many major cities, St Paul included, to grow food on boulevards to help combat hunger. Instead of handing out money to homeless on street corners why not grow an apple tree in front of your house and put up a sign to pick what they need! Take some to a local food shelf or soup kitchen.

Trade some of it with your neighbors. What better way to create a Shire-like community than to exchange food with the people in your community? Maybe you have too many tomatoes. Maybe your neighbor down the street has too many beans. Trade with each other! You could even arrange — via the internet and knocking on doors — a neighborhood food exchange system or swap-meet once a week to do just that! Could there be anything more Hobbity than sharing food and making conversation with your neighbors? Bring beer and wine and make it a party! You could also make a small profit from your excess food. Is there a local farmer's market nearby? If so, sell some of your produce there, which is another place to meet the neighbors and other like minded people.

## Lawns: Only Cows Eat Grass

Lawns can be nice things for kids to run on, play baseball, football, etc., but they are in many ways a waste of resources, especially water and contribute to pollution of our rivers and oceans. Lawns require a lot of water, especially in the hot summers of North America these days, and most people load them up with chemical fertilizers much of which runs off into the gutters on the street. As mentioned earlier once that water hits the river it flows into the Gulf of Mexico without passing GO or collecting $200, carrying with it all kinds of poisonous chemicals that mid-western, bread-basket Americans have dumped on their lawns, excreted from their cars, runoff from their farms, not to mention all the plastic trash that is swept off our streets. So, while lawns might look really nice — if you baby them all the time — they can be very wasteful things. It comes down to personal choices but if you want to maintain a lawn think about the following things to help minimize or eliminate some of the impact.

## Tips for Shire-friendly Lawns:

- **Reduce it's size.** The smaller the lawn the less of everything you have to do to it. It makes it manageable in so many ways, not the least of which is the time it will save you mowing it and fretting over the weeds that pop up. Less is better when it comes to lawns and you can put that space to better use growing food.

- **Water lawns infrequently but heavily when you do.** It is better for lawns and plants in general to get an inch or so of rain per week than to water it just a little every day. This encourages deeper roots which conserve water and make for a much better lawn. If you can afford it have an irrigation system installed by professionals to help conserve water. There are even systems that only water when a certain dryness level is detected.

- **Avoid all man-made fertilizers.** Personally, I would not fertilize it at all. It doesn't really need it. Allow grass clippings to fall into the ground. They will create mulch which holds moisture. Avoid cutting the grass when it's wet to avoid clumping.

- **Aerate your lawn.** Instead of fertilizer, aerating the lawn occasionally let's air, water, and other nutrients to get into the soil. It also loosens the soil so the roots can spread out.

- **USE NO ROUNDUP!** Roundup is one of the most insidious chemicals ever introduced to the Earth. It is toxic as hell and linked to all kinds of health problems, including cancer and respiratory diseases. I've been guilty of spraying this crap in my gardens too, but not any more. Not to mention, it's an orcish product from Monsanto, the most hated corporation on Earth—a well earned hatred I might add. Avoid using any herbicides in your garden. You don't need them, especially on your lawn. The best preventative for weeds in your lawn is aerating and mowing often.

- **Mow the lawn often.** You should mow your lawn every 5-7 days if not more often, depending on how fast it grows. The rule is that you should never cut more than about 1/3 of the leaf from your grass. There are two reasons for this. If you cut more than that the plant spends most of its energy attempting to grow new leaf instead of deeper, more dense roots. Denser roots help to choke out weed roots which lowers the amount of weeds in your lawn. Also, if you mow frequently — since weeds usually grow leaf faster than the surrounding grass — you are cutting more than 1/3 of *their* leaf which forces them to grow more leaf instead of more roots. This creates a big *double-whammy* on weeds. Also, make sure you are not cutting your lawn too low to start with. Chances are, you are cutting it too low. I've seen this so many times in my neighbors' lawns and have been guilty of the same mentality in the past. The idea is that if you cut it low you won't have to cut as often. It simply doesn't work this way and will instead create a situation where the weeds will win out, which means you have to cut *more* often in order to keep the weeds all the same length; it's a Catch 22 situation. So mow the proper length — ask your garden center — and mow often.

- **Consider getting one of the old fashioned 'reel' mowers.** Yes, that's right, a non-gas powered mower or a battery-powered weed-whipper. There are several benefits:

  - *It doesn't burn fossil fuels*, so no pollution or support for oil companies.

  - *You get more exercise*, which is an added perk.

  - *It's Quiet!* Honestly, this was the best thing about my mower even though I bought it for environmental reasons. The sound of it whizzing through the grass is comforting, and people — especially the retirees in the neighborhood — will stop and say stuff like "I didn't think they made those anymore!" And then you can have a conversation with your neighbors without the drone of a power mower in your ear while you both shout over it.

— *They rarely break down.* How many summers have you pushed your power mower out to discover that it has decided not to run? So you truck it off, sticking out the back of your trunk, banging against the trunk lid, to get it fixed. Then your lawn grows exponentially from the deluge of rain that inevitably comes when you don't have a mower to mow it. With a reel mower, maintenance consists mostly of getting the blades sharpened once or twice a season. Most repair can be done with a wrench.

— *Sam Gamgee would never use a noisy, nasty, orc machine.* Ok, that one was below the belt but I do hate power mowers. If you have lot of lawn, and must use a power mower, think of ways to reduce the size of your lawn so that it doesn't take long to mow. That will also save on fuel, not to mention time and the drone in your head for an hour after finishing!

# Natural Fertilizer

Now that we've finished trimming the verge, let's talk about garden nutrients and fertilizers. Manmade chemical fertilizers pollute our water supply because a great deal of them run off our properties and farms and into our rivers where they promote the growth of algae, which saps the oxygen from the water, killing fish and other aquatic animals. Luckily, this can be avoided if we abandon fertilizing our lawns and use more natural fertilizers as well as conserving some of our rainwater on the property. We need to think more in terms of *re-building* soil, instead of trying to artificially boost the soil we have depleted.

**Some Soil Building Tricks and Natural Fertilizers:**

- *Worm tea*: Yeah, I know, sounds appetizing right? "Hey honey, pour me a cold glass of worm tea!" Well, considering that it is worm waste—insert, worm *pee and poop*, you might want to pass on the drink but definitely put it in your garden. You can find instructions all over the internet on different ways to set up your own worm tea compost, but I'll give you a brief definition here. Basically what you do is set up a bin, larger one with a spout on the bottom of one side, another smaller bin inside it with holes in the bottom. Then you put in organic material and some soil. Then you add worms, and wait. After a few days the *tea* will collect in the bottom bin, and when there's enough, you can dispense it out the spout and spray it or pour it around your plants! Here's a website with instructions.

- *Fish Emulsion*: Fish emulsion can be purchased in most gardening centers. It smells like, well, fish, so you might not want to store it in your bedroom or kitchen. I'm sure it's full of pheromones but it's not gonna help you get a date, unless you're a Tuna. Instead, store it with the rest of your gardening supplies. Follow the instructions on the bottle to mix with water and pour or spray on your plant's roots.

- *Composting*: Making good ole fashioned compost is pretty simple. You put organic material into a pile, and it rots, turning into soil that you can use to fertilize your garden. If you do little else for your garden, start a compost pile. Plus you will eliminate the majority of your garbage every week. We must have cut our garbage output by over half, just by composting and recycling. We used to produce 5 or 6 bags of garbage per week; now it's down to about 2 or 3. Patience's dad, Greg, and I just built a simple compost bin out of used pallets. The whole thing was super cheap. If you want to see it you can find the photos on the Be a Hobbit, Facebook page. Eventually, I will have more detailed instructions but I think you can see basically how we put it together.

# Weed Control

Instead of using harmful chemical herbicides use more gentle forms to control unwanted grasses.

- *Let them grow.* The most gentle of course is to just let them grow. All so-called *weeds* are just wild grasses that aren't where you want them to be. Most of them are probably indigenous grasses to your area. Though to be accurate, a lot of the *indigenous* grasses in North America were actually introduced by Europeans during the colonial period. Some weeds have very pretty flowers. You might consider joining them if beating them has become a chore.

- *Mow often and Trim:* The best way to combat weeds in your lawn, as mentioned, is to mow often. Also you can use a weed-wacker/trimmer to clean up grasses that grow along barriers and walls. If you can, avoid the gas-powered ones. Yes, they work better—when they work that is—but their two cycle engines are heavy polluters and put money into the pockets of the orcish oil companies. Also, if you're trimming with a weed-wacker, avoid piles of dog-crap: just a warning. If you want the whole story you can find it on my blog, Weed Whippers, Dog S@*t, and an Alternative for RoundUp.

- *Pull them:* Instead of running trimmers just bend over and pull them. I have to confess, that this is the least attractive option for me personally. I'm kind of a lazy Hobbit, and very, very UN-bendy. I tell people all the time that if the work doesn't fall between thigh height to about head height, I leave it to someone else. I'm trying to break myself of this, but it's a long way to the ground and an even longer way back up! Weed pulling can be a kind of therapy or meditation though, so I recommend trying it, a little bit everyday. Just pick a small area of your garden/yard to weed or set a timer for 10 minutes or 15 and stop when you finish that section or the timer goes 'ding'. Before you know it your garden will be weeded. This works especially well if you can get the whole family doing it together.

- *Cardboard Landscape 'Fabric'*: Before planting many people put down landscape fabric under the mulch. This has never worked all that well for me because weeds will grow on top of the mulch anyway. Most of these fabrics are also made with fossil fuels, oil, so avoid them. Instead use *cardboard*! This summer we tried this and it worked really well. Save up cardboard boxes, break them down and store them over winter in the garage or basement. Then in the spring, before you put down fresh mulch around your plants, put down the cardboard like you would landscape fabric. Once you have it laid out, water it down with the hose really well and then cover it with mulch. It really did do a good job of choking out weeds and it will decompose and become soil over time.

## Gamgee's Grass-Slayer

There are some weeds that are just going to grow and they grow in places where we don't want them. For the ones in the sidewalk cracks or away from plants I do want, I use the following, simple, 100% non-toxic recipe that I call Gamgee's Grass-Slayer. You mix it all in a garden pump-sprayer and spray away! Don't get it on anything you don't want to kill though!

- 1 gallon white vinegar (organic preferably)
- 2 cups of table salt
- 2 tablespoons of dish soap
- For full instructions, see my website and the video: Weed Whippers, Dog S@*t, and an Alternative for RoundUp

# Midges & Mosquitoes: Pest Control

No one likes a bunch of 'skeeters flying around them, sucking the life's blood from their veins while trying to eat BBQ. Mosquitoes, while an important part of the food chain, I'm sure, are better off not in my yard or draining my veins. If you live in the Midgewater, like where I used to live in Eastern North Carolina — basically reclaimed swamp-land — then 'skeeters are just part of the 'lure' I reckon. But for the rest of us, we'd like to get rid of them as well as the gnats and horse flies!

One summer, years ago when I was living in N.C., a friend and I, while swimming in my pool killed over 50 horseflies in about an hour! The problem was that for almost every one of them, we had to stand still while the fly bit us so that our partner could smack it to death, on our skin! It became a mission though, so we just counted the bites as wounds suffered in a greater war on insects. We lined up the dead carcasses in an expansion joint in the walkway around the pool and watched ants complete the process by crawling on them and eating them. Ahhhh the beauty of Mother Nature. Well, I told you I was a bit Dwarvish. Here are some other ways to deal with flying pests that don't include being bitten by 50 horseflies:

**Natural Predators**

Insects do have enemies and not just us. All insects have natural predators who can help rid your yard of the pesky things.

- *Birds*: There are several species of birds that love to feast on flying insects. Do some research for your area and then try to attract those birds to your yard. NOTE: Birds are suffering from the pollutant and destructive practices of our culture. Many species are already extinct and many others are on the verge. The fact that flying insects are increasing, it seems, is due in large part to the lack of natural predators. We should do whatever we can individually and collectively to help bring back those birds that are still with us.

- *Bats*: No, they do not turn into vampires, unless of course they are Vampire Bats. They are also not major carriers of rabies, contrary to popular myth. In fact, dogs are at a much, much higher risk for that disease and are less afraid of humans than bats. Bats can eat their body weight in flying insects every night! There are towns where bat colonies are protected by law, and guess what? They don't have mosquitoes or other flying insects, hardly at all! The great thing about bats is that they do not move their home even when they've eaten the insects close to it. They just keep flying further and further out every night. So they expand the *Skeeter Free Zone* every season, starting at their nest and working outwards. So, if you had a nest or bat box in your yard, you'd have no insects to deal with! Setting up your own bat colony is tricky, but it can be done. Do some research online. Bats prefer a south-facing home so that they can take advantage of heat from the sun, and a spot where they won't be bothered by humans or any other predators, like snakes. To attract them you might have to spread some guano, translate, *bat poop*, around the bat house. You can get this at some garden centers, especially higher end ones. Give yours a call to see if they have it. Otherwise, you can probably order it online. If you have bats in your attic, which is not ideal, check out this site for information about how to get them out without killing them.

- *Ladybugs*: Is there a bug more cute than a ladybug? I think not. Plus, they are good luck if they land on you. All good Hobbits should have them flying around their garden. The reason they are good luck, at least in the garden, is that when they are in larvae form they eat aphids which eat your plants. You can usually get ladybugs from good garden centers, and release them in your garden.

## Natural Repellents and Prevention

There are also natural ways to discourage pests and to repel them with non-toxic alternatives.

- *Remove Weak Plants*: diseased plants can attract predator insects, so remove them.

- *Build Healthy Soil*: If you have healthy soil, built with good compost and mulch, then you'll have stronger plants which are less attractive to predators.

- *Rotate Plants and Crops*: Many pests are plant-specific: they only like to eat one thing. If you move them around from season to season or plant them next to other plants that the pests don't like, you'll discourage the orcish insects to move on.

- *Remove Insect Habitats*: This is especially true for mosquitoes who love standing water. You should have water in the garden but it should be *moving* to prevent mosquitoes from laying their eggs.

# Water in the Garden

No water, no garden is a true maxim. Even desert-Hobbits need *some* water or their cactuses will eventually die. Water sustains us all. After all, we Hobbits are like 98% water, ok, maybe 5% of that is beer, but beer is made from water, so there ya go! Other than the obvious use of water in the garden to water plants, it also serves other functions. While—indeed *because*—it's important to the success of all gardens, and to sustain life, it's also imperative that we conserve it and use it wisely. Here are some ideas on how save on water, and how to use it to attract some of those beneficial insects as well as soothe the Hobbit soul and bring Shire tranquility to your garden:

**Conserving Water**

- *Rain barrels*: One of the most efficient ways to save water is to trap rain water on your property in rain barrels. Most of us have probably seen these. They are large barrels positioned around the house under gutter downspouts to contain rainwater. Ideally, you would have one of these for every downspout on your house to capture the maximum amount of water from each rainy day. They have a hose connector on the bottom so you can run a hose to your garden. These are easy, and fairly cheap, to build yourself if you don't want to spend $100 or more on one from a store. Look for '50 gallon plastic barrels' on Craigslist. Try to get *food grade* ones so they won't be full of nasty, orcish chemicals. I found some that had stored honey, for about $15 a piece. They were blue, so I painted them brown to look more like wooden barrels and then painted Hobbity labels on them, like Longbottom Leaf, Old Toby, and Prancing Pony Ale.

- *Watering*: If you want to conserve water, install drip hoses or soaker hoses instead of sprinklers. Sprinklers, unless positioned perfectly, waste a lot of water. You could save up to, or more than, 50% of the water you've been using and that is a significant difference and impact on the environment not to mention the dragon gold you'll save. If you attach those hoses to a rain-barrel then you're saving 100%! Now *THAT* is impact. As with the lawn, water infrequently, not every day. When you water make sure your plants get a good bit, like an inch. This promotes root growth. Watering also depends on the plant species, so make sure you're not overwatering which is just as bad as not enough, and it's wasteful. If you have not installed barrels yet, or they are empty, then you'll have to resort to turning on the spigot and using the city/county water supply — unless you have a private well or spring on your property. Either way, stick to drip/soaker hoses; they will save you water and save water for everyone else on the planet. Also, the best time of the day to water is in the morning. This is because the ground is still cool, as well as the plants, so evaporation is minimized. In the heat of the day a lot of water is lost directly to evaporation and is not absorbed by your plants, which is the goal of watering.

- *Rain Gardens*: "What?" you ask, "Aren't all gardens, rain gardens?" No, they aren't. Rain gardens are a fairly new idea to help trap runoff from residential lots. In short, they are usually located in a spot on your property where water naturally runs. To build one, you essentially lower the ground by digging down to create a slight depression—to trap water—and then plant native grasses and wild flowers in the space. Emphasis is on plants that trap lots of water. For more information, look it up online. You may have a local group that installs rain gardens. I had one installed for free by a group testing the effect of rain gardens on the local water quality. They came and installed it one day, while I wasn't even home!

- *Mulch*: Another thing good gardeners usually do is to cover the soil around their plants with natural mulch. Mimicking the forest—where leaves and other organic debris fall to the forest floor where it slowly decomposes and becomes rich soil—we can do the same thing in our gardens with mulch. Of course you can go buy mulch from a garden center if you want one of those manicured gardens with matching pine straw, cedar, or other forms of mulch but you can also use natural stuff from your yard to do the same job, which is cheaper, and easier. Some mulch ideas:

  - **Buy mulch**: While this is the way most of us have done it in the past, I certainly have spent plenty on it, it is unnecessary. However, if you want a uniform look to your garden it's probably the easiest way to achieve that. Most of the time, though, it comes in plastic bags which we're trying to avoid. Personally, I'm getting away from it. I don't think Mr. Gamgee or the Gaffer would ever buy it that way. If you simply must buy it, try to buy it in bulk and have it delivered in a truck or trailer to your house—more on that below.

  - **Buy rock**: Another solution if you want a uniform look is to buy rock. Rock doesn't hold moisture in the soil quite as well as traditional mulch but it does help, and can look very nice. It's not cheap though, especially if you buy it in individual, orcish, plastic bags. The best way is to buy it by the truck or trailer load and have it delivered to your Hobbit-hole where it can be dumped in a location near where it will end up, or if in a trailer, shoveled out into wheelbarrows to dispense it where you want it. You can rent trailers and pickup trucks, even bigger trucks at larger home improvement stores. If you just need a pickup to rent you might also try Zipcar, or RelayRides.

- **Leaves and Needles**: While store-bought mulch and rock may look better, it is infinitely more expensive than just using what nature provides you, that is, if you have trees on your property. If you don't have trees, why not? Start planting them. A couple of nice oaks or maples or better yet, fruit trees would add real value to your home, not to mention provide shade in the summer. Also, they drop leaves and needles — if you have pines like we do back in N.C.. This is free mulch fellow Hobbits! Rake it up from the areas where you don't want mulch and put it where you do. It doesn't get any simpler than that and it gives your garden a more forest floor appearance, which is very Hobbity.

• *Call up the Shire*: Don't do all the work by yourself! Especially for larger jobs where you need to disperse a truckload of rock or mulch. Call up the family, friends and neighbors and make it a party! Seriously. Crank up the grill, chill some beer or other favorite beverages and get to work! You can knock that job out much quicker and it's way more fun with a team of Hobbits to help.

• **Reduce Lawn Size**: This has been covered above. Lawns need loads of water to survive. The smaller it is, the less water it needs.

## Water Features

One of the best ways to attract birds and honeybees to your property — which help to pollinate your garden and the food supply of the Earth — is by installing water features, like fountains, birdbaths, ponds, and streams. Birds love moving water the best. I can't wait to get out into my new yard next spring and install a fountain right in the center of the yard. I had one in my old house in Minneapolis and the birds were all over it! They loved it and I loved the sound of the cascading water and the chirping of my flying friends.

If you have a pond, you'll want to have some kind of pump to keep it moving. Why not design a little waterfall feature, running down a rock filled stream into your pond? It could be your own little Whithywindle! How awesome would that be? Pretty darned, I think. Not only birds love water; bees do too. Honey bees are disappearing quickly as mentioned in part I of the book. If they do, we are in deep trouble as a species because they pollinate about 1/3 of our food supply. Planting flowering plants without pesticides and having water features helps to promote the bee population.

## What to Grow

Now that we've covered *how* to grow your garden, let's talk a little more about what to grow. In general, plant foods that you and your family like to eat. You will be more motivated to do the work and the results will be more rewarding. As for the ornamental plants in your yard, if you pick plants that naturally do well in your climate zone and region you will have an easier time getting results and the results will be quicker. For instance, while I love palm trees, they're probably not going to grow well in my Minne*snow*ta backyard. If you're not a natural-born gardener — I'm definitely not — then it pays to do your research first.

Find out what is in your yard already! You may already have hidden gems in your landscape. Don't cut out a bunch of plants until you know what they are. Use the internet to find answers to any questions you have and to see what other gardeners are doing in your area. In my area the major concern is hardy plants that can withstand the sub zero temperatures of a Yankeeland winter. In your area it may be high temperatures and drought. Do your research before you plant. Also, don't forget to talk to people you know. Do you have a Sam Gamgee in your family? If so, invite them over for dinner and take a walk through your yard. If not, find one in your circle of friends or hire one to come look at your space. They can give you great advice on what you have and what you might plant.

## Trees: Your Own *Old Forest*

As mentioned above, trees are wonderful things because they give shade, store fresh water, and help to send it back into the atmosphere instead of running off into our rivers and oceans. They are home to countless birds and insects and help to shuffle nutrients through the soil from one place to another. So plant trees, and save the planet.

There is probably no other plant that is more important to saving the planet than the tree, and there might have been no bigger lovers of trees than J.R.R. Tolkien and his beloved Hobbits. So, if for no other reason, plant them in his honor. Maybe name them all after his characters. Encourage your neighborhood to plant trees of all kinds. There is a movement that has begun in some cities, like Tampa, Florida and Los Angeles, where organizations are planting fruit trees in public parks making food available for people to harvest. This helps to put a dent in hunger, especially in low-income neighborhoods and can be a major boost to those who are homeless and looking for food on a daily basis. Is there really a good reason for us not to plant food in public spaces? I think not. We'll return to that at the end of the book.

## Hobbit Veggies

Grow vegetables too, of course. I've already confessed that I'm not a big veggie fan, but that's just me. Most people like them more than I. This is one area where I'm more Dwarvish than Hobbity. I prefer roasted meats to green stuff which I usually refer to as *rabbit food*. But even *I* like a few, okay, a couple: green beans and tomatoes. Yeah, I know, tomatoes aren't vegetables. So what. This summer I've been trying to expand my horizons, as it were. Patience has even managed to get me to eat *kale*, which is about as green as it gets! I've even come up with a great chicken-vegetable soup with kale, carrots, peppers—even green ones, onions, and celery. So eat your veggies Hobbits! They're good for you, so plant your favorites in your new Victory Garden and tell Sauron and Monsanto to kiss off!

## Plant Pretty Stuff Too!

Ornamentals add beauty to your garden so choose flowering and colorful plants that you love. They will entice you out of your door and into the garden more often which is the point of having one. Spend time picking out and planning out your ornamentals. Some ornamentals complement vegetables and fruits. Do your research on this. For instance, marigolds are very good around tomatoes and other vegetables because many insects that would eat your veggies, do not like marigolds, so they act as a natural repellent. Again, consult your personal Gamgee about what is best to grow in your yard.

## Save the Pollinators: Bee Friendly Plants

Whatever you plant, make sure the plants are safe for the honey bees and other pollinators. Bees are in serious danger! The overall bee population has been drastically declining for the last ten years or so. Called *Honey Bee Colony Collapse Disorder*, the catastrophic problem has been somewhat of a mystery until recently. Bees pollinate about 1/3 of all the food in the World. If they disappear, so does that food! Human civilization would probably not survive the loss of the bees. Even if some of us did survive, the World would be a very different place. Scientist now know that there are several contributing factors to this collapse, the most egregious of which are insecticides, like RoundUp and others called ___neonicotinoids___, which is a mouthful to be sure. The problem with them — other than the fact that they are made by the fossil fuel industry — is that they are the main cause of the bee population decline. Be aware, that many of the major suppliers for garden plants are selling ones sprayed with neonicotinoids. Ask before buying. Make sure they DO NOT have this horrible crap on them. Instead, plant bee-safe plants that they are attracted to and help to save our food supply! President Obama has recently signed a memorandum to help bring awareness to this issue. For more information on bees, and how you can help to save them, and us, visit the Pollinator

Partnership and the Honey-Bee Haven where you can get your own Bee-Safe yard sign to let your neighbors know you love bees!

## The Hobbit Menagerie: Raising Your Own Farm Animals

Animals can also be part of your garden, especially if you live in the country. Your options are wide open there; you could raise just about anything your local climate will support. Make sure to do your research first because raising animals, any kind, is a commitment that should not be taken lightly. Animals require time, energy, and money but can be a great benefit to your food supply if you can afford to take care of them properly. If you decide to raise animals make sure to do it in an organic way. To do so any other way would be orcish, and there would be no point. You might as well go to the store and buy orcish meat and milk, but what Hobbit wants that?

What if you live in the city or suburbs? There's a growing trend to raise some small animals even in the city, especially chickens, bees, and bunnies! Hobbits love stewed rabbits and herbs! And don't forget all the honey-bees and honey at Beorn's House! Yum! You should check your city's website or call them about regulations on raising the particular animal you want to raise. Some city's still frown on it, though more and more are allowing people to do it.

### Fried Chicken and Eggs

Chickens are especially popular, but not roosters! Your neighbors probably won't be happy to wake up on a Saturday morning to the sound of your rooster crowing in their bedroom window at 4 or 5 a.m.!

Hens are the ticket. They will provide you with fresh, organic eggs, every day, probably so many you'll have to give some away or sell them. Try not to get too attached to them though because after the first two years they won't lay anymore eggs. What do you do with them then? Sounds like chicken-soup time to me! I've heard that the hens aren't that good for frying, unfortunately. Patience's mom, Dee, is planning on getting some hens. But she gets attached to animals and refuses to even think about eating them when their egg-laying days are up. She wants the grandkids to have one each and to give them names, so I told Duke and his cousins to name them Fried, Soupy, Grilled, and Roaster! She didn't find that as amusing as I did. Go figure.

Chickens also produce great fertilizer, i.e., *chicken-shit* which if you allow them to wander around your garden freely they will disperse and scratch into the ground for you. If you'd rather not have them wandering over the entire yard, you can create a movable chicken pen that you can relocate everyday to a different spot. They need a warm place to roost, a hen house, food to eat, and to have their coop cleaned out once a week or more. If you live in the Great White North, like me, there are other concerns but I know people up here who raise them so just do your research before you leap into raising chickens.

## Beorn's Bees: Producing Honey

Bees are another great option, if you love honey like I do. Of course, if you're allergic to bee sting or one of your family members are this is probably not a good option. That's not to say that bees are sting-happy but even if they never sting you or your family, anyone with an allergy may be less likely to spend time in your garden and that would defeat the purpose of having a garden. Tending bees is one of the most important things one can do to help save the planet. As mentioned above, they pollinate our food supply, and if you have them in your garden, guess what? Your garden will grow better because they will pollinate it! And, they'll make lots of yummy honey for you! Did I mention that they make honey?

You do need special equipment to raise bees: colony boxes — where they live and make all that honey, a bee suit, hat and gloves, and a smoker thingy — which is simply called a *bee smoker*, though I think *smoker thingy* is much catchier — to calm the bees down so you can tend to their boxes and extract honey when it's time. The price of honey has been climbing for years due to the failing bee population, especially in the U.S., so if you produce it you can make a bit of money, though to make a big profit, you'd have to live in the country because there are restrictions in the city on how many colonies one property can raise.

Definitely check on city regulations for beekeeping. One of the main concerns is possible negative interactions with neighbors. The best way to minimize that is to have a privacy fence around your yard—out of sight and mind. Plus bees tend to fly out from the hive at the same height from the ground so if they have to fly over a high privacy fence then they tend to stay at that height till they reach the flowers and plants they want to extract nectar from. If your fence is over 6 feet high, then they will avoid most of your neighbors, unless your neighbors are Strider and Boromir but they can probably hold their own against a few bees, I'm thinking.

**Stewed Rabbit and Herbs**

Another idea I've seen is to raise rabbits. Then you can make one of Sam Gamgee's most famous recipes, Coney Stew and Herbs! Rabbits are notoriously easy to breed so having enough of them should not be a problem. They need a cage, because if not, they will escape your yard and run rampant over the rest of the neighborhood. They will also eat up your plants which is not desirable. However, if you like rabbit meat, they could be a good steady supply of protein, unless you're Patience's mom— then they're only good for petting. Their poop is also very beneficial to your soil and compost pile. You can set up a collection bin under the cage to catch it, then sprinkle it in your compost bin, or directly into the garden.

# Where to Plant

There are myriad methods for planting gardens. Pretty much, if you get any sunlight at all in a spot and can get water to it a plant will grow there, if tended to. There are numerous books on garden planning, depending on your particular space. Two things to ask your local Gamgee is not only *what* to plant but *how* and *where* you should plant particular things. Do some research on the methods below first, then ask them how they might be employed for your garden.

## Raised Beds: Save the Old Hobbit Back

The most obvious place to grow plants, both food and ornamental, is in your backyard, front yard, or where ever you have outdoor space. That is if you have space outdoors and especially if you have a lot of sun on your property. One of the most successful ways to grow plants here is in raised beds. Raised beds have a couple of benefits. One, they are higher off the ground — which I love since I'm un-bendy. And that makes it easier to plant, weed, and harvest from them. Two, you usually add soil to them so it will be looser and hopefully more nutrient rich, if you pick good soil, or make it.

## Micro Gardens

Micro gardens are veggie gardens grown in a very small place to maximize both space and productivity. This is the way to go if you're one of those Condo-Hobbits living in the city in an apartment, or gardening in a small plot in your local community garden! I've seen numerous innovative ideas, from hanging herbs in windows, to vertical gardens on patios, to small 4'x4' gardens. Check out Anne Gibson's website on micro-gardening. She has loads of advice and tips.

## Vertical Gardens

If horizontal space is lacking, grow your food vertically! There are numerous ways to get your plants up off the ground. Do some research on it, and ask Gamgee about it. The most famous vertical gardens in history were the Great Hanging Gardens of Babylon, one of the Seven Ancient Wonders, an idea I'm sure they probably stole from the gardens of Gondor or Numenor: *copycats!* Why not create your own? If you want a lot of ideas, be a copycat, too, and follow Eunice Baurmeester on Pintrest! She has a bunch of them pinned!

## Window Gardens

A version of vertical gardening is the old standard of window boxes. You can put them outside the window, if your window opens, or inside on the window sill. This is particularly convenient if you're growing herbs, onions, and other sun-loving veggies in a kitchen window and especially windows that are south-facing with lots of sunlight. There are also ways to hang or attach shelves inside the window to maximize space.

## Personalize Your Garden

No matter how you plant your garden, what size it is, or what you plant *in it*, you should make it your *own*. Add your own personal touches to it. Make it a space that you, your family, and your friends will want to spend time in. Are you not particularly creative? That's okay; just do some research online and look for some ideas. In the next chapter I'll give you some of my ideas for turning your garden into a Middle Earth-ian sanctuary. What could be more fun than that? Nothing, I reckon.

# 32

# YOUR BACKYARD LOTHLORIEN: A SANCTUARY IN THE TREES

When his eyes were in turn uncovered, Frodo looked up and caught his breath. They were standing in an open space. To the left stood a great mound, covered with a sward of grass as green as Spring-time in the Elder Days. Upon it, as a double crown, grew two circles of trees: the outer had bark of snowy white, and were leafless but beautiful in their shapely nakedness; the inner were Mallorn-trees of great height, still arrayed in pale gold. High amid the branches of a towering tree that stood in the centre of all there gleamed a white flet. At the feet of the trees, and all about the green hillsides the grass was studded with small golden flowers shaped like stars. Among them, nodding on slender stalks, were other flowers, white and palest green: they glimmered as a mist amid the rich hue of the grass. Over all the sky was blue, and the sun of afternoon glowed upon the hill and cast long green shadows beneath the trees. — *LOTR*: I, *Lothlórien*

I remember reading that passage for the first time, sitting in my roach-infested, orcish apartment so long ago and thinking to myself, "That must be the most beautiful place in all of history." If a portal had opened up in the wall I would have walked through and never looked back. Alas, it did not, but I've dreamed of the golden trees and flowers of Lothlórien ever since. If it's the last thing I do on this Earth it will be to bring just a little of that magic to our world. My personal goal is to build a Hobbit-esque, garden, an urban Lothlórien, where my family, friends, and neighbors can come to relax, read, eat, party, socialize and let our minds get back to the things that are important in life: experiences, not things.

If you're a Condo-Hobbit, that's okay, find a local park or see if you can organize the people in your building to build a garden space outside somewhere, maybe even on the roof! Even if we can't yet get away from working with orcs and *for* Saruman we can at least come home to the Shire and let those stresses fall away for a few hours each day. Make your own space personal to you and your family. Maybe you'd like to make it as Hobbity as possible to transport your mind to another place, where trees talk, and Strider walks? If so, here are a few decorating and entertaining ideas to help you transform your outdoor spaces into a Middle Earth sanctuary.

## Essential Elements

### Gates and Paths

One of the most important things about gardens, that most people don't think about is the power of a wandering path through it. Don't forget Bilbo's words about setting your feet upon a path! It can sweep you off to lands unknown. A path winding through your garden will transform it. It can be as simple as a dirt path, worn down by walking year after year, barely defined by the plants that crowd over its edges, or it can be stark and hard of concrete, brick, or stone, or like the one I'm going to build of soft sand that massages your feet and sifts through your toes as you stroll through your garden—if I can figure out how to keep the cats of the Shire from crapping in it, that is.

Paths give structure to a garden. They lead you through it, or more accurately, pull you through and focus your attention to all areas of the garden. Winding paths are much more

Hobbit-y than straight ones of course, and far more interesting, especially if they wind around corners. This creates a sense of mystery. "What's around the next corner!?"

## The Garden Gate

If you can at all manage it, include a gate to your garden and make it as Hobbit-y as possible. A wooden gate under an arched trellis covered in roses, or a grape vine, or like mine, Virginia Creeper, will draw you towards it and create a heightened sense of mystery. "What's in THERE?!" It's not an exaggeration to say that the garden gate at the top of the driveway to our new house was the first thing that attracted me to it. When I drove up the driveway, I saw the gate, under all those vines. I could not resist its pull. The first thing I did was to walk through it to discover what was beyond. Paint your gate a bright Hobbit-y color! Maybe green or yellow? Use your imagination. Mine is still bare wood because I'm still cogitatin' on what color to paint it.

## Sit Down and Relax: Seating Areas

Make sure you have outdoor seating. Avoid plastics, of course, unless you already have them. Remember that the greenest option is to use what you already have. Sitting on plastic is okay though not optimal. If you don't already have furniture, good, opt for more earthy materials like wood, and metal, even stone or concrete. They are more attractive and more comfortable usually. Arrange seating around the garden as if you would in a house, with an eye on the view from the seat. You want to have something interesting or beautiful to look at from each area, and you may only have one area if you have a small yard.

## Second Breakfast Nooks

This is a Hobbit garden after all! Don't be one of those Elves in Rivendell who 'forgets to eat.' What's up with that anyway? If you've seen a picture of me, you'll note that I haven't skipped many second breakfasts. There should be places, or at least *one* place, to eat in your garden. There's nothing more relaxing than to eat breakfast, lunch, or dinner outdoors in a garden. Make sure you have a place to do this: a picnic table, small table and chairs, etc. And then get out there and eat! Invite friends over to eat with you!

## Cooking on the *Trail*: Outdoor Kitchens

Are you a master chef, or watch Iron Chef every week? Or maybe you just love cooking outdoors? Samwise Gamgee was known for his ability to rustle up dinner, even on the road to Mordor, so you should be able to do it in your own backyard! If you love cooking as much as I do, consider building an outdoor kitchen or at least set up an area as your cooking, grilling, and BBQ area. Make sure to equip it with the basics: a grill, a table or bench to put stuff on and somewhere for the beer cooler. One of the things I'm going to work on next summer, in my garden, is to build a *tin-shed* roof off the back of my garage which will be my outdoor kitchen. It will be home to my smoker grill—I'm a BBQ snob, another charcoal grill, a bar, tables to work on, maybe a little fridge, etc. Eventually I want to add a flat-top grill—like you see in diners—so I can make omelets, fried eggs, and sausage for outdoor Second Breakfasts!

I could write an entire book or series of books, on cooking, especially cooking outdoors. Maybe I will one day. But if you want to grill or BBQ, you need to burn some charcoal. Yes, it does release carbon into the atmosphere. But we have to eat, and so let's eat well. Propane grills are fine if you don't have time to fire up charcoal, but they are also pollutive, and they don't taste nearly as well. If you opt for charcoal, make sure to buy only the natural, *lump* charcoal, *not* the briquets. Most charcoal briquets are loaded with chemicals that you don't want to eat, or burn, or smell, and they're also chock full of fillers, like sand. Yes, I said sand. That's why you have all that *ash* in the bottom of your grill after you finish burning hotdogs on the 4th of July every summer. It's not ash, it's charred sand. Real hardwood charcoal is light weight and will leave very little ash in comparison. It's light because sand is heavy and there isn't any in it. So stop wasting money buying sand and chemicals. And when you go to light it, skip the lighter fluid too. You don't need it. Get a charcoal *chimney*. All that you need is the chimney, the charcoal, and some newspaper, or any paper really. You ball up the paper underneath, light it, then wait till the charcoal is white hot. Dump it in the grill, and bam! You're grilllin'!

### The One Ring, of Fire: Your Hobbity Fire-pit

A garden without the fourth element, fire, is seriously lacking something. What's better than sitting around a campfire roasting marshmallows and making s'mores? Possibly sitting around a campfire and roasting sausages, steaks, or pork chops! Greg and I recently built a fire pit in our backyard. It's simple to do and doesn't have to be expensive. I spent about $100 on bricks that I found on Craigslist, but you can find them for free, too, if you're willing to go get them. The ones I got were old bricks taken from University Avenue here in St. Paul, so they're old, and now they've been repurposed! There are endless ways to build a fire pit, from simple stones in a circle, a hole in the ground, to elaborate brick and stonework, to portable pits of cast iron and steel. It's really about your personal tastes and budget. You can find pictures of my fire pit and the process we went through on the *Be a Hobbit* Facebook Page. Check it out for one example of what can be done. Then look online for thousands of others!

# Décor

If you're a hard core Tolkien fan, and you must be if you've reached this point in the book, consider decorating your yard with Tolkien themed accents. All of my suggestions can be created at home with minimal costs and materials. Here are some suggestions that will add Hobbity flavor to your garden, home, and yard.

### Signs

Create place-name direction signs to hang around the garden, on posts, fences, side of the garage, wherever you can find a spot. I stole the idea years ago from the TV show M.A.S.H. If you were a fan of the show you will probably remember the central signpost in the middle of camp where everyone put up a hand-painted, wooden sign pointing to their home town, with a mileage. You can do the same but instead of Toledo, Ohio, you put the names of places from Middle Earth: You can paint an arrow, either left or right of the word, pointing wayfarers to places like Lothlórien, Lonely Mountain, Rivendell, the Shire, etc. The best are made with reclaimed lumber. One of the best ways to make them is to get a few old wooden pallets, cut or break them apart, and use the slats. I like to paint them with white, outdoor paint, because the white will reflect light in the evening, and even at night if you have torches or candles burning in the garden. These signs — one of the simplest things you can do — will add a lot of Hobbit flavor to your garden and help to transform the place.

### Shields

If you are more artistically inclined or if you have a child who is, or friend, or other family member, you can also create painted shields from the various races of Middle Earth and place them around the yard, on trees, fences, etc. Look up images or watch the movies and take ideas from there to design them. I originally used 3/4 inch plywood for mine. I cut them out with a jig saw or router, in round or 'kite' shaped forms then painted them up! They look fabulous hanging around the yard, and are a topic of conversation, especially for Tolkien fans who come to visit. The kids love them. I even had a sign for the Prancing Pony Inn which I had hanging next to the bar I built. Duke, Greg, and I made a couple for Middle Earth Day this year, plus a Prancing Pony Sign! You can find pictures of them as well as other pictures of our preparations on the Middle Earth Day Facebook Page.

### Music

Not all decoration is visual. What we hear goes a long way to setting a mood. People often overlook the power of music. Being an old musician myself I have always wondered why this is so. I suppose that most people get so worked up fretting over other party details that they just forget how important music is. Music, for instance, is one of the most important things in movies and television. If it's done right we rarely think about it. If it's missing, or done haphazardly, then it's jarring.

At some point in your design, I would strongly suggest you come up with a way to bring music outside. What music you play is less important than having it available, unless you are throwing a themed party, then you should follow me on Spotify.com because I've created quite a few themes on there, including a Tolkien one! I also have themes for stay-cations, with tunes from around the world arranged to create a mood for most geographically themed parties. I often create new ones. It's free, so why not check them out? One of these days maybe I'll write a stay-cation book. Keep an eye out for that one. Maybe I should start with a Tolkien theme?

Music was a key component of Tolkien's works, though I wish he had recorded his voice reading all of the books so that we could hear him sing all the songs as well as do the voices. There is a recording out there of him reading and singing key sections from *LOTR*. I once found it in the local library. There is a segment on Spotify as well though currently it does not contain the stuff on the recording I found in the library. Make sure to include music in your life, if you haven't already. Sign up for a free or premium Spotify account. It's my favorite software on my computers at home. You can get it on your smart phone, too. There is also an app that your friends can download so that when you have a party, you can let them set up requests for songs on your account. They can then add their selections to a cue to be played during the party. If you need another reason to join Spotify, it's also a more sustainable way to collect music.

The production of all that vinyl, and all those plastic CDs and the cases which inevitably break anyway, are adding to the enormous waste problems on the planet. Downloading music, seems to me to be the best way to go. It's simply the most *green* way to purchase or listen to music. Heck, with sites like Pandora and Spotify you don't even have to purchase the music. You can listen for free and the musicians are paid royalties based on how often their stuff is played. If you're concerned about music piracy, you should read my article on the topic, Why Hobbits Love Spotify and Music Piracy. How ever you collect your music, the next step is to set up some kind of sound system to play it in your garden.

**Ideas for bringing music to your garden:**

- *Hobbit-Hack It!*: If you can't afford an expensive stereo system all over your house here's an ingenious idea I stumbled across at my brother's house. He has an iPhone with Spotify installed. We were outside in his backyard, grilling burgers and dogs one evening. He was playing some tunes with his phone and for a while I didn't pay attention to how he was amplifying the music, until I looked over beside the grill. He had taken a tin game box—I think it was for the Simpson's Game actually—turned it on it's side and propped up his iPhone inside it against the back of the box which he had turned up on one side. The tin box amplified the sound enough so that all of us could hear it, even over conversations for quite some distance!

- *Live Music*: This is, of course, the *most* Hobbity way to bring music to any occasion. Hobbits didn't have electricity or a recording industry. If they wanted music they had to make it themselves, live. Most people aren't musicians, or at least not very good ones,—like myself—but if you are—or even if you aren't—tune up and play! Also, you can invite musician friends and neighbors to come over and bring *their* instruments. Depending on where you live you might want to keep it acoustic and keep the volume down; check the local regulations on noise first. I'm considering doing an 'open mic' night or something in my backyard, maybe once a month or so and inviting musicians from around my area to come and jam, share food, drinks, and conversation. Maybe I'll call it Green Dragon Jams or Prancing Pony jams or something like that?

- *Go Wireless*: There are many options if you want wireless music. Do some online research to figure out what will work best for you. If you already have a wireless router in your Hobbit-hole then it's just a matter of choosing a receiver unit and speakers that will work best for your set up. Some older homes, especially ones with stucco finishes or thick brick or concrete walls aren't suited for wireless outside the house, but you can check it to see. Take a laptop outside and see what your signal is like in different places around your yard. If it works then a music system probably will too.

- *Pro System Install*: If you're rich like Bilbo, you can always hire a professional to install a wired system connected to your interior entertainment system.

## Build a Hobbit-hole!

The coolest thing you could ever do to push the Tolkien theme over the top, would be to build an actual Hobbit-hole on your property! Maybe you live in the country and own 100+ acres and you want to build one to live in!? It's kind of a dream of mine, though I'm quite happy in my little *above ground* Hobbit-*house* for now. There are plans and ideas online for building Hobbit-like homes; see the *Resources* section for links to some.

Also, if you don't have 100 acres—I don't—you could instead build a Hobbit-hole playhouse! I'm planning on doing this at some point. I'd like to do it this summer or fall, but since we just moved in last fall and have been buried in snow since, there are other projects that will come first, but I'm going to do it! There are tons of ideas online on how to build them. How awesome would it be for your kids, and the neighborhood kids? You could put some chairs in there, a little electric or gas fireplace, some book shelves with Tolkien books, and invite kids over to check it out! I say kids, but really, we know it's more for us adults! Don't forget to make it big enough for *YOU* to enjoy as well! Hell, while you're at it, invite the entire Shire over! Throw a big ole' Hobbit party!

## Spruce Up the Party Tree!

I love parties. All my friends know that I put on some doozies. And I don't half-ass them either. Hell no! I go all out, but that doesn't mean I spend a fortune. I don't hire elephants, or camel racers, or belly dancers—though the last one sounds like fun. But I make sure that the food is great, the drinks are plentiful, and then I take care of the details that make it memorable. If you're not a big party-thrower, then maybe you should start! Or just throw small ones!

Throw backyard parties during the warmer months! Be creative. Give parties a theme! Try not to be boring. If you're not particularly creative, do some research online, or send me an email for ideas! Don't forget to decorate in the theme. You can usually put together stuff from friends, rent them, or make them. Some communities and neighborhoods have compiled a sort of Party supply library! They find a central location, or store the stuff separately and allow their neighbors to borrow things like plates, cloth napkins, utensils, grills, you name it, for parties. This is a very Shire-like idea! Plus it cuts down on the crappy, plastic plates, forks and cups that we all waste every time we throw a party. I want to form one in my new neighborhood! If you already have a Facebook page for your neighborhood, post the idea there! See if anyone wants to compile all the party stuff into one location or compile a list of what everyone has, so you can share!

# Middle Earth Day!

If you created a Middle Earth themed garden like we talked about earlier then throw a Middle Earth party! Better yet, join me and a growing number of modern Hobbits in our celebration of Middle Earth Day! While we Hobbits love the traditional Earth Day—April 22nd—and will continue to celebrate it, some of us realized that *one* day or even the entire month of April, just wasn't enough to bring attention to work that many people are doing to make our Earth a cleaner place to live. On August 10, 2014, my brother, Tim Bivans, remembered an idea that had crossed his mind months before. The idea was to hold another Earth Day, but exactly 6 months after the previous, and before the next, (on the 3rd Saturday of October), and call it 'Middle' Earth Day in celebration of the Hobbits' love for all things green and for their sense of community, or Shireness.

So Middle Earth Day was born, and so shall it be. We hope that you will join the movement too! By the time you are reading this we will have celebrated the first one, on October 18, 2014. I've given the date some thought in recent weeks, and come to the conclusion that we will probably change the date to the 3rd Saturday in September instead. Since so many Tolkien fans are already celebrating Bilbo and Frodo's birthday at that time, it only makes sense to combine the two ideas into Middle Earth Day and celebrate them all at once! For more information, you can visit my website www.stevebivans.com. But make sure to *like* the Middle Earth Day page on Facebook as well. There will be photos from the last event and you can send in yours so that we can all see how Hobbits everywhere are Saving the Earth!

**Build the Shire**

Whenever you decide to throw your Hobbit party, invite friends or neighbors who are Tolkien fans to it! Most kids these days have seen the movies and would probably love to attend. Open it up to all ages and you'll have more guests. Encourage them to dress as their favorite character. This is a perfect opportunity to discuss how you are trying to live the Hobbit Life and how everyone can make a difference by making gradual changes to the way they do things. Suggest this book or any number of other ones listed at the end of this book to get them started.

Don't think that you have to convert everyone at the party all at once, or that you will do so at any point. Pick and choose those who you feel are receptive to the message and forget about trying to convince them all. Lead by example is always the best way. Wait for moments when your friends, family and neighbors ask you advice on how you do things, to show them and explain, in brief, why you do it that way. Don't overdo the explanation though. Give it to them in little bits, between bites of appetizers.

Gardens are probably the most important things we can add to our Shire and to our own personal spaces. If you don't have room for a big one that's all right; grow plants inside or spend time in public gardens near to you. Maybe you can organize your neighborhood to find a spot to create a garden space for everyone to enjoy. It's a place to relax, exercise, read Tolkien books, have breakfast and second breakfast, socialize and get to know your neighbors. We need to reconnect with our neighbors, and relax. And gardens are the best place to do it. They're a reminder that there is beauty still in the world and they are the place where we can grow food: food that will enhance our health and help us to build our Shire by sharing it with our neighbors. And the best way to do that is to throw parties, whether they are of the *Un-*, or *Long-*, *Expected* variety.

# 33

# LAST SHIP TO VALINOR: A SUSTAINABLE HOBBIT FUNERAL

"To the sea, to the sea! The white gulls are crying,
The wind is blowing, and the white foam is flying.
West, west away, the round sun is falling,
Grey ship, grey ship, do you hear them calling,
The voices of my people that have gone before me?
I will leave, I will leave the woods that bore me;
For our days are ending and our years failing.
I will pass the wide waters lonely sailing.
Long are the waves on the Last Shore falling,
Sweet are the voices in the Lost Isle calling,
In Eressea, in Elvenhome that no man can discover,
Where the leaves fall not: land of my people forever!"
— *LOTR*: III, *The Field of Cormallen*

I am a poor wayfaring stranger
While traveling thru this world of woe
Yet there's no sickness, toil or danger
In that bright world to which I go
I'm going there to see my father
I'm going there no more to roam
I'm only going over Jordan
I'm only going over home  —Emmylou Harris,
*Wayfaring Stranger* (traditional folk song)

Let's talk about death. Yeah, I know that was an abrupt segue, especially since we were just discussing garden parties, but death waits for no one and you never know when it's coming so jamming it in between parties and a chapter on the family is just as good a spot as any. Though none of us like to think about our own mortality, or that of our friends and family members, preparing for the inevitable is something we all should do at some point in our lives. If you're not to that point then come back to this section later. If, however, you have begun to consider planning for the future, hopefully *distant* future, then read on.

In Middle Earth, all races were susceptible to death. While the Elves were immortal in the sense that they could not die of disease or old age, they *could* in some circumstances, die. They could be killed in battle or suffer accidental death. When they died their souls were swept off to the Halls of Mandos in Valinor over the Western Sea. All the other races were mortal. The fate of the souls of Humans, Hobbits, and Dwarves was unknown to all in Middle Earth, even the Elves. The Elves who lived outside of Valinor considered the fate of mortals to be a blessing, as they considered their own immortality to be a curse. The death of the things around them brought with it a mounting weariness, which could turn to sorrow and grief. Some Elves succumbed to this and died themselves. Most Elves who were still living in Middle Earth chose to sail into the West to be with the Valar and their fallen kindred.

You will remember my discussion of Boromir's funeral earlier in the book, where I described in great detail his journey to the sea and what would become of his remains and that of his vessel. A Western funeral today, while certainly ritualistic, containing most if not all of the aspects of Boromir's funeral send off, is more different than similar. Instead of returning the body of our loved one to the Earth, we embalm them with chemicals, hermetically seal them in an expensive coffin made of numerous materials that are now wasted forever—probably including many plastics—place that inside a concrete sarcophagus and then cover them with dirt, usually reciting from the Bible, "Ashes to ashes, dust to dust," which when you think of it, is completely absurd.

They are not ashes, nor will they ever be, nor will they completely turn to dust. We have preserved them with modern chemistry, as if that will give them some special place in the afterlife. This is ridiculous. Why do we do it this way? Is the process driven by modern science and chemistry, "Hey people! Your loved one will get to Heaven or Nirvana or Paradise in much better condition if you pump them full of manmade juice and send them off in a plastic box! Only $5,995!" Did modern chemists take an intro course to Ancient Egyptian History and think, "Cha Ching! Now there's a way to make some dough!"?

Surely there must be better ways to do it. I have been of the mind that I should be cremated and placed in a small wooden boat, much like ole Boromir, then pushed off into a lake doused in bourbon so that one of my friends—who hopefully isn't too drunk to pull it off, this means you, Keith—can shoot a flaming arrow into the boat, sending me up in smoke, returning me to the Ether and to Mother Nature. Problem is, they usually burn you in a coffin and expend vast amounts of fossil fuels to accomplish it, so I'm not sure it's really any greener than the coffin option. Maybe there are better ways to do it out there. Certainly there are people in other countries around the world practicing a more sustainable way.

## Plant a Mallorn Seed: *BE* the Party Tree!

The other day a fellow Hobbit posted a link to a company called Bios Urn that makes biodegradable urns. The urn itself is made of all biodegradable ingredients. The ashes of the deceased are placed in the bottom part which is separated from a top section where you place local dirt, compost, etc., and a tree seed! The seed will germinate fairly quickly, and over time the urn will disintegrate as the roots of the new tree absorb the nutrients from the ashes! So life springs from death and your loved one becomes a tree! As a tree, they will give life in the form of oxygen to all the Earth while standing as a living memorial to their spirit. I think this is the most Hobbity idea I've ever seen. Like Samwise, who planted Galadriel's Mallorn seed, they, or we can *become* a Party Tree where our friends and family can gather for decades to remember them and to celebrate important life events. We can name the tree after them, even place a permanent marker next to it! Instead of being hermetically sealed in an overpriced box pumped full of poisonous chemicals and buried in some cemetery — which takes up a ridiculous amount of land — and being left there, where most of us forget to visit, let's plant our loved ones in our yards! Then we can visit with them every day, sit under their cooling shade, watch them grow, shed leaves every fall, and return every spring. Plant flowers around the tree, perennials that will come back every year. And some day in the future, if we raise our children as good little Hobbits, they will take a seed from that tree and plant another one, or the seeds will just fall to the ground and a forest will spring up! I can think of nothing lovelier than that. Then, instead of hewers of trees, we will all *become* trees. We will have evolved from *Homo Hobbitla* to *Homo Entlus:* Hobbit, to Ent!

# 34

# THE HAPPY HOBBIT FAMILY: GETTING THE SIGNIFICANTS, YOUNG'UNS, AND FOUR-LEGGED HOBBITS ON THE ROAD!

If mama ain't happy, nobody's happy. —Traditional Wisdom

With any new changes to one's lifestyle, one of the biggest stumbling blocks to success, other than our own inaction or procrastination, is trying to get those closest to us to accept the changes and to join in on the work. There are many reasons for this, and my family is no different in that respect. I am lucky in that Patience is very supportive of what I do, whether that is historical research, or teaching, or my new passion: writing about environmental issues. I realize many people do not have that kind of support. Without it, major changes in a home will be minimal, at best, and impossible in the worst cases. It is therefore very important to get your family members onboard with the new Hobbit lifestyle.

# Some General Thoughts

Take your time and listen to your family's concerns. Try to remember how you felt when you first discovered how messed up our planet is. Maybe that was just a couple sections ago, in this very book. Or maybe you've known for a long time but were paralyzed—as many of us have been—by despair that your efforts might have no real consequence or weight, that the problem was just too big for one person to make a difference. These are natural reactions to bad news and most of the news is bad: rumors from Mordor. I hope I have made a strong argument for not despairing. Remember, don't be Denethor, be Frodo or Aragorn.

I am asking you, personally, for your help to save our Earth, our Middle Earth, if you will. If you cannot help, who will? This is not to guilt you into helping; guilt is a weak motivator. I want to empower you to help by showing you how you can make a difference. The more people we get to join our Fellowship of the Ring the more impactful that difference will be. The movement to save the Earth has long started, it is no longer a trickle; it is more than a stream, and it will soon be a river and then quickly, a flood. The tipping point I talked about earlier is very close. Come walk with us Hobbits and be the change in the world that you wish to see. Start in your own Hobbit-hole by gently easing your family to join you. Then you can slowly work to bring in the rest of your family, friends and then your neighborhood. Working all together, you can build your own little Shire, right in your city, or township.

Are your family members Tolkien fans? If so, read *The Hobbit* or *The Lord of the Rings* together as a family and point out comparisons with things in the stories, as this book has done, to things in the real world. There are few books as inspiring as Tolkien's and reading them as a family can help to create a positive attitude about the changes you want to make. You can explain how these changes are the way to 'live like Hobbits,' and who doesn't want to do that? Read parts of this book along with Tolkien! Share the book with your significant other; let them read it for themselves! Or better yet, re-read it to them or to each other. Maybe your family aren't big readers, but have seen the movies. Watch them again and then discuss ideas from this book that you see in the films.

# Questions and Reactions: Forming the Fellowship

Here are some common questions and reactions you will run into when trying to convince family members and friends to join you:

### How will we find time to do all of these changes?

In the long run, if you make the changes suggested you will actually save time by simplifying your lives and finding new ways to spend your free time together. As mentioned in the food section, we spend a great deal of time running around doing errands, especially food shopping, that could be more organized. Much of this is because we have been convinced, by advertising Sarumans like Edward Bernays—long rot his bones—that *convenient* products are in fact, convenient. They are not; they are wasteful. Anything worth having, or eating, is worth a little time researching, shopping for, and preparing. If you're in a hurry, just don't buy it.

### How much is this going to cost us?

Another problem that family members like to point out is the expense of all these projects. You need to point out that since you're not going to do it all at once the costs will be spread out and that in fact, in the long run you will save money. As I mentioned earlier, Bea Johnson, author of *Zero Waste*, cut her family's budget by 40% over time by eliminating waste of all kinds. I highly recommend you read it though you don't have to go to the extremes that she did to get positive results. Any amount of money saved while also saving the Earth, is a win-win. If you make the major changes in this book you will save money, especially on energy use: electricity, gasoline, water. You will also save money on food if you buy things in bulk and put them in your own containers. If you grow your own food you will save an enormous amount of money, every month.

Don't think you have to grow everything you eat. Start with the things you love the most, and expand over the years to include more things.

**Pass the Trash, Make some Cash**

You can also *make* money in the process of decluttering your Hobbit-hole. Sell off stuff you don't need or consider renting it out! Don't forget all the new cooperative consumption ways to share your possessions with your neighbors. Think Shire-like. If you have things you don't need, sell them, lend them, or give them away. Don't hang onto them. Storing stuff costs money! You're paying for that storage space, whether it's a rental space somewhere out in the suburbs or the space in your garage, basement, or closet. Is it being used in the most efficient way? If it's like mine, probably not.

I keep my mother's voice in my head when I walk into the garage, "If you think you're gonna *war* that tree together, you best drag it to the street right NOW!" So get rid of it. Clean it out. Reuse the space for something more fun. Turn it into a play space or work shop or Hobbit-man-cave/hole. Maybe turn it into a tool library for the neighborhood, or a book library? Put some old chairs and a sofa in there with some book shelves and Hobbity decor and let your neighbors come and hang out and read! Use your imagination.

**How can we speed this up, to save the Earth FASTER?**

This is a common reaction once you realize the scope of the world's problems. You want to save the Earth, all at once! What ever you do, <u>DO NOT try to make too many changes at once</u>! This is the kiss of death for any new lifestyle change. Take one small section of this book, like the food section, for example, and focus on that one for a month or two months, however long it takes to make the changes you want to make. Remember also, that the changes I suggest are only ideas of ways to help curb waste and pollution to the environment while at the same time improving the quality of life for you and your family.

You certainly must decide together what changes work for you, and which ones do not. Not all of them apply to everyone and everyone has their own ideas about what works and what does not. When it doubt, give a change a try to see if a particular strategy works for you or not. If it does, awesome! If not, then maybe try something different. You can also try <u>grouping smaller changes from different sections of the book</u> that seem related to your particular situation. That would work too as long as you don't try to do too much, too quickly. It took generations for us to develop the *Taker Mentality*; it cannot be dismantled in a day. The way of thinking can change very quickly indeed but the practical application of those ideals takes time to implement.

**Do I get a say in what we change?**

Let your significant other, wife, girlfriend, husband, boyfriend, know that you understand their reservations, that you experienced those too at some point and reassure them that you will work together and discuss changes before making them. They get a vote too. Coercion is a Saruman-ic way to get something done. Don't do it. Don't try to guilt them into it either. They will only push back, and you will get nowhere. Be accommodating and things in life will go easier. Nothing ever goes to plan. So be prepared to change the plan, constantly. There are infinite ways to be a Hobbit and just as many ways to do most of the things in this book.

# Seasons of Change: a Calendar for the Hobbit-hole

Some changes also lend themselves to particular seasons of the year. Instead of trying to do them all at once, consider breaking up projects according to seasonal considerations. Here is a suggested schedule for seasonal projects:

## Winter

Work on inside changes like the food you eat, how you store it, and organizing the kitchen. Get rid of poisonous chemicals and cleaning products. Start ridding the house of plastics, starting in the kitchen and working through the house. Weed out your closets of clothing that doesn't fit or isn't fit to wear. Start planning your vegetable garden for the spring! Don't think you can accomplish all of this in one season though, unless of course you live in the frozen wasteland like me, where winter is 6 months long!

## Spring

Get out in the garden once it warms up. Clean up, prune things that didn't get pruned in the fall, rake up debris, and prepare to start planting once it's warm enough, unless you have a greenhouse, or a place to start seeds earlier. Clean out the garage; garages are usually storehouses for hazardous chemicals. Make sure to take them to the proper disposal place. Check your local government website; search for 'hazardous waste disposal.' Another good thing to do during spring, or anytime, is to donate unwanted items or sell them on Craigslist.

## Summer

Get out in your garden and enjoy it! Sure, you can keep working on it and other projects but leave time to actually sit back, as Bilbo would, and enjoy what you are building and planting. Go on a vacation somewhere with the family. If going away isn't in the cards this year, take the family and friends on a picnic to a local park or nature area. Don't forget your picnic bag! Throw parties and cookouts for friends and family. Why not invite the entire neighborhood over for a BBQ? What better way to get to know everyone around you? Designate one of your trees as the Party Tree and decorate it with hanging lanterns or low wattage christmas lights. Set up a tent, or fly a tarp to give shade and to set atmosphere.

## Autumn

The Fall is a great time to clean up the yard and get ready for winter, but mostly it's about celebrating Middle Earth Day in September, and Halloween, and in the U.S., Thanksgiving. You can continue working on outdoor projects but it's really time to store up food from the garden so you can have that produce in the winter. It's time to *can*. I've never canned food in my life, until this fall. Patience, Duke, and I canned tomatoes for the winter. We didn't do a lot of them, because we didn't really know what we were doing and didn't want to get over ambitious our first time out. But I think we did a good job with the 'maters. I'm looking forward to eating them in the winter. While our 'tater plants didn't work out quite as well, we'll regroup, get some advice from friends, and try again next year. If you're storing food for the first time too, I would suggest you get the *Ball Complete Book of Home Preserving*, then buy a bunch of the *Ball* canning jars and get busy!

# Young'uns: Making it Fun for the Wee Hobbits

For those of us who are parents, we know how difficult it can be to get our children to do the simplest of tasks sometimes. How many times do we have to tell them to brush their teeth, comb their hair, and pick up their rooms? To get them to make the changes suggested in this book can be daunting but if presented in the right way we can make them strong allies for saving the Earth. If your young ones are already Tolkien fans the task is half accomplished already. It's pretty easy to draw comparisons between Middle Earth and our world and kids have fun trying to find them. If your kids aren't already Tolkien fans, read the stories to them, let them read them themselves, or watch the films as a family. Get them hooked into the wonderful world of Hobbits and half of your job is done.

**Be Positive**

Kids can be sensitive to negative information about the future, so it's best to ease them into the negative stuff about the environment. Too much of it at once and they will be overwhelmed. Expect that some things will upset them; the information is simply upsetting, even to us adults. That's not to say that you should shelter them from it, but it's best to show them some of the results of our culture's wasteful practices without scaring the heck out of them with predictions of impending doom, however true those predictions might turn out to be. Fear is not something that will motivate your kids. Well, a little healthy fear of mom and dad goes a long way but not the kind of paralyzing fear that can come from the realization that our planet is in dire straights. They can learn more about this as they get older, say in middle school or high school, but until then try to keep the message positive. You can tell them, "The world is kind of a mess but we can clean it up if we work hard at it, and live like Hobbits!" After all, it's true!

Enduring positivity is what will save the Earth no matter how negative the problems may be. Explain to them the benefits of each change that you make. Instead of terrifying them this will *empower* them and teach them a very valuable life lesson: If you face overwhelming odds, keep doing what is right, no matter what. This is what all true heroes do, like Frodo and Sam, like Merry and Pippen. It is perfectly okay to be afraid, but never, ever, ever give in to your fear and turn your back on your values or your duty to do what is right. Keep on walking. Like Winston Churchill once said, "If you're walking through hell, keep walking."

Use documentaries to help explain what is going on with the planet. There are some good ones that kids can handle, depending on their age. It's best if you watch them yourself first so you can gauge how they will react. Don't be too overprotective, however. Children are much more resilient to adversity than we think. It does them no good to grow up completely in the dark about the troubles on or planet. Many of us did, and look where it has gotten us. Two really good family-oriented documentaries are *Garbage: the Revolution Starts at Home* and *The Story of Stuff* They do a great job of showing how our modern, consumer lifestyle is out of control and how we can work to fix it. There are also a lot of really good TED talks which you can find on Netflix, and Youtube.

Now that we have the *human* children taken care of, let's not forget our other *kids*, you know, the real bosses of our families and the universe: the ones that walk on four legs.

## Hobbit Kitties and Pups, a.k.a. *Rulers of Middle Earth*: Sustainable Pets

We have three pets. Well, it would be more accurate to say we have two emperors and one dog. Bubble, the dog, mostly just follows orders from the cats, the two Emperor, Viking, Pirate kitties—Squish and Punkin'—who run everything on Earth, and in fact, in the entire universe from their favorite spot, the Ottoman Empire. That would be the ottoman in the office. Bubble is a Chow-Lab mix. She's old, lazy, and mellow. Basically, she's a Baggins. If she's not eating, she's sleeping and hanging out with the pack. The pirates, on the other hand, love to run around, play the *sock game* – dragging them up from the basement to place in the water dish—torture the dog, and then curl up and sleep on the Ottoman Empire, or the bed, or the chairs, or the dog. Squish is the dominant personality in the house. She runs the show. She's contemptuous of humans who she refers to as *huuuumonnns*—unless we are serving her needs at the moment. Punkin' is the cutest thing ever. We call her the Midgard Kitty because she spends 90% of her time curled up sucking on her tail like a binky, much as the Midgard Serpent of the Old Norse Myths. We love our pets. If you're a pet owner, I'm sure you do too.

There are some environmentalists I've read who argue that pets are a strain on the environment. Their food and litter create a strain on the system. Some of them go so far as to suggest that we get rid of our pets as if this would solve the problem. Would it? Of course not. It's not as simple as asking ourselves, "Should I have a pet?" If everyone said, "no," then what would we do with all of those animals? Release them into the wild? That would be an environmental disaster of massive proportions. Unless we euthanize them all which would be the most dastardly act in human history—and that's saying something— we have to find more sustainable ways to keep them. Animals have just as much right to live on this planet as we do; some— myself included—would argue they have *more*. Yes, there are costs involved in keeping pets. We should always be looking for ways to minimize their impact on the environment.

**Spay and Neuter**

The one thing that all pet owners should do is to spay and neuter their animals. There are already plenty of dogs and cats in the world and to continue to propagate them is irresponsible. They will not *all* be spayed or neutered, of course, so there will always be a supply of them. If, for some reason in the future, the cat and dog population of the Earth drops too low we could reconsider the practice, but until then we need to work to keep that population down.

### Rescue Them!

Please don't feed the *breeder* market. Pure-bred means nothing. There's no such thing as pure-bred anyway. All of the breeds can only be traced back a couple hundred years, if that long. And even if they could be traced back to Adam and Eve and the Fried Chicken Tree, who f'n cares? It's an elitist attitude, a waste of money, and it supports some of the most inhumane practices on Earth. Instead, adopt your pirate kitties and Baggins hounds from the Humane Society or other animal shelters. There are millions of animals sitting in cages who are looking for a warm Hobbit-hole to curl up in.

### Feeding the Beasts

Pets can eat a lot. Big dogs especially, but my cats aren't slackers either. There are environmental issues with how the food is raised, processed, delivered, etc., just like human food. The problems with GMOs, pesticides, and other nasty, orcish chemicals is an issue with their food as it is with ours. Buy the best food you can afford. If you can find it locally, great. Otherwise, try to buy organic or more naturally raised pet foods. Buy in big bags if you can. Bulk is even better. The biggest impact from pet food, however, is from the containers. Pet food cans CAN BE recycled. Just as drink cans, recycling aluminum from pet food cans takes 95% less energy than making a new can! That's a big deal Hobbits. So put those cans in the recycling bin! Of course, cans aren't the *only* waste generated by our pets.

### Scooping Poop the Hobbity Way

This summer I spent an entire afternoon crawling under spider-infested, dusty, old basement stairs to clean out ancient cat feces. That was fun, let me tell ya. The stench surely rivaled that of Shelob's Lair. Maybe you've had a similar experience? If you're a pet owner, you probably have. Pet ownership isn't *all* glamor after all. So what do respectable, sustainable Hobbits do with their kitty and puppy leavings? In some ways dog crap is easier to deal with. You take Bungo out, or let him out; he does his business and then you let him, or bring him, back inside. Of course, you then have piles of crap all over your yard, or your neighbor's. If you live next to the Sackville-Bagginses then maybe you're not all that concerned about the puppy gifts left on their lawn. But if you're trying to keep peace in the Shire it's probably best if you pick them up and dispose of them properly. That's where the choices come in, and where the environmental impact follows.

The easiest way to take care of dog poop, is to scoop it up, place it into a bag and throw it into your outside garbage can. But most of us use plastic or paper shopping bags for that purpose, both of which are harmful to the environment. Plastic is just plain orcish and paper uses up too many resources, in particular, water. But there are biodegradable bags out there made specifically for this purpose. BioBag makes a version from plant derivatives that is 100% compostable, though composting dog poop has to be done properly and the average residential compost bin won't reach the temperatures needed to do it. But the bags will break down in commercial compost piles. They could also be used to dispose of scoop-able cat litter, though most information you find online says to never compost cat litter. If you only have to deal with dog poop and want to compost it, there are factory-made systems that you can purchase, but Hobbits would rather make them, I'm sure, so here's a link to a good design. Basically, you're burying a vessel—anything from a 5 gallon bucket to 55 gallon barrel—where you drop the poop and grass clippings. Once it's full you can dig it up and use the contents as fertilizer.

I love kitties. I'm not really a dog person, though I love ours, Bubble, because she's an exceptionally laid-back dog. But cats? Love'em. That doesn't mean there aren't times when I'd like to cook'em. Like right now, for instance. Punkin' just attempted to jump over my laptop and landed with her back paws on the delete button, erasing the *n't* from 'are' in the last sentence. So yeah, sometimes I'd like to make kitty stew, but I don't. Mostly I just *smoosh* on them. They hate that. I call it corporal cuddling. I love it, they hate it. It works for me. But when it comes time to scooping the poop, and pee, I usually pass the job off to Duke. I mean, what are 12 year olds for? There are a couple of things to consider about cat litter, that is if your cats use a box indoors. Cats really shouldn't be outdoors because they live longer if they aren't. But if yours are, then you don't have to worry that much about litter. If they do stay indoors then you need a box, litter, and if you don't want to wash the box every time, box liners.

As for litter, the biggest problem is with traditional clay litters which are becoming a major problem in landfills. Clay, while natural, doesn't break down and much of it is strip-mined in the first place, which is another impact that we don't want. Common litters are also chock full of chemicals from Isengard and Mordor. Luckily there are more natural, sustainable alternatives to clay-based litters these days. Most of these are plant-based, either from wheat, corn, nut, or tree byproducts. We've been using SwheatScoop for about a year now, and it works pretty well. It's made with ground wheat. Another one is World's Best Cat Litter, made from corn. Another reason to switch to an alternative is that clay-based can be unhealthy for cats because they breath in the dust and consume it when they clean themselves, which can gum up their systems. I know I ate my share of Play-Doh growing up, as you probably did as well, and I'm fine, but kitties probably shouldn't be eating clay. Once we find a new litter there's the question of the box and liner.

I confess, I used to use disposable litter boxes for years. You know, the ones in Mordor-Mart made out of plastic. Yeah, just spank me. I deserve it. But no longer. We got a reusable box when we moved to our new house last year so at least we weren't constantly buying new ones and throwing them out to pile up in the landfill like some kind of ammonia-smelling Barad Dur. But there's still the problem of a box liner, which are pretty much all plastic bags. We could go without the liner, I reckon, and clean out the box every time, but as much as we have a 12 year old to do the job I'm not completely sure that it would get done to Squishy Kitty's satisfaction, and that would lead to disaster on a Nazgúl-ian scale. We'd just have to clean up the rest of the house instead. So we're still using the bags.

I've been searching for a non-plastic alternative but so far I've not been able to find one. Cats are individuals, and I've seen every solution in the book for this problem but none of them seem to apply to our kitties, so the quest continues. BioBag does make kitchen size, and larger, garbage bags that are compostable and non-plastic. They're not cheap, but we may be trying those soon. We still won't be able to compost the litter, but at least the bags won't be creating more plastic waste.

As I said, most experts tell you that you shouldn't compost kitty litter, but the reason being that carnivore and omnivore feces has bacteria and parasites that could be passed to other humans. I say *other* humans because if they're your kitties, you already have them. This is easily avoided if you don't apply this compost to your food plants, but there are some gardeners who do just that. I'm not sure that we'll be doing this at our house anytime soon—we're just learning how to compost *regular kitchen waste*, so don't have the expertise to venture into pet waste composting just yet—but if you're interested in the subject check out these two websites: The Compost-Gardener.com and Glen Brook North Zero Waste.

## Keep It Fun: Happy Hobbits Get More Done!

Life should be fun, even in the midst of tragedy and trials. A sense of humor is the most important trait for a person to have. If you can't laugh, at your self, with others, and see the absurdity of your own troubles then you will lose your mind and become like poor Gollum. Laugh like a Hobbit, then *live long and prosper*! Keep in touch with your neighbors, friends, and family. Stay in the loop. Don't become isolated in your attempt to become Hobbits! That would be very anti-Hobbit. Hobbits are not *hermits*. Just because we live in *holes* doesn't mean we don't come out of them and mingle with the rest of the Shire. And in order to save the Earth, at some point that's just what we have to do: come out and bring Shireness to the World. And that is the aim of the last section of the book.

# 35

# EXPORTING SHIRENESS: BUILDING THE GLOBAL SHIRE

It is best to love first what you are fitted to love, I suppose: you must start somewhere and have some roots, and the soil of the Shire is deep. —LOTR: III, The Houses of Healing

Start a huge, foolish project, like Noah...it makes absolutely no difference what people think of you. — Rumi, the Sufi Mystic

We're not on our journey to save the world but to save ourselves. But in doing that you save the world. The influence of a vital person vitalizes. —Joseph Campbell, The Power of Myth

"So what's next?" you ask. "What do we do after we Hobbitize ourselves and turn our own homes into modern Hobbit-holes?" "Will it really make a difference in the larger scheme of things?" The short answer is, yes it will. Any change that you make creates a ripple effect, even if you don't see the ripple or the effects. That's what Joseph Campbell was trying to say above. Actions *always* have consequences. Most of the time we would agree to that statement but we're usually focused on *negative* actions and karma. But it holds just as true for *positive* actions.

A couple of weeks ago, Patience and I were driving home from the market. It was a beautiful, late summer day. We had the windows down, the radio playing classical music. Everything was pretty darned perfect, if there is such a thing as a perfect day. We came to a stop at a light and I looked over to the right, where a group of high school students were walking home from school, girls and boys. They were talking, joking around like teens do. But one girl slowed down as she was passing a sidewalk planter, you know the type—with a tree and flowers planted in it. She looked down into the flowers planted there, and then reached over into them. My first reaction was negative—I have to admit. The first thought that popped into my head was, "Damn! She's gonna put some trash in there or something," even though I'd seen nothing in her hand to lead me to that negative conclusion. Then she did something truly simple, but amazing beyond belief. She pulled a fast-food bag, a plastic cup, and some other trash *from* the planter and carried it off! I was flabergasted. I looked over at Patience—who I hadn't realized was also watching—and she said, "Did you see that?"

"Yeah! I *did!*" I said, "That was f'n awesome!" "She's a *Hobbit!*"

I almost began to cry. I won't lie to you. It still affects me when I think about it. So, don't you fret, Frodo; you are not alone. There are many Hobbits out there already, even if you don't see them or they don't know they're Hobbits. The more you Hobbitize yourself the more likely you are to see Hobbit-ness in others. You will see things just like the scene above, over and over again. <u>But you have to **train your mind** to see the positive in people</u>. It's hard to do but it's essential. The more positive you become yourself the easier it will be. And remember that it's not just seeing *others* doing Hobbity things; you need to do them, too! This is how we begin to export Shireness to the rest of the World. You don't have to become Mother Teresa and feed all the starving people in India. But you can find something meaningful to accomplish in your own town, state, or country. Don't just clean up your house, plant a garden, and become a *respectable* Hobbit that never goes on adventures! Awaken the Took in yourself and head out into the great big world and stir up dragons, slay orcs and destroy

Rings! Where would Middle Earth have been without disrespect-able Hobbits? It would have been overrun by Sauron and Saruman. It would have all been Mordor.

The next step is to export our Shireness to our neighbors, cities, and the world, one Hobbit at a time, or if you're lucky, tens or hundreds at a time.

## Our New Global Story: Builders of Shires

> If the world is saved, it will not be saved by old minds with new programs but by new minds with no programs at all. —Daniel Quinn, *The Story of B: An Adventure of the Mind and Spirit*

Before we can export the ideas of Shireness to the rest of the planet we need to make sure they are solidly constructed in our own minds, the minds of our families, and our neighborhoods. We need a New Story. Our old one is dysfunctional and negative. We are part of the Earth. We are not its rulers. Until our New Story is engrained in our Hobbit-noggins, nothing good will happen. There will be no Global Shire. There will be no World Peace. Ignorance and Fear, Want and Greed, Violence, Corruption, and Disease will continue to rule. We have no *rights* to the resources of the Earth, no more than any other living creature upon it. We have the *priviledge* of living here, with our neighbors of the animal and plant kingdoms, as well as our fellow humans. We don't have to love them. We don't even have to like them. We just have to find a way to coexist with each other. That doesn't mean violence and wars will cease. That would be nice, but it's not realistic. But we should, as Hobbits, always strive to reach out to our fellow humans around the world and build bridges between cultures. This is the only way to undermine the Ignorance and Fear that drives so much conflict. This is true in all situations, from one Hobbit to another and between great nations of people.

What we need is a plan. We need a plan that is flexible enough to accommodate other points of view. That does not mean we should turn a blind eye to aggression, oppression, greed, and intolerance, however; those must be fiercely resisted. But differences of culture, religion, politics, and philosophy should no longer be the basis for wars. Arguments? Sure. Arguments, as long as they do not become violent or disrespectful are okay. But we need to remember each other's humanity while disagreeing. Is that easy to do? Nope. It isn't. But it's necessary. We need to examine our own Willful Ignorance and Fear, so that we can avoid it as much as possible. This is a block to accomplishing the New Shire. The problem is that most of us, probably all of us, think that *we* know the truth. But do we? Don't forget to employ <u>Bilbo's Personal Willful Ignorance Test</u> anytime you feel the urge to argue with someone. If you let the discussion degenerate into an argument you will accomplish nothing towards building the Shire. <u>Arguing is a form of coercion, and it doesn't work</u>. Instead of agreeing with you, your opponent will retreat into their own Barad Dur of Ignorance, and you will do the same. Nothing good ever comes of that.

We need to develop a plan to deal with the ignorance of others as well. We cannot attack Ignorance head on. That's been tried for millennia, with little positive effect. Instead, we need to tirelessly work toward building connections between people to foster understanding of our common humanity. The best way to do this is to return to ancient roots of communities: gardens, food, storytelling, art, music, humor, and hospitality. We need a plan to bring Shireness to the World, lots of plans. But be careful when making them. Why? Because they aren't going to work the way we plan for them to. But that's all right. There's always more than one way to get to the Lonely Mountain, and back again.

# 36

# BARBEQUING WITH LESBIANS: LETTING SHIRENESS BE

"It's dangerous business, Frodo, going out of your door," he used to say. " You step into the Road, and if you don't keep your feet, there is no knowing where you might be swept off to. — *LOTR*: I, *Three is Company*

Sometimes the light's all shinin' on me;
Other times I can barely see.
Lately it occurs to me
What a long, strange trip it's been. — The Grateful Dead, *Truckin'*

Life is just what happens to you,
While you're busy making other plans — John Lennon, *Beautiful Boy*

This summer, I barbequed with lesbians. Yep. That's what I said. And they were *married*. Yes, I said married, as in *hitched*, *tied the knot*, *walked the green mile*. Okay, the last one was my veiled shot at the institution of marriage itself, of which I've had little success. But the point I want to get across is that I barbequed with married lesbians, in Yankeeland, in Minnesota, the land of snow, and Germans, and Lut'erns — that's Lutherans for the rest of us — and Scandihoovians, and Vikings. I, Steve Bivans — southern     boy,     straight,     white,     used-to-be-

401

conservative — made proper barbeque with married lesbians. And you know what? It was pretty darned all right. In fact, it was a hell of a lot better'n all right. I loved every minute of it. In fact, *everyone* should do it!

But I was not always of that mindset. And it wasn't my fault. I had long held a prejudice against gays and lesbians — as well as other prejudices — because I grew up in a culture in which those attitudes were common. And I don't mean *Southern* culture. I mean the culture of white-bread America in the 1960s, 70s, and 80s. I'm old, that's when I grew up. When I was young, before my teens, I didn't even know gay and lesbian people existed. Once I learned of them, I was told that they were — like so many other people — "living in sin." That they're lifestyle was a choice, not something they were born with or into. Well, I'm not here to argue nurture vs nature. I personally believe everyone on Earth is a healthy combination of both. What I want to talk about is life and how strange it is. And how we have no control over where we end up. Not one bit. Why do I say we have no control? Because we don't. My life is a perfect example, as is everyone else's, but since I don't know your story, I'll tell you a bit more of mine.

Let's just say that ten years ago I walked into the fortune-teller's tent at the county fair. I didn't — and I never will because they're complete frauds — but let's just say for argument's sake that I did. And after gazing into her well-polished bowling ball, or Magic 8 Ball, she told me that in ten years I would be sitting in a lawn chair, in June, in a driveway in South Minneapolis, making barbeque with two women — recently married lesbians — to celebrate said marriage, I would have laughed in the charlatan's face and demanded my money back. But that's exactly what happened. And the series of events that led to that moment are staggering and almost none of them were planned by anyone. Sure, the wedding celebration was *planned,* in the sense that a group of people got together and laid out a list of things to do and get done. But the coincidences that led to me being there are almost beyond belief.

It all began ten or eleven years ago when I decided to go back to school to finish my bachelor's degree in history and to continue on to get a PhD. That one decision set off a chain of events that put me on a path towards making barbeque with married lesbians. Here's how it happened, and I'm going to go quickly so hold on. I finished my B.A. in history at East Carolina University from 2004-2007. I applied to about ten different graduate programs, mostly on the East coast. I had not even considered applying to the University of Minnesota until I was talking with one of my professors at East Carolina, who asked me, "Hey, have you looked at the medieval program at Minnesota?"

I said, "Uhhhh no. Why would I want to go there!?" But I did apply, and of the ten or eleven schools I applied to I was accepted to three, but the offer from Minnesota was too good to pass up, so off we were to the land of snow and Vikings. Before applying to the U of M, I had never really given the state a second thought in my entire life. I knew that the Minnesota Vikings football team was up here, of course, and the Minnesota Twins baseball team and that it was cold as a witch's tit in a brass bra in the winter, or all year, and that the Mary Tyler Moore show was set here, but that's about it. Why would anyone want to actually *move there*? Well, we did, and then I was divorced, houseless, moved back home for a bit and came back for a Yankee girl from Minnesota. No one could have ever predicted all that. And that's how I met Patience's sister, April, and her sister's girlfriend, Nicole and ended up making barbeque with them to celebrate their wedding which ten years ago, hell, two years ago, wasn't even legal in Minnesota and still isn't in most states of the Union.

What's my point? Just this. You have no freakin' clue where your life is going to lead. None. All plans dissolve as soon as you walk out the door, if they last that long. Your feet will be swept away and you'll end up climbing mountains and matching wits with dragons, battling giant spiders, and crawling up volcanoes, or moving to Yankeeland and making barbeque with lesbians. Plans are all fine and good as long as you don't actually think they're going to happen that way. Make plans. But then follow the words of Paul McCartney and "let it be." You cannot coerce things into being and this is also true of building Shires. Coercion is the myth of *control*. Coercion is what Saurons and Sarumans try to do, not Hobbits. Hobbits step into the road and let their feet be swept off to adventures unknown. They make plans, sure, but they soon discover that plans change, because Hobbits have no control, nor do they want to *control* anything. They would rather just let things be and admire them for what they are.

As we continue this journey that we've set out upon, keep this thought in mind. Making plans is okay but be prepared to constantly change them, because if you don't, you're going to miss out on the best opportunities. What if ole Bilbo had refused to go on that adventure with the Dwarves? Think about it? Would the Ring have found its way out of the mountains? Probably, but how? Would it have gone to someone as resistant to its power? I doubt it, and that would have been the ruin of all of Middle Earth. Bilbo had other plans that evening, but a wizard and twelve Dwarves offered him an alternative path. He had a choice. And luckily for Middle Earth, and for us, he chose the unexpected one. Would Bilbo, later in life, have regretted his choice? I think not. That doesn't mean that his choice wasn't fraught with danger and inconveniences, but in the end, those experiences were worth all the gold in Smaug's Lair. It is our experiences that define us in the end. Sure, we could choose the safe path: stay at home, eat second breakfast, sleep in late, never go anywhere, or do anything. But one day at the end of your life would you regret not having taken any chances in life? I think so. So take those risks but don't for one minute think you know where they will lead you. You don't. Just let it be. Give up coercion.

## Bye Bye Coercion, Hello Mr. Dao

In many ways I set out to write *Be a Hobbit, Save the Earth,* with the expressed personal intention of *saving the Earth,* as if somehow I could write words compelling enough to coerce others to just *do it.* Of course, that's ridiculous on the face of it, now that I look at it more objectively. That doesn't mean the Earth doesn't *need* saving; it just means I can't, or at least shouldn't, coerce people into doing it. Why can't we coerce people to do what we want? Because ancient Chinese sages say so. That's why.

Lately I've been studying Daoism, you know, the ancient Chinese philosophy. I'm certainly no expert—having read exactly one book on it—but I think I can convey the basic ideas. At the heart of the Dao, or *way-making*, or *making one's way in life*—however you translate it—is the idea that *things*—as discrete or determinate entities—don't really exist. In other words the chair you're sitting on right now does not exist as a static *thing*. In fact it is really an *event* or part of an event that is ever changing, moment to moment. The chair as a static *thing* is a momentary, mental snap-shot, a photograph if you will, taken by *you* and only you for the briefest of moments, then it's gone because the chair is continuously changing, aging, and if you were to observe it at the molecular or elemental level—using modern science and a microscope—you would see this transformation at work.

Ancient Daoist sages, of course, didn't have microscopes but they could see transformation over the long run and deduce that it was always happening, slowly, to everything around them. So *things* aren't really things they are just brief pictures of a *process* of *thing-ing*. How's that for deep *doo doo*? Yeah, I know. Damned Chinese philosophers. Those same sages—if you were to sit down with them—would tell you at some point in your learning process that since things are really processes, you can't force them to do what you want them too. In other words, coercion is out. You can try, but you will get results that are less than what you had hoped for. For example, you can divert the flow of a river but what will be the results? The sage will tell you that you can't possibly foresee the results and that most likely they will be radically different than you intended.

## Coercion of the Natural World

The U.S. Army Corps of Engineers will tell you, these days anyway, that the Sages were right. They've been trying to coerce American rivers to stay in their *natural* banks for about a century, and failed miserably. In fact many of the floods that happen today are actually the result of their attempts to coerce water to go where *they* wanted it to flow. The levy on Lake

Pontchartrain in Louisiana might be the most dramatic failure of this modern coercive *philosophy,* if indeed anything the U.S. Military does can be properly called "the love of wisdom."

The oil companies are trying to coerce the last drops of oil and natural gas to the surface by fracking the life out of the Earth's crust while poisoning the last remaining natural aquifers, the air we breathe, and the soil we plant our food in. It's not working either. It's time to stop and rethink our *philosophies.* Maybe it's just time to stop coercing things?

## Letting Shireness *Be*

In order to build strong Shires we have to abandon the idea that we can *make* them happen. We cannot. We must give up coercion. We can make plans but we can't make those plans come to fruition out of some act of will. Rather let's figure out how to lead by example or by story. *"Here's how I do it; how might you do it in your own special way?"* I know, it sounds kind of hippy dippy, like Spinal Tap singing about the "Flower People," but that's probably the only way to really accomplish building Shires and achieve the goal of saving the Earth; one person or Hobbit does something and another thinks, *"Hey, that was kind of cool; I could do something like that, but I have a different idea on how to do it."* And before you know it you have Shireness popping up everywhere! Have you ever made a plan to do something and then just kind of sat back and watched it take on a life of its own? How did it turn out? Better than you hoped? That's been my experience. The more I try to force things, the more they fall short of my expectations. When I manage to step back and just 'let it be,' things usually surpass my wildest dreams. Gardens are like this. They have a life of their own. Yeah, you can plan them, somewhat, but they tend to do what they want to and if you let them, they can amaze you.

Shires are more like gardens. You plant some seeds, and water them, let the sun shine on them, pull a few weeds here and there and return those to a pile of compost that you use on the garden and one day you have Kale, or carrots, or 'maters, or 'taters. So let's be little Gaffers and plant 'taters. Focus on planting seeds and pulling weeds and forget about saving the Earth. If we do the work without focussing on the results Shires will grow. Then we can harvest the produce, save the seeds, plant them again and one day bring Spring again to the trees.

# 37

# TO BRING SHIRENESS TO THE WORLD, AND SPRING AGAIN TO THE TREES

...it is now exactly twenty years since I began in earnest to complete the history of our renowned Hobbit-ancestors of the Third Age. I look East, West, North, South, and I do not see Sauron; but I see that Saruman has many descendants. We Hobbits have against them no magic weapons. Yet, my gentle Hobbits, I give you this toast: To the Hobbits. May they outlast the Sarumans and see spring again in the trees. —J.R.R. Tolkien, in a speech in Rotterdam, 1958.

## What is *Shireness*?

Before we can *bring* Shireness—*plant the seeds* of Shireness—if you will, we must first define what that something *is*. The Hobbit's Shire was a rural farm-scape surrounded by wild places, forests, streams and rivers. But I am coining the noun *Shireness* to describe an ideal living condition for humanity. Here's my not-so-formal definition:

Shire-ness: n., a sustainable, free, and open, 'Hobbit-like' way of living, rooted *in* Nature, cooperating as a community, with humanity, hospitality, and humor.

## Do We All Have to Move 'to the Country'?

No, as I mentioned early in the book, as idyllic as that sounds it would in fact be disastrous, as one of the biggest problems facing the Earth—especially in developed countries like the U.S.—is the loss of farmland to the suburbs. This must stop. But where will all 7 billion of us live then? Answer, mostly in cities. We need to address population problems—a much larger subject that I won't go into here—and to build UP, not OUT.

Shireness is rooted *IN* Nature. In other words it requires a different mind set about our place in the natural world; it doesn't suggest we should all move into Hobbit-holes and out in the country. What it means is that we need to stop thinking of the Earth as simply our *resource*, to use as we will. It is not. As we've already discussed, that is an ancient myth developed in the misty dawn of civilization, the patently false root of all our problems as a species. What we need to do in order to live in the Shire is not to move to country—the sticks, the boonies, boondocks, hicksville, etc—but to bring the *country* into our minds. I'll repeat something I said earlier. <u>We need to *change our story*. We need to rewrite our thinking so that it states that we are *PART* of Nature, not Nature's masters. Hobbits aren't perfect people. Just like *Leavers*, Hobbits are not *Saints* they're just *sustainable*.</u>

## Sustainability: a Hobbit Virtue

This word gets thrown around a lot these days, but is rarely defined. I'm using it to refer to a way of living within Nature, like mentioned above. Instead of a *Taker* mentality, we must begin thinking about how we can close the loop on all our systems to eliminate wastes—of all kinds—so that we stop polluting our environment and corrupting our systems of government. Waste of any kind is a sign of bad system design. In Nature—and all things *ARE* in Nature—everything returns to the system as a useable by-product; think of trees, leaves, forest floor mulch, soil, back to trees. Nature perpetuates itself in a closed loop. There is no *waste*, ever. We, however, have produced crap-tons of waste and are doing it as we speak, namely fossil fuel laden products like plastics which will never bio-degrade. We need to cease making such things and find other ways to make the same, or better, products that are made of bio-degradable materials.

## Free and Open

This is the one that will get me in trouble with my conservative friends. "Nothing is Free, man!" they will say. To which I will say, "Yes, and no." Sunlight is free; water should be—though that is almost locked up in the hands of Saruman too. When I say *free* I'm not referring to some communistic, utopian idea of society, where everyone works to produce stuff for their neighbors on the assumption that their neighbors will do the same, and that everyone will put in equal effort and produce equally valuable contributions to the group. That's a myth, and it falls apart under any scrutiny, or logic, not to mention actual experimentation.

No, *free* refers to freedom of person, like in the Declaration of Independence. Everyone on Earth should have the right to own their own body, soul, and mind. Not everyone does, even in places where we claim it, like in the U.S. As discussed earlier there are both actual slaves and practical slaves in the so-called *free world*. Millions of them, and their numbers are growing, especially the latter kind.

When I say *Open* I'm referring to the movement for *open source* resources. This is the way many products were produced in the past, but increasingly the world has moved to the idea that products, ideas, and governments need to be secret. It is a hoarding mentality based on the idea of proprietary ownership. Our world has become too complex as a result, and expensive. Such closed mentality benefits the large corporations but not the consumer or society. We need to start producing goods and services that are *open* in nature. In other words, instead of locking up the insides of your cell phone, the software that you use, the shadowy workings of our governments, they need to be transparent. It's ok to own a patent, but the formula should be open for other people to use — not for free necessarily — but open in a way that others can improve upon it, make off-shoot products from it. And governments need to allow the direct participation of society and to simplify the system so that people can understand what governments are up to. If you want to read more on the open source idea check out Robert David Steele's book, *The Open Source Everything: Transparency, Truth and Trust*. The link will take you to my full review. It's a fascinating book by a former head of the U.S. military intelligence community. Also read David Bollier's book, *Think Like a Commoner: A Short Introduction to the Life of the Commons*.

## Cooperating as Community

This seems simple, and it kind of is. Basically this refers to the human ability to work together in a group to achieve prosperity for the whole of the group, not in dog-eat-dog competition. Healthy, friendly competition is good for society but not if the participants are flouting the rules of Shireness. In other words, you can compete, yes, but it has to be in a spirit of working for the greater good of society not just for your own greed and gain. Wealth and prosperity are good things, Greed never is. It is rooted in fear. If you want a more in depth look at what I mean by *cooperating* I recommend Rachel Botsman's book, *What's Mine is Yours* or Lisa Gansky's, *The Mesh*. Basically, I'm talking about modern Hobbits working together, sharing resources, ideas, and expertise in a way that benefits everyone, not just a few Sarumans at the top. What's amazing is that if those Sarumans or corporate heads just thought about it for a bit, cooperation is actually good business, which is the message in both Botsman's and Gansky's books as well as one of the messages in Steele's book too. It's also my message to you. Cooperation is not antithetical to profit or commerce. It just isn't.

### Hobbit-like

If you're reading this book and managed to get this far, you probably already have a solid idea of what constitutes a Hobbit, both in Tolkien's stories and how I define a *modern* Hobbit. If you need more information then you simply must read, or reread J.R.R. Tolkien's books, or at a minimum watch Peter Jackson's movie renditions. But for me, Hobbit-like is summed up in the words, *humanity*, *hospitality*, and *humor*.

## Humanity

When I say *humanity*, I'm referring to all it's definitions. It includes the idea of community, the species of *homo sapiens sapiens*, but mostly the idea that despite what differences we might have we are all basically the same. We want the same core things, at least in this lifetime. We want to feel free to express ourselves. We want to be free from Fear—though we pretty much never are. We want our fair share of resources. Yes, there are those among us who seem to want more than their share of all of that and to dominate the rest of us. True. But they are working on faulty assumptions about the way the world *is*. Their stories are screwed up. They could rewrite their stories, just as we must, but many of them will not. That doesn't change the fact that deep down they want the same things, even if they've forgotten it.

## Hospitality

Hospitality refers to our innate ability to show compassion and generosity to our fellow human beings and to all living things. We do it all the time, especially in times of extreme crises. We tend to forget our differences and remember our shared humanity and that comes out in an outpouring of hospitality. We take in our neighbors, feed them, cloth them, and house them. This is an appeal to all of us to remember this, more often, and not just in times of crisis.

## Humor

Ahhhh Humor. Without a sense of humor you might as well eat a shotgun blast, and you probably will. We need to stop taking ourselves so damned seriously. I'm guilty as hell of doing that, but I'm also known for joking and laughing, sometimes at my own absurdities—like *being pissed off that I'm pissed off*—for instance. Yeah, I do that. Sue me. By humor, I also mean our natural bent for socializing which is linked to hospitality too. Most of us love to spend time talking with other people, sharing food and drink, and good times. Indeed, if not for humor and hospitality, I would argue that humans have no place on this Earth anyway. It is possibly our greatest contribution, maybe our only novel one. Most of us have managed to do this with a small group of family and friends but I'm suggesting that we need to include our neighborhoods, our SHIRES too. We can't socialize with everyone on Earth, not all at once anyway, but we can extend our social networks—and I don't just mean Facebook—to include those people living around us not just people we agree with or think we have something in common with. We have something in common with every human on Earth, and with all the living creatures upon it.

"Ok," you say, "But how do you propose to accomplish *bringing Shire-ness to the World?*" There are two ways to accomplish this, or two simultaneous and mutually supportive paths to building a Global Shire. One, and most importantly, we need a new way of thinking, a new wisdom, a new **story**. Without a new story, a new philosophy about our place on the Earth, we will fail. Two, we need new **wizardry**, innovative technologies and tools to help repair the damage that we've done to the Earth and to provide humanity with the basics of survival: food, shelter, and health care. Let's begin with our New Story, one that begins with our neighbors.

# 38

# FRIENDS AND NEIGHBORS: STARTING YOUR SHIRE AND DEFEATING FEAR

Our job is to love others without stopping to inquire whether or not they are worthy. That is not our business and, in fact, it is nobody's business. What we are asked to do is to love, and this love itself will render both ourselves and our neighbors worthy. —Thomas Merton

Do not waste time bothering whether you 'love' your neighbor; act as if you did. As soon as we do this we find one of the great secrets. When you are behaving as if you loved someone, you will presently come to love him. —C.S. Lewis

Do unto others as you would have them do unto you. —Jesus, *The Bible: Gospel of Matthew* 7:12

The phone rang.

It was 8 A.M., on a Thursday, in February, in North Carolina. I was studying for an exam on Alexander the Great that I had to take later that morning.

"Hello?" I answered the phone.

"Mr. Steve?" It was our neighbor's son from across the street.

"Hello Egan! What's up?" I was friendly but not overly chatty since I was engrossed in studying.

"Can you take me and Julie to school?" he asked, "My dad's sick and mom wants to stay with him."

"Sure, just knock on my door when y'all are ready."

Don, his dad, was the best neighbor we had. Really, he was the best one on the block. He was a few years older than I and an extremely smart guy, even if he did let you know it on occasion. But for the last several months or more he had been suffering from seizures and his doctors couldn't seem to figure out why. One of them had been very severe, to the point that he never quite recovered. He was never quite as *sharp* as he had been, and that ate away at him.

The night before the phone call, his wife, Callie, had called me to ask for my help. He was having another seizure and was on the back porch and wouldn't, or couldn't, manage to come back inside. I had helped her a couple of times before in a similar situation, so I rushed over to find him swaying and staggering. I helped him to the bathroom and then to bed. He was not a small guy either. Of course, neither am I. It was never easy to get him to his bedroom, but this evening the seizure seemed particularly bad. By the time we got to his bedroom, he went to his knees on the floor and I had to pick him up to put him in the bed. Not an easy task. So, when his son called the next morning I wasn't overly surprised, though they had never asked me to drive them to school before.

I hung up with Egan and got my school stuff together so that I could drop them off and head to the university to take my exam. Then the phone rang again.

"Mr. Steve?" It was Egan again.

"You guys ready?"

"Mom wants to know if *you* will watch dad while she drives us to school?"

I hesitated for just a second because it just seemed like an odd request, but not knowing what was going on over there, I told him that would be fine. I'd be there in a minute. I rushed downstairs, out the door, and across the street. Callie was at the door with the kids as I walked up the steps to the front porch.

"I'll be right back in a few minutes!" she said in a breathless tone. "He's really not doing well."

"Ok, I'll check on him." I said, and she and the kids left for school as I went into the house.

They lived in a big, Victorian home, with a large living room and a hallway beyond French doors. The master bedroom was to the right just past those doors. I walked in and stopped in my tracks. Don was lying on the floor at the foot of the bed, face down on the rug. I'm not sure if he had just crawled out of bed after Callie left him, or if he had been there for a while, but he had vomited on the floor and his breathing seemed labored.

"Don?" I called him. He did not respond. I then went to my knees beside him and rolled him over on his side. He was very pale, and even as I called to him repeatedly, he did not acknowledge my presence.

"Don! Are you okay man?!" Nothing. He didn't even really look at me.

Then I began to worry, I mean really worry. And his breathing started to slow down, noticeably. "Damn it! Don! Breath man!" I was beginning to panic. All this happened in about 30 seconds, though it seemed like 10 minutes or more. Then he stopped breathing. Completely. "Fuck!" Then I knew what to do. I snapped out of my paralysis and ran to the phone in the hallway. I dialed 911. The dispatcher came on and asked me what my emergency was.

"My friend is lying on his floor. He's stopped breathing. We need an ambulance NOW!"

"An ambulance is on its way." she said, calmly. "Can you perform CPR on him?"

"Yes, but I have to put the phone down because it's not cordless and it won't reach!"

"That's okay sir, just leave the line open and go do what you can."

As I went back into the room to attempt CPR, Callie came back. She walked into the bedroom, and went pale. I was panicked. "Callie, he isn't BREATHING! I called 911!"

"Oh my god Don!" she screamed, "What did you do?!"

The paramedics arrived before I could even start the CPR. They must have gotten there in less than a minute. I ran to the door to show them in. Callie and I stood in the hallway while they desperately worked to get him breathing again. They rushed him into the ambulance and Callie followed them in her car. I drove to school in a daze, took my exam, and then drove home. I don't really remember anything about the test, or the drive, but when I pulled into my driveway, Callie's car was already home. I knew that I had lost the best neighbor, and one of the best friends I'd ever had. I had watched him draw his last breath.

Don was the kind of friend and neighbor who would help you fix plumbing, or anything. He wasn't really an expert handyman—you would never tell him that—but he had all the tools, and probably had the part you needed somewhere in his junk heap of a garage. He'd be one of the first to every party, and one of the last to leave. He was intelligent, witty, and always willing to give advice. I miss him still, even though I'm thousands of miles away, and he is gone. I kind of lost touch with the kids and Callie when we moved to Minnesota, though I've recently reconnected on Facebook. It was never the same after Don died, though. He and his family were such amazing neighbors that if I had to sacrifice our friendship to bring him back, I suppose I would do it, though it would be an enormous loss of great memories to do so. Of course, that's not how it works anyway. Bringing him back isn't an option, so I'll just hang on to my memories. Great neighbors are treasures greater than dragon's gold, or mithril. That reminds me, Don and his family were huge Tolkien fans, too.

## Say Goodbye to Fear, Hello to Friends

Can you name all the neighbors on your block? I bet not. I can't. Bilbo and Frodo knew every Hobbit in the Shire, or nearly. Why don't we? Fear is why. We are afraid. We are afraid to talk to strangers. Why? Lots of reasons, probably as many reasons as there are people, but they can be boiled down to a handful of categories I think. There's the fear of violence and that can be a powerful one in some neighborhoods, or if you've experienced violence in your own life. There's the one that most of us suffer to some degree or another: lack of self esteem. We fear that we're not good enough, or pretty enough, or smart enough and people will discover those things if we open up to them. There's the fear of not being accepted for one of the reasons just mentioned, or some other reason. Sometimes we are "afraid we will be annoying someone" if we bother them by speaking to them on the street. But I think the deepest fear is that if we make a new acquaintance we will then be obligated to them in some way, and this is not unfounded; friendship *is* an obligation and sometimes that involves very unpleasant things, like fixing plumbing, or holding their hands while they die.

I've suffered from all of those fears at one point another and I'm sure you have as well. I'm usually a pretty outgoing guy but I find excuses not to wave, or say, 'hello' to my neighbors if I don't already know them. We must break this. Nothing is more important to the future of our planet, to *saving the Earth*, than getting to know our neighbors. Other than your own mental, philosophical transition, that is, there is nothing more important. Because we cannot *bring Shireness* to the world if we are afraid to talk to them. And our neighbors can be, if we let them, the strongest allies and friends that we'll ever have. So get outside and go for a walk around the block. If you see neighbors, at least wave to them for starters. If you're feeling particularly *Tookish* actually speak to them. Say, "hello." Start a short conversation about the weather, their begonias, or 'mater plants, or a big tree in their yard. Find *something* to talk about! These are the seeds of that Shire-garden, the human one. Plant a few every time you go out.

Or if talking to complete strangers is too daunting, start closer to home. Have you already waved to, or said, 'hello' to your neighbors next door? What about on the other side of you? Take them some cookies, or a pie. Invite them over for dinner or drinks. After you've made friends with one neighbor, ask them if they know the people on the other side of them? Would they introduce you? Get over your fear. They're just people. Hell, they might even be huge Tolkien geeks like us!

## Recruiting Friends and Neighbors: Lead by Example

One of the best ways, if not the fastest to get your message across is through the things you *do*. Leading through example can be quite powerful. For instance, if your neighbors see you planting food in your front yard on the boulevard instead of grass or ornamentals, it begs questions. Questions are dangerous things. They're capable of driving a person mad until they find a suitable answer. And if they screw up the courage to ask you one day, be ready to talk about it.

Hopefully your neighbors will ask you what you're doing, and why. Then you have an opportunity to drop a few ideas or to start a conversation. You never know how much other people are already thinking about the problems presented in this book till you start talking to them. I've been amazed at how many of my friends, neighbors, and coworkers are trying to work out answers to many of the problems in this book. I find that once I get a chance to talk to them, it's usually best if I just drop a few hints or bits of the whole, instead of launching into an hour long sermon on the evils of corporate greed, plastic pollution, etc. Trust me, I can do it. Just ask my friends. Resist it. The last thing you want to do is to run them away just when they've shown some interest.

For instance, if they ask you about your garden, try to stick to topics directly related to growing food like the anti-GMO movement and the benefits of organic food versus non-organic. You could talk about trying to help out those less fortunate in the community by providing vegetables and fruits near the street for them to harvest. By the way, if you *do* that make sure to put up signage so that people know it's okay to harvest it. The sign can also spark questions and conversations. Hopefully your neighbor will be a gardener, too and then the conversation can move along.

## Small Bites at First

You have to gauge each person by their interest in each part of your conversation to see whether they are ready for more information. If it seems they are, suggest a book for them to read, like this one — if they are a Tolkien fan — or another book more related to your conversation and their interests, like

Quinn's books or any of the others listed in my Resources section at the end of this book. Whatever you do, don't force it. No one likes to be preached to. Remember that *coercion* is the friend of Sauron and Saruman, so take it easy and slow until you hit a chord with someone. Eventually you will run across someone that just *clicks* with what you say because they've already been thinking about it. When you find like minds you can give them much more information and more quickly. Always remember though that we don't have to convert *everyone*. We are just trying to get enough people on Earth to reach a tipping point, where Shireness becomes the *way to do things*. Once that happens then everyone else will be faced with the decision to jump onboard, or be left out. Then the our little Hobbit *stream* will become the great Anduin River, flowing to the sea. But start off by planting little seeds, if you will, and before you know it you will have a Shire Garden. Speaking of that, guess where we're going?

# 39

# PLANTING SHIRE-GARDENS: TOPPLING THE TOWERS WITH VEGGIES

"You are a new people and a new world to me. Are all your kin of like sort? Your land must be a realm of peace and content, and there must gardeners be in high honour."

"Not all is well there," said Frodo, "but certainly gardeners are honoured." —*LOTR*: II, *The Window on the West*

Gardens are to Shires, as seeds are to gardens. —Me, *see below*

Is there anything more Hobbity than food? I think not. And even more Hobbity than that is planting your *own* food. If there is one thing that every community on Earth needs to do to help save the Earth, it's to make sure that everyone in the community has access to healthy food. The first step towards that goal is to make sure that everyone has a *place* to grow food, a community garden, or Shire Garden.

# Ron Finley, Hobbit Warrior Gardener

A few years ago, Ron Finley, an independent sportswear designer from South-Central Los Angeles was staring at the empty, weedy boulevard in front of his house when the idea occurred to him to plant vegetables there. Since the city required him to *maintain* it, he didn't really think they'd care *how* he went about accomplishing the task. So he planted vegetables. And then the city—Sauron—sent in their Black Riders to tell him that he couldn't do that. He resisted and called in his Rangers—the local media—who picked up the story and before you know it, the city was all behind him.

He has proven in the last few years that putting a shovel in the hands of people in the *food deserts* of Los Angeles can empower them in ways that no one ever imagined. He and his organization are transforming boulevards and empty lots all over the City of Angels and he hopes that other cities will catch on, and they are! Urban gardening is exploding all over the U.S., and there's nothing that Sauron and Saruman hate more than empowered urban Hobbits planting their own organic produce instead of buying their chemically induced, genetically modified, crap. According to Ron, and I agree, "Gardening is the most therapeutic and defiant act you can do. Plus you get strawberries." If you want to absorb some of his infectious energy-and you do–then check out his TED Talk video.

# Plant a Garden, Destroy the Towers

Other than our own mental transformation and the destruction of the Ring, there is no idea more important in this entire book than this short little section. The solution to almost every problem on Earth is in the dirt, the dust, the soil. And you have the power to do it. We have the power to do it. Forget the negative story that says food comes from Sauron and Saruman. If you want to destroy their power over us you must start growing food. Must. It doesn't have to be much in the beginning; just plant some 'maters for Bilbo's sake, but plant *something*. Ron Finley is absolutely right; gardening is the most defiant thing you can do that will actually WORK. Yes, you can join protests on Wall Street, at your city hall, in the park, but none of that is as effective as just planting seeds, watching them grow, pickin' 'maters, makin' salsa, and eating it! Your personal garden is important, as we've already discussed but if you really want to build a strong Shire, a resilient community that can resist the whims of the *market*, of the Sarumans of the corporate Isengard, if you want to bring their Orthancs crashing down upon their heads then you need to get out, meet your neighbors and plant a community garden. Why is this so important? That's a very good question.

## Real Food, Real Cheap

The food from Saruman's factories is poison. We're eating it and he's raking in the profits while eating organic produce himself. That should be enough reason to grow your own food, or some of it. But there are some of our neighbors really suffering out there. They aren't all lazy, unambitious, welfare slobs, as the elite of this country want us to believe. So many of us — myself included — have bought, or are still buying, this lie. It's simply not true. If you don't believe me get out there and meet some of your less fortunate neighbors. What you're going to find is that the vast majority are hard-working people, or people who *would* work hard if they could find a job that actually paid them a livable wage. They and their children are killing themselves every day by eating the poison from Isengard and they struggle just to pay for what little of that they can manage. Many of them are on public assistance just to survive. Their self esteem is damaged, broken in many cases. I've been there myself. Poverty and unemployment are the handmaidens of depression. They sap your will to live, to move, to even *breathe* some days. Unless you've been in it, it's impossible to fathom the depth of despair it can drive one to. So instead of blaming the poor for their condition we need to start thinking about how we can help them claw their way out of it. Welfare is a band-aid at best. It's an inefficient system, but right now it's all we have. But that's starting to change, thanks to leaders like Mr. Finley and many others around the World. They're starting to realize that they can teach the poor, the rich, and the rest of us to take control of our food supply and in the process build a community.

## A Young Hobbit Mama

Pamela is a young, single mother in my Shire who I know is struggling to make ends meet. You can see it in her face, at least when she's not smiling and laughing, which she does a lot. But you can see the weariness in her eyes. I know that look. I met her this summer in our community garden. Recently I sat down with her to find out how she got into gardening and how she got into community gardening. She told me that one day the idea came to her to start planting vegetables in her kitchen. She said, "I had no idea *where* I was going to plant them after *that!* But I was like, 'I don't care! I'm gonna start them anyway!'" She took some sweet potatoes that she had, cut them into pieces and put them in glasses of water to see if they would sprout, and they did! She was amazed and excited. But because she lives in an apartment, she still had nowhere to plant them. Then she ran into Carol.

Carol runs our community garden, the Stryker Community Garden. Carol told her about the garden and how it was only $20 a year for a box, so Pamela rented one and started planting. She'd never planted a garden in her life but she dove in head first. Nearly every time I went over to check on our box, she was there, with about 5 kids in tow — she has one son that lives with her and she watches kids for other people. I remember the first time I met her. I was quickly covering my plot with a tarp because hail had been predicted for that evening. She came over and asked me what I was doing. When I told her, she was very concerned, "Oh my! Do you think I should cover mine too? I don't really have anything to cover it with. This is my first time growing a garden."

I said, "Oh, I'm probably being overly cautious, you'll probably be fine." Her plants fared better than mine so I probably won't be covering mine next year when the lightning strikes.

On another day, she showed Patience and I how to harvest kale because neither of us had ever done it and she had just learned herself. But the best day was in late September when we were volunteering to help clean up the garden. She was there harvesting her sweet potatoes. Those same sweet potatoes she had started in her kitchen. She was so nervous before she began to dig into the dirt. Then something magical happened; sweet potatoes began to come out of the ground! And I mean some big-assed 'taters man. Loads of'em! I've never seen the face of a child at Christmas as happy as her face that day. I thought she was gonna cry and she probably would have if she weren't so busy running around the garden showing off her harvest to everyone. She had planted little chunks of 'taters and reaped a harvest any farmer would have been proud to claim. But I think it was much more than that, though she didn't say it. She didn't have to. She had not just grown sweet potatoes, no, she had fed her family! SHE had done it. Not some grocery store, not welfare, not Saruman. Nothing can replace that feeling. By planting sweet potatoes she had not only created food for her family, she had found something much more important: her self confidence — which I don't think Pamela really lacked anyway — it would be more accurate to say *more* self confidence. And that feeling is worth more than all the dragon gold on the planet.

If we want to attack Greed and Want, planting community gardens is the first thing we need to do. In the process we can also help to defeat that other Tower: Ignorance and Fear.

## Killing Fear and Ignorance with 'Taters

Planting food as a community, as a Shire, is the best way to bring people of different races, ages, religions, and cultures together. Everyone on Earth has to eat. Food and water are the two things that are absolutely universal. What we grow and eat, and how we cook it and share it differs from one culture to the next, but we all eat. If you want to get to know the neighbors in your Shire or on the rest of the planet, eat their food. Better yet, eat their food *with them.* Sharing food, produce, and recipes is one of the best ways to build friendships. Hobbits know this. Food reminds us of our shared humanity, the importance of hospitality and that some people in our Shires are suffering from the lack of healthy food, and sometimes just *enough* food of any kind. There is no excuse for starving people anywhere on this planet. There's plenty of food to feed every mouth but it's locked up by the elites and by the myth of the *market*. <u>Food is a right, same as water</u>. The beauty of growing your own, and growing it along with your neighbors is that you take back control of what goes into it. You reconnect with the origins of food, the Earth, the dirt, the dust, the rain. You connect, maybe for the first time ever, with your fellow human beings, the Hobbits of your Shire. This leads imperceptibly to the banishing of Ignorance, the ignorance of your neighbors' sufferings, their culture and their humanity. You begin to see that you are not really all that different after all. <u>Gardens are to Shires as seeds are to gardens</u>. So plant some seeds and join your community. Forget your ignorant fears of other people. Get the hell out there and meet them, and plant a garden!

## Growing Green Stuff and Killing Corruption

While we're feeding our families with healthier food and building stronger relationships with our fellow Hobbits, dispelling Fear, Ignorance, Greed, and Want, we will also be taking money out of the pockets of the Saurons and Sarumans who are used to reaping in record profits by controlling our food supply. Let's show them who's really boss! Every 'mater, 'tater, and head of lettuce you grow takes money from the pockets of corporate farmers. The money stays in *your* pocket. And if we stop buying their poisoned food they will dry up and blow away. They worship the *market* and we can use it against them. The rules of the market say that business is dependent upon demand for a product. If we produce our own produce, we don't have to buy it from them. They will stop producing it. That's how their economic system works.

If they no longer have our money, guess what? They can't spend it to bribe politicians, turning them against the people who they're supposed to serve. It's really simple. But it goes further than just the food supply. Growing your own food, locally, also puts a dent in the fossil fuel industry.

## Gardening and the End of Fossil Fuels

As mentioned in Part I, some 60% of the food produced in the U.S. is dependent upon fossil fuels. And it's not just the transportation from farm to market either. As mentioned, there's a ton of fossil fuel consumed in the production of food at the farm level: fertilizers, pesticides, tractors, plows, etc. So every harvest of kale from your community garden plot takes a chip out of the fossil fuel industry, too! There will be some who argue, and *have* argued that these little cuts matter not. Sure, my three kale plants this summer weren't in danger of bringing down Exxon. But if ten percent of the citizens of the U.S. started planting their own kale? Things would start to add up quickly. Individually we are insignificant; collectively we are *invincible*. So plant some kale and kick Exxon's ass! Plus, it's really good for you and you'll know what went into it.

## Food is Medicine: Community Garden as Community Clinic

Food grown by the Sarumans of this world is laden with orcish chemicals that have been linked to a laundry list of phyiscal and mental disorders, including cancers. Why are we eating this stuff? Because we were ignorant of what was really going on. We've been duped into thinking that our food was safe. We believed our government officials when they told us that everything was fine. It is not fine. Their lies are at best criminal, at worst, pure evil. No more. We will not stand for it. The line has been drawn in the sand. We will not buy their poison anymore. And we do not have to. If we want to improve our health and that of our families, friends, neighbors, and the world, we must begin with cleaning up our food. We are what we eat. Do we want to be *RoundUp*? Or would we rather be the organic cherry tomatoes our neighbor gave us in exchange for the kale. And there's no better way to do that than to grow it, and grow it in a Shire garden. Why? Why not just grow it all in your own yard? Because you probably can't. But if you work with your neighbors you can.

## Cooperation

Every yard is different. Some have more sun, more shade, more water, less water. Planting a community garden can help to stabilize your food supply against these variations. By building a community garden you can plan for a sunny spot, and most vegetables love the sun, as do we up here in snowy Yankeeland. And in a Shire garden, once again, you meet your neighbors.

Maybe they are very good at growing 'taters, like Pamela; maybe you are a master of 'maters. If you're both growing in the community garden you can trade produce! You can trade ideas! You can trade tips and recipes! You can invite them over for dinner. You can make friends. And friends can work together to dispel Fear, violence, and crime.

## Growing 'Cukes and Cutting Crime

Lack of resources and lack of hope leads to desperation and Fear. It leaves one with a sense of apathy and distrust. These are all ingredients for crime and violence. Desperate, hopeless people, especially the young are at risk for slipping into crime and violence if they aren't quickly given something positive to focus on. There's nothing more positive than growing food. Even teenagers eat, as most of us who've had them in our homes already know. A recent study about children's eating habits discovered that most of them knew very little about vegetables and most didn't really eat them. I know my mom tried to get us to eat our veggies. I resisted. I didn't like them. Of course, we didn't grow our own. Most of them came from cans. But the study discovered something else, too. It turns out that if kids *grow* vegetables, kids *eat* vegetables. Go figure. So the best thing we can do is to get them interested in growing food. Get them out in our Shire gardens to plant some green beans. Ron Finley has been working on this idea for a few years now with some amazing results. To the youngsters who think they're tough, street-smart criminals, he says, "If you ain't a gardener, you ain't gangsta!" In other words, if you want to stick it to *the man*, you need to do something that actually does some damage, like growing your own food. This takes money out of *his* pocket and puts it in *yours*. Finley also tells them that, "Growing food is like printing your own money." And he's right. And it's probably the only way that the human population is going to survive in the future.

## Feeding the World, One Shire Garden at a Time

One way that Monsanto and others like them justify genetically engineered crops is to claim that they are "feeding the world." That if it weren't for their amazing breakthroughs in science and

428

food technology the world would starve. This is complete bullshit. We've already discussed it so I won't go into it too much again, but if their claim were true there wouldn't be so many starving people on this planet. GMO food isn't about feeding the starving masses it's about feeding Greed. The best solution to feeding the planet is to DE-centralize food supply and production, not to centralize it further in the hands of a few elite douchebags. This has recently been confirmed by a study done by the United Nations which concluded that the best way to feed the growing population of the Earth is through small, urban gardens: Shire Gardens basically.

We have to rethink the way we grow food. It's no longer the job of some poor, ignorant, dirty, stupid, redneck farmer out in the *sticks*. It's everyone's job. First off, farmers are none of those things. Well, they do get dirty, but if you think that farming is something for the stupid you better try it some time. We planted 'taters this year—twelve plants and we pulled seven potatoes out of the ground, and I'm no idiot. So I'm going to talk to my Pamela about what she did with hers, because ours were pathetic. Farming is hard work and it requires a lot of knowledge of a lot of things. So we need to rethink our image of farmers and farming. There is no more noble profession on Earth. Without them we would not be here. So thank a farmer next time you see one and then start growing your own food. Maybe your neighborhood already has a garden! If you're not sure, do a quick search online, or if you're in the U.S., check with the American Community Garden Association, where many gardens have registered. If you don't have a Shire garden near you, start one.

## Building a Community Garden

I really believe that any community can get a garden going. First you must gather your Fellowship of Hobbits, Wizards, Dwarves and Elves to help organize the project. Remember, this is a community project, not necessarily a Middle Earth-Geek-a-Thon Project, so my geek terminology is mainly for our benefit. Your neighbors might not be as cool as we are so we have to give them a pass and keep the Hobbit theme in our own head. But who knows? Maybe your entire neighborhood is chock full of Tolkien fans! That would be awesome. But I digress. Gather together a handful of neighbors interested in building a garden and get started. If you have a lot of people interested, great! Pick or elect a handful to serve as the organization committee.

Then you can begin to see what kind of resources you already have among the members of the committee and interested neighbors. You're going to need a lot of things, but most importantly you need people who are excellent gardeners or at least have some experience growing food. Make sure to talk to the Elders of the Shire. You never know how many Gaffer Gamgees you might have living around you; many of them garden, or they used to do it when they were younger. From there you can start to look for a suitable location. Empty lots are sometimes owned by the city, or you can contact the current owners and see about renting or leasing the property. You want to try to get a long term lease if you can because building a garden is a multi-year process and it would be best if you can find a place to call *home* for many years.

To cover the initial expenses, you're going to need money. Be creative with this, unless you happen to have a billionaire living down the street who wants to write a check! There are many ways to raise money for gardens, including grants. But you definitely want to look into the newest Hobbity way to raise funds through *crowd-funding*. It's a great way to raise money for community projects. Kickstarter is the most popular platform but Indiegogo, GoFundme, and others are gaining ground and broadening the scope for types of projects that can find funding online. If you're unfamiliar with crowd-funding you should do some reading on the sites above, but the here's the basic idea. Crowd-funding is a way for individuals, organizations, and companies to raise funds for a variety of projects. Instead of going to a traditional bank—i.e., Sauron—to get funds, you start a crowd-funding project online and people who think it sounds cool can contribute funds towards the goal. This book is such a project. I raised $5000 to help finish and polish it. The contributors are listed at the beginning and end of the book. There's a lot more involved than just posting a campaign, of course, but that's basically how it works. Look into it! It's worth it.

## Seeding the Shire: Growing West Side and the Birth of a Mini Farmer's Market

Maureen has been living in St. Paul's 'West Side' community for over 17 years. She's one of those neighbors who is everywhere at once and knows everyone. She's a *connector* of people. I met her this spring. She had posted a call on the Growing West Side Facebook page for a *flash* weeding event to pull weeds and clean up some raised garden beds in a neighborhood garden where she planned to plant a salsa garden for the residents of the *District del Sol*, the predominantly Hispanic area of our community. I was immediately enamored with her energy, friendliness and her commitment to the community. In the coming months, Patience and I became more and more involved with Growing West Side, the organization that she and a handful of others have organically constructed over the last few years.

Several years ago, Maureen and another neighbor decided to raise chickens. Instead of reading "too much" into the city regulations—which actually require you to keep them in a coop—they decided to let them roam around the fenced-in yards. As it turned out, the roaming fowl became a natural conversation starter with wandering neighbors. This brought about connections with the neighborhood that they had never thought would happen. Maureen thought that maybe there was a way to expand on that community-building idea. Then she came up with an idea one day to plant some beans on her boulevard and to try to get a handful of others to do the same. She says, "Originally, I'd emailed the idea out to about 30 neighbors I knew, and I figured about 15 of them would respond. Of those, I calculated that about half would humor me and agree to do it. But before it was done, we had 85 people wanting to grow beans on their boulevards!" Maureen had originally thought that she would have enough supplies—poles, string, seeds—to supply the 7 to 10 she had predicted but there was no way she had enough scrap supplies to pull off 85. So she contacted the West Side Community Organization who gave her a small grant to purchase the supplies for the project and Beans on the Boulevard was off! But that's not the end of the story.

Maureen was also growing garlic in her home garden—among many other things—and was selling it at various farmer's markets around St. Paul when she and her partner, Martha, decided to try to open up their own little market behind the local coffee shop, Jerebek's, which for many years had operated on the corner around from my house. Jerebek's agreed and the little market was up and running with two vendors. Shortly thereafter a couple more friends joined, Leah and Ellen, and a local CSA farm, Tusan Tack. This worked well for awhile until a baker asked them for permission to set up next to them. Since Jerebek's was a bakery and coffeeshop, that didn't work out so well, so they went looking for another spot and managed to make a sweet deal with Pompeo, the owner of the local ice cream joint, The Icy Cup, who has a fairly large parking lot.

That was three years ago and the Growing West Side Farmer's Market has really taken off. Don't get me wrong, it's still a small, neighborhood market but that's what's so awesome about it. It's cute and friendly as hell. They have a steady number of vegetable farmers, Todd—the organic chicken-egg farmer, and Tony, a neighbor who's started his own hot sauce line, Isabel Street Heat. He used the market as his testing ground and after some great success selling his sauces to the neighborhood—I've had them and they're pretty kick-ass—he's expanding his operations for next year!

There's almost always live music and entertainment and the police department occasionally brings out their mounted unit, and the fire department brings out trucks, which are a big hit with the kids. They hold gardening and cooking classes to give tips on how to grow and prepare many of the things found at the market. All of this was accomplished by a small team of volunteers in the neighborhood. The collective talents of local farmers, gardeners, cooks, bakers, musicians, entertainers, and the generosity of the neighborhood, and that of Pompeo, the owner of the Icy Cup.

Any neighborhood can do what Growing West Side has done in our little Shire. And that's not the end of the plans. We're working on raising funds to expand the market, and among other ideas, to plant orchards in the neighborhood to bring fresh fruit to those who could use a little help.

## Shire Orchards: Fruit Trees in Public Places

For a couple of years now Growing West Side has been talking about, and planning to plant a handful of orchards in the neighborhood. Maureen has had three fruit trees sitting in her driveway waiting to be planted, but due to time constraints, lack of funds, and labor, and a few other red-tape issues they were still sitting there, until a couple weeks ago. Then at our last monthly meeting she announced that she and another lady had just decided "It's time to plant these things!" so they just went and did it. Now, the West Side Community has the beginning of an orchard in front of our local fire station. We plan to turn it into a permaculture orchard, with companion plantings, and the fruit from the trees — once it comes in — will be freely available to the people of the neighborhood to harvest. And there are plans to plant similar orchards in other places around the Shire. This idea has been growing for sometime nationwide, and in other countries too. Some cities have taken it to an even higher level by planting Food Forests! The city of Seattle, Washington is one of them. You can read more about it in this article.

## Shire Greenhouses: Growing Year Round

Another way to bring healthy, organic produce to your Shire is to build community greenhouses. A greenhouse lets you grow produce year round, even in freezing Yankeeland. Obviously this requires a great deal of planning, and materials, but it needn't be overly expensive if you collect free and cheap materials from fellow Hobbits in the Shire, via Craigslist and social media and store them up until you're ready to build. Old glass windows or plastic roofing shingles make good materials, as do glass doors, pvc gutters—for vertical gardening, barrels—for water, and various other materials. I'm no expert on building greenhouses, having never done it, but I hope to build one next to my house, maybe next spring. Eventually, I'd love to see Growing West Side build one in our little Shire. Planning it isn't much different than putting together a Shire garden, except there's a bit more building to do. It's a great place for neighbors to meet, to teach people how to garden all year long, and to keep all the Hobbits eating well during the winter months. It's a great place for the young Hobbits to learn, as well.

In our neighborhood we have a Youth Farm that does just that: teach kids of all ages how to grow their own produce. This is an empowering tool to keep kids out of trouble, give them something positive to do—especially during the summer when they're out of school—and teach them a skill that cannot be overvalued, especially if we're trying to build Shires and take back control of our food, money, and communities. Food is the key and the young Hobbits of the world are the future. What better way to secure it than to teach them to feed themselves and tell the Sarumans to go to Mordor.

## Protecting the Food Commons: Shire Seed Libraries

Another project of Growing West Side, and many other local organizations around the U.S. and the world, is a grass-roots attempt to combat the imperialistic seizure of our food supply by the likes of Monsanto, and others, who are rapidly laying claim to the diversity of food crops by engineering and patenting the very seeds needed to feed the world. This is one of the most insidious practices by a company famous for insidious practices. As a result, as much as 90% of our historic food varieties have disappeared! For example, in the late 1800s there were about 7000 varieties of apples; today there are fewer than 100! Many Shires are fighting back by organizing Seed Libraries. The libraries collect heirloom and organic seeds and distribute them to local Hobbits who plant them and then collect seeds from the plants, and return some of them to the library for others to use. In this way, they can assure the perpetuation and preservation of our seed and food diversity for the future. Without this work the corporations would soon destroy that diversity by homogenizing the remaining species of plants.

Growing West Side started a seed library, in large part, from seeds that senior community members had been planting and saving for decades, if not longer! And their currently working to increase the number and variety of seeds in hope of doubling their outreach next year. This is one of the cheapest ways for Hobbits to help to save the Earth and it's one of the most important. Diversity of food species is essential to survival of our own species. If you only grow one kind of apple or potato and a disease infects them—as happened in Ireland in the 1850s—millions of people could starve to death or be severely malnourished. The more varieties there are the less the impact of one disaster on the system. Our seed library is actually housed in our little local public library, The Riverview Branch Library—just up the street from our house, who have been very helpful, giving us space to hold classes on seeds and gardening. If you're looking for a beginning project that isn't expensive, start a seed library. All you need is something—preferably portable—to keep the seed packets in, and some seeds! Then you just announce it on Facebook or your website, or good ole word of mouth, and get started! You can ask Hobbits in your Shire for heirloom, non-GMO, organic seeds and then find someone who knows how to save seeds from the plants they grow, and in that way, increase your library over time.

## A Note to Hobbit Farmers and Gardeners

There are many people in our world and even in the U.S. that are suffering from poverty. As a result they are essentially forced to buy prepackaged, GMO laden, nutrient depleted produce and meat. They are living in what some scholars have coined, a *food desert*. In many cases, even if they wanted to buy fresh, nutritious produce there simply isn't a source for it within the limits of their transportation. Many do not own cars. Many live in the inner city and because their neighborhood is lower income or poor, grocery stores choose to build elsewhere. This is a real issue and one that needs to be addressed immediately.

In my area, the Twin Cities—Saint Paul and Minneapolis—there is a growing movement of little farmer's markets and Shire gardens. These help out in the warm months, but of course, it's not always warm in Minnesota. However, many of the poor in our country are working poor; some work 2 or 3 jobs just to make ends meet. They do not have time to grow food. What can be done about this?

I am making a plea to you, especially to the farmers trying to blaze a new trail, or re-blaze an old one by growing organic and natural foods, to try to find ways to help out those at the bottom of the economic scale. I've been there myself and it is neither a fun, nor healthy place to be. Consider donating some of your produce to local soup kitchens, or sell some of it at a reduced rate at a farmer's market in the inner city? Maybe set up a CSA that accepts EBT and deliver directly to those neighborhoods that need it most. Only you can know what works best for you. What we have though is a gap between what people WANT to eat, i.e. your healthy produce, and what many people can AFFORD to eat: GMO crap. Somehow we must figure out how to bridge that gap.

Educating people on the inherent value of good food can only go so far if they simply cannot afford to buy it. The good thing is that organic prices, at least on some items, seem to be coming down as supply and demand go up. I remember years ago when I started buying organic milk—the first organic food I ever purchased—it was considerably more expensive than the regular stuff but so much better in taste—I love milk—that it was worth it to me to spend that extra. I have noticed that the price seems to have come down over the years, a bit, while at the same time, the price of regular milk has gone up so the gap is closing. I challenge you to keep working on ways to make your entire operation more efficient, so that prices can come down. Don't forget to make a profit too; there's nothing wrong with that.

While we're on the topic of efficiency, please try to find alternatives to plastic to package your organic and natural products. This is something that bugs me when I go to buy organic produce. So often it's packaged in plastic. I know most of you are aware of this conundrum, but keep looking for better alternatives. Can you sell more in bulk? What about glass or ceramics—allow people to bring them back for a deposit? Keep an eye out for new alternative packaging options—cellulose *plastics*, more on that later.

# 40

# TELLING STORIES: FINDING OUR COMMON HUMANITY

> Storytellers are the most powerful people on earth. They might not be the best paid—but they are the most powerful. Storytellers have the power to move the human heart—and there is no greater power on earth. —Laurie H. Hutzler

> Storytellers are a threat. They threaten all champions of control, they frighten usurpers of the right-to-freedom of the human spirit—in state, in church or mosque, in party congress, in the university or wherever. —Chinua Achebe, *Anthills of the Savannah*

The other day I was interviewing my friend Maureen about the origins of Growing West Side and the Farmer's Market, the Beans on the Boulevard, and how it was working to bring a sense of community or Shireness to our little neighborhood. Then she began to lament that the Beans project seemed to have kind of stalled out in the last year or so, even though this last year twenty new people joined the project. She was worried that maybe the idea had run its course and that maybe it was time to let it go and move on to something new. But she had just told me a story of one of her bean farmers, a local lady, who had as a child, made fun of her foster-mother for digging around in the dirt planting vegetables, and now *she* was doing the same! And she was *proud of it!* Maureen then admitted that maybe she was viewing the project from an *objective* viewpoint instead of remembering the impact that it had had on real people and their lives. I said, "Yeaaaahh! That's what it's *about* Maureen!"

"I suppose," she said, "But it's not what people want to hear about. They just want to hear the numbers."

"No the hell they don't!" I said, "Who the hell cares about numbers? Numbers are boring! I guess if you're one of those accountant types sitting around counting other peoples' money you like numbers, or a scientist or mathematician!"

"Yeah, I guess."

"I guess my ass! What people want to hear are *STORIES* Maureen! Stories are what move people, not numbers! Like that story you just told me! What we need to tell to ordinary people, are stories!"

We've spent some time in this book talking about stories and the power within them to move people in both negative and positive ways. I've told you parts of my story which—until recently—I had been telling in a very negative way, to myself and to others. We've reexamined Tolkien's great stories to give us a lens through which to examine our own collective story, the story of our culture, our civilization, which has been very negative, too. But it doesn't have to end on a sour note. Like my father always used to tell us when he was teaching us to play horns, or sing, "People usually only remember two notes, the *first* one, and the *last* one, so if you mess up everything else in the song, make sure to get those two right!" There's nothing we can do about the first note our civilization played; it was too long ago, but that's okay, there's no one around who remembers it. But we can get the last one right. We rewrite the song, the story. We can change it. We can rewrite the ending. Indeed, we can rewrite the entire thing! And we need too.

Stories bring us together as a species. They allow us to understand each other, not just our friends, but also our enemies. Most stories can be told in such a way as to place almost anyone as the protagonist. Well, it's difficult to do that with Hitler's story, true, but I'm sure he could have told it in a way that might give us some insight into why he did the horrendous things he did. Hell, maybe even the board members and stockholders of Monsanto could do the same thing? And I'm not talking about just some *spin*, another lie to cover their tracks, but the real story. But more important than the *Story of Monsanto*, which I really don't care to hear, is the story of all the regular, hard-working, real people of the world. If we can find ways to tell their stories, or allow them to tell their own, it would go a long way to striking death blows to Ignorance, Fear, Bigotry, Greed, Want, and Hate. It's much more difficult to hate someone when you've read their story or seen it on the screen. And we need to tell stories in every way possible: books, articles, blogs, television, movies, documentaries, songs, plays, and video games.

It's easy to hate someone who's wronged us or wronged someone we care about, or even a stranger that seems to be driven by evil. But if we knew their story maybe we'd realize that they were not that different, that they had, and have, feelings and emotions, trials and troubles, just like us. Sometimes they choose to do things that hurt others, or hurt us, but that doesn't mean they intended to hurt anyone. How many times have you, have I, lashed out at people near us when what we really wanted was someone to just listen to our story. We need to listen to the stories of others, and we need to tell them ours, and help them share theirs.

I realize that not everyone is a writer, musician, actor or director, but everyone on Earth has a story to tell and they need to share them with their friends, neighbors, and with the world. We need inspiring stories that demonstrate how people can look past their differences and come together to build Shires instead of perpetuating Fear and Ignorance. In some ways this *is* a call to people with storytelling talent. Too much time, money, and talent have been wasted in the entertainment industry to produce absolute garbage, on the theory that *that* is what people want. No it isn't. Not really. The great movies, the great songs, reached into us and moved us in positive ways. That is what we should be aspiring to do as artists, as writers, as musicians. Forget about the bottom line and tell stories with passion that help to heal the divisions between us. The stories of Hobbits have done a great deal towards that goal, but not everyone is a Tolkien fan — weird, I know — so we have to look for stories that appeal to a wide variety of audiences.

Let's stop creating mindless crap. We've had enough of that. That doesn't mean that you can't make art that's humorous — we could all do with a few more laughs — but make sure it also has substance. Tell stories and make art that drives people to aspire to the "higher angels of our nature," as Abraham Lincoln once said. Don't aim for the lowest common denominator. Much of what you see today does. It focusses on the negative emotions of the human experience: Greed, Fear, and Ignorance. Stop! It's time to start telling stories that champion the highest common denominators: humanity, humor, hospitality, love, compassion, self sacrifice, charity, and empathy. The same goes for all the other genres, and for music genres, art, and dance. In many ways art is designed to bring people together, to *say* something. Just make sure it says something that mends, not rends. That doesn't mean that all art has to be *positive* in its message. Much truth is negative, it seems, but try to look past that and find the positive. It's there. Negative things happen in life; people make mistakes. Sometimes they do absolutely evil things, but they can change. It is that transformation that we need to work towards.

## Games to Save the Earth and Tell Stories

Jane McGonigal, in her book, *Reality Is Broken: Why Games Make Us Better and How They Can Change the World*, argues that playing games is essential to our species and that in fact they just might be the key to solving some of the world's biggest problems. For instance, medical researchers are using the collective computing power of thousands of the world's most avid gamers, by borrowing their computers during off hours to run computations that would otherwise take years to accomplish. McGonigal has personally been involved in designing some amazing games, like *Evoke*, in which players were given missions to actually help come up with solutions to some of the World's largest problems, like food security, energy and water shortages, the future of money, and empowering women. *World Without Oil* is another of her games in which players were given scenarios to work through in a *post-oil* world. Her latest game, *Superbetter*, has helped nearly half a million people relieve symptoms of depression, anxiety, insomnia, chronic pain and traumatic brain injury. If you love games — or especially if you *don't* — I challenge you to read her book. If you want a synopsis of her argument, check out her TED Talk. I would rank her as a Modern Wizard, for the scale of her work and her innate ability to attack the World's problems from outside the box. She's like a young, curly-haired Gandalf, but without the hat, the staff and the wrinkles.

Not only should we design games that solve real-world problems but also ones that tell positive *stories* and help to bring people together to work in a spirit of Shireness. Build games, both video and *real* that give people the tools to actually make a difference in the World, and that are *FUN TO PLAY*! If they're not fun, no one will play them and nothing will be saved. Fun first, positive action second. How can your game help to build Shires? My brother, Tim, is a game designer, and we've been talking about different ideas for video games. Maybe we'll develop one based on the ideas in *Be a Hobbit*? Keep an eye out on my website and Facebook page. The potential for video games to spread the ideas in this book is enormous. Are you a game developer or artist? If so, then please do contact me if you're interested in putting together a team. We're looking for talented people. You can also contact Tim at Enlītānment Studios, LLC.

# 41

# SHIRE-MINDED BUSINESS: VALUE FOR PROFIT

"'Are these magic cloaks?' asked Pippin, looking at them with wonder.

"I do not know what you mean by that," answered the leader of the Elves. "They are fair garments, and the web is good, for it was made in this land. They are elvish robes certainly, if that is what you mean. Leaf and branch, water and stone: they have the hue and beauty of all these things under the twilight of Lorien that we love; for *we put the thought of all that we love into all that we make.*" —*LOTR*: I, *Farewell to Lórien*

Guess what percentage of total material flow through this system [modern capitalism] is still in product or use 6 months after their sale in North America. Fifty percent? Twenty? NO. One percent. One! In other words . . . 99 percent of the stuff we run through this system is trashed within 6 months. —Rachel Botsman, *What's Mine is Yours: the Rise of Collaborative Consumption*

Mankind was my business. The common welfare was my business; charity, mercy, forbearance, benevolence, were all my business. The dealings of my trade were but a drop of water in the comprehensive ocean of my business! —Charles Dickens, *A Christmas Carol*

If Shireness isn't anti-commerce what would a Hobbit business person look like?

Short answer? A generous one. How do Hobbit business people build Shire-Minded businesses? Shire-minded businesses produce goods and services that added *value* to the Shire and society at large and make a profit doing it. At the same time, they take care of *all* of their assets which includes their *value-makers*: their employee-owners. They produce things, not just because they *can* or because they *can convince someone else that they need them* but because the products fill an *actual need*. Like the Elves of Lothlórien they put "the thought of all that [they] love into all that [they] make." Shire-Minded businesses make the very best product possible. Those products or services are of a quality that the business owners and employees themselves would want in their own houses or feed to their own children, and of such quality that they are proud to put their own name and face on the label. If as a business person, you cannot say these things about what you make or sell or the companies you invest your money in then you should consider changing the way you do business, do something else for a living, or find a better company to back with your money.

## Value or Profit? Costs and Assets

The problem with so many capitalist businesses today is that they seem to pursue profit to the exclusion of everything else. The anonymous *shareholder* is often blamed for this and they do of course have to shoulder much of the blame because the purpose of the corporate structure is to pay dividends to shareholders. But many a decision has been made by CEO — that might not have been approved by a great number of the shareholders — had they known or foreseen the consequences. There seem to be a couple of reasons that modern business have lost the path and strayed into the depths of Mirkwood Forest. One is the conflation of *profit* with *value*, and the other is the *externalization* of costs and the conflation of some *investments*, with costs.

These days it seems that if you ask a business person what *value* their company provides they break out an Excel Spreadsheet to show you the bottom line: their profits. The two words have been conflated and they are *NOT* the same word, nor are they synonyms. Profit is the bottom line. It is what is left over after you take in revenue and subtract all your costs of doing business. It's what you can reinvest in the business and pay off your shareholders. Value on the other hand, is a measurement of worth. Does a product, or service, provide something valuable to the customer or society at large. This should be *true* value not *perceived* value.

One might argue that sugar-covered breakfast cereal provides value to the customer, because they can eat it. True, it does provide a certain number of calories and will in fact *fuel* the body for a period of time. But are these really valuable calories? Is it truly nutritious? Does the product contain ingredients that are harmful in the short- or long-term to the consumer? If so, then its *true value* drops considerably. If, however, the product *is* nutritious, safe, and healthy, then we can say that it has true value. In other words, whether a product has true value has very little to do with whether it will be, or can be, profitable. If we can say that it does indeed provide value, then we need to consider the impact of production on the environment: from the standpoint of the employee's, the community's, and the Earth's health and well-being.

## Sustainable or Sarumanic? Externalizing Costs

One reason most modern companies can hold down *costs* and uphold *profits* is that they just refuse to count ALL the costs. They externalize them. This is particularly important when it comes to environmental impact. Most modern companies never take into account the impact of their products or services on the physical environment, or on the health and well-being of their employees, or the communities in which they operate. This allows them to cut costs, or as I like to say, *cut corners*, to keep their prices down. But this is an artificial cost reduction. This is one of the main reasons so many companies relocated to Mexico and to China in the 90s, and early 2000s. Those countries had lower regulations on pollution, wages, working conditions, and waste disposal. This was the "big sucking sound" that Ross Perot warned us about when four living presidents signed NAFTA. [Note: *When four presidents agree on something, run the other way.*] Instead of working within the legal parameters in the U.S., many American companies just pulled up stakes and moved so they could create even cheaper products or drive up profit margins. But the true costs of doing business was elevated pollution, slave-wages, sweat shops, and mountains of toxic chemical and plastic wastes dumped in the backyards of China and Mexico and many other places around the world. This is not sustainable business. This is Saruman-ic business. It is Shire Scouring business. If we keep this up the entire planet will be ruined in a decade's time.

It's time to start calculating the true costs of doing business so that we can find ways to produce things more sustainably. The first thing is to ask ourselves if the product we want to make is actually adding *value*. If so, then is it *needed*? Then and only then, should we consider making it. Just because we *can* make something doesn't mean we *should*.

## Labor: Investment or Cost?

The other problem with modern business is the confusion between *investments* and *costs*. So many business people are still arguing that *labor* is a *cost*. Yes, labor costs money, but labor is not a *cost*, it is an *investment*. You put money into an employee. You spend money training them to do their job efficiently, and they in turn produce products and services that make you *profit*. Employees are investments. I hesitate to compare people to other types of investments, but it might be instructive to do so. As business people, we invest money in infrastructure and tools to help us produce goods and services. These tools are an investment, not a *cost*. They can be used over and over again. Costs are something that you spend money on, and then it is gone. Energy to run our businesses is a cost. Certain materials, chemicals, or other ingredients can be calculated as costs. They are used up and gone. Eventually tools break down, but if we take care of our employees they should not break down. They may retire one day, but they don't break down. But because we think of them as costs we tend to use them like ingredients, not tools. We burn them up like fossil fuels in our Saruman-ic factories and then just find a new one to take their place. This *becomes* a cost because the constant retraining of new employees—as long as it's not seen as an investment—is a drain on a company. What we need is to invest more in the workers we have, and not just in their training but their well-being, as well.

## Saruman's Slaves: the Overwhelmed Modern Worker

A huge problem, especially in the U.S., is the over-working of employees. Workers in every industry are wearing out. The American *work ethic* is unsustainable. The idea that the worker must sacrifice family, social life, and leisure time for the good of the company is still the paradigm. And it is literally killing the work force. Brigid Schulte, in her book *Overwhelmed: Work, Love, and Play When No One Has the Time*, points out that the insistence upon *face-time* at work, the sacrificial work ethic, and set hours instead of productivity is dragging the modern worker into an early grave. The average health of the American worker is declining every decade. The problem with this *work ethic*—or one that should matter to business leaders—Schulte points out, is that it has been scientifically demonstrated to be not only destructive—in terms of employee health and well-being—but very <u>inefficient and unproductive</u>. It turns out, go figure, that unhealthy, stressed-out, over-worked employees with broken family relationships and no down-time, or vacation time really suck at doing their jobs. Recent studies show that the average American worker is only productive about 2 to 3 hours per day! If you think that's low, a study of *Fortune* 500 CEOs showed that because of their constantly interrupted schedules they only average about 28 uninterrupted, productive minutes per day! A half an hour! This is not productive, either for the bottom line or for the health of everyone involved. A new way of thinking about work is needed.

## Shire-Owned Business

Author Daniel Quinn talks about forming *Tribal* Businesses, or what I'll call Shire-Owned Businesses. The idea has been around for some time and there are a growing number of them popping up everywhere, but there needs to be many, many more. Shire-Owned Businesses are essentially employee-owned. Every employee has a vote or say in the way the business operates, or at least a share in its profits as well as what ever wages were agreed upon. This way employees have a stake in the success of the company and many times an actual vote when it comes to company policies and direction. This is how most business should run. Instead, we have share-holder run corporations who hire and fire CEOs to do one thing: maximize profits at the expense of everything else. Employees in this old-school way of thinking are little more than wage-slaves who can be hired and fired (freely in most cases), and have no say in what the company does, or how it is run. The true costs of doing business, the costs to the environment and to society, is of little concern to the shareholders, it seems. As long as the dividends keep rolling in the effects on the future of our planet are inconsequential.

Shire-Owned Businesses oppose such thinking. First and foremost, they should be designed or *redesigned* with the mission to help clean up the planet and to promote others to join along. And they don't have to be built from scratch; existing businesses can be transitioned into employee owned companies. They must also be profitable, of course. But there are businesses out there doing this. For more information, read Cat Johnson's article on "How To Convert a Business into a Worker-owned Cooperative." Be creative and use your talents, whatever they are, to create your own business. And don't forget to ask for help from your neighbors! You live in a Shire remember. Whether you work solo, or build a multi-employee based company make sure that your employees are properly treated. Never forget how it was to be a wage-slave yourself. The last thing we need in the New Shire are slaves. We need empowered individuals who believe in their job and its importance, not only to making a living but to saving the Earth from the force of

Saruman-ic corporations and the Dark Lord of Mordor. If you can create such a job for yourself, and for others, you will dispense with the soul-sucking depression that can set in when you hate what you do for a living. You will then be happier and that means healthier. If you can create a business that also promotes Shireness, a sense of community, then you can be a Hobbit business revolutionary!

## The New Model: Hobbit Cooperative Consumption

Not only do we need to rethink the way we run our businesses from a philosophical and organizational point of view. We also need to rethink *what* we make, *how* we make it, and *how* we sell it. Rachel Botsman and Lisa Gansky have identified a couple of related world-wide movements that've been going on for sometime that they call *Cooperative Consumption* and *The Mesh*. Essentially, what they are talking about is the birth of businesses and sharing platforms designed to better use resources and that break outside of the old formula for business, 'I-buy-cheap, sell-it-to-you, good-bye-till-next-time,' mentality.

Instead of focusing on selling cheaply made goods and services with built in obsolescence — with the intent on getting you back into the store as soon as possible to buy another version after throwing out the old one when it breaks — *Mesh* businesses focus instead on making products that last and that are more sustainable, both in their materials and in their potential to be reused, or recycled, many times by the company itself. This seems to be counter intuitive to making a profit, but in reality it's not. Instead of trying to sell you a new model every year, or every week, *Mesh* companies offer service and repair, exchanges, or rentals of products to keep customers coming back.

Botsman's idea of *Cooperative Consumption*, is similar to Gansky's *Mesh* in that most cooperative consumption companies are created to fill a need for consumers who are selling, renting, or giving away things they already own or providing shared ownership, or rental service for products that haven't been traditionally offered that way. Botsman points out that shared ownership, or temporary rental of things is really a very old concept. Most of us still think ideas like shared ownership of vehicles as *weird*, but how many times have we all shared rented beds with strangers? I'm not talking about *simultaneously*; you can keep that story to yourself. I'm talking about renting a hotel room. And how many of us have rented cars while on vacation or on work trips? So the idea isn't *weird* at all. It's just hasn't been applied on a large scale to other items that we use occasionally, like tools, toys, our guest room, cookware, party decorations, etc. But some of these businesses already exist, too!

## Goodbye Consumerism, Hello Experientialism!

The difference now, is that the newest generation, the Millennials — in part because they are young and adventurous but in large part because they are under-employed and lack the finances to keep up with the *Joneses* — are latching onto the ideas of shared ownership in new ways and with a new enthusiasm. They are moving away from consumerism and towards what James Wallman calls, *Experientialism.* Wallman, in his book *Stuffocation: How We've Had Enough of Stuff and Why You Need Experience More than Ever,* argues that there is a growing movement, and a large one, walking away from the consumerism/materialism model that most of us in the West have been following for the last 80 to 100 years. He points to recent studies that show that only half of us still hold materialistic values, and that two-thirds of us would like to live more simply, with less *stuff.* If these numbers are correct, and I suspect they are near the mark, it is an encouraging sign.

Wallman says more and more people are opting instead to fill their lives with *experiences,* instead of more things. What's funny is that in many ways it is the Greed of the Sarumans of the world that is pushing the rest of us to withdraw from the consumerism model because we can't afford it any longer. As a result, their Greed is destroying the very system that supplied them with wealth. That's not to say that we shouldn't buy things at all. Just that instead of buying lots of low priced, low quality crap, we should purchase better quality things, and less of of them. Also, those items should enhance experiences, like cooking, sports, travel, instead of filling up garages and basements with so-called *status symbols.* So let's reject Saruman's consumerism, and follow Bilbo's *Experientialism.*

We'll return to the idea later, but if you are a business person or dreaming of opening a business, consider this new trend and read Wallman's book. It would pay to do so because his *day job* is advising Fortune 500 companies on future trends, and he's damned good at it. So if he says that the trend is towards Experientialism, and away from consumerism it would be best to give that some thought in your business plans. Plus it's more Hobbity anyway. At the same time, don't forget to incorporate the ideas of the *Mesh*, and *Cooperative Consumption*. If you can come up with a product or service that provides, or facilitates *experience*, is open to the feedback of your customers, offers them ways to share ownership and costs, reduces waste and pollution, and promotes Shireness and community you're well on your way loads of dragon gold, I suspect. If you can do all that, take care of your labor investments and save your customers money, too? Then you'll be striking a blow on Saruman's corporate domination of our political institutions by siphoning money away from greedy, capitalistic businesses who have lost touch with their customers. But what if you're not an entrepreneur or business person? Can you still make a difference in how companies do business? Yes. Yes you can!

## The Power of Protest: Hobbit Boycotts and Social Media

In 2012, Sarah Kavanagh was a 15 year old high school student from Hattiesburg, Mississippi. She's a Hobbit *and* a vegetarian — which I know sounds like a contradiction, but trust me, she is both — so she's understandably picky about what she eats and drinks. One day she was getting ready to drink a bottle of Gatorade but before she did she took a moment to read the ingredients label. I know, the story sounds incredible — I mean, a teenager that actually *reads*? But alas, Sarah can, and did, and what she found puzzled her. One of the many ingredients in this chemical soup was something called BVO — bromated vegetable oil. Since she had never heard of BVO before she did what every red-blooded, American teenager would do, she looked it up on the internet. When she Googled the additive she discovered that it was linked to a long list of issues, including neurological disorders and altered thyroid hormones.

Now Sarah could have just said, "Oh well, I won't drink that," thrown the drink in the trash, and went along her merry, teenaged way. She could have responded, "No adventures for *this* Hobbit! They're such *nasty, disturbing, uncomfortable things*! Make you late for dinner!" "My friends are waiting for me at the mall," or "I have some texting to do," or some other self-indulgent response. But no, Miss Kavanagh was concerned, not just for her own health but for those of everyone consuming Gatorade. So she took up the challenge — like Frodo accepted the burden of carrying the One Ring — and she marched it straight to the source: Pepsi Cola! To get them to listen, she started a campaign on Change.org to get them to remove it from Gatorade!

After she garnered over 200,000 signatures, Pepsi agreed to remove it from the product, which they did last year and then announced that they would work to remove it from the rest of their Gatorade products!

Yay Sarah! But this little Hobbit didn't stop *there*! Oh no! She then took on the biggest dog in the industry, Coca Cola itself! And after only 60,000 signatures, *THEY* agreed to remove it from *their* products! I'm sure her original success with Pepsi had something to do with that! I mean, it's hard to say no when your main competitor has agreed to do something that consumers are demanding. This story actually makes me tear up — and I'm a big ole manly-man usually — but it exemplifies everything this book is about: <u>how one little Hobbit can make a huge change in the World</u> by speaking out, blowing her little Horn of Rohan and gathering other Hobbits to fight to clean up our Shire!

What Sarah's story demonstrates is the effectiveness, and power that one Hobbit can wield, even on the biggest corporations on Earth. Pepsi Co. and Coca Cola are two of the biggest dogs in the World. Coke is unarguably the most recognized trademark on the planet, selling billions of dollars in product every year but they are not immune from the pressure of the market, a market they helped to build I might add. If one teenager from Mississippi can convince major corporations to change their practices, *anyone can*! That means you, it means me, it means *EVERYONE*! Not only *can we* but we *should*. The boycott of products is one power that Sarumans can never really take away. It's their game and their rules. They claim to want a *free market*, but the problem with free markets is it assumes that the customer is free to choose. If in fact the market *is free* — or maintaining the illusion that it is — then the customer *is* free to choose. As long as we have choices we can choose to buy something else and that is the most powerful weapon we have as Hobbits.

We DO NOT have to buy crappy products anymore, products with secret ingredients, loaded with GMOs, with pesticides, with chemicals, products produced by employees paid slave wages or by children pressed into labor at starvation wages, products containing components, or ingredients raped from the Earth, leaving behind devastation and destruction. We can say NO! We simply do not have to buy them and we SHOULD NOT. To knowingly buy a product produced in these ways is to be complicit in the crimes committed by the corporation making them. If we continue to buy them then we are just as guilty as the company producing them because we are telling them, "It's ok if you act like Saruman, rape the Earth, enslave people, and poison us; here's my vote for what you're doing; here's my money!" Hobbits would never do such a thing, unless they're Sackville-Bagginses, of course. So stand up! Say NO! And if there's a product you really love and it's not completely poisoned tell the company that you will boycott them until they change it. Start a campaign on Change.org, like our little Hobbit Hero, Sarah Kavanagh! Hobbits like her are making changes like this all the time. The Shire Revolution has begun! It is HERE!

Let this also be a warning to the Sarumans of the World, the CEOs of all those massive corporations, and to their shareholders.

You are on notice! We the people, the Hobbits of the Earth, are saying that we will not buy your products anymore. We are tired of being lied to, bamboozled, and poisoned. Stop enslaving your workers for poverty wages and worse! Stop poisoning our water, our air, our Earth. Join with us to clean up what you have done in our name for your gain. If you cannot honestly tell us what is *in* your products, produce them ethically, morally, and with respect for the environment and the future of the planet's inhabitants then there is only one logical conclusion that we can assume. YOU have something to HIDE, and that is all we need to know when we reach for our wallets!

And while you're at it, stop buying our politicians to vote against our interests. "Wait a minute!" you say. "I *work* for a company like that!" "What can I do?" Maybe you're in the unenviable position of an orc in Isengard, who would rather be a Hobbit, or a Dwarf. What do you do then?

## From Orc to Dwarf: Striking Saruman from Within the Tower

Do you feel like an Orc? Maybe you have become a bit Wraithish working for a Sauron, or Saruman? This is a likely scenario with most people. I've been there. I have friends and family stuck in such a predicament. What can we do if the very income we depend upon to feed our families comes from the pocket of Saruman? Leaving your job might not be an option, at least not yet, but maybe you can leverage your position to the good of Hobbits everywhere? Think about it. How can you make a difference *right where you are*? If you're just an employee, like most of us, those changes might be tiny indeed, but never underestimate the tiniest of changes. They are like butterflies flapping their wings that may just cause a tsunami one day, so keep at it. A friend I know works for a bank and often feels that his soul is draining away, but the other day he convinced one of his clients to *not* invest in fracking by telling her how destructive it was to the environment, and that instead she should invest in new green companies. And the client *took the advice*! Then she proceeded to tell all her friends the same information! So save the Earth, from *where you are*, first. You can change jobs later if you want.

But what if you *are* in a position of more influence? What if you're the boss? What if you *are* a Saruman or you're afraid you're becoming one? Do you already own or run a large business? Are you the heir to one, but are tired of seeing how your family's business has been run? Are you a stockholder in a large corporation? Are you secretly a Hobbit too? You know what? It's not too late. Just like ole Scrooge, consider me your

Marley. Stop forging those chains! "Mankind [is our] business! The common welfare [is our] business; charity, mercy, forbearance, benevolence, [are our] business!" Maybe, instead of becoming an Orc or Wraith, you can be a Gandalf, Legolas, or Gimli! Which epitaph would you choose for your grave-stone: "He made lots of money." or "He saved the Earth"? And don't think I'm being sarcastic, because for once, I'm not. We're all going to die. What will be your legacy? Smaug-loads of money? or Saving the Earth? It's your choice. If you're in a position of power you can make sweeping changes to the way things are done by applying your new Hobbit mentality to the business world. Not only can you do immense good at the sweep of a pen but you can also take down the enemies of Earth: your competition, all those other Sarumans who chose the path of Greed!

Contrary to what some think, environmental sustainability, ethics, generosity, and fair-play are not the enemies of profit. In fact, there is growing evidence that they are the new way to ensure it. The current corporate mentality is *profit* at all costs, even the cost of destroying the business itself, the environment, and the future of the planet. It is an insane mentality. No logical argument can be made for running a business that way. It is purely about Greed driven by the lust for *more*. Of course, legally, every corporation must seek to maximize profits for their shareholders but destroying the very planet from which the profits are derived is not a sound business strategy in the long-term; it is a short-term murder, not a long-term marriage.

At the root of this insanity is the shareholder. Corporations live to serve their shareholders; it's the law, actually. In many ways, this is their strength. With ownership spread out among many people, risk is lessened, while capital is maximized. Blame can also be dispersed when things go wrong, as we see many companies attempting to do these days. "We serve our shareholders! We answer only to them! If there is blame to be had they are to blame, not the board or the CEO!" How convenient an excuse. What sucks is that the excuse is grounded in an element of truth. Shareholders are the driving force in large corporations. If a CEO attempts to make sweeping changes without the support of her holders, she's doomed and she'll be looking for a new job. But what corporations and most stockholders don't realize or even consider, is that shareholders can also become Hobbits, or at least Gimlis. How's *THAT* for an idea!? If you own stock in a company, are you concerned about the future of our planet? I will assume you are since you've reached this part of the book. If so, then use your vote and voice to make changes, big changes. You, like company owners and CEOs, have a unique power that can be used for good. Use it, we need you! The Earth needs you! Be Gandalf in the rising sun! Be Bard! Loose your Black Arrow into the belly of Smaug! He will never see it coming! And you will be scoring a win against corporate corruption of politics.

# 42

# SHIRE-MOOT:
# DIS-SPELL-ING SARUMAN
# WITH SOLIDARITY

"Alas for the folly of these days!" said Legolas. "Here all are enemies of the one Enemy, and yet I must walk blind, while the sun is merry in the woodland under leaves of gold!"

"Folly it may seem," said Haldir. "Indeed in nothing is the power of the dark Lord more clearly shown than in the estrangement that divides all those who still oppose him. Yet so little faith and trust do we find now in the world beyond Lothlórien, unless maybe in Rivendell, that we dare not by or own trust endanger our land." — *LOTR*: I, *Lothlórien*

If the common people do not
hold your authority in awe,
Then some greater authority is on its way.
Do not reduce the size of their places of residence
And do not lower their standard of living.
It is only because you do not lower their
standard of living
That they do not become disaffected.
It is for this reason that sages know themselves
But do not show off;
They love themselves

But are not *precious*.
Hence, eschewing one they take the other.
— *Dao De Jing*, Chapter 72

Suppose you were an idiot. And suppose you were a member of Congress. But I repeat myself.
— Mark Twain


I hate voting. Don't get me wrong; I do it. I do it everytime the damned polls open. But if you asked me, "why?" I couldn't give you a logical reason. I honestly don't know why I waste my time doing it or why anyone does. I do it every single time and walk away wondering what was the point of the entire exercise. It seems to make no substantive difference. I feel like I need a shower as I walk to my car or back across the street to my new home. Yeah, I know, you're gonna argue otherwise; trust me, I've heard all the arguments *for* exercising my *right to vote*. There are some valid points made for it, I'll grant, but in the end, there's really only one thing that decides *who* wins an election, in the U.S. anyway: money.

As Russell Brand points out in his recent book, *Revolution*, every election in U.S. history has gone to the party that raised the most money towards the campaign, so why not just wait to see who raises the most and forget about it. I'm not going to spend a lot of time researching the accuracy of his statement; it's not important, because while one might find a handful of exceptions to the *rule* or hold exception to Mr. Brand's life-choices, or politics, we all know that in essence he's right. Money talks, and we walk. The system is so corrupt that no matter who you vote for — with very few exceptions — you're voting for a career politician who is going to go to Congress, or the White House, or Downing Street and vote to support the interests of international corporations, the Sarumans of the World, not yours. The few lone voices of honesty in government, like Senator Elizabeth Warren and Bernie Sanders, have repeatedly preached this message in the last few years but nothing has changed about the system; in fact, it's gotten worse, especially since the passing of Citizens United. So why do I vote? I don't know. Maybe it's because I still, somewhere deep inside believe in the ideal of democracy. It is a great ideal. If only we lived in a democracy. We do not; we live in an oligarchy, a world dominated by Saruman, and Sauron.

## I'm an Ent: a Political Atheist.

What the hell does that mean? Just that I don't *believe* in political solutions to our problems anymore. Like Treebeard, when asked what part he might play in the War, "I am not altogether on anybody's *side*, because nobody is altogether on my *side*" — *LOTR*: II, *Treebeard* I don't really have a *side* or a *party* per se. That doesn't mean I don't care, just that I know that politicians don't represent me, my interests, or the interest of the planet. Politics, like the Capitalism that drives it, has become a substitute religion in America, or wedded to it. The situation isn't that different in most countries of the world. People put their beliefs, their dreams into political solutions, into politicians! Is this wise? Uhhh no. Yeah, I'm sure you can make some argument about your favorite politician, how he or she has *saved the world*, or kissed babies, or improved the economy, or whatever. No they didn't. Things aren't essentially different today than they were four years ago, or twelve, or twenty. Not in essence anyway. Unless you want to argue that they are worse. Corporations have gained more power, more influence, more profits, and raped the Earth and the citizens of the Earth with ever increasing efficiency but the situation is no different, and it doesn't matter which *party* is in office. That's why I'm an atheist when it comes to politics. All sides are corrupt and we are left standing in line waiting for table scraps from the feasts of Saruman. Why is it so? Because we *believe* that there's a substantive difference between political parties.

Is there? Maybe. There are certainly differences in opinion about how to go about running the economy, social and domestic programs, the military and foreign policy. Basically, the Republican Party stands on a platform that things would be better if we just let the *free* market be to do its own thing: everything would balance out in the end. The Democratic Party points out, correctly I might add, that to allow big business to run unfettered leads to disastrous situations, like the collapse in 2008 and the ridiculous disparity in wealth between those at the top and the rest of us. But before you start thinking I'm a card-carrying Democrat, let me say that the similarities between the two parties are more important in the long run, than their differences. Because while the Democratic Party, and most liberals in general, point to big money as a problem they are still working on the base premise that big business and markets are essential to the economy and to the health of the country; in other words, they still *believe* in the religion of Capitalism, and the *free* — if somewhat tethered — *market*. Because they are still married to this belief any solutions they come up with have to jive with it or they are thrown out as, shutter, gasp, *Socialism*, or even worse, *Communism*! And we can't have that! Everyone knows those things are inherently evil. Our leaders — like the late Senator Joseph McCarthy, the asshat from the 50s *Red Scare* — have been telling us that for decades! Hell, they even teach it to us in school! *Ergo*, it must be right.

Well, I'm not going to argue for a Communist revolution, or even a Socialist one, but a revolution is needed, and that's a fact. Russell Brand is arguing for one, a peaceful one, and I'm in agreement 100% on that. We need it. Our system, as it currently exists is not working. All that wealth generated by international corporations is running rampant like a virus through the political systems of the entire planet corrupting everything in its path and literally killing us. People die every second on this planet because the resources they need — resources that used to be common property to everyone — are being usurped by Sarumans and Sauronic governments under their influence, so they can sell us those products and reap record profits, none of which any of us ever see. In the process they corrupt almost every major politician they come into contact with, regardless of party affiliation. So we, as Hobbits, Dwarves, Elves, Wizards, whatever, need to stop arguing about which crooked politician we should *vote* for and start working together to take back control of our governments!

## Be Gimli or Legolas: We're All on the Same *Side*

In *LOTR*, there are two characters who manage to put aside their prejudices, their petty squabbles, their Fear, and their Willful Ignorance to join together in a common struggle against evil, against the forces of Sauron and Saruman: Gimli the Dwarf and Legolas of Mirkwood. Elves and Dwarves had long been rivals, and at times enemies, thanks to the corruptive power of Sauron who stoked the long-existing animosities between the two races to keep them fighting each other, while ignoring what he, Sauron, had planned for Middle Earth. Too often his plan worked. Great battles had erupted in the past between Dwarves and Elves and that hatred and mistrust spills out a few times between Gimli and Legolas, especially when they reach Lothlórien:

"Here we are at last!" said Gandalf. "Here the Elven-way from Hollin ended. Holly was the token of the people of that land, and they planted it here to mark the end of their domain; for the West-door was made chiefly for their use in their traffic with the Lords of Moria. Those were happier days, when there was still *close friendship between folk of different race*, even between Dwarves and Elves."

"It was not the fault of the Dwarves that the friendship waned," said Gimli.

"I have not heard that it was the fault of the Elves," said Legolas.

"I have heard both," said Gandalf; "and I will not give judgement now. But I beg of you two, Legolas and Gimli, at least to be friends, and to help me. *I need you both*. The *doors are shut* and hidden, and the sooner we find them the better. *Night is at hand!*" —*LOTR*: I, 316 [italics mine]

Here is a perfect example of Willful Ignorance and Fear rearing their ugly heads. If only Legolas and Gimli had learned Bilbo's Willful Ignorance Test! Don't you forget it either; if you're in an argument and you think the other person is the only one being willfully ignorant, stop yourself, because so are you. Gandalf, always the voice of wisdom and reason, points out that the two of them should forget about past grievances, be friends, and work together to accomplish the goal of saving Middle Earth. Gimli and Legolas follow his advice, to the benefit of all races. Of course, *race*, in *LOTR* refers more to species, but the word is appropriate for our purposes. Race, as we've already mentioned, is mostly an illusion. The DNA differences between one human *race* and another are almost unrecognizable, even if it were it shouldn't matter; we are all human beings struggling for survival in an increasingly hostile climate and against other humans who wish to horde all the resources to themselves. Race should be irrelevant, as should *class* distinctions, which are only a luck of the draw.

We modern Hobbits, Dwarves, and Elves need to start talking to each other in more civil ways. We need to realize that despite our differences of opinion on how to fix our problems, we are not enemies; we are all in the same boat. If you aren't one of the 1% of the Earth who can afford to fly *over our boat* to Paris for lunch, and San Fran for dinner, then you have more in common with our fellow Hobbits at the bottom, and visa versa. You are being screwed by the Sarumans and you need to realize it. If you don't, and soon, it will be too late once you do. The goal of the elite of our planet is to take it *all*; that is evident, or it should be. That means what *you* have not just what that poor guy flipping your burger has; he has nothing, and pretty soon, neither will you. We need to get to know each other: burger flippers, middle-class managers, and even millionaires. Continuing to vote for and support political parties, to blame the poor, the *other race*, the other *religion,* isn't going to solve the problem. We need to cultivate friendships and alliances with the people we *disagree* with, not just those who think we're brilliant. The late, great President Thomas Jefferson once said, "I never considered a difference of opinion in politics, in religion, in philosophy, as cause for withdrawing from a friend." We should take his advice if we hope to save the Earth. We will not do it by squabbling over scraps; we will only do it by joining together. We need to start *throwing parties*, instead of *voting* for them.

### Political Parties: a Warning from the Past

While most of us think of ourselves as being either Democrat or Republican—and yes, I know there are other parties out there— our founding fathers, or some of them warned us of the dangers of forming such parties. Our first president, and the man who led the rebellion against England, George Washington, was emphatic that political parties were dangerous to a democratic republic. Among the many dangers, the most important was that they were easily corrupted by those with money to do so:

However [political parties] may now and then answer popular ends, they are likely in the course of time and things, to become potent engines, by which cunning, ambitious, and unprincipled men will be enabled to *subvert the power of the people* and to usurp for themselves the reins of government, destroying afterwards the very engines which have lifted them to unjust dominion.

Now, I don't for a minute think that we are going to abolish political parties, and I'm not really calling for it, though it would be a good thing if we did. I'm just calling attention to the simple fact that parties are too easily led around by those with the cash to control them, and the two main parties in the U.S. are corrupt to the core. It's fine to be conservative or liberal, yourself. Just don't put your faith in politicians and don't forget your shared humanity with those who disagree with you. The kind of people who are attracted to power, are exactly the kind that shouldn't be given any. Tolkien himself warned of it:

Government is an abstract noun meaning the art and process of governing and it should be an offense to write it with a capital G or so to refer to people … The most improper job of any, even saints (who at any rate were at least unwilling to take it on), is bossing other men. Not one in a million is fit for it, and least of all those who seek the opportunity. — *The Letters of J.R.R. Tolkien*

In Middle Earth, the struggle for power is more cut and dry, except for Saruman's betrayal of the Council. Sauron is evil, Saruman covets the Ring and Gandalf and the Hobbits are pitted against them as the forces for good. It's simple enough. Tolkien however suggests another perspective that we might take. He says:

But if you have, as it were taken 'a vow of poverty', renounced control, and take your delight in things for themselves without reference to yourself, watching, observing, and to some extent knowing, then the question of the rights and wrongs of power and control might become utterly meaningless to you, and the means of power quite valueless. — *The Letters of J.R.R. Tolkien*, No. 144

What the professor seems to be saying is to remove ourselves from the struggle altogether, but I'm not sure that is exactly what he intended. Tolkien was outspoken against the evils he saw in the 20th century, especially those dealing with the environment and with government and power. What I think he means here is that we should not seek power, either for good or evil, as it is corruptive. I think the idea is similar to the epigraph from the *Dao* at the top of the chapter:

> It is for this reason that sages know themselves
> But do not show off;
> They love themselves
> But are not *precious.*
> Hence, eschewing one they take the other.

True leaders lead with a light hand, and a fair one. They do not take too much for themselves. They do not make a show of their position, or grasp for power. We should always seek to share it equally with our fellow human beings, our fellow Hobbits: a true democracy, where everyone's input is valued and considered.

What I'm arguing for, or *suggesting* — there's been enough arguing about politics lately — is that we Hobbits start thinking as a Shire instead of thinking as Democrats, Republicans, Libertarians, Socialists, Communists, or whatever. We are allowing our politicians and their puppeteers to dazzle us with bullshit. Stop the madness people! We are arguing about shadows on the wall of a cave. Step outside of your Hobbit-hole and see the politicians for what they are: puppets. Let's start thinking like Hobbits and forget about political parties, or at least stop worshiping them like they hold some universal truths or something. They don't. Let's do as conservative Gimli and liberal Legolas; let's focus on our shared humanity, our shared struggles, our similarities instead of our differences for a change. If you want to remain a member of a party, fine. In fact, it could be quite useful when it comes time to vote, but don't expect too much from politicians. They have been corrupted by the Ring, and the Greed of Saruman. Instead, put your faith in yourself, your family, your friends, and your neighbors. Work together as a Shire to make real changes <u>where you live</u> and then make alliances with other Shires next door in your town, county, or city, to push larger agendas. Let's start with supporting initiatives to clean up our Earth, like renewable energy projects, clean water projects, food security, and the like. So, what I'm suggesting I reckon is Hobbits UNITE! It's the best way to start mending our broken system.

**Our Shire-Moot Philosophy**

Instead of thinking as divided individuals and clinging to our out-dated political parties, let's think more about what we have in common, our shared goals. Cannot we agree on the following, or some version of it?

- All work should be towards 'Saving the Earth' in all its aspects.

- Work to minimize Fear, Ignorance, Want, and Greed.

- Shireness: Keep our dialogue civil. Avoid personalizing your arguments. Remain friends, or at least allies. Remember Jefferson's quote, and Bilbo's Willful Ignorance Test.

- Remember our shared Humanity. This is an extension of Shireness. Just because we disagree doesn't mean the other person is evil. They might be, if they're a murderous Ringwraith, but most people aren't. Let's try to remember that we're supposed to be on the same side.

- We all have a story that contributed to our personal world view. Just don't forget that the other person *also* has reasons for thinking the way they do.

# Taking On Saruman's Horde: Politics on the Macro-Scale

I don't want to completely discourage anyone from attempting to make changes via the political system. Taking on politics in a head on fashion occasionally brings results. While I believe that the only *sure* way for us to save our earth is to destroy our metaphorical Ring—through changing minds and then actions on a personal level, slowly gaining more and more allies—that does not mean that we should abandon efforts to make larger changes through politics. In *LOTR* the efforts of Boromir, Isildur, Aragorn, Faramir, Gimli, and Legolas were not wasted. They played an extremely important part in the destruction of the Ring. Even the little Hobbits, Merry and Pippin, did not walk into Mordor to destroy the Ring. They found other ways to bring the fight to the enemies of Middle Earth, first by attending the Entmoot—a democratic caucus, if you will—where they convinced the Ents to march to war against Isengard and Saruman's hordes and then separately as retainers of great kings, Merry as a warrior of Rohan, and Pippin as a Tower Guard of Gondor. Both fought valiantly. In fact, if not for Merry, Eówyn might have been crushed by the Witch King on the Fields of the Pelennor. It was his timely thrust that distracted the evil Nazgul, just as Eowyn screwed up the courage to ram her sword into his face—or into the space where his face *would* have been if he in fact, had a face. True, Merry's attack was from the rear. How very stealthy of him and very Hobbit-like: just as Frodo and Sam snuck in the back door to Mordor! Brave Pippin faces evil head on in the battle at the Black Gates, an encounter he barely survived, being crushed under the weight of a fat troll which just might be the best example of what happens when we small Hobbits try to take on the *big folk* in politics, who have the weight of so much dragon gold backing them up.

## Be Like Merriadoc: Look for Your *Moment*

Usually, when gains are made in the real world it has to be accomplished by convincing those with power that the change will benefit them in some way. Infrastructure projects used to be viewed this way, though I'm not sure they are anymore. Things like building roads, bridges, public spaces, parks, were once important to the elite in the U.S., and still are in some places around the world. The increasingly *international* ties of most corporations means that they have no loyalty to national governments; instead, they just barge in, bribe politicians and take what they want without paying taxes. So they have little concern these days for the infrastructure of the host countries. They aren't there to *build,* only to *extract,* either resources or profits. The most useful motivator for those at the top is Greed. And as such, the best way to get them to do what we want is to vote with our money, though occasionally, larger opportunities present themselves.

In our world and time, big political gains are usually precipitated by a chaotic event that opens up small, exploitable opportunities, much as Smaug, the symbol of greed, had a tiny, forgotten chink in his scales that Bard exploited with his Black Arrow. As Gar Alperovitz argues in his book *What Then Must We Do?: Straight Talk about the Next American Revolution,* big events in history such as the Depression and WWII opened up opportunities for large scale change that did not exist before. In Middle Earth, Sauron and Saruman's impatience and malice led them into offensives before they were fully prepared, exposing weaknesses that our heros exploited. Smaug's hubris and forgetfulness led to his fiery crash into Long Lake.

We should be alert for such blunders by our political leaders and their corporate masters. They screw up often. Corporations seem to think they are unsinkable but many of the largest disappeared during the current economic crisis. General Motors' Pontiac division, is the best example. Corporations are very conservative in the way they view the market these days. They tend to think in old ways believing that their past business strategies will continue to work indefinitely. The world is changing, as you now know, and businesses that ignore these changes will suffer for it. They may just find themselves blindsided by Gandalf on the dawn of the third day at Helms Deep or be deceived into thinking those black sails on the river are allies, only to find Aragorn and company sailing in behind them on the fields of the Pelennor, or transfixed by a Black Arrow as they plummet in smoking ruin into the depths of Long Lake!

Most people are paralyzed by the size of the world's problems. They see things like *global warming,* economics, corruption, poverty, and war and throw their hands in the air in defeat. They become Denethors. I can totally relate. I've been

there myself, and it wasn't that long ago. But we must keep trying, and the best way to save the Earth is to make changes in our own lives and then work on our friends and family to help them do it, too. If you want to make a difference on a larger scale, most of us will have more impact by refusing to spend our money with companies that are destroying our planet and doing other orcish things, like not paying a fair wage to their employees. Stop spending money with them. Eventually they will either change, or dry up and blow away. After all, it is our money they are using to corrupt the political system, and use it against us. If you're feeling bolder, a bit more *Tookish* than that, then start a Change.org campaign to gather the support of other Hobbits out there to influence a corporation, like Sarah Kavanagh, or form a coalition of citizens to stop government corruption on a local level, like in Tallahassee, Florida, and a handful of other cities recently did.

## Dwarves, Elves, and Hobbits in Action: Anti-Corruption Laws by Popular Support

There is a political movement in many states to force an amendment of the U.S. Constitution to do away with Citizens United and to curb corruption on a national scale. Only time will tell whether that will succeed. A similar proposal was put forward in Congress in 2014, but was defeated in the Senate. One hopes that the state level initiative will fare better, but I wouldn't hold my breath on that one. It's best for Hobbits to work locally to develop a model that might work elsewhere, in other localities, states, the nation, who knows, even internationally. Such a movement has already begun and had some early success.

On 4 November, 2014, the citizens of Tallahassee, Florida, and other cities around the U.S. voted to end government and election corruption in their municipalities. And they did it without the help of politicians, who traditionally aren't that hyped about ending a system that puts dirty money into their pockets. And what's more impressive about their victory was not just that it passed with an overwhelming majority of the vote, but *who* put it together: a coalition of political *enemies*. Democrats, Republicans, Tea-Party members, and others got together to tackle the corruption in their towns and cities. They worked in tandem with lawyers from around the nation to draft a law that they could all agree on, and that has a lot of teeth. Then they garnered a butt-load of signatures, way more than needed to get the referendum on the ballot, and rallied the people to vote for it, and vote they did. Now here is something worth voting for! To be honest, I was shocked when I heard about it, because I'm a political atheist, and other than diverting out money away from corporations, I haven't thought of another truly successful political strategy to defeat big money in the political arena. Kudos to these resourceful Dwarves and Elves! And to all the Hobbits who signed the petitions and voted to put it through! If you want to know more about this initiative and how they hope to spread it around the country, and to scale it to the nationwide level, check out the website for the movement. Maybe you will be the next Hobbit to score a blow on the Sarumans of your Shire!

If we look for our openings, work together as a Shire, we can slowly, town by town, city by city, state by state, begin to regain control of our political system. At some point, the movement will *tip*, and before you know it we'll have our Shire cleaned up. Then the really hard work begins. I know, I'm full of good news. But it is good news. Because once we clean up the corruption, then we can rebuild the Shire the way *we want it to be*.

# 43

# SHIRE GOVERNMENT: HOW HOBBITS SHOULD RULE

That we should wish to cast him down and have *no one* in his place is not a thought that occurs to his mind. [bold mine] — *LOTR*: III, *The White Rider*

I'll tip my hat to the new constitution
Take a bow for the new revolution
Smile and grin at the change all around
Pick up my guitar and play
Just like yesterday
Then I'll get on my knees and pray
We don't get fooled again
Don't get fooled again. — The Who, *Won't Get Fooled Again*

If some wants to rule the world,
and goes about trying to do so,
I foresee that they simply will not succeed.
The world is a sacred vessel,
And is not something that can be ruled.
Those who would control it lost it. — *Dao De Jing*, Chapter 29

# Meet the New Boss: No Boss

The problem with revolutions, all of them up to this point in history is that they were all conceived in violence. One might argue that Gandhi's revolution overthrowing the British domination of India was a peaceful one. That's mostly true, at least from the standpoint of Gandhi's personal actions. But there was a lot of violence between factions in India, especially between Muslims and Hindis that threatened at times the success of the resistance. During Gandhi's lifetime he was able to quell much of this but of course, was himself assassinated, and so ended the peaceful part of the revolution. All the other revolutions, with one exception that I can think of, were violent. Yes, many would argue that the American Revolution was successful, and I won't argue too much against that, but to say that the reason we need a new one is because the old one was incomplete and essentially just traded one elite, an English Monarchic/aristocratic one for an American, mercantilist, soon-to-be capitalist one, which then managed to dominate the politics of the planet and the freedoms of its own people. Violence is not an option for the Shire Revolution that I'm calling for. If we resort to it, we will fail. Trust me, I'm an historian. I know stuff. If we want to succeed then we have to find ways to do it non-violently.

Non-violent, doesn't mean *pacifist*. Gandhi was accused of calling for pacifism and he soundly denounced it. There's nothing pacifist about revolution. Pacifism is just accepting the world the way it is, and dealing with it. Revolution requires resistance; it requires that we fight back. *How* we fight is what matters. There are infinite ways to resist without resorting to violence. We've already covered some of them in the last chapter. In this chapter we're going to assume that we've managed to gain some semblance of control of our governmental institutions, through non-violent means and that we're all sitting around a big table, in my backyard, eating BBQ—because what else would we have if we're celebrating a victory—attempting to lay out a plan of action for our new government. We'll start by assuming that we have only managed to get control of our local government—town, city, county—first, and then we'll think about what happens after that, at the state, national, and international levels. Most of that is beyond the scope of this not-so-little book. Volumes have been, can be, and should be written on what to do about that, but I have to end this book somewhere, so I think that some thoughts on local government—then a brief look at how we can clean up the planet, and the national government—will suffice. Then we'll go to the final section of the book where we'll look at how technology can assist us in that quest.

Frodo and his companions, when they returned home to find their Shire destroyed, rallied their neighbors and threw out Saruman and Wormtongue. But their revolution was more a *repelling* of an invader, not a true revolution from within. Hobbits had not devolved over centuries into a corrupt system; the corruption wormed its way in and then invaded wholesale. So, while their story serves as inspiration to us, the comparison can only go so far. We, in the so-called *civilized* world have allowed ourselves to be corrupted. Our Ring is really *ours*; we own it, though it was handed down to us as an ancient heirloom. Our corrupt political systems are that way because we designed them to be corruptible—which of course is not the fault of anyone living today—and then let them be corrupted—which is our fault to some extent. We bought the lies told to us by the elite of the World, that they had our best interests at heart, that our *democratic* governments were just that: democratic. They aren't. We do not live in a democracy, or a republic; we live in an oligarchy—the rule of many by the few, the rich, the elite. We are ruled by Sarumans and not a few Saurons. The only way we can kick them out, I have argued, is from the bottom up. And let's assume we've managed to do that in our local area. What then? How would this new government function?

What we want to avoid when putting together a new, more democratic form of government, and democracy is what we're calling for, is to do it in a coercive way, or to think of government in the old way: top down. We must think bottom up. We must make new rules and laws that are fair for everyone and that have the interests of the Shire as a whole, at heart. Anything else and we're just reviving the Saruman formula. We should resist any attempts, by anyone—most importantly ourselves—to assert *control* over our fellow Hobbits. Remember, accomodation not coercion. How can we accomodate everyone and their needs and talents? Resist the attempts of anyone to be *the leader*. Leaders should be changed often. Term limits of office should be written into every new charter, or constitution, or into old ones if they are revised. That doesn't mean we don't need leaders, we do, but that they should work within fairly strict parameters to keep corruption from starting, or spreading. Term limits, at the very least, make corruption a short-term affair. It's when people stay in office for too long or spend their lives as politicians, that corruption, which may have begun as a seed, becomes a thicket of briars and weeds. The best way to avoid this is through democratic elections to elect temporary politicians.

## Liquid Democracy: Electing Hobbit Experts to Represent Us

I've thought for a long time, at least since the invention and proliferation of the internet that it was ridiculous to hold onto the old way of holding elections, especially in modernized countries with solid, internet infrastructure, like the U.S. Why is it that in a country with so many computers, iPads, and smart phones, we still have people coloring in little dots on a piece of paper? Seriously, in some places, like my district, in a major metropolitan area like St. Paul we are still using a pen and paper to vote. At least it's not the *punch card* type they used in Florida for the 2000 presidential election. Before that, I had never heard of a *hanging chad*, and now I wish I never had. What a clusterfuck. I mean, in the digital age, the year 2000, we had to wait a couple of *WEEKS* to find out who the next president of the *free* World was going to be? The point I'm trying to make here is that there's no reason whatsoever that we should still be using these outdated systems to elect our officials, at any level. The technology exists to institute *DIRECT DEMOCRACY* to most of the planet, if not all of it.

Why haven't we? Just ask the 1%; they'll ignore the question because they don't like to vocalize the answer. They could not possibly hold onto power if they allowed direct democracy. The American republican form of government was installed specifically to keep control in the hands of as few people as possible; that's why we have an Electoral College who actually chooses the president. In the 18th Century, it made sense to have elected officials, representatives and senators to go to Washington, or to our state capitals to do the hard decision making and voting. We didn't have an internet. It simply wasn't possible for people to vote directly on the laws and issues; they had to be at home running farms, milking cows, making babies, and cleaning the outhouses of their elite employers. So we elected men — and it was *only* men, and *white* men back then — to go do our voting for us. But it's not 1776 anymore, people. We need to move into the 21st Century. We need a ONE CITIZEN, ONE VOTE democracy, in every country of the world.

The problem with direct democracy, even in the digital-internet age, is that we don't all have time to vote on every issue that comes up at the various levels of government. I mean, think about it. You have town-city governments, counties, states, and national governments, all constantly working on new laws, and new government programs that are supposed to serve *us*, the public. So there's no way that the average person can keep up with all of that. That's one of the main arguments still put forward for representative style government. But who says that we can't use the internet technology to revolutionize the *way* we choose our representatives? Well, the entrenched elite do, of course, but there's no *technical* or *philosophical* reason why we cannot. The elite, if you catch them behind closed doors, will admit that they don't think the rest of us are smart enough to actually vote on the issues, and due to our lack of intellect and expertise, we *need them* to do the thinking for us. What a bunch of crap. We don't. And we don't need expertise in every field to participate in our government. In fact, most of our so-called, *expert* representatives have proven, time and again, that they are more incompetent than the average two year old. Sorry two year olds, for the insult.

One of the ideas in Russell Brand's book, was that of a *Liquid Democracy*, put forward by a friend of his, Dave DeGraw, a leader in the Occupy Movement, In a liquid democracy, DeGraw argues, we could use technology to choose people who *do* have the expertise in a particular issue to represent us on that particular issue or a category of issues. Let's see if I can simplify this a bit. For example, let's say you had a cousin or an old college professor who you knew was an expert on genetic engineering, you know, the science that Monsanto is abusing to poison our food. In a liquid democratic system you would have the choice to either vote on every issue *or* choose someone to cast your vote, or votes, for you. So you choose your old professor, whose viewpoint on the subject is well known to you, and you assign your vote on an issue to him. Maybe a thousand other people do the same. All of this is done online. On the day of the vote, or ahead of time, the professor can schedule his vote — along with all the votes given to him by people like you — and when the time comes for the actually vote, all his votes are cast. You would have the option of choosing someone like your professor, or your uncle the Army Colonel, to vote for categories of issues. The professor votes on scientific issues for you, and your uncle on military, foreign policy, and things of that nature. If you discover they're not going to vote in the way you like, you just simply *unclick* them, and they're no longer your representative. You can then choose another one, or choose to do the voting yourself.

What's beautiful about this idea, is that it's so flexible and scalable. It can even be slowly introduced by using our current system of representation, which is probably how it would work at the beginning, and probably on a very local level, even at the level of the neighborhood, and then city. Instead of choosing a random person to cast your votes, you could choose *any* existing, elected representative to cast your votes. This would entirely eliminate gerrymandering of districts, or at least remove the power of it. Let's say that your city councilor doesn't seem to represent your views. Fine, you can just choose one that does, on a particular issue or category of issues. You give them your vote to cast, and they cast it. The reason this is different, is that their vote isn't just one vote, it's a collection of all the votes that were assigned to that councilor. It's still one citizen, one vote; you just don't have to be there to do the voting in person. Eventually, it would be better if we move away from the traditional elected representative system altogether. We don't need it. The proxy system like I laid out above, would be preferable. That way the voter, the citizen, has many more options to choose experts on particular topics to cast their votes via proxy. This is just one idea on how we could do it; there are many others out there and I'm sure that more will arise as the Shire Revolution develops. However we vote, we need to have a plan on *what* government should *do* for us. What kinds of things *should* they do? How should they do it? How best can government serve *us*, the people, not the corporations?

# The Role of Government in the New Shire

For all of human history, written history that is, governments have been top-down structures. From the earliest priest-kings of Mesopotamia and Egypt, to the so-called democratic republics of today, the system is designed in an hierarchical way. Rule comes from the top and rains down upon those at the bottom. If we are to have a true revolution, this must change. A certain amount of hierarchy and centralization is necessary, at least once you get to a city-sized to larger institution, but the role of that system, of that beauracracy — a word I destest, not so much the word as what it has come to represent — should always be to *serve the people*, not special interests or the elite. It also should be decentralized in the sense that it is there to support local efforts, not to dictate them.

### Government: a Hobbit Tool Box, Not a Box of *Tools*

In, *The Gardens of Democracy: A New American Story of Citizenship, the Economy, and the Role of Government,* Eric Liu and Nick Hanauer, suggest that government should serve as a tool box. They argue that one of the problems with large, centralized government is their propensity to dictate *how* to do things without providing the *means* by which to do them. Instead of saying, "Here's some money, you figure out how to make it work for you," they tend to say, "You must do it this way and raise the money yourselves." Even when they *do* fund projects or programs they run them with dictatorial fervor. Instead, Liu and Hanauer argue they should be "big on the what, and little on the how." In other words, government should set the goals, the direction that they think the city, state, country should go and then let the people and their local representatives decide *how* to accomplish those goals. But that's not the end of their role.

Government has to support those goals, not just with money, though that's crucial; they also need to support them by developing *tools* to accomplish those goals. This can be a myriad of things, including infrastructure—both physical and virtual, resources—money and other, education, and expertise. The virtual infrastructure could be anything from a free and open internet, to apps, to websites, videos, and a host of other things to assist the public and local governments in solving their problems, and creating a better world. This could be immensely helpful in solving some of the huge problems that face every community, especially hunger and want. With the right expertise and resources, we could make sure every person has access to healthy, organic food and the means to grow it themselves if they so choose. So as you're forming your new Shire, keep this idea in mind: *big on what, little on how.* Let people be creative in their solutions, as long as they follow basic guidelines that keep the environment and human rights in mind. Don't try to micro-manage people; we're all used to that already. That's coercion! We don't need any more of that crap. Governments should be a tool *boxes*, not boxes of *tools*—which is what we already have. Once we set up local governments on these principles then we can start to tackle larger issues.

# 44

# SNAPPING SARUMAN'S STAFF: THE DIS-CORPORATION OF OLIGARCHY

"You have become a fool, Saruman, and yet pitiable. You might still have turned away from folly and evil, and have been of service. But you choose to stay and gnaw the ends of your old lots. Stay then! But I warn you, you will not easily come out again. Not unless the dark hands of the East stretch out to take you. Saruman!" he cried, and his voice grew in power and authority. "Behold, I am not Gandalf the Grey, whom you betrayed. I am Gandalf the White, who has returned from death. You have no color now, and I cast you from the order and from the Council."

He raised his hand, and spoke slowly in a clear cold voice. "Saruman, your staff is broken." There was a crack, and the staff split asunder in Sarumans's hand, and the head of it fell down at Gandalf's feet. "Go!" said Gandalf. With a cry Saruman fell back and crawled away. —*LOTR*: II, *The Voice of Saruman*

Corporations haven't been around that long, only a couple of hundred years, and I think one of the problems we have in our *hypnotized state of despondency* is that we forget that we are not listless little subjects but glorious creatures that can imagine new lives for ourselves. Succinctly, all we have to do to rid ourselves of a problem like corporate tyranny is to imagine doing it, then do it. —Russell Brand, *Revolution* [italics mine]

Fill the streets with ordinary people of every color, alignment, and faith and together demand our country back. Demand a fair deal. Demand that which is already ours but will never be freely given and can never be achieved until we overlook the superficial differences and distinctions that they lower like a veil between us and we unite to overcome them. Then, if in a few years, if that hasn't changed the world, let's go back to killing one another.

For now, though, let's kill a corporation. —Russell Brand, *Revolution*


The voice of Saruman was strong. All those within earshot were in danger of being drawn into his web of lies. Only those with extraordinary strength of will were able to resist. Gandalf of course was well up to the task, as was Theoden, but are we modern Hobbits made of stern enough fiber to resist the voice of our corporate Sarumans? We must be. There is no option. Like Russell Brand points out, we have been hypnotized for decades, generations by the lies of the corporate world. It's as if they were Sith warriors employing *The Dark-side of the Force* in some kind of Star Wars-ian, Jedi Mind Trick, "We are not the enemy you seek. We are your friend. We mean you no harm. We are the only thing separating you from starvation, from poverty, from violence, from the chaos of a world without Capitalism! We are not the enemy. Look over *there*. The enemy is the tired, the poor, the huddled masses, the wretched refuse of alien nations, the homeless, the immigrants who have been tossed upon our shores by the storms of the untamed, wild places of the world, where we have yet to extend our benevolent hand to quell the tempest of war, oppression, and dispel the evils of anarchy, communism and socialism, where chaos reigns."

Wake up already! Shake off Saruman's spell. Open your eyes and measure the words of the corporations against their actions. Are they really doing what they say they are? Do they really have our best interests at heart? Do they have a *heart* at all? In most cases, the answer is a resounding NO! As with the spell their products, their brands had over us, so it is with the institution of the corporation itself. We have come to think that they are essential to our survival—like the *too big to fail* banks in 2008—as if they have always existed, but they have not. They are a relatively new phenomenon, but the clock on the wall is tick-tocking and their time is running out.

# A Brief History of Corporations

There is not space to go into depth on the entire history of corporations; that would require another book almost as long as this one. But rest assured that they have not been with us for long. The earliest ones only go back a couple hundred years, and until the late 1800s they were temporary entities, not the permanent, global empires that they have become. Originally corporations were set up to solve a particular need, or problem, and they had an expiration date. After the job was finished, or after a set date, they were dissolved. They could argue to extend their charter if there was sufficient reason, but if not, they ceased to exist. But in the late 1800s they managed to argue in court and get the support from judges, to extend their life indefinitely. As a result, corporations have since expanded their original charters to become international, power-hungry empires with the strength to corrupt and overthrow national governments and international governing organizations, all in the pursuit of Greed. It is past time to put a stop to them.

### But Aren't They Needed to Drive the Global Economy?

In short, no, they are not. Not if they don't play by the rules, at least. As we've argued in this book over and over again, localized businesses are more sustainable and more important than large corporations who answer only to the Greed of their shareholders. No matter how much they might *say* they have our interests at heart, it is mostly a pack of lies. Unless you're a shareholder, they simply don't care about you. Hell, unless you're a *major shareholder* they couldn't care less what you think.

They have some care for your bank account, but not you. You are simply someone to sell something to. You are a *number,* a demographic, nothing else. Most of us inherently know this these days. We can feel it when we interact with corporations. How far has customer *service* fallen. Whole companies have sprung up just to deal with the customer service of other corporations. In most cases this is farmed out to external companies who seem to have little knowledge or training with the products which they are hired to represent. And the quality of the products is far less than it used to be.

Everything is designed to be obsolete within a couple of years, if not sooner. How often does a company really need to come out with a new smart phone design, new textbooks, new tennis shoes? We don't need what corporations bring to us, with very few exceptions. Almost all of it can be found in local stores, from local suppliers, and much more of it would be available from those sources if they weren't so often squeezed out of existence by corporations that don't play fairly. On top of that, they are usurping common resources, like water, power, the internet, and others and claiming proprietary ownership over them. We don't need more *me-me-me* from businesses. What we need, as we've already mentioned, is openess, and sharing of information, ideas, technology and resources. We need *co-operation, not corporations.* We need our institutions and businesses to work together for *OUR GOOD* not just the good of the elite shareholders. How do we break this hold on commerce, and our governments? We start by killing some corporations.

## Dis-Corporating Business and Killing Oligarchy

Before you start to hyperventilate, let me say that I'm not necessarily calling for the end of all corporations. Some of them do play by the rules, are working to be more sustainable, and aren't killing the planet. But most of them? They need to either clean up their act pronto, or they need to go. Let's continue with our *what if we manage to gain control of our government again* scenario, and entertain some ideas about how we can kill, and then Shire-ize corporations. What would that look like? The following are some criteria that we Hobbits might use to judge the continuation of corporate charters in the New Shire, and some basic laws and tools to keep them in check.

## Is it Useful? Is it Fair? Is it Safe?

The main criteria by which to judge all corporations would be whether what they produce actually serves the public need, and in a sustainable, fair, safe way. Are they producing something we actually need? or at least want? If not, break them up. If we need the product, then is it produced in a fair way? Are they paying their employees a livable wage? Do their employees have a stake in the company? Do they have a vote on company policy an direction? If not, break them up. Are their products safe for us, for the environment, for the future of our existence on this planet? If not, or if there is any real doubt, break them up. We do not need corporations that continue to pollute our Earth, enslave and exploit workers, and produce crappy trinkets of no real value. Break them up.

## Saruman, Pay Your Damned Taxes!

Corporations should be taxed at the highest rate on all profits, a rate to be determined by democratic vote. I'm thinking something like 90%. It used to be this high in the U.S., and when it was we built amazing infrastructure and experienced a great deal of economic prosperity, rising wages and quality of life. Deductions should be standard and include actual costs of doing business expenses, not *jet-setting* around the globe in private planes or taking million dollar lunches. Corporations have been dodging taxes all around the world for decades. That money is trickling to the top, and leaving the rest of us scrambling to survive. It's time to pay up. If they won't? Break'em up!

## Keep Accurate Books: Stop Exporting Costs

As we discussed earlier in the book, corporations have been exporting many of the costs of doing business onto the public, the environment, and to other countries. This is unacceptable. All costs must be calculated in the same *book* as the other expenses of doing business. If you can't make the product, or provide the service without damaging the future of the planet, then you can't afford to make the product. Period. If they're caught with cooked books? Break'em up.

## *Day of Judgment* Date

We need to return corporations to their temporary status that they once held. No longer can they continue to exist indefinitely, which leads to domination of markets and corruption of governments around the World. All corporations, those existing and those that develop in the future need an expiration date, a term limit. How long? I think five years is a good term, just off the top of my head, but that can be determined through a democratic process. Whatever the length, I would argue that shorter is better than longer. There should be an option to renew their charter at the end of the term but they would have to make their case to the public, who would then vote on whether it should be extended, and for how long. <u>At no point, should any corporation be given permanent status</u>. This should be written into the constitutions of every country on Earth. [NOTE: In order to put these laws into effect, we would need to redefine the legal term, *corporation*. As I understand it, most businesses these days—even small ones—constitute a *corporation* by law. This would need to change. Small, local businesses—while subject to laws—might not necessarily be considered *corporations*.]

## Subject to Public Scrutiny: Bounders and Watch Dogs

Another check on the power of corporations, one that is already in place and growing in strength, is the public themselves. With the use of an unfettered, open, neutral internet, the public can keep watchful eyes on the doings of corporations as well as government officials and government and non-government agencies. If not for the work of these watch dog groups, much of what I'm writing in this book would not be possible; the information simply would not be available. In the New Shire, this is the job of the Bounders, the deputies of the Shire. But instead of official titles, everyone is deputized to keep an eye on corporations and other institutions of power. Any suspect activity should be brought to the attention of the public, to the attention of the corporation itself, and should be investigated to determine the veracity of the suspicions. If a corporation is found to be in violation of serious laws, their charter should be revoked, and depending on the severity of the crime, appropriate penalties and jail-time should be enforced, including the dissolution of the corporation for a period of time, or permanently if the situation warrants it. With the use of social media we can keep the information flowing in a non-linear way, and balance out any bias in the mainstream media.

## Real News: Dis-*spell*ing Propaganda

While social media is an important tool in keeping the public informed, there is still a role for mass media news. Television, radio, and newspapers are still important sources of condensed news, and they can still function in that capacity in the New Shire, but in order for that to happen we have to clean them up, too, and subject them to the same limitations and decentralization that we did other corporations. As I mentioned in the early sections of the book, in the U.S., six corporations own the majority of media outlets in the country. This has to be broken up, and should never be allowed to incorporate that way again. Such centralization of news only serves one purpose: to allow control of the flow of news and vital information to be concentrated in the hands of the elite. Such a situation is probably the most damaging to any society that aspires to democracy. Democracy cannot exist when information is in the hands of those in control. Local news should return in force but be owned by local companies who are not in any way controlled by corporations of any kind. News should all be open source, though credit and remuneration should be allocated to those who break the stories: the journalists. Censorship of any kind should be abolished; it has no place in a democracy. It is, in fact, the first tool used to gain control of a population because it restricts free speech. Without free speech there can be no freedom.

## They Should Be *Open-Source*

I don't mean, *open for business*, of course, I mean they should be producing open source products. That doesn't mean *free*. Every company has the right to make a fair profit, but we need to end proprietary ownership of products and ideas. No idea is truly novel; they just aren't. The old adage, *nothing new under the sun* is an absolute. The science-guru, Carl Sagan, said, "If you wish to make an apple pie from scratch, you must first invent the universe." All ideas, all products, all services, are derived from something that existed before. The ideas come from infinite directions. Think of all the things you've learned in your life, from your parents, your teachers, your work, your friends, the list goes on. Do they *own* all of those ideas? Do you? No one does. They come spontaneously. That doesn't mean that if you write a song or a book that someone else can just take it, put their name on it, and start collecting royalties; that's theft. But as long as someone gives credit and pays royalties where due, there is no reason why they shouldn't be able to take your song, your book, incorporate the ideas, add them to their own and come up with something new. The same goes for technology and scientific research. Corporations are rapidly usurping what were once Common resources. They have wormed their way into our public universities, taking over research, patenting valuable research for their own gain and supressing research that might undermine their own profitability. This needs to stop. If we hold coroporations to the idea of open source information then the products they make might spark improvements that benefit us all, not just their shareholders.

## Get the Hell Out of Politics!

Citizens United must be repealed, as mentioned already, and elections financed by public money. No private money will be allowed to be spent in the name of a candidate, either directly, or by placing ads. This will remove the main source of corruption from the political arena. And to remove the rest of it, lobbying should be made illegal; it is simply a form of bribery and in many cases it involves *actual* bribery. If companies, organizations, or individuals want to influence politics, they should attend debates, or join in online discussion of the issues, then vote on the issues directly or via proxy representatives as laid out in the section on Liquid Democracy. Money needs to be removed from the system as much as possible.

## International Status?

One of the biggest problems with modern corporations is that they have no boundaries, either legally — they have been nearly impossible to convict or punish — or physically — they stretch around the Earth, toppling and corrupting governments while killing the environment, and the people. Should corporations, even under the limitations put forth here, be allowed to extend their business over borders? Maybe. International commerce isn't necessarily the problem. But if corporations form in one country, then exploit other countries for their resources, they could in theory claim that they were only *following the law* in a country with laws less stringent than in their home country. My thought is this: If a corporation forms in the U.S. under the ideas set forward in this chapter, and then wants to do business in Africa, their practices in Africa should be held to the same standards as they are in the U.S. Bounder-Watchdogs would have to keep an eye on them and their dealings overseas. If they are found to be exploiting another country, their charter should be revoked and the corporation dissolved. The same would go for a corporation from Japan, who wanted to do business in the U.S. or some other country. The home country could revoke their charter for infractions in the U.S. Also, before a corporation could enter as a guest into the U.S., their charter would have to be ratified by the people of the U.S. through a democratic vote and be subject to the same rules as any other corporation.

With these basic laws and practices in place, corporations could make profits, share their wealth with their employees and shareholders, but be limited in both time and legal parameters to prevent them from attempting to dominate the globe. To begin this process, we should start with those corporations that are attempting to dominate the world's food supply. Those that manage to withstand the revolution should be dismantled. Let's break'em up!

# Reclaiming Our Food: the Destruction of Sauron's Seeds

In 2014, GMO manufactuers took a blow from two Shires in the Amerian North West. Josephine and Jackson Counties in Oregon both voted to ban genetically modified crops from the farms in their jurisdiction. They managed this despite the influx of money from corporations like Monsanto. In November of 2014, the island of Maui, Hawaii, which has been overrun with GMO crop testing, accomplished the same thing, though a federal judge might just throw out the law. As I am writing this the entire state of Oregon is waiting with bated breath for the outcome of an initiative to ban GMOs from the state. At the moment, GMO supporters slightly outnumber their Hobbit counterparts, but there are over 13,000 contested votes, and the Hobbits have closed to within 1000 votes of carrying the measure, triggering an official recount. This is a model for how we as Hobbits can take back control of our towns, counties, and cities, by coming together to draft new laws to protect our food supply, as well as to affect other changes. But what needs to happen, once we take back control of our governments is a world-wide ban on genetically engineered seeds and crops until such time that they can be proven to be safe. Along with that ban, we need to ban the use of orcish pesticides like RoundUp, which are designed to kill everything but the GMO crops. They're also designed to kill us. I say *designed*, not *intended*, though I sometimes wonder if the latter isn't more accurate. After we ban GMOs we need to dismantle the corporations who developed these products, permanently.

With corporations reigned in we can finish the job of cleaning up our governments and solving the myriad of other problems that we face. Next we'll look at what Hobbit Justice might look like.

# 45

# THE PAX HOBBITLA: PEACE AND JUSTICE IN THE SHIRE

Black day in July
Black day in July
In the streets of Motor City is a deadly silent sound
And the body of a dead youth lies stretched upon the
ground
Upon the filthy pavement
No reason can be found.

Black day in July
Black day in July
The streets of Motor City now are quiet and serene
But the shapes of gutted buildings
Strike terror to the heart
And you say how did it happen
And you say how did it start
Why can't we all be brothers
Why can't we live in peace
**But the hands of the have-nots**
**Keep falling out of reach.** —Gordon Lightfoot, *Black Day in July*

When a man carries a gun all the time, the respect he thinks he's gettin' might really be *fear*. So I don't carry a gun because I don't want the people of Mayberry to fear a gun. I'd rather they would respect me. —Sheriff Andy Taylor, *The Andy Griffith Show*

## The Mayor of Michel Delving: a New Model for Justice

In the Shire, the nominal ruler was the Mayor of Michel Delving, but that was mostly an honorary title. He served as the master of ceremonies and as the Postmaster for the Shire. He had like four deputies, called Bounders, one for each Farthing. Their duty was to keep the law. In reality, most of their time was spent rounding up cows, goats, and sheep that had wandered out of broken fences. Crime was basically unheard of, until Saruman came to town that is.

My favorite law man, of all time, was the Sheriff of Mayberry, N.C., Andy Taylor, played by Andy Griffith. I actually met Mr. Griffith many years ago, okay, 3 decades and a half ago. Maybe I'll tell that story some other time, on my blog or something, but here I'll just say that he was the most down-to-Earth guy you'll ever meet. Nothing like you would expect from most TV or movie stars. When I met him, I was twelve years old. He was shirtless, and spent an entire afternoon helping my dad, and a group of us load stuff from his five car garage into a moving truck to donate it to the Salvation Army. Such was my brush with fame. I've never forgotten it. But I was in awe, not so much from my encounter with the actor, as with the character he played on TV. Sherrif Andy Taylor was, I think, the model for leadership: then and now. Yeah, there was a mayor of Mayberry, but everyone knew that Andy was the real leader of the community. Andy had an innate ability to see through the facades that people put up, a Solomonic wisdom that ecshewed the *book* in favor of the *spirit* of the law. He was fair, he was compassionate, he was honest, but when needed, he could bring justice down upon the wicked swiftly. The world today needs leaders like this.

I still have a great deal of respect for the job of the policeman. It's not a job I would want. The stress is high, the pay not that great, and the image is suffering. Thanks to the ramping up of Fear, the police forces of the world are slipping out of control. Violence perpetrated *on* police officers, and *by* police seems to be on the rise. There are many factors involved, but the nexus of racism and the militarization of American law enforcement agencies seems to be fueling an increasing cyclone of Fear that's spiraling out of control. Why do police forces need tanks, automatic weapons, tasers, tear gas? Did you know that tear gas is included in the United Nations' list of banned chemical warfare weapons? Yeah, it is. It's basically a war crime for any government in the world to use it as a weapon of war, but the U.S. government uses it all the time, on its own *free* citizens. Is our government at war with us? It seems so. Are we free? It seems not. Whatever happened to *protect and serve*? That used to be painted on the side of every police car in the U.S. That doesn't mean they always lived up to that slogan, far from it, but at least they *aspired* to it enough to put it on their cars. I suspect that most police officers still aspire to that code, but the job is getting tougher.

Why is this happening? There are lots of reasons, but the excuse goes back to 9/11, and the government's response to the *new* threat of terrorism. After the attacks of that September, the U.S. government started allocating military equipment to local police forces, and that trend continues, even under the nominally liberal president, Barack Obama. This massive influx of war gear seems to have gone to the head of many police chiefs and their officers. The problem with a lot of this gear is that the officers aren't receiving adequate training in their proper use or safety. I've seen video and still photographs of police in Fergusson, MO. stopping civilians — unarmed civilians mind you — with their assault rifles pointed as if ready to fire. This is bad training — bad training combined with Fear; that's never a good combination. That's how innocent civilians get shot. Even I KNOW that you never pull a gun unless you intend to use it, and you certainly don't AIM it at an unarmed person, or anyone, unless you are ready to pull the trigger. It provokes violence because it further ramps up the Fear. Just stop already. Put your guns down. Take off the helmets. Park your tanks. In fact, take off your guns and leave them at the office, metaphorically if not physically. It's time to stop shooting people, unless they are shooting at *you*.

Andy Taylor never carried a gun. I know, he lived in a fictional town where there was little to no violence, but the lesson is valid. Fear begets Fear; Violence begets more Violence. I'm not saying that police shouldn't carry guns, necessarily, but the rhetoric, the Fear, needs to be turned down, not up. If you want to save the lives of law enforcement officers, let them be who they really are: human beings, Hobbit Bounders, not Stormtroopers or Ringwraiths. In the new Shire we need more Sheriff Taylors, more Mayors of Michel Delving, less S.W.A.T., and *no* Rambos or Terminators.

Now I'm going to address the other responsible party in this ramping up of Fear and Violence: the public. One reason some law enforcement officers wear all that body armor, carry the firepower, and feel that they *need* tanks and teargas, is that they would like to come home at night to eat dinner with their families. Sometimes they don't. Sometimes they sacrifice their lives to keep the rest of us safe. Just recently, not a mile from our home, a local police-officer was shot and killed in a routine traffic stop by a fugitive. Officer Patrick—universally recognized as a good cop—was gunned down before he could even pull his weapon. This happens, more often than it should, which is never. It is this kind of situation that leads to a growing Fear in the minds of law enforcement officers all over the world. If you want the police to do their job of protecting us, then we need to put pressure on our fellow citizens to give up crime, put their weapons down, and take part in a new revolution with us.

## Fewer Laws, Fewer Criminals: Crime & Punishment in the New Shire

As we laid out in Part I, the American justice system is overwhelmed. Prisons are overcrowded, the courts dockets are packed, and everyone in the system, both prisoners and law enforcement personel, are feeling the pressure. Much of this could be relieved with a few small changes in our attitudes towards crime and by taking some of the control out of the hands of private interests.

## Decriminalize Drugs

One of the more controversial solutions to lower crime would be to decriminalize some behaviors that are loading the system unnecessarily. The fastest, and easiest way to do this would be to decriminalize drug *use*. Drug use, like alcoholism—a drug problem, or smoking—another, are health and mental health issues. They cannot be cured by throwing people into prison, nor can the desire to do drugs be hampered in any way, by legality. Drug users and abusers, addicts in other words, simply do not *care* if their habit is illegal. They are addicted; they aren't thinking straight. Drug use has been illegal in the U.S. for a very long time now, long enough to prove that laws do not cure addiction; treatment does. Instead of spending billions of dollars a year to incarcerate and feed *inmates* in prison, why not spend a fraction of that money helping *addicts* to kick their habits and become productive, *employed* members of society again? At the same time we could spend a little of that money educating the public on the true nature of drugs, including those that are *legal*.

## Close the Prisons of Isengard: No More Corporate Prisons

Remember, that one of the corporate take overs still advancing as we speak is the privatization of American prisons. Prisons should be run by the government, not corporations, the same corporations that lobby the government for stricter and broader laws. The proliferation of laws directly correlates to the number of criminals. Every time a law is made, another portion of the public become criminals and subject to being incarcerated in a corporate run prison. This is a serious conflict of interest and it must be stopped. Return the institutions of justice back to the people, the Hobbits, not the Sarumans.

## Racism, Crime, and Punishment

In these prisons the proportion of whites to people of color is grossly out of balance. Why is this? Partly it is the result of a long-standing racial bias that exists in many places in the world. We've already discussed race in brief, and ways that we can all work to open our minds, dispel irrational fears of those of different races, and work to build a Shire together. Always keep in mind the example of Legolas and Gimli, who began as rivals from two different races—at times *enemies*—but who managed to put that aside to work toward the common goal of defeating Sauron and Saruman. In the process of that common struggle they saw through their prejudices, recognized their shared *humanity*—as peace-loving creatures of Middle Earth—and became lasting friends. Keep working to rid yourself of the Fear that leads to racism.

Another reason minorities end up in prisons more often is probably due to the debilitating pressure of poverty in their communities. In areas of lower incomes and lower resources, crime prevails. We all know this. Without access to decent jobs, healthy food, safe neighborhoods, and decent education those who live in depressed conditions often turn to crime as a *way out*. Unfortunately many of them achieve this; they end up in prison, or worse. Many end up in an early grave. If we want to lower the number of people committing crimes and landing in prison we need to build Shires, plant gardens, empower people to take control of their resources, especially food, and we need better education. Most racism is driven by Fear. Much of this Fear is driven by Ignorance. So anything our new Shire governments can do to undermine that nasty tower will go a long way to building peaceful communities. The best place to start that process, is *everywhere*, but it's best to teach it early, and often. Start with the young Hobbits; start in the schools.

# 46

# Ignorant Hobbits, Bad Hobbits: Education Reform in the Shire

Give me a man or woman who has read a thousand
books and you give me an interesting companion.
Give me a man or woman who has read perhaps three
and you give me a very dangerous enemy indeed.
—Anne Rice, *The Witching Hour*

There is a cult of ignorance in the United States, and
there has always been. The strain of anti-
intellectualism has been a constant thread winding its
way through our political and cultural life, nurtured
by the false notion that democracy means that 'my
ignorance is just as good as your knowledge.
—Isaac Asimov

Fighting Ignorance is the most difficult battle of our war of the
Ring. Ignorance is rampant and much of it is of the Willful kind.
Since we've already covered how to tackle it in our own lives,
recognize it in others, and how to deal with that, let's spend a
short space talking about education reform. This is an enormous
topic to put it mildly. There isn't time or space to deal with all

the ins and outs in this book so we're going to focus mostly on higher education, and only briefly with that.

I'm a graduate student, as I've mentioned already. I came to Minnesota in 2007 to pursue a Ph.D. in history. There were or are many problems with that decision but the most poignant one has to do with economics. My pursuit of an advanced college degree seemed to make sense when I originally decided to do it, back in 2004. That's when I went back to school at East Carolina University to finish my bachelor's degree in history, but I already knew that I wanted to continue to get my doctorate. Because I wasn't independently wealthy at the time, or now, I had to take out quite a few loans to finish up my undergraduate degree. I won't say how much, but more than some students and less than others. The debt is enough to buy one hell of a car, but not a particularly nice home, especially not in the Twin Cities. Personally, I don't like to think about it much, though I just got the bill a couple weeks ago for the first time; it was a bit of a shock which required a larger than small dose of bourbon to ease the throbbing in my cranium.

The cost of a college education in the U.S. has skyrocketed in the last 40-50 years. At the same time the pressure to get an undergraduate degree is suffocating and real. Without one, your prospects for livable wages are slim. Even with it, your chances aren't great. But most of us just suck it up, take out the loans and hope for the best. Mostly, we're disappointed. In some cases, that disappointment turns to depression, deep depression. I've been there. Even with a *master's* degree I spent a year in 2012-13 looking for a employment before landing a job paying less than $15 per hour. Of course that's almost twice the minimum wage, which is what most college students can expect to be paid if they take a part-time job while in school. I've seen people, usually my age or older, say uninformed things, like, "When I WAS in school, I worked 170 hours a week — there's only 168 — and walked up hill in the snow both ways to work to pay for MY education!" you know, the ole *bootstrap* argument. My bullshit meter goes off every time I hear this and then I blow a mental gasket. It takes all my Hobbity, Taoist restraint not to go all Gimli on them! Arrrrrgh!

First off, these old geezers — and I'm just as old as they are — have no clue what college costs these days. Most of them are single, or married with no college-age children and have had their heads buried up their collective asses for the last 30 years or more. Back in the 60s and 70s, you could work about seven weeks a year, at minimum wage, and pay for your tuition to college: 7 WEEKS! <u>The figure is closer to 50 weeks now</u>, and that's just for the tuition! That doesn't include books, food, lodging, transportation, clothing, you know, the luxuries in life. The cost of college in the U.S. has gone up drastically since the 60s. Hell, just since 2000 the cost of public college tuition and fees — don't forget the fees — has jumped over 30%! The rise is well above the cost of living increase or even the rate of inflation! And we're expecting our youngest and brightest kids to shoulder this enormous debt when they haven't even secured a job? It's insane. And stupid. The cost of education is out of control, and if it is not reigned in soon we're going to have a disaster on our hands. It might already be too late to avert it. The student loan debt in the U.S. is so enormous — 1.2 Trillion Dollars — that it's hard to fathom how those students are ever going to repay it, especially since the job market is so bad. But how can we fix this?

## Loan Forgiveness: an Investment in the Future of the Planet

A handful of representatives at the federal level have proposed that we bail out our students, instead of the banks, and corporations that have put us into the financial situation we find ourselves. Obviously this has gone nowhere. When that suggestion was shot down, Elizabeth Warren and Bernie Sanders proposed that we extend the ridiculous interest rates that the banks get from the government when they borrow money — which is under 1%, by the way — to student loans. Student loan interest rates are much higher, and they aren't afforded the option to wipe those loans out through bankruptcy. If you owe a student loan and work for peanuts for a corporation, there is NO WAY for you ever get out of that loan. You're screwed. However, if the billion dollar corporation you work for gets into financial doo doo, they can file for bankruptcy, cancel their debt — all of it — and walk away. Many times they remain in business! We loaned out over 29 Trillion Dollars—more than twice our GDP—bailing out the banks in 2008, but the students? the homeowners? "Sorry, pay up, or move out!" So for the moment you can forget about real reform from the top. Those institutions are too entrenched in our political system to ever allow such a thing. We will have to remove them from the loop before real reform can come, but let's suppose--for argument's sake—that we had already cleaned up our government, and removed the influence of corporate money from the formula. What then?

## Shire Jubilee! Clean Slate Time

Then we could, and should, cancel all student loans, both federal and private. "Sorry banks, you had your chance and you screwed us all. Pay up, or move out!"

"But we can't do THAT!" someone will say, lots of someones, "The banks will fail, and the economy will crash with them!" If they do, good. But I don't think the economy will do any such thing. Why? Because that debt, owed by ordinary citizens is depressing the economy in ways that hasn't been truly discussed, not in the media anyway. Let's say you have a large student loan and your payment is three to four hundred dollars a month—which is not uncommon. What could you do with that extra money every month? Eat real food? Go out to eat? Purchase a fuel efficient or electric car? Install solar panels on your house? Build a garden, a greenhouse, or make a large donation to your local neighborhood charity? Actually live without incurring more debt—usually via credit cards—just to cover the essentials? How about all of that? How do you think that would affect the economy? Can we do it? Yes, and there's historical and legal precedent for doing it. Cancelling debt was a common thing in ancient cultures. Read your Bible, the Old Testament. Every 50 years the Hebrews would declare a Jubilee, a year in which all debts were cancelled. Big parties were thrown, people danced in the streets, sang songs. Sounds like a good idea to me.

The problem with *trickle-down* economics—which I used to think was a logical idea—is that the wealth never actually trickles down, it *runs* up! Up to the top, where it stays. I've not seen any of it trickle MY WAY, have you? And I've been waiting for 34 years, since ole Ronnie took office in 1981. It hasn't happened. And if it hasn't, it's not going to. It doesn't work that way. The point here is, if we can give 29 Trillion to the criminally run banks, to bail them out after crashing the economy we can afford to take that back from them in the form of debt cancellation on student debts. There's no difference between the two, except the second option would be way cheaper and actually help real, average Americans who *need* it, not fat-cat bankers who don't, and don't deserve bail outs and bonuses for cheating us into a depression. Yeah, I said *depression*, because that's what it is. *Recession* is a bullshit term invented by bankers to keep us from throwing them out of windows onto the pavement of Wall Street. It worked, last time. The next time it crashes? And it will. I wouldn't lay a plugged nickel on a banker in *that* race.

**Free Education: a Real Investment**

While we're at it, let's eliminate the need for student loans to begin with; let's make higher education, public universities, free for our citizens. "No way! How can we afford that?!" you ask. Well, let's ask Denmark, or Germany, or a host of other countries around the world who have already done it, some of them a long time ago. By the way, all of these countries are ahead of us economically, if you measure the right things and I'm not talking about GDP, which is outdated and only measures *profit*, not *value*, which we've already discussed. The standard of living in Scandinavia and Germany is significantly higher than the U.S., and a big part of that is their investment in the future of their citizens through education and other ways, like health care. More on that later.

If we, in the U.S., and other places that have similar problems with public higher education, want to compete— *contribute* might be a better word—in the future of the planet in a real way, then we need people with great educations who aren't saddled with oppressive debt as soon as they enter the job market. The average American graduate these days is so in debt by the time they reach the market that they can barely survive on the wages they can expect to find at an entry level position, and that's *IF* they find a job at all. So many of them end up back in minimum wage jobs like flipping burgers at McDonald's or wading through hot grease at Burger King in their holey tennis shoes. Of course, at the time, I had not finished college but I know plenty of people now that are stuck in low-paying jobs with degrees hanging on their mold-infested apartment wall. It's a sad statement for the *most powerful country in the world.* And it's not acceptable. Let's put our money where our mouth is; let's *invest* in the future by investing in the education of our youth and the re-education of those who need it and *aren't* so young anymore. It's **not** *charity*; it's an investment in the mental, intellectual, and social infrastructure of our country and our planet. Charity is something you give to corporations when they commit crimes of fraud and plunge the world into economic turmoil. I say we put an end to charity and start investing in what matters, the minds of our future leaders. But let's not forget to also invest in their bodies. Because an unhealthy body is unable to sustain a healthy mind or to learn anything. And that brings us to the next major issue we need to work on in the New Shire: health care.

# 47

# HANDS OF THE KING: REBUILDING THE HOUSES OF HEALING

"Awake, Éowyn, Lady of Rohan!" said Aragorn again, and he took her right hand in his and felt it warm with life returning. "Awake! The shadow is gone and all darkness is washed clean!" Then he laid her hand in Éomer's and stepped away. "Call her!" he said, and he passed silently from the chamber.

"Éowyn, Éowyn!" cried Éomer amid his tears. But she opened her eyes and said: Éomer! What joy is this? For they said that you were slain. Nay, but that was only the dark voices in my dream." —*LOTR*: III, *The Houses of Healing*

New Rule: Not everything in America has to make a profit. If conservatives get to call universal health care "socialized medicine," I get to call private, for-profit health care "soulless vampire bastards making money off human pain." Now, I know what you're thinking: "But, Bill, the profit motive is what sustains capitalism." Yes, and our sex drive is what sustains the human species, but we don't try to fuck everything. — Bill Maher, *The New New Rules: A Funny Look At How Everybody But Me Has Their Head Up Their Ass*

This will be a very short chapter, for two reasons. One, we've already discussed the major issues facing health care in the U.S., and two, the topic is entirely too large to do justice to it in a chapter, indeed, in an entire book. And there's a third reason: I'm not qualified to solve the problems of the the health care system, either in the U.S. or anywhere else. Of course, many critics will probably claim I'm not qualified to speak on *any* of the topics in this book — I won't argue with them too much — but that hasn't stopped me so far, so why now. That being said, I'll look at a couple of the key problems and offer some suggestions to discuss once we've cleaned up the Shire and kicked the Sarumans out on their asses. Quite frankly, when we do *that* a great deal of the problems with our health care system will probably resolve themselves. That's because the biggest issue, especially in the United States, is that we're all eating unhealthy, chemical-laden food. That we have discussed at great length so we'll move on to the health care system itself and some possible solutions to the remaining problems. We'll return to food in the next chapter, briefly.

## So Long to Saruman's Snake Oil: Removing Greed from Health Care

As mentioned earlier, the biggest problem with health care in America, and other places, is that it has become a *for profit* business. Since *profit* and *value* aren't the same thing we can never be sure that we'll get the latter, if the provider of the service — in this case, health care — is mostly concerned with increasing the former. Health care in the U.S. has been slowly usurped by private companies for decades while the cost of that care has steadily risen. One of the issues not fully addressed by President Obama's Affordable Heath Care Act was the *cost* of health care. While the idea of giving universal health care to those who cannot afford insurance is a noble goal, the cost of that care makes it nearly impossible to finance such a goal. Until health care is seen as a *right* of citizenship or a *human right*, then we are not going to solve this problem. Everyone who is a citizen of a country—especially one as rich as the U.S.—should have basic health care. It's simply not fair that reliable and preventative health care should only be available to those who can afford to pay for it. We are punishing those at the bottom who are mostly there because the elite of the world refuse to pay their fair share of the burden. What we need is *public* health care; and we *CAN* do it.

"But why would anyone be a doctor in a publicly owned system?" you ask, "They won't be able to pay off their medical school debt if they're working for less money in a public system!" Ah ha! Now we're getting somewhere. That problem is already solved! Remember in the last chapter when we made public education free and forgave all the student loans? Now those bright high school students who want to become doctors—for the right reasons—can do so, and not have to worry about going into debt the rest of their lives to do it! And those current doctors suffering from crushing debt will get some relief. Yes, doctors salaries will probably come down in a public health system, maybe, but if you don't have that debt hanging over you, you can afford to take less pay. And with a public system of universal health care we can also eliminate another Sarumanic institution: Health Insurance Companies.

As we've discussed, health insurance companies have wormed their way into our system to the point where they are really calling all the shots about what care you get, what drugs are prescribed—translate: over-prescribed—what tests your doctor can run, what treatments are available, who bills you, how much they bill you and your *provider* and a host of other Sarumanic practices. No more! Once we uncorrupt the political system we can *actually* vote on what kind of health care system we want, and I would argue that health care should be extended to all citizens, at the very minimum, if not to all legal residents of the country. And I did say *legal*. People who are not legally residing in a country should not be given the same rights as those who played by the rules. To do that only encourages others to break the rules. What the rules *are* would be up to us to vote on, of course! We can debate those and come up with a consensus with our new *liquid* democratic system.

Of course the best solution to solving many of our health issues is to clean up the environment we live in, starting with our food. But since we've already discussed that at length, we can now look at the ways in which technology might come to our aid. It's time now for some New Wizardry. It's time for science to do what it's supposed to do: work *for* us, not *kill* us.

# 48

# NEW WIZARDRY: SCIENCE, TECHNOLOGY, AND SAVING THE PLANET

> When maybe a thousand years had passed, and the first shadow had fallen on Greenwood the Great, the *Istari* or Wizards appeared in Middle-earth. It was afterwards said that they...were messengers sent to contest the power of Sauron, and to unite all those who had the will to resist him; but they were *forbidden to match his power with power*, or to seek to dominate Elves or Men by *force and fear*. [italics and bold, mine]
> —*LOTR: Appendix B, The Third Age*

> Science cuts two ways, of course; its products can be used for both good and evil. But there's no turning back from science. The early warnings about technological dangers also come from science.
> —Carl Sagan, *Pale Blue Dot: A Vision of the Human Future in Space*

We've examined some of the ways that modern Hobbits can solve some of the biggest, social, economic, and political problems we face. But some of the biggest issues or looming disasters are ecological and environmental. The biggest problem is the effect of Climate Change on our future survival. As we've already discussed, rising temperatures due to greenhouse gasses are changing the global climate, speeding up a natural process. If we want to survive as a species we need to come together and make some major changes to the way we live and the way we think about the environment. First, of course, we have to destroy our Ring; we must stop acting as if the Earth belongs to us. That is key. Then we can look at the ways we have damaged our Earth and stop doing that. Once we've stopped doing harm we can try to clean up and reverse some of the damage already done. To do that, we need wizards; we need new scientists and new science, new magic if you will. Many people today are making the mistake of putting technology and science ahead of the philosophical and social changes. That's unfortunate because a lot of the problems we face in the modern world are a product of doing just that. We discover new technology or science and immediately try to apply it to solve problems, without a full understanding of the ramifications or dangers of those new developments. Think of some of the major breakthroughs in modern science: steam engines, fossil fuels, electric light, firearms, automobiles, aircraft, nuclear weapons, biological and chemical weapons, plastics, and GMOs. Have some of those technologies given us positive advancements? Yes, of course they have. Others? Not so much. But all of them have also given us a planet overwhelmed with pollution. We seem to be serving science, these days, instead of the other way around. Science and technology are supposed to serve *us*. We need to turn that around again and put it back to work cleaning up the messes we've made. Like the wizards in Middle Earth, science should not employ force and fear to dominate us. Nor should scien*tists* allow themselves to be coerced into doing damage in the name of *power*.

Luckily there are a lot of new discoveries, new wizardry going on every day that promises to help us undo the dark *shadows* that have fallen over our Earth. New developments in energy production, water conservation, pollution control, and communications may allow us to reverse much of the damage we have done. This section could be an entire book. It's not. You're welcome. But we should take a brief look at some of these new wizards and their wizardry.

# Shire Power: Energy Solutions for the Shire Age

Did you know that enough sunlight falls in *one day* to power the Earth for an entire *year*? One of the first problems that our new wizards need to work on is our addiction to fossil fuels. There are viable alternatives out there already including solar and wind generated power. The problem, of course, is breaking our addiction to fossil fuels and making the transition, which includes spending money on new infrastructure.

Once we regain control of our governments, we can divert money and resources that would have otherwise been wasted on wars—on foreign and domestic enemies, as well as on mental disorders like drug addiction—to solving our energy crisis. Even before we retake control, we can work towards this goal. There are scientists and lay-people doing just that. The Solutions Project is a collective of Hollywood actors, scientists, and others that are pushing for 100% renewable energy in the U.S. All Hobbits should join this movement and support it in any way we can. The future of the Earth depends on alternative sources of power. Fossil fuels are the major contributor to climate change, and the pollution of our air, water and soil. And in the U.S. we would only need about 1% of the land space to capture enough solar energy to power the country for a year, and since the technology is rapidly advancing, pretty soon we won't need a fraction of that. Wind power could make up the slack in those areas, like where I live, where the sun is more *prodigal* than *present*. We certainly have enough North-wind in Minnesota to keep the lights on for eternity.

While the U.S. is still addicted to fossil fuels to run its cars and light its homes other countries are finding more sustainable alternatives. One of the leading countries is Germany. They have a written plan to eliminate all of its nuclear power plants by 2022 and replace them with solar power. If Germany can do it certainly the world's richest country can do it. There is enough sunlight in the southern and south western sections of the U.S. to power most of the country, if not all of it. Germany should be commended for taking the lead on alternative power! We do not have to continue to burn fossil fuels indefinitely.

The fossil fuel industry and their supporters—so-called scientists—like to point out the downsides of solar and wind, like the lack of rare-earth minerals needed for the former, and other materials needed for the latter, but this is all just *warm rain* running down our backs with a distinct ammonia odor. There are new technologies for solar being developed as we speak that greatly increase their collection power and reduce their reliance on rare materials. Some of these are up to 100 times as efficient as the ones currently in use. Storing that energy is still an issue, but there are scientist working on new break-throughs on that, too. As for wind, yes, a giant windmill does require a great deal of materials. But so does an oil rig in the Gulf of Mexico. It, or one of its thousands of cousins will spill millions of gallons of oil into our oceans, not to mention the leaks and spills that pipelines and train derailments will add to that total. It's past time for those of us in the Western world to wake up and clean up. Just say no to the fossil fuel industry! Join the Shire and demand alternatives! When we do that we will really be able to clean up all the mess we've made.

# Wizards of Anti-Pollution

Not only are a new breed of wizard-scientists finding innovative ways to power our World, they're also discovering ways to use Nature to clean up the pollution we've strewn all over the planet.

### Making Sauron's Poop Go '*Poof*'!

One of the most promising innovations in the works is by Paul Stamets, a biologist working with mushrooms. If there is a candidate for the title of Radagast, it's Stamets. Hobbits should love his innovations for a couple of reasons. First off, is there anything more Hobbity than mushrooms? Second, mushrooms might prove to be one of the best solutions to clean up the mess that fossil fuels are doing to our planet. Stamets has discovered that a certain strain of mycelium, or mushroom, can actually eat oil and other pollution! I don't mean they just absorb them, which would be helpful in and of itself. No, I mean they actually absorb, then *break down* oil and gas spills and turn them into carbohydrates! If you want to know more about this, and I suggest you do read more about it, you should watch Stamet's TED talk video or read about it HERE. He has also developed a mushroom 'sandbag', essentially a sandbag with soil and mushrooms in it, that can be placed down hill from chemical or industrial runoff to capture pollution before it makes it into our streams and rivers. The vision is to use these worldwide, anywhere where this is toxic runoff water to clean up our water supply before it makes its way to the sea. The ramifications are very promising and Stamets isn't the only wizard working with mushrooms to solve pollution problems.

Students at Yale are currently testing another strain of mycelium that might be able to eat *plastic*! Yes, that's what I said, eat plastic. It is still early, I think, to tell if this one will work as they hope but initial experiments look promising. If it works out the way they hope, they will have a strain of mushroom that can actually *decompose* plastic much like the other strain that breaks down oil/gas into carbohydrates. Read about it for yourself or watch this short video on it. Can you imagine the possibilities for cleaning up our planet if they do figure this one out? All the plastic sitting in landfills could be eliminated, forever. Now that is real wizardry!

And in the meantime, two high school girls, Miranda Wang and Jeanny Yao—working on a project for science class—have discovered a way to break down phthalates— one of the most toxic chemicals in most plastics. These little Hobbit-Wizard heroes demonstrate again, that age and size have nothing to do with the ability to save the Earth; anyone can do it if they set their minds to the task. Of course, a lot of our plastic doesn't end up in landfills; it ends up in our oceans, like Boromir's boat. How on Earth will we ever clean all THAT up?

### Get That Milk Jug Out of My Ocean!

Hang on Denethor. There's a solution to that, too! Two years ago Boyan Slat, a 17 year old high-school student from the Netherlands, was swimming in the Mediterranean. He was astonished to discover so much plastic debris floating around and thought, "Why can't we clean this up?" Why not indeed! So he went back home and got to work designing a solution to clean up all the plastic crap in the world's oceans, as a science project for school. His design is nothing short of wizardry, a masterpiece that even old Gandalf would be proud of. Basically, he drew up a plan for a stationary tower linked to the ocean's floor, with flexible arms extending outwards around it that can trap floating plastic debris and funnel it into one area where a conveyor belt thingy can pick it up and deposit it all into a huge tank which can then be picked up periodically by ship and taken off to be recycled. He's even discovered a way to recycle much of it back into oil! He was planning on going to college this year, but he has put that on hold so he can Save the Earth—my words, but it's true. In the summer of 2014 he raised over two million dollars to build the first prototypes! If you'd like to read more about it check out his website and become part of the solution! You can still donate to the project. If his idea works then we can begin the process of cleaning up our oceans and with the help of plastic eating mushrooms, we can dispose of this plastic once and for all. Now you're probably thinking, "Yeah, but we keep making plastic by the tons every day! Is there a substitute?" Why yes, there is.

**No More Plastic! No More Plastic!**

It turns out that mushrooms are also a good alternative for plastic, especially when it comes to replacing styrofoam packing materials! A couple of young scientists, Eben Bayer and Gavin McIntyre, have invented a way to grow mushrooms into any shape including packing materials, to replace styrofoam. These can be produced on any scale, anywhere, and the best thing of all, is when they are done doing their job of protecting your, hopefully, non-plastic dinnerware you can just throw them into your compost pile in the backyard and they will break down into soil! How awesome is that? Pretty darned awesome, I think! Check out there company, Evocative Design, especially if your business is looking for alternatives to styrofoam packaging. But of course, packaging is only one plastic problem. There is the problem of all the other stuff made of plastic. "What do we do about that?" you ask. Yep, you guessed it, there's a solution for that one too.

Other scientists have recently come up with ways of replacing plastic goods all together. Turns out that you can make a durable poly material with cellulose! No, not cellulite. That would truly be a blessing for us all. But no, I said cellu*lose*, i.e. the membrane that exists around every plant cell on earth. These wizards, Robert Bramsteidl, Martin Ernegg, Horst Dodfner, and their company, Zeoform, have come up with a way to make durable products—dinnerware, toothbrushes, chairs, pretty much anything you can imagine currently made with plastic—and they're doing it with plant cells, not petroleum! So when this stuff finally breaks it can be decomposed instead of floating around in our oceans or filling up landfills. While reducing our dependence on more and more stuff is a better solution in the long run, it is good to know that there are wizards finding new ways, and more sustainable ways to make the things we need and want, without polluting the earth, air, and water.

## Water, Water Everywhere

> Water, water, every where,
> And all the boards did shrink;
> Water, water, every where,
> Nor any drop to drink. —Samuel Taylor Coleridge,
> *Rhyme of the Ancient Mariner*

As we've discovered, our fresh water supply is dwindling due to overuse and pollution. Demand will only increase. We need to clean up and conserve the water we have. And find ways to desalinate ocean water to keep up with the increased demands of the World's population. We've already discussed at some length how to conserve what we have and how to stop the pollution. But there are new innovations out there for desalination that look promising. The biggest stumbling block to overcome is the fact that the process requires a lot of energy, heat energy. Right now the cheapest way to generate that kind of heat is through burning fossil fuels, which is obviously not a sustainable method. But pretty soon, solar power should be able to do the job at a mere fraction of the cost and in a much more sustainable way. That will be a major breakthrough for sure. We also need to expand well-drilling in Third World countries where safe water supply is a life-threatening problem. As part of a plan to break up Sarumanic corporations, we need to dissolve the ones consuming the water resources—like Nestle—who are attempting to privatize our water supply. The water should be returned to the Commons, to be distributed by local democratic institutions, not exploited by centralized corporate asshats.

## Raising Beef and Curing Desertification?

We talked about Smaug's desolation and desertification in Part I. I'm not an expert on this subject, or on many of the subjects in the book but Allan Savory is an expert on this particular subject, and I think he's on to something that might just be the cure. Savory, who has spent decades researching the topic, world-wide, argues that what is killing the grasslands and leading to desertification is not *overgrazing* of livestock, which has been the theory for ages but is, in fact, the *under-grazing* by the large herds of wild animals who once roamed the savannas of the world. I'm going to try to boil this down to it's basics, for space reasons. If you want more, please read his book, *The Grazing Revolution: A Radical Plan to Save the Earth*. Basically, large herds would wander around grazing on the grass, tramping it down while crapping and pissing all over it. This creates a natural fertilizer and mulch, much like you would put in your garden. This mulch, and the subsequent rainy season would help to soak up rain and hold it on the land, instead of allowing it to run quickly off into the creeks and rivers. The dead grasses would rot, fuel the soil, and reseed it, which would come back every year. But the herds aren't there any more. Neither are the predators that used to keep them in large herds. And the grasslands are dying, or dead.

But Savory has discovered, and tested on millions of acres around the globe, a process of introducing livestock—cattle, goats, sheep—to these areas, keeping them in large, packed herds, and moving them around on a precise schedule to mimic the natural movements of wild herds. Basically humans take the place of the predators and keep the herds from overgrazing any one spot. What he has accomplished with this method is astonishing. Unfortunately, naysayers and anti-carnivores have attempted to debunk his theories by requiring him to replicate his results as if one plot of land is the same as another. In defense, Savory argues that because every spot is different, you have to adapt the plan for the particular conditions. It's not like a chemical experiment under lab conditions. There are no lab conditions on a grassland, or anywhere in nature. Nature doesn't work that way; it's a system — more like a garden — not a machine. I will just say this in his defense. The only thing we need to know about his theory and method is *if it in fact works*! That is easy enough to test. You give him a plot of desert land, and let him do his thing. If he's able to restore grass to it, then it works; if he can't, then it doesn't. Who cares about the minutia of *why*? Sure, it might be interesting to know how and why it works, but in Nature there are too many uncontrolled variables, and you can't have a scientific experiment if there are more than ONE. In Nature, there are infinite variables that you cannot control, let alone fathom.

If Savory's method works, we could knock out at least three major problems facing the Earth today: food shortage, water supply, and climate change. Millions of acres of reclaimed desert — feeding livestock — could feed billions of people. Grasslands keep fresh water in the soil, and return it to the atmosphere instead of allowing it to run off into rivers and oceans where it becomes salt water. Those same grasslands also store carbon in the plants and in the soil, instead of allowing it to escape into the atmosphere where it contributes to global warming. Bare soil also increases ambient temperature in a desert, which heats up the air, and the Earth. Grasslands are cooler than deserts, which also helps to bring down warming. The logic is solid. We need to give the man a chance to test it on a much larger scale. If we don't, we might one day wish we had.

But whatever you do, don't despair and set yourself on fire in your family tomb. There be wizards at work out there! Just like those four little Hobbits had mighty Gandalf fighting for them and alongside them, we have scientists at work trying to solve the world's problems. Are some of their ideas radical? Yeah, they are. But so are the dangers we face. Gandalf's idea was to send the Ring to the heart of Mordor suspended from the pale neck of a tiny Hobbit. It was a fool's errand, possibly, but it was the only option left that offered a final end to the evils of Sauron. As Gandalf said as he advised Aragorn, Eomer, and the brave defenders in the clearing smoke of the Battle of the Pelennor, to march to what seemed certain death at the Black Gates of Mordor:

Concerning this thing [the One Ring], my lords, you know all know enough for the understanding of our plight, and of Sauron's. If he regains it, your valour is vain, and his victory will be swift and complete: so complete that none can foresee the end of it while this world lasts. If it is destroyed, then he will fall; and his fall will be so low that none can foresee his arising ever again. For he will lose the best part of the strength that was native to him in his beginning, and all that was made or begun with that power will crumble, and he will be maimed for ever, becoming a mere spirit of malice that gnaws itself in the shadows, but cannot again grow or take shape. And so a great evil of this world will be removed.

Other evils there are that may come; for Sauron is himself but a servant or emissary. Yet it is *not our part to master all the tides of the world, but to do what is in us for the succour of those years wherein we are set*, uprooting the evil in the fields that we know, so that those who live after may have clean earth to till. What weather they shall have is not ours to rule. — *LOTR: III, The Last Debate*

We know that their attack on the Black Gates was not in vain. It allowed Frodo and Sam to cross Mordor more-or-less unheeded, and to reach the fiery mountain while the Dark Lord's gaze fixed on their friends and allies. So it is with our plight. Unless we try some radical ideas, the population of the Earth is going to suffer increasing deprivations and possibly the collapse of civilization. At the root of all these problems is one thing: our Ring, the mistaken and misbegotten belief that we are the rulers of the Earth, and that it is a resource to use and abuse as we will. It is this mentality that has allowed us to spread our species all over the planet, consuming everything in our path. Our population is out of control. We need to destroy the Ring and then figure out how to lighten our load on the planet.

# 49

# GLOBAL POPULATION IN THE NEW SHIRE

There's nothing fundamentally wrong with people. Given a story to enact that puts them in accord with the world, they will live in accord with the world. But given a story to enact that puts them at odds with the world, as yours does, they will live at odds with the world. Given a story to enact in which they are the lords of the world, they will ACT like lords of the world. And, given a story to enact in which the world is a foe to be conquered, they will conquer it like a foe, and one day, inevitably, their foe will lie bleeding to death at their feet, as the world is now. —Daniel Quinn, *Ishmael: An Adventure of the Mind and Spirit*

And now I return to where I began so many months ago, with the issues that set me off on this amazing journey and produced this book you have slogged through. We have travelled *there and back again*. Thank you, by the way, for sticking with me through it. What was first intended to be a *little* book about *saving the Earth* turned into a manifesto, and a long one at that. As I mentioned in Part II, this book began with the reading of Dan Brown's *Inferno*. The basic premise of that book had to do with this very same topic: over-population. The antagonist, a micro-biologist named Bertrand Zobrist, like a dark wizard, came up with a solution to the problem if a rather arbitrarily applied one. I will warn you that I'm about to tell you the plot and end of the story. Mr. Zobrist developed a biological solution to the problem, and it's not what you think. It was not a Stephen King, *Stand*-like super flu to kill off 98% of all humans. Instead, he developed a vector virus that rendered one third of all the Earth's population, infertile. While the solution is a bit radical, if somewhat humane, the implications could be sinister if such a technology got into the hands of those with less philanthropic tendencies. In other words, these new viruses could be employed to kill, not just curb, population. So, that's probably not the solution to our problem. But what is? Well, the answer to that is not so simple.

Of all the subjects that Daniel Quinn tried to tackle, this is the one that got him into more controversy than any. It's a tough topic, for sure. How many times—and be honest with yourself, no one's listening to your thoughts—have you said, either to yourself or out loud, "There's just too many people living on the Earth!"? Maybe you're one of those saintly people who never think such things, or it just hasn't occurred to you that human population is exploding geometrically every year. As we discussed, we are expected to reach 9 to 10 Billion by 2050 and that is a conservative number; it could be much higher. We are already at 7 Billion. The Earth will not support that number for long and that's if we all don't lose our happy-helmets and kill each other off before then.

I used to argue—usually at a party with a beer in my hand—that the Earth's human population was just the macrocosm of a cocktail party at someone's house, ok, it's probably more like a *kegger* at a frat house on a Saturday night. If you have 10 or 15 frat brothers hanging out drinking beer, they will probably get along fairly well even after several keg stands and beer bongs. If you jack that number up to around 50, there will be some kind of argument during the night. It might not lead to blows but a couple of drunk guys will argue about something. If you push it to 100 or more, you can bet yer damned life there will be a fight before the nights over with. I mean a fists flying, blood sprayin', shirt tearin' fight! Outside the frat house, in the larger world, it's really not much different. Too many people in too little space means that violence will break out. If it were just violence that were the problem, we might be ok, but it's not.

As mentioned in the first part of the book, each person on the planet represents transformed biomass; people are made of food and water, nothing else. In order to make them, their parents must eat. In order for a child to survive, she must eat. I know, it sounds dumb to say it out loud but I never really thought about it that way. There is no new biomass on Earth. We do not create new biomass; the system is essentially closed. Yes, we can grow more crops, which looks like more biomass. But where do we grow them? We grow them on land that once held other types of biomass: trees, grasses, swamp plants, etc. So we exchange those things for corn, soybeans, potatoes, cows, and the other things we humans like to eat. For every crop or cow we grow, some other species must be pushed aside or destroyed to make room. For every person that's born, something else must die. It's the *circle of life* if you will—cue Elton John again. How many more species of plants and animals will we consume in the goal of *more people*?

In LOTR, the only parallel to over-population is really the propagation of orcs by Sauron and especially Saruman, who was breeding his new GMO strain, the Uruk-Hai. Just like *Takers*, the orcs of Middle Earth were increasing daily, it seems, intent on consuming everything in sight. We must not be orcs. We must find a solution to this problem and stop thinking that it will go away if we refuse to look at it. It will not. Once we regain control of our political institutions through our peaceful Hobbit revolution, we can then have a serious discussion about many things. But near the top of the list needs to be population. The following are some ideas that we could consider.

## Possible Solutions to Over-Population

### More Education, and *Leaver* Mindset

First we have to destroy and forget our Ring. The last thing we need are more *Takers*. That mentality is what got us here, on the brink of disaster. The earth simply won't support that kind of mind set. There is a direct correlation between education and lower birth rates especially in countries where girls and women are more educated. This is perfectly logical. Women who know more about their reproductive health and family planning and who are given the freedom and sovereignty over their own bodies tend to have fewer children. One of the greatest things we can do as a species of Hobbits is to work to improve the status, education, and health of women, worldwide. First off, it's the right thing to do. It's time to end the outdated mindset of male superiority and the subjugation of women. Only weak men need to dominate women, or for that matter, dominate anyone or anything! It is simply unacceptable behavior for civilized men. In places where this behavior is rampant the spotlight should be trained until the perpetrators hang their heads in shame, renounce their insanity and put women in the position they should have always been: as equals.

## Birth Control is Not Really the Solution

In order for birth control to work, it would have to be mandatory in Third World countries, as well as the rest of the planet and that would require coercion which isn't right or Hobbity. Also, it doesn't work. China, a country with well over a seventh of the World's population have employed Draconian tactics for decades, with little success. Birth control can help but only if girls and women are educated and free to make those kinds of choices. A more effective strategy for the Third World would be to eliminate poverty.

## Kill Poverty, Not the Poor

Poverty is a major issue when it comes to population, even if that seems counter intuitive. Developed, modern countries have lower birth rates than those that are poor and undeveloped. This might seem illogical since you need food to make people. But it's true, nonetheless. In the Third World, where poverty is ubiquitous, children are seen as assets, and they are. They perform many tasks and are a sort of built-in social security for the elderly when they grow too old to work. In order to do all the work it takes to reap a harvest from desert soil, families produce more children to help with the work, which of course means more mouths to feed.

Propping this system up is the food aid coming in from the First World, which seems like a good thing on the surface. But if we examine it with a detached eye it is only increasing the problem of starvation, thanks to the fact that more food equals more people. When a population, any population, is left to survive on what they already have and produce, they will naturally limit their population, over time, to match the food supply. This has been observed in many animal species, over and over and over again. But we, as humans, you know — the *rulers of the Earth* — think we can ignore such laws of Nature. We keep thinking that if we just produce more food then the starving people of the Earth will stop starving. Every year we produce more food with the expectation that the result will be different, and every year more people appear. HELLOOOOOOO. This isn't working. Food aid is a band-aid tactic. Band-aids are great to cover a scratch from my sweet kitty, Punkin', but if Squishy Kitty gets ahold of you, you better have a surgeon handy; a Band-aid ain't gonna stop the hemorrhaging, and the Third World is bleeding out while we keep handing them tiny, self-adhesive bandages in the form of bags of rice. Time for some new strategies. Let's teach them to fish, metaphorically, instead of giving them fish. Maybe if we let Allan Savory test his livestock grassland method those people can start to produce their *own food*, and reclaim land from the desert to boot.

## End GMO *Food* Production

This may sound controversial because most people will assume that I'm suggesting we let the poor of the world starve. I'm suggesting no such thing. What we need is to scale back food production slowly, by cutting out non-organic, genetically engineered foods — which are not good for us anyway — and replacing them with more sustainably grown crops and livestock that both enhance the environment and are more nutritious. Remember, by the time most engineered food reaches your table, it only supplies about 50% of the nutrients that locally grown organic produce does. That's a waste of 50%

of the food! On top of that, in the U.S., every day, we throw away between 30-40% of our food! That is driven in large part by the fact that we overproduce it in the first place. Food isn't precious to most of us in the U.S. because most of us don't have to go without it. In other words, if we stopped wasting food, if food was grown locally and organically, we would only need to grow about *HALF* of what we currently grow. Chew on that for a few minutes — pun intended.

What Third World people need — besides no longer being referred to as *Third* — is not chemically grown, nutrient drained produce shipped from the other side of the world. What they need is to learn to grow their own in a sustainable way. What they need is education and the freedom to rule their own affairs. They do not need our orcish food or Sauronic bank loans that drive them further into debt; what they need is freedom and education. What they need and want is access to more of their *own* resources: clean water, renewable electricity, education, sustainable farming practices, stable *Leaver* economies, Mesh ideas, etc. In short, they need their Shires back, to give them the kind of support they need to take care of the problems or tasks that children now perform.

It is the imposed *Taker* mentality that is keeping them in poverty. Centuries of Totalitarian Agriculture have ravaged their landscapes, leaving deserts in its wake. If the land can even be brought back, it will be through *Leaver*, Shire-like strategies that work *WITH* nature, not against it. Until the people of the earth, of *Taker* culture, destroy their Rings, and decide to be *Leavers*, population will be a problem. When the Shire is rebuilt, worldwide, it will curb population in a natural way and find an equilibrium that we all can live with. *All*, meaning *homo sapiens sapiens* or *homo Hobbitla* and the rest of the species of our Earth. The time for the Hobbit-Shire Revolution has come. We have reached the end of the book, and the beginning of the journey and the job.

# CONCLUSION:
# SPRING AGAIN IN THE TREES

Sky of blackness and sorrow (a dream of life)
Sky of love, sky of tears (a dream of life)
Sky of glory and sadness (a dream of life)
Sky of mercy, sky of fear (a dream of life)
Sky of memory and shadow (a dream of life)
Your burnin' wind fills my arms tonight
Sky of longing and emptiness (a dream of life)
Sky of fullness, sky of blessed life (a dream of life)

Come on up for the rising
Come on up, lay your hands in mine
Come on up for the rising
Come on up for the rising tonight.
—Bruce Springstein, *The Rising*

The moment is dire. The problems we face are daunting indeed. *Taker* culture has ravaged Mother Nature to the point where she might just decide that we aren't needed anymore. If we choose to continue on this path, a century from now there may not be any or many of us left. Be careful, Frodo, when you step out on the road. Choose that road with care. Some roads lead to Lothlórien, others to Mordor. We are on the latter. Our air is becoming a poisonous fume. Our rivers, lakes, and oceans gleam with the sheen of oil; continents of plastic debris are floating on their surface. People murder each other over resources and religion, driven by Fear, Ignorance, Want, and

Greed. Guiltiest of all are the the massive corporations and banks who use debt to enslave millions, nay, billions to pay back loans conjured from thin air in the first place, like some Sarumanic slight of hand. Fellow human beings lose their homes, their jobs and, many times, their lives in the name of Smaug's hoard: money to line the pockets of the richest, entitled of the species who barely note the increase to their own overburdened treasure hoards. To what purpose do they employ it? They enlist it to bribe politicians around the world to look the other way while they take more and more and more from the Earth and from the less fortunate of their own species. In their wake are the smoking ruins of Mordor: wastelands where there were forests, deserts where there were fields, gurgling sludge where there once was a crystal stream, oil where there was water, heat where there were cooling breezes, garbage in place of green pasture, and silence where once the singing of birds.

Why do they do this? Why do *WE* do this? Because we are infected with a disease: the toxic belief that the planet and all of its resources are ours to do with as we will. It belongs to us, like some kind of mongrel dog that we can feed when it suits us, beat when it barks, or leave out in the yard chained to a rotting tree stump till we need something from it. This is how we treat our planet. This is how we tend The Garden while expecting it to feed our ravenous hunger. Those of us who hold onto this belief, and many of us who should know better, grasp our *preciousss* with whitening knuckles as our fingers grow hot then cold with avarice and apathy. Like Frodo perched at the Crack of Doom we cannot drop it into the abyss whence it came. Even those of us who *know* that we hold this ring, find it nearly impossible to relinquish it to the flames.

Most of our culture have forgotten, eons ago, that such a Ring ever existed, though its evidence is all around in the blackened ruin of our groaning planet. Drop the Ring, Frodo! Do it now. Wait not for Gollum to sever it from your hand. "Take off your golden ring! Your hand's more fair without it. Come back! Leave your game...Tom must teach you the right road, and keep your feet from wandering." Drop it into the fire. Walk out of the cave. Heed not the shadows on the wall; they are the shades of the puppeteer only. They are not real. They are Sauron's smoke and mirrors, Saruman's velvet lies, a pale reflection of the light you will find outside. **Frodo, come forth!** Step into the light of the Sun; walk into the light of the Shire! Come home. <u>You are needed</u>!

There is work to be done. Long have the Sarumans of our world ravaged the homestead. Let us undo their poisonous handiwork. Let us rebuild our communities, replant our gardens, our Party Trees, and grow Shires. Let's be *Hobbits* again and not far-wandering adventurers. Plant the seeds of peace and harmony. Let's work together to clean up the mess we've made and return Shireness and greenness to the Earth. Let's throw a party! Let's celebrate the destruction of the Ring by forming renewed connections with our Shire and with Nature! Let's walk the paths of the Old Forest, Fangorn and Mirkwood. Let's renew our friendship with Treebeard, Bombadil and Old Man Willow. Bring not axes and fire; bring only Hobbit feet and Hobbit senses. Feel the earth in your toes, smell the forest breath, hear it speak and sing, taste the air upon your tongue and see the roots that bind all living things together as one. We are not separate from the willow. We are not severed from the stream. We are the rain. We are the trees. We are the birds who sing in its branches. We are the streaming beams of light through its leaves, dancing on the forest floor with billions of teeming, waltzing neighbors. We are Nature. We do not rule. Shall we rule ourselves? Folly! We control nothing! We rule no one! We dance with the Ents, or we die with the orcs. Be not an orc. Be not a Wraith to the Ring. Be a Hobbit. Save the Earth.

> *Farewell! wherever you fare, till your eyries receive you at the journey's end!*
> *May the wind under your wings bear you where the sun sails and the moon walks.*

# OFFICIAL SHIRE-HOBBITS!

## Official Shire Hobbits

I want to specially thank the following people for their support on the Kickstarter Campaign in August of 2014. If not for you Shire Hobbits, this book might never have seen the light of day. Thank you for helping me drag the Ring to the top of Mt. Doom!

**Patience Felt** best girlfriend in history!
**Kellie, (K.M) Rice**
**Corena K. Panaccione**
**Ben Utter**

**Professor Nicole Nolan-Sidhu,** thank you for teaching me to write, though please lay no blame on her for any mistakes herein; they are my own.

**Bonnie T. Marques**
**Niina Mitter**
**Jenn Watts**
**NW Permaculture Institute**
**Jackie Kennedy (Go Pirates!)**
**Holly Dagan Rastegari**
**Amy Cooper**
**Annie Lewine**
**Bonnie Gordon**
**Bernadette Barnes**
**Kitty West** (the Hobbit-mama, Elven-Goldberry)

**Dr. Peter Stein**
**John Carlson**
**Asha Goodwin & Keith Smith** (axe throwin' and BBQ are in order)
**Marty & Nell 'Yes We Are' Kauls**
**Dr. Diane Anderson**
**Jo Lynne Navarre**
**Nicole Zuber & April Felt**
**Dr. Heidi Coplin**

# CALL TO ACTION

Thank you for reading

# BE A HOBBIT, SAVE THE EARTH!

Sign up for free articles, news updates, give aways and new book announcements.

## Subscribe to Be a Hobbit!

http://eepurl.com/Vghp5
Please consider writing a short review of the book for Goodreads!

# About the Author

## Steve Bivans

is a Viking scholar by training. He holds a master's degree in history, and when not writing a 500 page book on 'being a Hobbit' is working on a dissertation on Viking Warfare to obtain a Ph.D. in history. At some point or another he's worked about every job known to man. More recently he's been a special education assistant, and an instructor of history and graduate assistant at the University of Minnesota. In the past he's been a working sous-chef, a burger-flipper, a landscaper, a pizza delivery driver, a rock-god guitar player, a concert promoter, a window washer, and a Salvation Army Christmas Kettle bell-ringer. These days? Mostly he's a writer, a freelance blogger, a BBQ expert, the best cook he knows, and a Dwarf dreaming of being a Hobbit, though he looks more like Theoden and is grumpier than Gollum, at least before second breakfast.

When he's not dreaming of building his own Hobbit-hole, or traveling the Earth, you might find him preaching sustainability in a bar with 'a splash of cola in his bourbon,' researching Viking battle-axes—throwing them at stumps in the back yard, writing, cooking, reading, partying, watching Buffy, mindlessly playing WOW or LOTRO, and/or eating. Always eating. "Pass the butter, please. And while you're at it the bacon. And he's as dusty as the desert and as dry as the road through Mordor, so pass the beer too!"

Steve is available for conferences, lectures, camps, school talks! Hire him to come speak to your school, civic group, or TED Talk (hint, hint). He loves speaking in public! Getting him to shut up might be the hard part. Send him an email and find out what he can do for your next gathering of Hobbits! If you have any spare food lying around you might twist his arm to cook you dinner, or second breakfast.

Find Steve everywhere online!

## Subscribe to Be a Hobbit! If you love the book, sign up for free articles, news updates, giveaways and new book announcements. http://eepurl.com/Vghp5

- Follow him on **Goodreads**!

- On Facebook: *Be a Hobbit, Save the Earth*. Come join the Shire Movement on FB! Make sure to 'like' the page, so you'll get updates.

- **Find him on Youtube!** Steve have several 'Hobbit Hacks' videos uploaded, and there will be many more.

- **Follow Steve on Twitter** and get the latest news, advice, how-to articles and news on book releases!

- **Yep! Steve is on Pintrest too!** If you have cool pictures of something you think he'll like, PIN THEM TO Steve's profile!

- **Contact Steve!** He loves to hear from his readers! And I promise I will respond! I can talk all day, and will. You can reach me at bivans.steve@gmail.com

# HOBBIT RECIPES,
# RESOURCES AND REFERENCES

# Hobbit Recipes

## Hobbit Mama's Shire-friendly Recipes and Resources

The following are the recipes and resources mentioned in the book for cleaning up your Hobbit-hole. You can thank Patience for much of this—as I have—because she did a lot of the research to find these alternatives to which she has added her own twists.

One of the books you'll need once you get to preserving food is the *Ball Complete Book of Home Preserving* It's pretty much *The Bible* on the subject. Everything you need to know is in there, and lots of recipes, too.

### Hobbit Mama's Cleaners

### Hobbit Mama's All-Purpose Shire-Cleaner

This simple spray cleaner will replace most of the orcish ones in your house. We use it on all surfaces, especially in the kitchen and bathroom. You need a 1 quart spray bottle, in which you mix the following ingredients:

- 3/4 cup of water
- 1/4 cup of vodka or other clear alcohol

- 1 tablespoon of liquid Castille soap. You can get it unscented, or with scents.

- 3 cups of distilled white vinegar

- Shake it up and spray anywhere you would normally use a spray cleaner.

## Hobbit Mama's Carpet Cleaner

This is for use in a rental carpet cleaner — like Rug Doctor — instead of their chemical laden product. It's cheaper, too. In one gallon jug/container, mix the following:

- 1/4 cup Super Washing Soda

- 3/4 cup Apple Cider Vinegar

- 1/4 cup organic liquid dish detergent/or laundry detergent

- Fill with very hot tap water, and shake to make sure powder dissolves.

- Fill machine tank and clean away!

## Hobbit Mama's Middle-Earth Friendly Laundry Detergent

Mix the following dry ingredients in a large container — Patience reused our old laundry powder container (20 lb size from Costco).

- 1 box of Twenty Mule Team Borax (76oz)

- 1 box Super Washing Soda (55oz)

- 1 bar all natural soap (she used Dr. Brommer's Castille Lavender w/hemp)

- grate the bar soap, finely (you can use a cheese grater, or put it in your food processor — the finer the better)

- Use as you would normal laundry powder.

### Hobbit Mama's Baking Soda Toothpaste

A fluoride free toothpaste that eliminates not only the orcish poison, but also the orcish plastic tube that most paste comes in. Since the following recipe is so simple, we're just going to send you to another Hobbit for the recipe, over at DIY Natural.

### Gamgee's Garden Tips

### Gamgee's Grass-Slayer

There are some weeds that are just going to grow and they grow in places where we don't want them. For the ones in the sidewalk cracks or away from plants I do want, I use the following, simple, 100% non-toxic recipe that I call Gamgee's Grass-Slayer. You mix it all in a garden pump-sprayer and spray away! Don't get it on anything you don't want to kill though!

- 1 gallon white vinegar (organic preferably)
- 2 cups of table salt
- 2 tablespoons of dish soap
- For full instructions, see my website and the video: Weed Whippers, Dog S@*t, and an Alternative for RoundUp

# Shire General Store

Here you will find the various resources mentioned in the book according to topic. I plan to put this up to www.stevebivans.com soon, so that it can be updated continuously with new resources and ideas for the modern Hobbit.

# Hobbit Activisim Resources

Change.org: If you have a cause that you want to create a petition for, this is the place to do it, just like our Hobbit Hero, Sarah Kavanagh did!

GMO Awareness.com: has lots of information on which products are GMO laden, and how to avoid them.

# Stuff You Might Need

Cottage Craft Works; they have a bunch of hand-cranked kitchen gadgets, including a kit to convert KitchenAid mixers.

www.etsy.com: Great source for everyday items from individual artisans. Good source to find recycled things.

Brush With Bamboo: they make bamboo toothbrushes that are compostable.

GlassDharma glass drinking straws for your Hobbit Dine-Out Bag!

# Shire Power Alternatives and DYI

SolarCity offers leasing options to homeowners.

Unitedwind has a leasing program, similar to the SolarCity deal.

Build your own wind turbine: instructions on how to do it yourself!

Plan for building your own 'tiny house' with mostly shipping pallets!

How to make a T-shirt shopping bag from old t-shirts!

The Solutions Project: to move the U.S. towards 100% sustainable, clean energy.

## Hobbit Transportation

Zipcar the leader in car sharing.

HOURCAR which works in a similar way to Zipcar.

RelayRides is a fairly new company that arranges for car rentals between people, kind of like Craigslist, but with safeguards to protect your vehicle.

## Gamgee's Garden Links

American Community Garden Association: for information on how to start and maintain a Shire Garden.

Seatle's Food Forest Initiative: For information on how cities can use public property to feed their citizens.

How to make worm tea! A great natural fertilizer for your garden.

How to make pallet wood compost bins: Plenty of photos to get you through the process.

Pollinator Partnership, and the Honey-Bee Haven, for more information on how bees are essential to the Shire garden, and how you can help protect them.

Anne Gibson's Micro Gardening Tips: On how to garden in small spaces.

Eunice Baurmeester on Pintrest! Vertical garden ideas for Hobbits with limited space.

Fire Pit pictures: Photos of construction of Steve's backyard firepit.

How to build a Hobbit-hole?
There are lots of sites about building Hobbit-holes and homes, either full-sized, or for playhouses. But most of them aren't that helpful. Here is a really good video on a cob house in Texas. The method he used could be easily adapted to build an actual Hobbit-hole.

## Shire Funding Sources

Kickstarter: If you have a creative project, this is probably the best crowdfunding site, and most popular.

Indiegogo: Indiegogo has fewer restrictions on the types of projects that can be funded, than does Kickstarter, so this is a good place for non-profits to check out.

GoFundMe: If you want to raise money, for any purpose, GoFundMe has the fewest restrictions on the type of project.

## Hobbit Entertainment and Exercise

Middle Earth Day Facebook Page. Join all of the Shire Movement next September to celebrate a new Holiday, Middle Earth Day!

Hobbit style golf: Get back to the original game, like ole Bullroarer played it! Pasture Golf!

Geocaching.com, Get out there and find your own dragon gold!

Letterboxing.org: If you like riddles and mysteries, this is the adventurous game for you!

## Hobbit Pet Care

BioBag: a compostable alternative for puppy poop.

Good design for a dog compost bin.

SwheatScoop: a more sustainable kitty litter.

World's Best Cat Litter: another alternative.

Composting pet waste: The Compost-Gardener.com, and Glen Brook North Zero Waste

## Last Ship to Valinor

Party Tree Funeral: if you want to become an Ent, or tree when you pass on to Vallinor, this company can arrange for that.

# BILBO'S BOOKSHELF AND EDUCATIONAL RESOURCES

I've tried to organize the following books, websites, and videos in some kind of logical order based on topic. There are some here that I've read that for one reason or another haven't made it into the book, per se. This is my way of giving credit to those authors who I haven't mentioned, as well as those I have. I recommend every book, website, and video on this list. If I didn't think they were worth reading or watching I wouldn't have put them here. Some of them I have reviewed for Goodreads. If so, I've tried to link to my review so that you can see what I thought about it before you buy it.

**Subscribe to Be a Hobbit!** (http://eepurl.com/Vghp5) **If you want to get my latests rantings and ravings. If you want to know what books I'm reading and recommend, follow me on Goodreads!**

## General Tolkien Books and Resources

Tolkien reading and singing: There is a recording out there of him reading, and singing key sections from *LOTR*. I once found it in the local library. There is a segment on Spotify as well. These recordings are some of the most amazing things you're ever going to hear. Trust me on that one.

TheOneRing.net: If you want to know about Tolkien, his books, the movies, and join the largest community of fans on the web, this is it. These guys rock.

The Happy Hobbit: This is the home of the biggest Tolkien fans on Earth. Check out Kili and Fili, for a ton of dorky, fun, happy Hobbity videos, recipes, stories, advice, and laughs. These two sisters are big contributors to TheOneRing.net and have interviewed many of the stars from the movies. Plus, they're nuts.

Be a Hobbit, Save the Earth on Facebook:
Don't forget to 'like' the official page for the book for updates on the Hobbit Revolution, recipes, Hobbity projects, photos, events, etc.

Patrick Curry, *Defending Middle-Earth: Tolkien: Myth and Modernity*

> Curry examines Tolkien's work to find spiritual and ethical lessons for our modern world. At the same time he examines Tolkien's view on ecology and the environment.

John Garth, *Tolkien and the Great War: The Threshold of Middle-earth*

> Excellent examination of Tolkien's war years and how those experiences influenced the creation of Middle Earth and the story of the War of the Ring.

# Being a Hobbit: The Inner Journey

The following are books, articles, and videos about our inner psychology. This is probably the most important stuff on the list. These books have been indispensable to me, and will continue to be so. If you are struggling with anxiety, anger, depression, or just a negative story, like me, then this is the starting point.

Jim Carrey's full graduation speech at Maharishi University of Management.

> This might be the most inspiration speech ever given. I'm not kidding you. If you don't weep, you're wearing toe-tags and lying in a freezer on a sliding tray. Any time I need an uplift, I watch this, and the next one on the list.

Matt Harding, Where the Hell is Matt?

> If there was ever a modern Hobbit, it is Matt Harding. He has literally been 'There and Back Again" several times, and wherever he goes he spreads goodwill, happiness, and his kick-ass dance moves. He should be given a Noble Peace Prize. Watch'em! It will revive your faith in our shared humanity.

Andrea Balt, 30 Questions you should answer before you die

> After the videos, START HERE! Don't be afraid, Frodo. I dare ya! This list of question is the reason you have my book in your hand. You'll be amazed what happens when you answer them.

**Daniel Quinn, *Ishmael.***

> Read everything he's written after that. Without this book my book would never have been written. Period. Quinn is a Gandalf and a Zen Master Monk.

Jim Loehr, The Power of Story : Rewrite Your Destiny in Business and in Life.

> Loehr is one of the pioneers of sports psychology, and this book is a perfect follow up to the 30 Questions. Read it and discover your life's purpose. Without that? You have nothing.

Martin E.P. Seligman, Flourish: A Visionary New Understanding of Happiness and Well-being.

Seligman is a pioneer in 'positive psychology' and there are some effective strategies in his book that dovetail nicely with Loehr's, and can help you in the process of rewriting your negative story.

Brigid Schulte, *Overwhelmed: Work, Love, and Play When No One Has the Time*

Don't have *time* to change your life, or save the Earth? Brigid's book will reveal *why* we don't have that time, and give you some hints at how to fix that.

S.J. Scott's 23 Anti-Procrastination Habits: How to Stop Being Lazy and Get Results in Your Life.

S. J.'s book helped me to get organized so that I could write a 500 page book about saving the Earth. Without it, I doubt I would have been able to do it. This is a short book, unlike mine, but indispensable.

Tom Shadyac, *Life's Operating Manual: With the Fear and Truth Dialogues*

Director of many films, including *Bruce Almighty,* and another Daniel Quinn fan, like me. I didn't mention his book in the text—I don't think—but the story of how he was exposed to the Ring—Quinn's thesis—is a fun read.

# The Shire Revolution

The following books, articles deal with the pieces and parts of what I call the Shire Revolution which is already in motion. The more you read from this list, the more you will see that Hobbits are on the move, all around you. We just need to start linking them all together.

Russell Brand, *Revolution.*

If you want to read an *on point* rant about what's wrong with the planet, and why, this is the book to read. Plus you'll laugh your ass off. Russell will tell you that the revolution is already happening and that all we need to accomplish it is to believe we can. He's right. He's more Dwarf than Hobbit, but that's why I like him; so am I.

Ron Finley's TED Talk video.

This Hobbit is the master gardener of the inner city. He is leading a revolution of community gardening, and you absolutely must watch his video, then follow him on Faceboo, Twitter, his website.

Malcolm Gladwell, *The Tipping Point: How Little Things Can Make a Big Difference*

One of the most important books on how movements and revolutions begin.

James Wallman, *Stuffocation: How We've Had Enough of Stuff and Why You Need Experience More than Ever.*

Wallman is an expert in the business world at predicting future trends. He says the future is in *Experientialism*. He's right. Read it. It will give you some hope for the future, and some ideas on how you can help to save the planet.

Rachel Botsman, *What's Mine Is Yours: The Rise of Collaborative Consumption*

Botsman argues that a new economic revolution has already begun, and that it is based on cooperation, and shared ownership. Indispensable for Hobbits and Hobbit business people.

Lisa Gansky, *The Mesh: Why the Future of Business Is Sharing*

Gansky lays out the new business model for the 21st Century, and it's not some huggy-wuggy, theoretical model either; businesses all over the world are making millions following the new way. If you want to run a Shire-minded business, you need her book.

Gar Alperovitz, *What Then Must We Do?: Straight Talk about the Next American Revolution*

> Gar's book is dark because the situation in American politics is nasty. He lays out some possible solutions, which includes a bottom up, local approach.

Eric Liu and Nick Hanauer, *The Gardens of Democracy: A New American Story of Citizenship, the Economy, and the Role of Government*

> Written by an ex-presidential speech writer (Liu) and a dot.com billionaire (Hanauer), Gardens of Democracy lays out their plan for a new, or revised, form of American democracy, that promises to solve the crises that now face the United States, if not the world at large. Their proposal is mostly top-down, but their 'ends' are very interesting reading, and their insight into the 1% is enlightening.

Robert David Steele's book, *The Open Source Everything: Transparency, Truth and Trust.*

> Steele argues that instead, the new revolution must come from the bottom-up, a peaceful grass-roots change of mind about how we govern and organize ourselves. Instead of focusing on secret intelligence, like governments, militaries, and corporations have been doing forever, he argues that we need Open Source Intelligence, on every aspect of life, from government to business, food production to technology, in order to tap into the most effective resource available to us: the collective human brain (all 7 billion of them).

Jane McGonigal's games to change the world: http://janemcgonigal.com/play-me/ and her book, *Reality Is*

*Broken: Why Games Make Us Better and How They Can Change the World*

> It's not just about games, but about why the real world is not what it should be, and then, how games can fix that. Not just fix it, but literally 'change the world.' Read it if you love games. If you don't love games, then you should be duct-taped to a chair and forced to read it.

Enlītānment Studios, LLC.

> My brother, Tim's computer game company. He's really just getting started but he has some very interesting ideas about creating fun games that will also help to make the world a better place. Please check it out and make sure to like the page and keep an eye on his projects! If you're interested in helping him, and me, develop a Hobbity-Shire-y game based on the ideas in this book, please contact us!

David Bollier, *Think Like a Commoner: A Short Introduction to the Life of the Commons*

> Bollier reveals how the corporate world has been encroaching and usurping the resources that were once held in Common by the citizens of Earth. If you want to know how the Sarumans operate, this is a good book for you. Also, he gives us hope by showing how modern Hobbits are resisting these efforts and creating new commons. A very good read.

Cat Johnson, "How To Convert a Business into a Worker-owned Cooperative."

Joseph Parent's, *Zen Golf: Mastering the Mental Game*

> The great Bullroarer Took would have killed to have this book in his Hobbit-hole. If you're a fan of the game, and want to know how playing it can make your life better? This is the book. Hint: It's not really about golf. Well, not really.

# Cleaning Up the Hobbit-hole, the Shire and the Earth

The following are resources to help you with the details of cleaning up your homes, farms, communities, and governments.

**Garbage: the Revolution Starts at Home** and *The Story of Stuff*

> Two very good documentaries on the pile of crap that consumerism is creating, and what we can do about it.

Allan Savory, The Grazing Revolution: A Radical Plan to Save the Earth

Bea Johnson, *Zero Waste Home: The Ultimate Guide to Simplifying Your Life by Reducing Your Waste*

> An essential guide for modern Hobbits to cut your waste impact, and save money.

Beth Terry, Plastic-Free: How I Kicked the Plastic Habit and How You Can Too

> Best guide out there when you get ready to rid your Hobbit-hole of orcish plastics.

H.C. Flores, *Food Not Lawns: How to Turn Your Yard into a Garden And Your Neighborhood into a Community*

Elizabeth Warren, *A Fighting Chance*

> And excellent look at the corruption and greed that runs America, from the inside by one of the only — dare I say—honest politicians on Earth. If you're into politics and solving things from the top down, read her book.

**Lansing Shepard**, Daniel Imhoff, Paula Westmoreland, Mark Ritchie, *This Perennial Land: Third Crops, Blue Earth, and the Road to a Restorative Agriculture*

Lays out the problems of modern agriculture, mono-crops, cultivating marginal lands, chemical runnoff, water pollution, and how some farms in Minnesota are working to restore the land to a more sustainable form of agriculture.

Linda Sue Park, *A Long Walk to Water: Based on a True Story*

Via a true story, examines the plight of children in Sub-Saharan Africa, especially the girls, who have to carry water for miles.

Sheryl's Blog for full instructions on how to season a cast iron pan with flax seed oil.

# Our Burning Shire

These are some of the books I read during my binge before writing Be a Hobbit. If you really want to know more about what's wrong with our planet and the way we are treating it, proceed. But do it with caution. I warn you, the picture is even bleaker than I had time to reveal in the book. Make sure to have some bourbon handy.

The World Watch Institute, *State of the World 2013: Is Sustainability Still Possible?*

If you want the hard truth about the state of the world, this is it. Warning, it isn't pretty, but you need to know it. The articles aren't written by journalists, either, but by the scientists and academics who are studying these topics, every day. I disagree with some of their arguments, especially that the only real solutions to the problems can come from big government. On that one, I strongly disagree. But their assessments of what is wrong? Dead on, I'm afraid.

David Graeber, *Debt: The First 5,000 Years*

> This book, written by an anthropologist, will kick you right in the balls. If you want to know why everyone on Earth is in debt, Graeber will tell you. This is an excellent book on the evils of uncontrolled corporate capitalism.

Thom Hartmann, *The Last Hours of Ancient Sunlight: The Fate of the World and What We Can Do Before It's Too Late*

> Hartmann paints a bleak picture of our Earth as we run up to the end of fossil fuels, and makes a plea to abandon them before it's too late.

Alfred W. Crosby, *Ecological Imperialism: The Biological Expansion of Europe, 900-1900*

> Examines the factors that allowed Europeans to imperialize some areas of the globe while failing to do so in others.

Made in the USA
San Bernardino, CA
13 March 2018